ANUNAKI   ANU –   100%.
           Father ⟍ enlil - human
           Human ⟍ enke ½ reptilian ½ human

we are: Sagittarius dwarf galaxy

INCREDULOUS

By

Joseph *"Five Eagles"* Reyna

2016
Prometheus Media Group

Prometheus Media Group
Houston, Texas
1-866-289-1777 fax

ISBN's

Perfect Binding	978-0-9854426-6-8
eBook/.MOBI	978-0-9854426-4-4
eBook/.ePub	978-0-9854426-5-1

Book Team
Book Packager and Project Coordinator — Rita Mills
Editors — Mark Rice, Debbie Frontiera
Cover Design — Mark Bender, Joseph Reyna, Deena Rae Schoenfeldt
Cover Production — Martin Vives

Printed in The United States of America

To my Mother who encouraged me
to pursue this path regardless of what
direction it would take me.

For the Reader

This story is a historical. fact-based, action / adventure work of fiction and the sole creation of the author. It does not reflect the official policy or position of any department, agency or government bureau. Views, preferences and facts expressed by the author do not attempt to bring any harm or disrespect to individuals (foreign or domestic) who might feel offended by the written content (or lack thereof).

That said, this work is not based solely on the author's imagination. It varies from the traditional orthodox teachings of events surrounding the Crucifixion. Information pertaining to the prophecies, arrests, trials and execution of the Nazarene were derived from the oldest known manuscripts of the Old and New Testaments of *The Bible*. The author wrote it as much for his own understanding as for the enlightenment of others. Having a different perspective, he observed things that had escaped those who were more directly involved in studying scripture.

Remote viewing was used, but the information obtained by this means was only added to the story after having been validated through extensive research; a process that often took years. The author has elected to spell some of the words in this book as they appeared in antiquity. This does not affect how they are pronounced. The calendar-era signifiers BC / AD, signifying Before Christ and Anno Domini, are not used. The author has elected to designate events that occurred before the birth of Christ with the alternative designation BCE: "Before the Christian Era". Dates after the year 1 shall be designated CE: Christian Era. The two designations are numerically equivalent. Neither designation uses the year zero; thus, 2016 AD corresponds to 2016 CE.

Foreword

> *If the world would meet the Christ of the Christians,*
> *they'd be saved; but sadly, they have met the*
> *Christians of the Christ and have rejected him.*
>
> **—Mahatma Gandhi**

According to legend, Cassandra was given the gift of prophecy by Apollo but was later cursed by him so that no one would ever believe her. Prophecies of impending doom are rarely heeded. Among the few examples where an entire nation consciously chose to make the necessary changes is the story of the prophet Jonah. After having delivered God's message to the people of Nineveh, regarding their imminent destruction, Jonah looked forward to their annihilation. Unfortunately, the citizens of Nineveh had taken the warning seriously. Grateful for having been alerted to the coming dangers, the people of Nineveh averted disaster by choosing to make the necessary changes. One would think the prophet might have been pleased—he was not.

Like Jonah, many well-meaning Christians have studied the prophecies of the *Book of Revelation* and look forward to the expected Apocalypse. But instead of a world hell-bent on destroying Israel, they see an Israel that is hell-bent on destroying the world.

The last quarter of the twentieth century has witnessed reforms in South Africa, the collapse of the Berlin Wall, and the alleged collapse of Communism. Tyrannical regimes across the globe are collapsing under the weight of their own oppression.

The last quarter of the twentieth century has also witnessed the largest spiritual awakening in human history. In their quest for a closer spiritual connection with the Divine, many mistakenly turned to organized religion, only to discover that direct communion with their Creator is strictly forbidden. As a result, there are now far too many disillusioned souls seeking spiritual guidance, and far too few capable of giving it.

My work is dedicated to those awakened individuals who seek Truth: a thing not easily recognized. Jesus Christ himself forewarned those who would seek after such things, cautioning:

> *Those who seek should not stop seeking until they find.*
> *When they find, they will be disturbed,*
> *after which they will marvel...*
> (The Gospel of Thomas)

Five Eagles

INCREDULOUS

The Strange Newness of a
Once Familiar World

...this message was for the ears of man alone,
they who walk between the worlds of Earth and Heaven.

—Excerpt from The Dead Sea Scrolls

Dia de los Muertos (Day of the Dead)
November 2, 2011

Torrential rains, brought about by an oncoming hurricane, had been punishing the dangerous muddy jungle roads all day. The bone-jarring seven-hour ride by military transport to the mountain village was brutal. Joshua had taken part in dozens of exorcisms over the past year, but nothing like this. The Church never went to these lengths for anyone. If anything, it seemed to ignore the flock's pleas for help. The Church's official stance on dæmons (demons) was that they did not exist in this day and age, which is why Joshua was surprised to see so many exorcists assigned to one case. With so many dæmonic outbreaks lately, exorcists had been spread rather thinly. Why were so many priests involved in this exorcism and why the urgency?

Artimus had been Joshua's closest friend and instructor for the past year, ever since Joshua had decided to make exorcism his profession. After only six months at his new assignment, Joshua had started wondering if this was what he wanted to do for the remainder of his life. Having grown up in a haunted house, he understood the dire urgency and need for exorcists. He did not believe in the lengthy process of going through proper channels if a Christian family was pleading for help. Joshua quickly became a problem for the archdiocese. When offered the chance to become a full-time exorcist, he had jumped at the opportunity.

Joshua knew of no official listing of exorcists. The men he met were usually engaged in active ministry and few held postgraduate degrees. It was rare to find an exorcist who was a recently ordained priest. Their median age ranged between forty-five and sixty-five. At thirty-one, Joshua stood out from the older men. And although a muscular athletic physique was not a characteristic of a run-of-the-mill exorcist, it could certainly come in handy should a possessed individual pounce.

As a rule, exorcists were not the scholarly type. After years of aloofness, most were lacking in social skills. For the most part, exorcists did not possess a vivid imagination: a valuable asset, thought Joshua. After growing up afraid of the dark, he could easily generate images of unmitigated horror. Having joined the Marine Corps at eighteen, Joshua had been around seasoned combatants most of his life: men who, like the exorcists, knew their enemy and were no strangers to death.

The Church chose its exorcists carefully. The qualities it looked for in a priest were soundness of mind and strong personal faith. A candidate's judgment and personal behavior had to remain rational under adverse and chaotic conditions. To the best of Joshua's knowledge, none had ever undergone post-exorcism psychiatric evaluations to prepare them for the skepticism they would meet in the outside world and within the Vatican.

There is not much written about possessions or the Devil in the ancient Hebrew Scriptures we call the Old Testament. In the New Testament, however, exorcism seems to be a standard operating procedure for Jesus and his disciples.

"Archbishop, would you please brief these men," said Artimus, startling Joshua back to reality. Artimus had been an exorcist now for thirty-one years and had never told Joshua much about his personal past.

Joshua wasn't sure how old Father Artimus was. His hair was almost completely white, and he was about Joshua's height: five feet, ten inches. Joshua had never seen Artimus so silent and secretive before. He'd been trying to goad him into revealing something about their latest mission. Usually Father Artimus would give everyone involved an in-depth briefing on who was possessed, how it had happened and the dæmon's name, if it was known.

'*What is a bishop, especially one who is not a spiritual man, doing at an exorcism?*' wondered Joshua.

"These men will be forming my team," announced Artimus, "and I will need them to know what we are up against. You can start with the circumstances of the haunting and take them through to the possession. I'll finish up with what information I feel they should know about the dæmon Asmodeus."

"Do you think that is wise, Artimus?" asked a balding, heavy-set Jesuit priest. The only thing denoting his rank was the amethyst bishop's ring and purple shirt with the traditional black cassock. Normally he would be sporting a purple cincture around his waist. "The Vatican was very explicit, Artimus—as few people as possible need to know all the details of this operation."

"Archbishop, I doubt that you have ever been involved with an exorcism. The lives of these men will be in danger. This is no poltergeist we're dealing with. Asmodeus is no ordinary dæmon. He is a prince among dæmons, making him more powerful than thrones, dominions or powers. And that is something none of these men have ever been up against. So either you tell them or I will!"

At the repeated sound of the word dæmon, the soldier wrestling with the wheel of the transport convulsed ever so slightly. He crossed himself, making the sign of the cross over his forehead, torso, and shoulders.

'*I will never understand why most Catholics in this part of the world tend to cross themselves so often. It gets annoying after a while,*' thought Joshua.

Archbishop Felipe Espindola considered for a moment and then spoke. "As things stand now, the dæmon leaves the possessed alone until nightfall. The possessed is a young girl named Ysenia. She is fourteen and the seventh daughter of a seventh daughter, if that means anything. The dæmon first took control of the girl's grandmother, a curandera, someone who is well versed in herb remedies and heals by the laying on of hands. Although the word curandera literally means healer, many in the village consider this woman to be a witch or bruja."

"Someone who heals by the laying on of hands hardly sounds like a witch," challenged Joshua.

"Curanderas are well known for placing curses on people and practicing black magic or brujeria," countered the archbishop. "About two months ago, thumping noises were heard in the grandmother's bedroom by the girl and her grandmother. After that, pictures of Christ on the walls shook and clawing or scratching noises were heard under the floorboards and on the roof. In the morning, objects would be found positioned in peculiar ways throughout the house."

"At first, Padre Antonio Gutierrez, the Priest who makes the rounds to this remote village, did not concern himself with the stories of the haunting, since the curandera did not attend regular mass or consider herself subject to the Church's authority. As a favor to the family, Padre Antonio stayed in their home while visiting the village. By this time the grandmother, Guadalupe, was said to be possessed. Antonio noticed nothing unusual about the woman during the day."

"That night he was awakened by screams. Horrified, he made his way toward the grandmother's room, where he witnessed three men in the process of restraining the woman, who seemed to possess tremendous strength. She had been bound to the bedpost to prevent her from scratching her face off. According to Padre Antonio, Guadalupe's eyes seemed enormous—an obvious sign of possession," commented the archbishop in an attempt to impress the group. "Also, the area under her eyes was incredibly dark and her tongue was protruding about twelve inches."

"That's always a dead giveaway, the tongue hanging out like that," remarked Joshua from the front seat, to the laughter of everyone but the archbishop, who was not amused.

"Padre Antonio also reported a commotion outside the house," continued the annoyed archbishop. "He was told Guadalupe only behaved this way when lechuzas circled over the house, shrieking and whistling."

"Lechuzas? You mean owls flew around the house whistling?" asked Doctor Facundo Lazo, scratching his granite-colored stubble.

'Doctors are only required on the most dangerous cases,' thought Joshua. He was not sure where the doctor originated from, but his English was excellent. Doctor Lazo, a distinguished-looking gentleman in his mid-fifties who peered through wire-frame glasses, had been waiting with the team of soldiers when Joshua and Artimus arrived at the military base that morning. It was obvious to Joshua that this doctor had never attended an exorcism.

"No, not owls, Doctor. Around here owls are called techolotes. Dees tings are as large as full-grown turkeys and have dee face of an old woman and not dat of a bird. I have seen one up close. It had dee long white hair of a woman and stood about a meter in height," added Padre Ricardo, who was accustomed to dealing with these creatures.

The padre, a parish priest from Cartagena, Colombia, was no stranger to exorcisms. Padre Ricardo Valencia was in his mid-forties and had been a priest all his adult life. The Vatican had recruited him for this mission at the last minute. "It seems none of us have been brought up to date on dee case. Why is dee Vatican acting so fast in dis case? Dee Cardinals usually drag dare feet when it comes to exorcisms," remarked Padre Ricardo in a heavy Spanish accent.

"How is it you got such a good look at one if it was flying in the dark?" asked the astonished archbishop.

"You don't have to see one to know what they look like. I have seen some myself. I know what he is describing," explained Artimus. "The whistle from one of these creatures will cause your skin to crawl and the hair on the back of your neck to stand on end. It is a sound you will never forget."

The archbishop continued apprehensively. "The Church originally refused to grant permission for an exorcism since Guadalupe does not consider herself a Catholic. After a time, things quieted down and Padre Antonio thought the dæmon had left. But it soon became apparent that the young girl Ysenia had become the dæmon's new target. It is believed that at some point in the possession the granddaughter, Ysenia, called the dæmon into herself in an attempt to save her grandmother. While Ysenia was at school, her desk started shuffling around the schoolroom floor on its own, frightening the other children. An exorcism was requested at this point. Once it was authorized, the priests involved continued the Black Fast for two weeks, trying to get the dæmon to identify itself."

"What relic were the priests using?" asked Joshua.

"At first they did not have one, nor did they know they could use one. When they called me from the military base at the foot of the mountain, I told them to remove the relic that was under the altar. This is a very old village, and church altars were originally sanctified with the relic of a saint. This one turned out to be a piece of spinal vertebrae. I do not remember who the saint was," added the Archbishop, shrugging his shoulders.

"An actual bone from the skeleton of a saint, a piece of his body?" asked the doctor, incredulously.

"Yes, that's why they call it a relic, Doc," explained Joshua.

"This relic, did it have any effect on the dæmon?" asked Artimus.

"Oh yes, it burned the girl when they touched her with it. They were not expecting this. In the morning, however, there was no sign of a burn on the girl, so they continued using it. After one more week, the dæmon identified itself as Asmodeus, apparently one of the princes of Hell. When I reported this to Cardinal Bishop Pablo de la Torre at the Vatican, he became very interested in the case."

"Why have dey not been able to cast out dee dæmon? And why are so many exorcists assigned to dees case?" inquired Padre Ricardo Valencia.

"That's just it. They are no longer trying to exorcize the dæmon, Padre. The Vatican wants this one captured and taken back to Rome for questioning," explained Artimus, to the surprise of everyone in the personnel transport. "Not long after the Vatican learned of the dæmon's identity, arrangements were made to have the girl brought to Rome. She has been under careful watch by the exorcists for several days now."

"So we're supposed to catch this thing and bring it back with us?" deduced Joshua, not certain he understood.

"The young girl will play host to the dæmon. If the winds allow, a military helicopter will arrive tomorrow and fly us to the nearest airport. She is to be heavily sedated for the flight to Rome. Father Artimus and Joshua will accompany her and her father back to Rome under special Vatican guard," announced the Archbishop, convinced this plan would work.

"Why doesn't a priest just call the dæmon into himself? Then you could all go back to Rome and question it at your leisure?" said Joshua with a wry smirk.

"Excellent idea, Joshua—would you like to volunteer?" asked his mentor, Father Artimus.

"*Hell no!*" retorted Joshua. "I never volunteer for anything! If I learned nothing else during my tour in the Marine Corps, I learned that much."

"Joshua, the Vatican has placed the highest priority on this case," Archbishop Felipe Espindola reminded him. "Your team is here to relieve the entire team of exorcists who have been with this family for nearly a month. The Black Fast has taken its toll on them. I'm not sure how much longer they could have endured this ordeal on a diet of bread and water." Turning to Joshua, he asked, "Have you started your fast yet, young man? And have you been absolved of your sins? This is a very powerful dæmon we're dealing with!"

"Yes, two days ago, sir. As soon as we were notified." Joshua remembered the old priest's breath coming from the other side of the cloth during confession. It had a hint of alcohol, probably whiskey, he thought. "Asmodeus! Isn't that the same dæmon associated with Rennes-le-Château? I visited the place when I was in France, and was mystified by what Saunière could have possibly found there. But you know what I found strangest of all? Inside the church are two large ornate statues, one on each side of the altar. One statue is Mother Mary. The other is St. Joseph. I thought it strange that each of the statues was depicted holding a Christ child."

"Joshua, I tell you this as a friend, young man. If you value your career as a priest, I suggest you stop looking for whatever it was Abbé Bérenger Saunière found at that infernal place," cautioned the archbishop.

The driver, who only spoke Spanish, informed the bishop that they were almost to the village of El Hormiguero. Due to the heavy rains, there didn't seem to be any villagers around.

"The name of this village, El Hormiguero, means the ant hill or ant infestation," said Doctor Lazo. "I'm glad there aren't any villagers around. They always get on my nerves!"

"How's that, Doc?" asked Joshua, trying to suppress a smile.

"These people, they're always so damn happy. They don't have shit! They're dirt poor. Why in the world should they be so happy? Hell, I drive a Mercedes and I'm never that damn happy."

"The poor still have hope," said Joshua. "They think money will help."

"The poor never seem to have enough for themselves, yet they somehow always seem to have enough to share with others who have even less," added Artimus, settling the matter.

As the military transport stopped in front of the Hospital Santa Rosa's entrance, Doctor Lazo wiped the fog off the small window with the sleeve of his rain jacket. He looked around, then up at the leaden gray sky. "Shouldn't these people have been evacuated for the oncoming hurricane?" he asked.

"Where to? There's no such thing as FEMA in this country, and the people would have nowhere to go if they left," explained Artimus. Noticing

Joshua trying to suppress a grin, he asked him to share the joke with the rest of the group. Artimus had discovered long ago that Joshua's mind could come up with the most amusing links to similar events.

"I remember seeing someone wearing a T-shirt at Mardi Gras after hurricane Katrina hit New Orleans," explained Joshua. "It read, 'FEMA Evacuation Plan: Run Motherfucker, Run!'"

Surprisingly, this village had a hospital, the Santa Rosa: an architectural eyesore. The hospital was located on the edge of a mountain ridge. Other than its barrel-tile roof, the three-story building had no outstanding features. It stood out because it did not blend in with the older buildings around it. A constant breeze from the Gulf of Darien helped to keep the mosquitoes at bay. The Santa Rosa had started out as a convent in which seven nuns ran a small clinic to treat minor ailments. The general population, being poor and uneducated, soon began to strain the clinic's resources. Seeing the opportunity to attract more converts, the archdiocese sanctioned the building of a hospital. Although the funding had been meager as hospitals go, the unexpected turnout of many volunteers, mostly young men, allowed the money allocated for labor to be used for equipment and medical supplies instead. The families of these men had wanted to repay the nuns for their kindness.

'*I hate the smell of hospitals. The smell of that yellow stuff they put all over wounds brings back unwelcome memories,*' thought Joshua as he ran into the building that stood next to the hospital.

The second truck pulled up and soldiers began unloading equipment into the old church. Joshua followed them toward a small room in the back, wondering what had been sent in all those waterproof plastic containers. Breaking the seal on one, he opened it and examined its contents

"Joshua, what is all this stuff you're unpacking here?" asked the doctor, motioning toward the equipment stacked against the walls.

"I think I just figured out why I'm on this team, Doc. I was in electrical-equipment repair in the Marines. They must have figured I would know how to operate all this stuff. This is definitely not a normal exorcism. The cameras are interesting. We have infrared and night-vision," said Joshua, almost to himself.

"You're awfully young for an exorcist, Joshua," observed Doctor Lazo. "How did you end up an exorcist anyway? No offense, but I would think a smart young man like yourself would have higher ambitions."

"When I was a child, my experiences with the paranormal and supernatural terrified me, Doc. Growing up Roman Catholic, I became fascinated with the supernatural. From a very young age, I wanted to become an exorcist, hoping I could help others who were going through what I had experienced." That seemed to satisfy the doctor's curiosity.

"You know, Joshua, when I find that some of my patients think they might need an exorcist, I usually direct them to a theologian rather than a psychiatrist. Most psychiatrists consider exorcisms to be religious in nature and based on a medieval supernatural nonsense that has no support in science."

"So what do you do if the possessed refuses to believe God even exists, let alone the Devil?" asked an incredulous Joshua.

"Well, I've only come across a couple of cases, but it was evident that they had suffered some sort of neglect, possibly physical or sexual abuse. Their behavior was bordering on psychotic. Multiple personality disorders, that sort of thing."

"How would you account for the freezing temperatures often associated with paranormal events?" asked Joshua. "A figment of the imagination, I suppose, Doc? Please don't tell me you presume that human memory is not reliable, and so the exorcist only thinks he witnessed floating beds, jumping tables, growling black apparitions and flaming candles."

"You have seen all these things?" asked the doctor, astonished at Joshua's sincerity.

"I sure have and with any luck, tonight I might even get to videotape them," said Joshua as he unpacked the last crate.

"You will be videotaping?" asked Antonio, as he entered the room.

"Padre, you look like Hell," blurted out the doctor. "Are you alright?"

"A month-long Black Fast will do this to you, señor," said the old village priest. Shaking the doctor's hand, he added, "I am Padre Antonio Gutierrez. I have been leading this exorcism since it began."

"Padre Antonio, I'm Doctor Lazo. I'll be the attending physician."

"I'm Joshua, and I guess I'm supposed to set this stuff up," said Joshua, motioning toward a camera mount with the cordless drill in his hand.

"Yes, you're supposed to mount some cameras on the walls. Do not worry about removing them. I will have someone else do that when you are gone," explained Padre Antonio.

"Joshua, I have never attended one of these…events before. What can I expect?" asked the doctor.

"Well, you're in for a treat, Doc, because I have never seen anything like this. I've been instructed to record what transpires during the exorcism, or whatever it is we are supposed to be doing tonight, but, I find the use of video-recording equipment and infrared cameras a bit odd. Normally no records of exorcisms are ever kept. I have never been allowed to take any video recordings before. This is by no means a normal exorcism. We have far more priests than necessary."

"Isn't that a good thing? With more exorcists, you should stand a better chance, shouldn't you?" reasoned the doctor.

"A formal Church-sanctioned exorcism requires only one exorcist and a junior colleague. The priests involved are usually appointed by diocesan authorities. There is no official training program to become an exorcist, so the junior colleagues usually attend for their own training. During this particular exorcism, I will be the only junior colleague. The rest of the exorcists are seasoned veterans. The number of assistants usually depends on how much violence is expected. Four is the usual number. We are using six, not including you. But do not deceive yourself into thinking there is safety in numbers.

"As the junior colleague, my job will be to monitor the words and actions of the exorcist in charge, and warn him if I feel he is making a mistake. Since there are many of us, we will help him if he weakens, and replace him if he collapses or flees in horror," Joshua said with a laugh. "We will also replace him if he becomes physically or emotionally battered beyond endurance, or dies, all of which have happened during exorcisms," he added in a more somber tone. "Once an exorcism has begun, there are no timeouts, except on the rarest of occasions. Then again, we are not trying to expel this dæmon, are we?

"Before performing any exorcism, everyone involved must make a good confession and be absolved of all sins that the dæmon may try to use against them. I usually prepare by spending my time alone in prayer, fasting and meditating. In preparation for an exorcism, priests are usually required to undergo the 'Black Fast'. During this time, we eat only small amounts of bread and drink only water. The Black Fast is one of the most physically demanding rites in the Church. It will take its toll on you if the exorcism is lengthy, as it did in Padre Antonio's case.

"Doc, it is very important that you also perform confession. Anything you're hiding in the closet will be used as a weapon. Like the exorcists, you must be able to endure horrible personal insults and be prepared to have your darkest secrets screeched before all those assembled. That happens routinely during exorcisms."

"How should I dress? What should I wear?" asked the doctor.

"You're fine just the way you are, Doc. The only people who need to wear special attire are the exorcists and the assistant priests. Each of us will wear a long black cassock that covers the length of our bodies. Over this will be a waist-length white surplice. A narrow purple stole will be worn around our necks, hanging loosely about the length of our torso," Joshua said as he stepped from the small room containing the electronic equipment into the main church, followed by his reluctant companion.

"Father Artimus wants the exorcism held in the church because of the recent paranormal outbreaks," continued Joshua, his arms outstretched. "Because we are using a church for the exorcism, the holy wafers are to be removed to prevent possible sacrilege. The room where the exorcism will be conducted must be cleared of anything that can be moved. Any religious iconography that's not anchored in place needs to go. Objects such as pictures, tables and chairs tend to fly around the room. During exorcisms, even large objects can move about, rock back and forth, or skitter across the floor. These have been known to strike the exorcist, his assistants or the possessed. All that sort of stuff will have to be removed.

"I have witnessed wallpaper peeling off walls. Sometimes there are strange rumblings, scratching sounds, hisses, and other noises that have no apparent source. Walls and furniture have cracked. Often, the temperature in the room containing the possessed drops dramatically. At times, an acrid and distinctive stench accompanies the possessed. I once tried wearing a gas mask—it didn't help. It is also quite common to emerge from an exorcism with serious physical injuries. For that reason, we are required to have a medical doctor among the team members."

"What are we talking about here? Bruises? Carpet burns?" asked the doctor.

Joshua laughed at the thought of carpet burns. Running a hand over his left sleeve, he said, "Once, during an exorcism, the sleeves of Father Artimus's black cassock kept bursting into flames. At one point, his purple stole slid off from around his neck and began thrashing on the floor like a wounded snake."

"Could the flames have been an illusion or a hallucination?" asked the doctor, intrigued.

"If they were hallucinations, the smoke alarm must have been hallucinating as well. When it went off, I just about jumped out of my skin. After the ordeal, I examined the cassock and found it to be severely scorched."

Gesturing toward the two large wooden doors at the entrance, Joshua continued. "Doors will open and shut uncontrollably but, because exorcisms can go on for days, doors cannot be nailed shut. And few exorcists wish to be locked in a room with a dæmon. On the other hand, the doorway must be kept covered. Otherwise, the physical forces released from within the room could affect individuals in the immediate vicinity.

"Windows must be closed securely. Sometimes they can be boarded over in order to keep flying objects from crashing through them. For some diabolic reason, the possessed seem to take great pleasure in hurling priests through closed windows. Luckily this old church does not seem to have any windows that we need to worry about.

"Normally a bed or couch is left in the room, and that is where the possessed person is placed. In this case, we are using a hospital stretcher complete with restraints and wheels locked in the raised position," said Joshua, tugging on the stretcher's heavy leather restraints. The stretcher had been placed on top of the pews, where it would serve as a makeshift bed. "A small table is usually needed. On it is placed a crucifix with one candle on either side, as well as holy water and a prayer book." For this purpose, a wooden box had been placed on one of the pews supporting the stretcher. "Although we will carry a saint's relic, we will more than likely not be using it. Padre Ricardo has placed a large picture of the 'Virgen de Guadalupe' on the box. He has probably learned that the possessed considers this image especially significant. And finally, once we've prepared the room, Father Artimus will enter—last and alone.

"Assistants are given three cardinal rules, Doc," cautioned Joshua, holding up three fingers and counting them off. "They are to obey the exorcist's commands immediately and without question, no matter how absurd or unsympathetic they may appear to be. They are not to take any initiative. And they are never, ever to speak to the possessed person. I trust that you, being a doctor, will not grow pale at the site of blood, excrement or urine. And remember to be prepared for obscene behavior or foul language beyond your wildest imaginings."

"Are all exorcisms this grueling?" asked Doctor Lazo.

Joshua looked about to see who might be within hearing distance before answering. "No, they are not," he said in a hushed tone. "And I've gotten myself in a lot of trouble for performing several unsanctioned exorcisms in the past. When Jesus sent his disciples out, they never had to request written permission from the High Priest in order to perform an exorcism. So I don't see why I need the Pope's permission. The way I see it, if he a-no-play-a-the-game, he a-no-make-a-the-rules.

"Elementals, earth or nature spirits, are probably the easiest to deal with," continued Joshua in a slightly louder voice. "Then you have your disembodied spirits. Restless souls, really. These are followed by more specialized evil spirits— lust, anger, that sort of thing. And finally you have the dæmons, the most unruly and by far the hardest to deal with." Joshua pulled out his iPhone® and began fidgeting with it.

"You can get a signal up here?" asked the doctor.

"No, Doc, I'm activating the Electromagnetic Field meter application," explained Joshua. "This gadget is nowhere near as sensitive as my real EMF meter, but it doesn't have to be, because the entities we deal with are usually very powerful. What I like about this application is that it allows me to record the event." Joshua held up a second device about the size of a carton of cigarettes. "This is our primary EMF meter. It is far more sensitive in detecting electromagnetic fields and can detect any changes in the room. A remote sensor connects at the base, much like a microphone. The top half is made of red plastic and lights up with an accompanying beep to alert the user when a change occurs. Because the constant beeping would interfere with the exorcism, I modified the device to beep only once, while the red light remains on during the entire time the signal is picked up."

"You know how to modify electronics?" asked Padre Ricardo, who had overheard the conversation.

"I know how to build them," beamed Joshua, having installed the last camera.

"Joshua, it is getting late," cautioned Padre Ricardo examining his watch. Hefting a large statue from its nook, in the thick adobe wall, he added, "You'll need to finish up positioning dee equipment before we begin."

"Yes, sir," replied Joshua. Returning to the equipment in the small room, he added, "If you'll excuse me, Doc, I forgot how late it was. I still have to test the visual on the infrared and UV cameras. I have no idea how this full-range spectrometer works," he added, examining the controls on its surface panel.

"Yes, of course. Thank you, Joshua. You have been very informative. I'll make sure I am prepared on my end," said the doctor. "Is this where I should confess?" he asked, pointing toward a narrow desk with a ledge at the bottom for kneeling.

"No, that is the prie-bieu. It's what the priest kneels on to offer his private devotions before saying Mass," explained Joshua. "For confession, you should use one of the two booths near the main entrance. A priest is required to absolve you of your sins."

Flirting with Disaster

The girl was brought in and asked to lie down on the stretcher. The heavy leather harnesses were placed over her body, and the straps secured. Her body was then covered with a blanket. The girl's father positioned himself among the three soldiers who would be doubling as assistants. Joshua entered the room fidgeting with something under his cassock. Artimus entered last and alone.

Turning to address the small group, Father Artimus announced, "Listen carefully. Do whatever is commanded of you by the archbishop or myself. If addressed by the dæmon, do not converse with it. Joshua, I have more than enough assistants. I think it would be best if you prayed at the foot of the stretcher during the entire exorcism. You might want to kneel on a cushion, son. I have a feeling it's going to be a long night." Artimus repeated his commands in Spanish to the assistants.

Without another word, Joshua grabbed a cushion from a bench near the altar and took his position. He activated one recording device on the floor and another that hung around his neck. In a loud voice, Joshua summed up the events of the previous month. He then gave the date and time followed by the girl's name, age and condition, adding that her parents had given permission for the Rite of Exorcism to be performed.

"Cardinal Bishop Pablo de la Torre has given permission for Padre Artimus Murphy to begin the formal Ritus Exorcizandi Obsessos A Dæmonio." Joshua named all the accompanying priests, the girl's father and Sergeant Martinez, adding that four soldiers stood guard outside the church.

"You forgot to mention we are being pummeled by hurricane winds and each of us is soaking wet," added Archbishop Felipe.

Ignoring the archbishop, Joshua opened the Roman Pontifical or Book of Exorcism. Beginning with the 54th Psalm, he recited in a low voice, "Deus, in nomine tuo salvum me fac: et in virtute tua judica me. Deus, exaudi orationem…"

On the pew next to Joshua was a crucifix, a plastic bottle of holy water, a small hand bell, and the relic belonging to the saint, in case Father Artimus had need of them. In addition to the psalm, other prescribed prayers were the Litanies of the Saints, the Pater Noster (the Lord's Prayer), and Ave Maria (Hail Mary). Artimus preferred that Joshua recite the prayers in Latin. That seemed to be more effective. In addition to these duties, Joshua would normally be required to make certain that special candles remained lit, and that cruets for water and wine remained full. For tonight, though, Padre Ricardo would be in charge of those duties.

Artimus began reciting the opening salutation in a commanding and authoritative voice. Normally he would have recited from The Ritus Exorcizandi, the Roman Ritual of Christian Exorcism. The ritual is spoken in Latin and translates into something like, 'I cast thee out, thou unclean spirit, along with the least encroachment of the wicked enemy and every phantom and diabolical legion. In the name of our Lord Jesus Christ, depart and vanish from this child of God....' Except that in this case, the Exorcist was under strict instructions not to expel this particular dæmon. Artimus called upon the dæmon to make itself known. As it was rare to find only one dæmon involved, Artimus wanted to ascertain the names and the natures of any others that might be involved. He demanded that they speak out and identify themselves.

Ysenia became maniacal, but the thick leather straps managed to keep her restrained. Artimus continued the ritual, demanding to know why the dæmon was here. Ysenia responded with a screaming tantrum. Her face began to distort. Loud thumps and scratching noises seemed to emanate from within the walls.

Joshua noticed his breath becoming visible as the temperature in the old church dropped drastically. His words became strained. He felt weighed down by a suffocating pressure. The possessed girl became physically immovable, anchored to the ground by 'possessed gravity': the opposite of levitation, where a possessed person rises off the ground.

The dæmon spoke, confirming its identity. Its breath reeked of an acrid yet distinctive stench that quickly filled the room. The disgusting odor made it difficult for the priests to breathe, and many in the room covered their mouths and noses.

Had this been a normal exorcism, the exorcist would have demanded to know when the dæmon would depart. This departure would usually be accompanied by the dæmon proclaiming Jesus Christ as Lord, sometimes uttering the words in Latin, "Christus Domini," at which point the exorcism would be over.

Archbishop Felipe Espindola approached Ysenia. "You are familiar with the parish church at Rennes-le-Château in France?" He pronounced the French name flawlessly then added, "You should be. There is a statue dedicated to you near its entrance."

Joseph "Five Eagles" Reyna

'*Didn't this hypocrite just finish telling me not to ask questions about that chapel?*' thought Joshua. As he continued reciting aloud, Joshua wondered if the archbishop would ask why Abbé Bérenger Saunière placed the bizarre inscription "TERRIBIL IS EST" over the porch lintel. The Latin's literal translation was 'terrible is this place' but the actual meaning was more along the lines of 'This Place is Awesome'.

As a priest, Joshua was fascinated by the bizarre inconsistencies of the plaques depicting the Stations of the Cross, at Rennes-le-Château. The plaques were positioned in reverse order. One displayed a child swathed in Scottish plaid. Another showed Pontius Pilate wearing a veil over his face. But the most intriguing mystery of all involved the statues that stood behind the altar. The ornate statues of St. Joseph and Mother Mary were each depicted holding a Christ child—what some might term identical twins.

"These are the questions to which we seek answers," continued the archbishop. "My first question deals with a riddle hidden within a coded parchment:

SHEPHERDESS NO TEMPTATION
THAT POUSSIN TENIERS HOLD THE KEY
PEACE 681 BY THE CROSS
AND THIS HORSE OF GOD I COMPLETE
THIS DAEMON GUARDIAN
AT MIDDAY BLUE APPLES

"The phrase I'm most interested in is, 'Blue Apples at Midday'. We have reason to believe that the phrase is somehow associated with the statue dedicated to you."

"You speak of the message deciphered by the Knight's Tour," responded Asmodeus in a deep, hissing voice, "a logic puzzle which has only one solution—as does the coded message."

"Now we're getting somewhere," said the archbishop.

"You seek to understand the code," said Asmodeus, "but fail to understand the men who created it...the Knights of the Temple...."

"I have no interest in medieval heretics," interrupted the archbishop. "All that is required from you is the meaning of Blue Apples at Noon. Do you understand?"

"Understand? Oh, I understand," responded Asmodeus. "Your focus is on the Blue Apples and their connection to the Annunaki Star Gates. If I were you, I would be more concerned with the two painters so prominently mentioned within the code itself." Suddenly the box positioned next to the stretcher was thrust across the room. It smashed against the wall with a thunderous crash. This was followed by a long, low and mournful wail in the distance.

"Un lobo!" exclaimed a soldier.

'*Whatever made that howl was much larger than a wolf*,' thought Joshua. The silence was broken by the yelp of a small dog then many larger dogs barking like hounds on the hunt. The sound of their baying made it obvious that they were headed for the old church. Asmodeus's deep guttural laughter slowly transformed into the melodious glee of a beautiful enchantress. The laughter ceased abruptly as she locked eyes with the archbishop. "Now I'll ask you a question. Think carefully, for it pertains to you, priest! What is the meaning of 'Blue Balls at Midnight'?"

Trying to contain his laughter, Joshua looked up, locking eyes with the gorgeous creature secured by the restraints. Ysenia's black hair had turned coppery-red. Her sapphire-blue eyes were set against an unnatural bronze complexion. He gaped in awe at her intoxicating beauty.

Artimus nudged Joshua's shoulder, bringing him back to reality. Sheepishly, he glanced down at the book in his hands. The dreadful wailing of hounds in the distance sounded much closer now. Joshua had heard these Hellhounds before. In fact, he had once seen the dreadful creature that initiated the K9 chorus when he was only four years old. His imagination began to run wild as he struggled to find the place where he'd left off. His inventive mind easily tracked the large pack as they hurried up the winding mountain roads toward the village.

Outraged, and oblivious to the approaching danger, the archbishop continued barking out his demands.

Ignoring his inquires, the dæmon continued asking questions. "What is the Horse of God, and why are there two astride it?"

Sergeant Martinez, a short portly individual who had begun to tire of guarding the door, asked the doctor, "Dis ting, it is a demonio, huhh?" But before the doctor could respond Martinez screamed, "*Ahiiii!!! Dios mio!*" Clutching for his sidearm, he gazed at the ceiling above.

"My God, was that a lechuza?" asked Doctor Lazo.

Still kneeling at the foot of the stretcher, Joshua heard something large land on the roof. As it tried furiously to tear its way into the old church from above, Joshua felt the presence of something that did not want them to be there. Then the stretcher before him began to bounce on the pews.

"It had to be one," exclaimed Sergeant Martinez in a heavy Spanish accent. "Dey used to fly over my grandmother's house when I was a little boy. My grandfather would shoot at dem with bullets he had prepared by scratching a crucifix on them. Otherwise de bullets would not go off," he explained.

"You heard a lechuza just now?" asked Joshua, knowing he shouldn't have asked.

"Yes, there was a horribly loud whistle, almost a shriek, and then a loud thump followed by the sound of scratching on the roof," said Doctor Lazo.

"You did not hear it?" asked Padre Ricardo.

"No, I heard it land and start clawing at the roof—was it really that loud?" asked Joshua.

"What are you talking about? My entire body shook! You didn't hear that damned thing?" asked Doctor Lazo.

"You may want to start scratching crosses on some of your bullets, Sergeant," suggested Padre Ricardo.

"Si, yes dat's a good idea," agreed Martinez.

Padre Ricardo instructed Martinez to scratch one cross on the firing cap and another cross to each side of it.

Joshua's knees began to throb. The rain, wind and thunder outside intensified, making it difficult to hear what was being said inside the old church. Joshua suspected that the recordings would be inaudible. He decided to stop praying and began repeating the demands of the archbishop, and the dæmon's responses, into the recorder suspended around his neck.

Joshua was startled by bright red flashes that lit up the interior of the small church. He had always been able to see these intense bursts of energy. They came as a result of someone being frightened or startled. He doubted the other priests would understand his ability to see auras and so had always kept these insights to himself.

Sergeant Martinez jumped at the sound of machine-gun fire erupting outside, dropping the handful of bullets into which he'd begun scratching crosses. Martinez turned in terror, looking wide eyed in the direction of the double doors. A strong gust of wind had blown them open. Rain poured in as a long mournful howl reverberated off the walls of the interior.

Joshua felt his lungs resonate as the hair on the back of his neck pricked up. He sprang to his feet but his legs were slow to respond, having knelt for so long. The hounds drew closer as he rushed for the doors. Shit, he thought, as his pre-combat jitters kicked in and his stomach began to wrench with gut-twisting fear. Probably why exorcists fasted, he thought. "Don't look, just don't look," he told himself.

Sergeant Martinez hurried to barricade the doors as he called for his men, over the sound of the wind and automatic weapons fire, to get inside the old church. But the Sergeant's commands were interrupted by the horrible cries of his soldiers.

"I have heard dat howling before…" shouted Padre Ricardo as he assisted in slamming the doors shut.

Joshua barricaded the oak doors by fitting a large timber into the iron brackets, securing the main entrance. Mercifully, they'd managed to stop the infernal beasts. All other doors had been locked before the exorcism began.

"Twice, I have heard dees dogs. It is said dat death comes to claim you if you hear dee dogs three times," shouted Padre Ricardo over the baying of the Hellhounds.

"Death stalks us all this night, Padre," said Artimus, arriving at the doors to see if he could be of assistance. "It is just a little closer today than usual."

'Luckily, this old church was built more like a fortress than a temple of worship,' thought Joshua. He tugged on the heavy, solid-oak crossbeam wedged into its iron supports and felt the frantic scratching of heavy paws on the hard wood. It had never occurred to Joshua that he might have to lock the doors to keep something from getting in.

A hysterical archbishop screamed instructions that were already known to everyone.

"What happened to the men outside?" asked the doctor.

"Hellhounds," answered Joshua, backing away from the doors. To his horror, he saw Doctor Lazo reach for the heavy oak crossbeam as if to lift it.

The sensation of frantic scratching and clawing from the other side of the doors seemed to startle the doctor and he drew back in horror. "What is scratching at the doors? And why is everyone yelling?" he asked in an almost inaudible voice.

"The howling and barking from the Hellhounds is so loud I can barely hear you, Doc," explained Joshua.

"He doesn't hear them, Joshua," deduced Artimus, "but then, neither do I. What are they doing now?"

The remainder of the pack was running circles around the old structure, baying and wailing in a most unnatural manner. "Dey are circling de church," answered Padre Ricardo.

Satisfied that the doors would hold, Joshua returned to assist with Ysenia. Two soldiers were holding down the stretcher. The girl's father appeared terrified but remained near his daughter. Time seemed to stand still. Joshua stared in disbelief as the ceiling slowly rose and was torn from the structure. The voices of the other priests became inaudible. His mind, frozen in fear, was useless. Intuitively, he knew what he had to do.

Looking up, he saw raindrops as they hovered, suspended in the air. Brilliant flashes of lightning illuminated the funnel cloud of a tornado. Joshua could hear the muted thumping of his heart in the silence that followed. Running instinctively toward Ysenia, who was still strapped to the stretcher in the form of an enchantress, he pulled the blanket over himself and covered the girl's upper body, shielding her face. The pews rose off the ground and bounced violently, smashing into one another. Soon after that, the area inside the small building was filled with foliage, mud and debris swirling in the confined space. Joshua struggled with the blanket, trying to keep their faces covered in order to prevent inhaling the suffocating sludge that was swirling within the enclosure.

As the deafening sound of the tornado began to subside, the young priest looked about in the darkness and turned on a small but powerful LED flashlight. Joshua gazed forlornly at the devastation, hoping to see something recognizable in the wreckage. Grimacing at the filthy scene, he could not make out any of the priests or assistants amongst the mud-splattered pile of pews that littered the tiny space. He could still hear the hounds running around the church and decided to shut off the flashlight.

His mind flashed back to his days of pilot training. "What should we do if the carburetor ices up?" a curious student had asked. "If you're flying at night, I suggest you turn off your headlights," the instructor had advised. "Why? So we'll have enough juice to try and restart the engine?" another student had asked. "No, it's so that you don't have to see the earth coming at you—just before you die," the old pilot had explained.

The skies began to clear and the winds subsided. '*We must be entering the eye of the hurricane,*' thought Joshua. Gazing up at the cliff-like formation of clouds that seemed to reach to the stars, he could make out three large silhouettes descending against the backdrop of stars. '*Lechuzas,*' he thought.

The three large figures began attacking something on the floor. Against his better judgment, Joshua shone the flashlight at them. He saw three white birdlike creatures, with long white hair, ripping a thick *Bible* to shreds. The light startled the creatures. All three stood motionless, staring directly at him. In appearance, each was somewhere between a harpy and an owl with a slender, goose-like neck and a head the size of a large lemon. Beady black eyes squinted in the bright light. These things had the faces of old women, not of birds. Joshua tried to stand but an intense pain shot through the right side of his ribcage, preventing him from doing so.

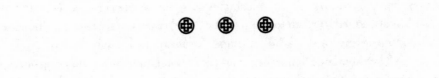

We Find Ourselves in Uncharted Waters —
Here There Be Dragons!

Twenty-four hours earlier, and approximately sixty-three miles east of Jacksonville Beach, Florida, a massive electrical disturbance had crippled the treasure hunting submersible, *Defiant's*, navigation capabilities. The seas above the submersible flashed with brilliant colors as balls of lightning struck the water. Trying to maintain its position, *Defiant* hovered thirty meters below the surface. In appearance, the ship resembled a cross between a Great White shark and a Manta Ray. No viewing ports were visible on the hull's sleek exterior. Its wide body provided spacious work areas and living quarters. The main vertical stabilizers, positioned to the rear, resembled the space shuttle's swept-back wings. Two dorsal vanes extended outward at a forty-five-degree angle, much like the F-18 Hornet fighter jet's twin tails. These acted as rudders and controlled pitch.

The ship's smooth shark-like nosecone gave it a predator's appearance. *Defiant's* hull was smooth and rubbery, like the skin of an orca, for noise suppression and radar dampening. Her hull was treated with an anechoic coating that absorbed microwave radiation, effectively making the ship invisible to radar while on the surface. The bottom of the nosecone was flat, and necked down towards two massive propulsor shrouds which flanked a transparent bullet-shaped command center. The shroud's ejection ports were equipped with "tail feathers": moveable fins that flexed and rotated in order to direct the flow of the propulsion thrust. This helped to stabilize the ship over a work area. The ship's engines were massive, the silent propulsion system taking up most of the space below decks.

All ships of the treasure fleet sported dazzle camouflage. The design resembled fragments of various multi-colored material glued together helter-skelter, like a collage. Dazzle camouflage had been developed by the Allies towards the end of World War II. Not a single ship painted with the dazzle camouflage design was ever torpedoed by enemy submarines. The pattern helped to break up the submersibles' outlines when viewed from the air. This was crucial because most of the Spanish fleet's sunken treasure galleons lay in the clear shallow waters of the Caribbean.

At the moment, the *Defiant* was trapped in an unexpected electromagnetic storm within the Bermuda Triangle. Although submerged, the ship's instrumentation was being affected. All compasses were either spinning slowly or completely erratic. All communications had been out for some time.

Due to its critical mission, the ship had to remain positioned over an area known to disrupt the Earth's natural magnetic field. The ship was able to maintain neutral buoyancy using pressure sensor feedback loops. The system did not rely on computers to maintain the ship's depth.

Aboard the craft, technicians gathered around a horizontal cylinder-shaped deprivation chamber. The compartment was spacious, with full overhead room fore and aft. The port and starboard bulkheads tapered to a forty-five-degree angle just behind the chamber. Sealed within the electro-magnetic shielded chamber lay their commander, Teryk, who was conducting a remote viewing exercise. Teryk had once been an exorcist for the Roman Catholic Church. He'd left the order, having become disillusioned with Church dogma and the bureaucracy of an incredibly inefficient system. It did not help matters that any records of Teryk's ancestry had been obliterated by Spanish conquistadors and Catholic priests.

A rogue priest turned treasure hunter, Teryk had learned to combine his special ability to bilocate with a technique known as remote viewing. The procedures for remote viewing were pioneered and developed by black ops contractors for the CIA. The recently declassified military intelligence project was known as Star Gate. The understanding that our unique awareness is not restricted to our biological life forms is central to remote viewing, which offered the ability to locate targets across time and space. Through the use of remote viewing, Teryk's treasure-hunting teams had managed to locate and recover nearly half of the Spanish treasure galleons lost in the Pacific Ocean. Locating targets in the past was normally not an easy task but the intense human emotions and excitement generated during the sinking of a ship proved an easy target for the remote viewers. The technique seemed ideal for locating sunken treasure ships.

Few individuals are aware that every year for two hundred and fifty years, between 1565 and 1815, Spain had sent one galleon to Manila, in the Philippines. The Manila galleons, as they came to be known, required an entire year to complete the round-trip journey across the Pacific. In the Philippines, the ships were laden with gold, Chinese porcelain, gems, and jewelry. The galleon would then make the six-month return trip to Acapulco, Mexico. From there, the cargo was transferred overland by burro to the Gulf of Mexico. During that quarter millennium, Spain lost a total of one hundred and thirty Manila galleons, each ship sinking with nearly a billion in treasure. A few ended up off the coast of California. One was lost as far north as Oregon.

The Spanish kept detailed records of manifests and shipwreck locations for each of the lost Manila galleons. Before the implementation of remote viewing, treasure-hunting teams had relied heavily on the efforts of specialized research teams. These researchers scoured archives and libraries around the world, locating and translating such records. Unfortunately, the records of the lost Manila galleons had been destroyed during the Mexican Revolution, in both Acapulco and Mexico City. The records on the other side of the Pacific met with a similar fate when U.S. forces bombed the Philippine National Archives during WW II.

During this particular remote-viewing session, Teryk was targeting the Spanish galleon *Nuestra Señora de las Maravillas*. The ship had been lost in the Atlantic, off the Little Bahamas Bank during a hurricane on 4 January 1656.

Military-trained 'operational' remote viewers, at least in the Star Gate Project, had been directed to specific targets, on their information-gathering missions, by Guides. The individuals guiding remote viewers through these exercises were unaware of the targets' identities. A target could be a person, place or thing. Targets were not restricted to the present moment or this planet, for that matter. To prevent what had been termed '*loading the target*, a simple code number was used to designate each target. In other words, each mission was conducted as a sort of double-blind test. The target's identity was not known to the guide and could not have been known by the remote viewer. Although the military denounced the Star Gate Project as a failure, 95% of all data retrieved by their remote viewers remains classified to this day.

Teryk's technique did not require a guide. He already had a rough understanding of where his targets were located and the approximate time and date they'd sunk or been destroyed by a hurricane. Loading the target, aka (also known as) letting one's imagination run wild, was always a danger. For this reason, Teryk employed a vast network of researchers. Once the researchers were given the information retrieved by Teryk and knew what to look for, they'd set out to either verify or discredit the information received.

To date, modern treasure hunters and archaeologists had only managed to locate about one hundred of the more than one thousand four hundred treasure ships scattered throughout an area known as the *Spanish Main*. The treasures recovered by Teryk's teams had originally been pillaged from his ancient ancestors by the Spanish conquistadors. Having recovered billions in sunken treasure throughout the Pacific, Teryk's teams had established a vast network of secret bases from which to conduct their operations. Through the use of highly sophisticated submersibles, like *Defiant*, these modern-day pirates had managed to avoid the attention of the evolving global fascist dictatorship calling itself the New World Order.

The transparent bullet-shaped compartment that extended into the sea offered an exceptional panoramic view of the work area below the ship during recovery operations. From the command center, all of the robotic arms, lights, vacuum guns and blowers could easily be operated. The transparent walls were six inches thick and made from dense, clear vacuformed plastic. Aurora sat in a command chair observing the colored balls of lightning as they struck the ocean's surface in the distance. Aurora's Asian appearance made her stand out from the other crew members; that and her being only twelve years old. She was one of the 'lost girls of China'. Chinese Government restrictions permitted families to have only one child. Because of the ancient preference for boys, to carry on the family name, an estimated one hundred thousand Chinese girls have been aborted, killed or abandoned when only days old. Aurora never knew her father or mother. Abandoned shortly after birth, she had been discovered by an expedition team sent into China to explore an ancient pyramid structure.

Aurora had been named after the Roman goddess of the Dawn: the time of day when she was found. Her long black hair contrasted sharply with the beautifully embroidered white silk kimono she wore. She abhorred wearing anything that resembled a uniform, preferring to dress in traditional Chinese silk garments.

Aurora was a Star Child, and like the Indigo Children before her, she was highly telepathic. Normally her telepathic abilities permitted her to communicate with the other Star Children aboard nearby vessels. These children's telepathic abilities had enabled the treasure fleet to remain secretive for as long as it had. Aurora wondered if normal people felt the way she felt now: alone and enclosed by the walls that surrounded her. She could sense the presence of a few of her friends onboard the ship. But beyond that, there was only emptiness.

Aurora observed that the brilliant fireballs penetrating the surface of the sea continued burning for some distance. In the forward observation area below the ship's hull, the open sea should have been brighter, the dimness most likely due to the storm. Earlier, Raven, the ship's captain, had activated the searchlights but could not detect the ocean floor. She had ordered that the lights remain on, so that the ship would not be in danger of running aground. Aurora was fascinated by the sharks that were drawn to the work lights.

"Hey kiddo, anything new?" asked Raven in her throaty English accent, her thick ebony-black hair falling off her shoulders as she leaned forward to ask the question. It was Raven who had discovered and adopted Aurora. Raven's name was derived from her beautiful, perfectly straight hair. Her face was not overly pretty, but

Joseph "Five Eagles"Reyna

she was striking in her captain's uniform. She was a strict vegetarian, and her athletic build concealed the fact that she would be a senior citizen in a few years.

"No sir, I can't sense the presence of anyone beyond this ship," said Aurora, removing her special observation helmet.

"Aurora, the crew is considering awakening the commander so we can try to get out of this storm…"

"No, you cannot! I can't sense him either. I think Teryk is somehow linked with the storm, trapped in it maybe. I get glimpses of him, and then he's gone. We have to hold our position, captain," Aurora assured her. "And we cannot remove him from the chamber."

"The equipment is malfunctioning. We are not getting any reliable vital signs on him. He could be in danger, Aurora."

Monique entered the forward command center and informed the captain that the ship was still not responding to the helm's commands. "Even if we did wake him, we would not be able to escape this storm. There are mechanical levers he can activate to alert us if he needs assistance, and so far he has not used them. I recommend we follow Aurora's request to leave him in the deprivation chamber until his mission is complete, captain." Monique's French accent somehow took the edge off her words. "I have never encountered a situation like this in all my years of guarding the commander. If Teryk is choosing to remain in the deprivation chamber, we must trust that it is for a good reason." Monique's eyes, usually topped by a frown, were an intense kelly-green so bright that it appeared she was wearing contact lenses to change the color of the iris. Ironically, she was color blind and could not see the shade of her eyes; a shame, for they were rather striking.

Although Monique radiated a personal confidence, an indefinable sadness added to the officer's seriousness. Locks of her thick burgundy hair fell un-styled past her shoulders. She was hauntingly beautiful, shapely almost to the point of distraction. Knowing this about herself, she usually dressed in battle gear in order to draw less attention.

"What Spanish galleon was he trying to locate, Raven?" asked Aurora, attempting to steer the conversation in a new direction.

"The *Nuestra Señora de las Maravillas*—it's Spanish for 'Our Lady of the Miracles'. The ship was also referred to as the Almiranta, because the admiral of the fleet commanded her."

"Who was the lady?"

"Mother Mary, I suppose."

"What miracles did she perform?" asked Aurora.

"I'm not sure, but she must have performed some for them to call her that," Raven assured her. "As I understand it, the combined armada was made up of twenty-two Spanish ships, mostly merchant vessels on their voyages back to

Spain. In the Archivo General de Indias—General Archive of the Indies—in Seville, Spain, one of our researchers located the diary of Padre Diego Rivadeneira, who survived the wreck along with forty-four others. According to him, the lead ship *Capitana* and the rear ship *Almiranta* carried the main treasure. They were the fleet's two most heavily armed war galleons. Along with its share of treasure, the *Almiranta* carried a sixteen-hundred-pound, solid-gold, life-sized statue of the Madonna and child: Mother Mary and the infant Jesus. There was also a three-thousand-pound golden table encrusted with emeralds. These are what Teryk was targeting.

"On 4 January 1656, the *Jesus Maria*, one of the merchant ships, struck a coral reef that tore off her rudder," continued Raven. "Her captain anchored the disabled vessel and fired her cannon as a warning to the rest of the fleet to avoid the shoals. But the crew of the *Maravillas* panicked. Thinking that they were under attack, they changed course and collided with the *Capitana*. The two warships remained lodged together for some time. When they finally disengaged, the *Capitana* appeared to be unharmed and continued sailing, but the *Maravillas's* bow had been damaged below the water line. She began to take on water. The admiral ordered the anchors to be jettisoned in an effort to lighten the load. But the ship was carrying over two hundred and fifty tons of silver bars and more than six hundred passengers.

"In an effort to save lives and treasure, the admiral ordered that the ship be run aground on the shoals that the merchant ship, the *Jesus Maria*, had struck," explained Raven. "She struck bottom half a dozen times. When she finally hit the reef, it is believed her hull was so damaged she simply slipped over the reef and came to rest on a sandbank in fifty feet of water. Both her stern and fore castles were out of the water. Do you remember the drawings of the old Spanish galleons?" Raven asked Aurora. "The castles are the parts that stick up out of the ship in the front and back.

"Everyone was safe and everything seemed fine but soon strong northerly winds began to blow and giant seas began to build," continued Raven. "Huge waves, generated by the hurricane, broke the galleon into three pieces. The bow with the silver remained in place, while the fore and aft castles were carried away by the winds and waves of the storm. It is this top portion of the wreck that contained the Madonna and child and possibly the gold table as well. All those who were on the castles were never seen again."

"Why would anyone want to have a three-thousand pound table?" asked Aurora in disbelief.

"Well, back then if you brought back gold in the form of money or bars, it was taxed by the king and the Church. If you had coins, they would divide them up. If you brought back a gold bar, they would chisel off a piece from one end and stamp it with a seal, to indicate you had paid the tax. But if the gold or silver was in the form of dinnerware, jewelry or furniture it was not considered money. The table would not be very useful if the king and the Church each removed a leg to cover their ten percent, would it?"

"Cap'n, the hatch is opening. He's out!" called a technician from the open hatch. The three headed up toward the deprivation tank.

Emerging from the deprivation tank, Teryk did not bother disconnecting the array of electrical sensors still attached to his muscular six-foot frame. Grabbing a towel, he headed for the captain's quarters with two technicians trailing after him.

Seeing Teryk enter her quarters, Raven followed wondering what could be wrong. Upon entering the compartment, she noticed Teryk attempting to activate the computer. She informed him that the electronic systems were operating erratically and that all communications were out.

Teryk considered her statement but gave no reply. He stood and approached the bulkhead to his left. Opening a compartment, he drew out a *Bible*, one of many versions from Raven's personal library. Noticing he was still soaking wet, he dried his hands, not wishing to damage the book. He wrapped the towel on his head in order to absorb the water from his long black hair. Without a word, he opened the book and began skimming over the Gospels, beginning with Matthew.

"Commander, you were in the chamber for a long time, sir. Are you all right?" asked Raven, concern clouding her face.

"Is anything wrong, monsieur?" inquired Monique.

"Oui! Something is very, very wrong, Monique." Turning to the ship's captain, he stated, "Raven, you and I have read over and discussed these Gospels countless times. Tell me, what day of the week was Jesus crucified on?" asked Teryk, not bothering to look up. "In other words, on what specific day of the week did the crucifixion take place?"

"Friday. Yes, it had to have been on a Friday..."

"Exactly!" interrupted Teryk. "That's the story that's been handed down by the Church for ages."

"That's why we celebrate Good Friday, isn't it?" she asked.

"Friday. That's what we've been taught since Sunday school," acknowledged Teryk. With his index finger firmly marking his place in the Gospel of Luke, he added, "Come closer. I need you to see this." Pointing to Luke 23:56, he read, "'...after the Crucifixion the women rested on the day of the *annual high Sabbath...*' This account is similar to the version given in Mark's Gospel. Unfamiliar with Jewish customs, I took it to mean Saturday, the Sabbath. But according to what just transpired, the Annual High Sabbath has nothing to do with Saturday," Teryk explained.

"During the time of Jesus, the Jews did not flock to Jerusalem merely to celebrate for one day. The festivities of Passover actually lasted for a total of eight days!" proclaimed Teryk, pausing for effect. "The day of Passover was followed by the week-long celebration of Unleavened Bread. The first day of this seven-day feasts was recognized by the Jews as the Annual High Sabbath."

Teryk read aloud from the Gospel of Luke. "'...After the high Sabbath *they* [meaning the women] prepared their spices...' This passage refers to a day, immediately following the high Sabbath, on which women were permitted to perform work: '...then *they* [the women] rested [again] on the Sabbath day *according to the commandment.*' Luke acknowledges that the Crucifixion occurred on the Passover. He then goes on to say that the following day was the Annual High Sabbath, a day on which the women were required to rest. On the next day, the women were permitted to perform work. Luke then records that the women rested again on the following day, in keeping with the fourth commandment. Do you understand the implications of what I've just read?" he asked, excited.

"I'm perplexed," admitted Raven. "Luke doesn't seem to be making any sense, Commander."

Flipping back through the pages, Teryk explained that, "Most Christians are not aware that Luke was not one of the twelve apostles chosen by Jesus. Luke was a Greek physician, and a follower of Paul. Luke's Greek is far more refined than that found in the Gospels of Mark and Matthew. His style is more eloquent." Pointing to the first verse in chapter one, he added, "Luke states from the outset that he carefully and personally investigated everything. He affirms that he found it to be well supported by witnesses from the story's beginning. To state from the onset that your account was as accurate as possible was a common practice among Greek historians."

"Luke explains that the 'day' on which the women made their preparations was enclosed by two very distinct and separate Sabbath days," added Teryk. "The first Sabbath day was the annual High Holy Sabbath, a day that occurs only once a year. This High Holy Sabbath coincides with Thursday. The following day, Friday, allowed the women to make their preparations. Saturday follows Friday and accounts for the additional Sabbath day that was observed, according to the fourth commandment."

Looking up at the two astonished women, Teryk posed the question, "Is it possible that Jesus was crucified on a Wednesday and not on a Friday, as we have been led to believe? And if they got something that simple so screwed up, what else did they get wrong?"

"There must be some mistake, sir. Perhaps that translation is in error," suggested Raven, reaching for another version of the *Bible* from the compartment in her captain's quarters. After reading the verse, she stared in astonishment and asked, "How on Earth did you come by this information?"

"Well, that is what I will need my entire team of researchers to investigate," said Teryk. Writing feverishly, he began to compose a list of questions far more embarrassing and dangerous to the Church than anything he'd ever thought to ask his superiors during his time as a priest. "Raven, what I just experienced in that deprivation tank goes far beyond remote viewing or bilocating. I'm not sure what actually happened in there," he said, handing the list to Raven. "The researchers are to select whatever topic they feel most comfortable with. Recall all of them to Antares as soon as humanly possible."

Antares was a floating city, and one of several secret bases designed to conduct covert underwater treasure-hunting operations. Being a Scorpio, Teryk had named the base after the brightest star in that constellation. Because of its color and position, Antares is known as the red heart of Scorpio. The city was saucer shaped and measured five hundred meters in diameter. At the moment, it was stationed in the Caribbean Sea north of Venezuela.

Raven glanced down at the sheet and read aloud. "Investigate these possibilities regarding the story of Jesus Christ:

- Did a town called Nazareth exist before Jesus' birth?
- Was the betrayal of Jesus actually based upon prophecies from the Old Testament and if so which prophecies?
- Is it possible that Jesus' arrest was conducted by Romans for having committed an offense to Caesar's personage—sedition, a crime punishable by death?
- Is it possible Jesus was guilty of the charges against him?
- Was Jesus crucified on Friday Passover 33 CE—'Good Friday'? Or was he crucified on a Wednesday Passover years earlier?
- Investigate the possibility that his body was wrapped in the Shroud of Turin.
- Investigate the legends of the savior-gods born of virgin mothers; more specifically, any similarities between the legends and Church dogma.
- Are there any written records in history that can verify an eclipse occurred on the day Jesus was crucified, and more importantly that it lasted three and a half hours?
- Investigate the legends concerning a double or identical twin brother of Jesus.
- Lastly, and most importantly, investigate the possibility that Judas remained a faithful disciple who never betrayed Jesus, never committed suicide, and was counted among those who saw him resurrected.

"Jesus—guilty of the charges leveled against him!" blurted out Raven in dismay. "Judas never killed himself. He was counted among those who saw Jesus resurrected! What on Earth?"

"Raven, you and I are both aware that the gospels were heavily edited by the founding Church leaders during the first few centuries. Having just read this verse in the Gospel of Luke, I am convinced that enough evidence still remains in the New Testament to prove…"

"Prove that Jesus was guilty!" Raven interrupted. "Sir, Jesus was innocent. Pilate later recanted his actions and tried to pardon him, remember?"

"That's what I thought too, Raven," agreed Teryk, "but one does not pardon an innocent man. An innocent man would have been acquitted of the charges."

"Commander, I doubt that we will need the entire team of researchers to track down proof of…"

Teryk cut her off. "I am willing to allocate the time and assets for this task. Assemble the entire team at our underwater base, Antares. The floating city's massive library should provide sufficient resources for the investigation. I need to know if the truth is still in the Gospels. Because if what I just experienced is a more accurate account of events surrounding the Crucifixion, it means the Church has managed to edit and twist the truth beyond all recognition." Looking down at his hands and staring at his water-wrinkled fingers, he asked, "Just how long was I in there?"

"We are uncertain, Commander," explained Raven. "The ship's chronometers are malfunctioning. All communications are out. The compasses are gyrating wildly, making it impossible for us to verify that we are holding our position."

"What about the gyroscopic nonmagnetic compasses?"

"The gyroscopic compasses are slowly spinning counterclockwise. The acoustic imaging systems are also erratic but they seem to indicate the ship is not turning. We have no idea how long you were in the deprivation tank. Probably no more than a few hours. Why do you ask? Did it feel longer?"

"It felt much longer. How did I manage to remain waterlogged in the deprivation tank for so long?" Teryk inquired.

"That was Aurora's doing," said Monique. "She was adamant that we not disturb you. Should we have wakened you, Commander?"

"No, I am grateful that you did not. You did well to follow Aurora's recommendation."

"She seemed to be the only one in contact with you," said Raven. "She has not been able to contact any of the Indigo or Star children telepathically, though. It's as if we've lost contact with the rest of Earth's inhabitants."

"While I was in there it felt as if time or reality shifted. Perhaps the entire ship shifted with me," reasoned Teryk. "Instead of simply observing, which is what normally happens when I bilocate during remote viewing, I became part of what was unfolding before me. I found myself in another body, in another time. I still had an awareness of who I was, but I also had control of another person's body and access to their memories, as if I had somehow lived that life and was reliving the events. While you waited hours out here, I experienced years in there. I was back in the time of Christ, before and after Jesus' crucifixion, and although I was in a position to try and avert its outcome, it still came to pass. Everything led up to it, but there were strange irregularities. For instance, Jesus' death is remembered as occurring on Good Friday. The crucifixion I observed happened in the middle of the week, and was accompanied by massive earthquakes as well as an eclipse, if you can call it that. The Moon certainly appeared to move in front of the Sun, but then it just hung there suspended for hours."

"That sounds wild," agreed Raven.

"You don't understand," Teryk explained, "while I was in there, I discovered that Passovers only take place during full moons, something I'd never heard of. Don't you see, Raven? If that's true, the Moon was on the wrong side of the world. It should not have been able to cause a solar eclipse of any kind. Stranger still, that night, there was another eclipse, a red lunar eclipse..."

"A red eclipse on the night of the crucifixion?" interrupted Raven excitedly.

Teryk nodded, and continued, "What I experienced seemed incredibly real. That is why I need the help of my research teams. Astronomical computer programs should be able to confirm the lunar eclipse easily enough. But why leave something like that out of the Gospels? Raven, if what I experienced was an actual event, it would mean that the Church has deliberately preserved a false version of what transpired!"

At that moment a crackly voice squawked over the intercom. "Captain, we are still having some electronic difficulties, but we've managed to re-establish contact with a satellite. I've confirmed our position and time, and it's not when or where we should be! Captain, we lost communication for three hours and eighteen minutes. Our present position is just south of the strait between the Cuban Peninsula and the Yucatan."

"Yucatan? That's over eight hundred miles from our last known position? Helm, can you confirm that?" asked Raven.

"The position is correct, Captain. According to incoming reports, several ships in this area had already gone to red alert when *Defiant* went missing. I sent a brief situation report but Atlantic Command is requesting we come in for a full diagnostic."

"What of Hypnautica, the ship's Artificial Intelligence computer? Is she still not responding?" asked Raven.

"The A.I. is still not responding, Captain," answered the helm.

"Raven, it sounds like communications are still a bit sketchy," said Teryk. "Once the A.I. comes online, encrypt a message. Order all researchers and investigators to be taken off whatever designated assignments they are presently involved with. Tell them to report to Antares as soon as possible. Issue a red alert along with the message. I want to recall everyone with as little resistance on their part as possible. I know this order will make little or no sense to them. Emphasize that I need everything they can find on the Gnostic mystery religions regarding the legends of the savior-gods. More specifically, any beliefs of that ancient religion that smack of Church dogma."

"What is this dog-ma of the Church?" asked a puzzled Monique.

"Dogma means you do not question the authority of the Church or anything they teach," said Aurora, who had just re-entered the captain's quarters with additional towels. "It means you are to accept what you are told, *without* question."

Raven started to leave the Captain's quarter for the Command Center. She turned abruptly and stood at the entrance, straightening out her jacket. "Sir, what do I give as the reason we chose to start your remote view at this specific location just minutes before the storm began in my Sit Rep?"

"In your Situation Report, state that I chose the time and location based on the position of the Galactic Center and the Sun's zenith in relation to the ship's horizon. If they do not understand, have them contact ESPionage for details. As of this moment, all details of what has transpired during this operation are to remain classified. Do not transmit any information pertaining to this mission over the airwaves unless it's encrypted. Based on what I observed, there is a very real possibility that the End of Days are upon us."

"Understood," Raven said, biting the corner of her lower lip. "Sir, I do not know if you have ever noticed the titles of the books in my personal library."

"How could I not notice them? It was you who led me to some amazing authors. And I think I can now answer some of those questions we pondered over…at least I hope I can."

"Was he actually married, sir? Jesus, I mean." said Raven hesitantly.

"Very much so, in accordance with the Hebrew customs of that time," explained Teryk. "The Mishnah, an oral rabbinic tradition, made it clear that any young man who was not married by the age of twenty was considered 'Accursed of God'. If Jesus had not been married, the scribes would have been quick to point it out. One thing that did surprise me was how incredibly young Mary Magdalene was. She was still a teenager and Lazarus, her little brother, was only about ten years old at the time."

"Then I take it you saw the disciple Thomas?" she asked excitedly. "When I return, will you tell me of him? Of all the apostles, he is my favorite."

Exhaling briefly while starring into nothing, Teryk settled back into the spacious ebony captain's chair and pursed his lips, wondering where to begin. "There was no disciple named Thomas…by that I do not mean the man did not exist. There was a disciple who was known by that nickname. Thomas is not a formal name. The Aramaic word means twin. It was a nickname applied to one of the disciples of Jesus' inner circle, because he looked so much like the Master."

"I knew the name Thomas meant twin, but you're saying this was a nickname applied to one of the Twelve? Wait a minute! If Thomas is a nickname, that would insinuate there were only eleven disciples!"

"Oh, you caught that? Well, that didn't take you too long. Jesus did select twelve disciples. It would appear one has been erased from memory—but not from history, I would think. And that, mon capitan, is why I am recalling all researchers to the Round Table of Antares. This brings me to my next topic. Raven, would you consider joining my group of investigators? I could really use someone with your knowledge and experience on the team. When we dock at Antares, you could transplant your extensive library ashore and assist with the investigation into the matters surrounding the crucifixion."

"If the *Defiant* remains docked at Antares, I could simply use my captain's quarters. You know how much I dislike being around large groups of people for too long."

"That's an excellent idea," Teryk agreed as he rose from the chair and took a second towel Aurora was offering him, "but I think you will find the energy from this group exhilarating as opposed to draining, as large gatherings normally are. Raven, at this point you know more than the rest regarding Thomas. Would you do me the honor of spearheading the investigation into the true identity of Jesus' lookalike?"

"Commander, you know very well that I don't believe Jesus died on the cross," contested Raven. "My research, has led me to believe that Jesus may have been given a drug that induced death-like symptoms. I believe that his uncle, Joseph of Arimathaea, with the help of the Essenes, nursed Jesus back to life, after which he traveled to Persia, where he had spent most of the missing eighteen years."

"That is exactly why I need you on the team," Teryk assured her. "You know that most of my beliefs are based on Church dogma. And by-the-way, those masters Jesus learned from in Persia achieved their light bodies after twenty-six years of intense meditation. How many of us could occupy our minds with thoughts of love, joy and peace for twenty-six years? Jesus mastered this technique and accomplished his transformation in only three days. Raven, if what I just experienced actually took place, there is an 'Event' about to unfold. And some of us will be expected to make this transition in the twinkling-of-an-eye!"

"Why would any of this information pose a danger to Antares?" asked Raven. "I would think that our ship having moved thirteen hundred kilometers from the Bahamas to our present location, off the western coast of Cuba, should pose a greater threat!"

"What do you mean, Captain?" asked Aurora, "We never moved from our position. We are still floating over the underwater Pyramid City."

"What Pyramid City? What are you talking about, Aurora?" asked Monique.

"Below us is a beautiful city of pyramids. I saw it when I was wearing the helmet in the command center. We were floating over the sunken city when the storm began, and we are still over it now. So the ship could not have moved!"

"Come, Aurora. Show me the Pyramid City you saw," said Monique as she led Aurora out of the captain's quarters.

"Raven, Jesus spoke of specific prophecies concerning the age we are now living in. What I need the research teams to do is validate my experience. If what I just witnessed is a more accurate account of events that transpired during the Crucifixion, then humanity is in grave danger. I have a tremendous amount of information to disclose, and I will do so when the team is completely assembled."

"Walk with me to the forward command center. I'll explain on the way," suggested Teryk. "I want to see what Aurora was talking about."

Raven turned and retrieved a thick towel coat from a bulkhead compartment. Handing it to Teryk, she said, "I'm not used to seeing you wander about the ship out of uniform, Commander."

Teryk nodded and continued with his conversation. "To the ancients, there were originally two words that meant 'to know'. One word meant you had an academic knowledge of a thing. The other 'know' was spelled with a G instead of a K, as in the word gnostic (noss-stick). To 'gnow' was pronounced the same way. The word meant you understood with absolute certainty, even if you could not comprehend fully how you arrived at that awareness. It is this word I am now using, when I tell you that I gnow we are in perilous times…"

"Mon Capitan, Commandant," Monique called over the intercom, "please come down to the work station's command center. You're not going to believe this. I've taken the liberty of launching an AUP (Autonomous Underwater Probe) to investigate the site."

Teryk gazed through the virtual reality helmet's display. The sunlight was fading, and the seas were growing dark. Far below him appeared pyramids and other structures illuminated by the blue-green laser from the AUP's optics array. The probe had not reached the site yet, and lights would be useless at that great a distance. He set the helmet down and instructed Raven to launch a second probe. They would have to return and make a full investigation later. He also gave orders for a squadron of AUPs to be launched at the coordinates the ship was believed to have started its mission from. "If Aurora believes the ship remained over the sunken city the entire time, there should be pyramids at our previous location as well."

"Captain," said a voice on the intercom.

"This is the captain. Go ahead," replied Raven.

"Captain, Atlantic Fleet is unable to comply with your request to launch an AUP squadron over our last known location. It appears there is still

Joseph "Five Eagles" Reyna

a tremendous amount of US Naval activity in the area. This activity is what had caused their original concerns when *Defiant* first went missing. Also, we've just received an urgent dispatch for Teryk. It is classified *Seven Seals*."

"Understood. Have the dispatch sent to my quarters. He'll take it in there," ordered Raven.

After reading the encrypted message, Teryk handed it to Raven and added, "Raven, I'll need a map of Colombia so I can dowse the location. I doubt the small village mentioned in the communiqué by Father Artimus shows up on any of our maps. I'll need you to arrange transport as well."

Raven nodded her understanding and asked, "Another helpless family the Church has turned its back on?" as Teryk handed her the message. "Asmodeus, where have I read that name before?"

"Asmodeus was one of the dæmons summoned before Solomon. The dæmon of secrets and buried treasure, if I'm not mistaken," said Teryk, recalling his reading of the Keys of Solomon.

"Solomon requested information from it during the construction of the First Temple, right?" asked Raven, not sure if she remembered correctly.

"It would appear the dæmon has resurfaced, and now the cardinals on the committee overseeing the exorcism intend to transport its host to the Vatican, where they hope to extract information from it. The hiding place of the Ark of the Covenant and the Templar treasure would be my guess."

"Do you think such a thing is possible?" asked Raven in disbelief. "Asmodeus is no ordinary dæmon. Do you think you're up to it, Commander? After what you've just been through, I mean!"

"Another exorcism, monsieur?" asked a concerned Monique entering the cabin. Her words, richly adorned by her accent, never seemed to alarm anyone.

"That ordeal is probably the only thing that's going to get me through it. You forget I've just spent the last few years under Jesus' tutelage…"

"You can't stake your life and endanger Monique's on delusions of grandeur, Teryk," cautioned Raven.

"I guess we're about to find out if I was hallucinating—the hard-way!" grinned Teryk. "How are we doing on that transport? Any of the Sea Wraiths nearby?"

"A Sea Wraith transport will rendezvous with us within the hour, Commander," Monique informed him. "Weather conditions over northern Colombia are not favorable. There's a slow-moving hurricane skirting the northern shores of Venezuela and Colombia. As soon as headquarters receives your landing coordinates they'll be able to calculate if it's possible to get you in as the hurricane's eye passes over the area. If that doesn't happen, I do not see how we will be able to get to Colombia within the next few hours, sir."

Turning towards Monique, Teryk ordered, "Prepare my ExoSkeleton and make sure I'm equipped with tracer-rounds. This will be a night-time operation. As always, I'll need you to accompany me, Number One," a term he'd taken to calling her.

"I've set a course to intercept the Sea Wraith, mon Capitan," said Monique. "Sea conditions will be calm when we surface, due to our distance from the incoming hurricane," she added in a whimsical tone, giving them a mischievous look as she exited the work station.

Where Angels Fear to Tread

Teryk hesitated, his internal self-preservation alarms warning not to enter the demolished building. Tugging on the rope one last time to ensure it was secure, he repelled from the hovering Battle Cruiser into the darkened structure, with much trepidation. As he touched down, his body froze momentarily. The internal cavities of the old church resonated from the howl of some infernal creature just outside the main doors. That howl... was the same hellish wail he remembered from childhood. The howling had always been a distant cry, never before this close to him. A chorus of barks and yelps accompanied the mournful wail that was echoing off the cavernous walls of the old church.

As his first officer touched down, Teryk signaled to the craft that was hovering silently overhead to depart. Only a shimmer of stars gave away the position of the Battle Dragon as it moved away. They had descended through the eye of the hurricane and would need to depart the same way. That gave them less than forty-five minutes to complete their task and get the hell out of there.

Teryk and Monique were both wearing dark hooded robes over their armored ExoSkeletons. Their helmets' night vision permitted them to see the destruction within the old church. Amazingly, its thick adobe walls had remained intact.

Teryk's night vision displayed three lechuzas tearing at a large *Bible* near the altar. He drew his sidearm and quickly dispatched them. The bullets in his Hellfire weapon did not rely on firing pins to detonate the gunpowder.

Suddenly a swirling cloud of shredded onion-paper strips enveloped Teryk. Retracting his storm shield momentarily he noticed the swirling mass split into two columns: whirlwinds which branched out, taking the form of two angels, each about twelve feet tall. The thrones moved in unison, flanking Teryk.

"Behold, a servant of the Most High," mocked Asmodeus. "You are too late to save them."

Teryk turned to see an ominous gleam emanating from the corner. A glow from its eyes was all that escaped the murky shadows. The thing seemed genderless, something powerful enough to be male but with female characteristics. A cold breeze lifted the long black hair off its face at that exact moment—as if it had power over the very elements. Teryk wondered why it was acting like a cornered animal. Activating several blue glow-sticks, Teryk tossed them about the enclosure.

Asmodeus moved towards Artimus.

Recognizing his old mentor, Teryk moved to intervene.

With undisguised hostility, Asmodeus snarled at the old priest, "Curse God and die, priest!"

"Perhaps this tragedy has come from God, but I charge him with no wrong doing," replied Artimus.

"Is this one proving a tough nut to crack?" asked Teryk. "His faith frustrates you, doesn't it? He is a man of the cloth but he is not cut from the same fabric of clergy you're used to dealing with."

The dæmon's voice intensified, "Why are you here?"

"I believe you already know the answer to that question," Teryk shot back.

Asmodeus circled like a wary animal, instinctively sensing something was very wrong. Then the expression on its face began to change, transforming into something easier on the eyes. The creature standing before Teryk was now a beautiful enchantress, whose well-proportioned body was barely contained in the tattered remnants of the young girl's dress.

Asmodeus eyed the two angels suspiciously, then looked up to the sky as if searching for something. The dæmon then exercised its powers of lust, which were this dæmon's domain. Inching closer to Teryk, she attempted to seduce him with promises of power and pleasure.

Teryk grasped her by the throat with blinding speed. "You will find that my powers are far greater than when last we met." He detected fear in her smoldering gaze, something he had not expected to see, at least not from this dæmon.

Still in shock, Asmodeus whispered, "Incredible, you've augmented your power base and lost nothing in the transformation. Is that why you returned to this world?"

"I never had any intentions of returning to this world," countered Teryk, releasing his grip on her neck.

"You were volunteered…again!" she laughed while massaging her throat. Asmodeus looked at Teryk as if he'd lost his mind. "Will you never learn? Tell me, are you as powerful as uhh…?" she asked, nodding toward the crucifix to indicate Jesus without having to utter his name.

"No. Y'shua is far greater, although I have performed miraculous healings that even I find hard to believe." Lowering his storm shield, he added, "I can also control the weather and the clouds to some extent. But before I get carried away, I should stress that the healings were actually the work of Faith and the Holy Spirit."

"Pity…his powers and your temper would make for a hell of a combination," said Asmodeus, winding her way through the mud-covered wreckage. She stood before Teryk and tried to stare into his eyes but the storm shield prevented it.

Against his better judgment, Teryk raised his visor. The soft blue shimmer of the glow sticks made her look truly exotic as she gazed with awe and bewilderment into his eyes.

"You've consumed the Bread of Life," said the dæmon, recoiling in disbelief, "haven't you?"

Teryk nodded, not sure where this was going. "I underwent a forty-day fast as part of ah…," he said almost reflexively before he could stop himself, "and…"

"And now you seem to be exhibiting unique abilities and powers," interrupted Asmodeus. "A forty-day fast on *shewbread* has one of only two outcomes. You either die a horrible death or your spirit-body morphs." Astonished at her adversary's audacity, she added, "But you couldn't have known what it was going to do to you or you would never have taken it." She stopped and looked directly into his eyes. "I would never have taken it!"

"Would it surprise you to know that I took it while I was in another physical form, a different body, in another time?"

"Manna supercharges the spiritual body. Release me!" She demanded. "Set me free and I will fill in the gaps for you. I will tell you exactly what you've done to yourself and what sort of changes you can expect."

"Don't do it," pleaded Joshua. Clutching at his ribs, he shook his head in pain. "Send that dæmon straight to Hell, where it belongs."

"There is only one place I send dæmons… the Abyss," replied Teryk.

"The Abyss? But there is no escape from that place," stated Asmodeus.

"Exactly! You won't be there forever, though. Christ will eventually release you."

"Yeah—after His thousand-year reign on Earth is over. Have you any idea how long a minute in that place lasts? And you want to send me there for a thousand years. I have no desire to hang around Apolyion for that long." Asmodeus held up a beautifully manicured hand and gestured for Teryk to hold off. "Teryk, what you've done can have horribly fatal consequences. Were you made aware of the dangers before you submitted to the fast?"

"Now you're just stalling," Teryk scoffed. "This is unbecoming. Come, let's get this over with…."

"Herod, yes Herod Antipas, underwent the forty-day fast when he was proclaimed Messiah by the Sanhedrin," said Asmodeus excitedly. "He died over a five-day period as worms slowly consumed his flesh. Herod the Great, his father, had access to the powder as well," she said, backing away from Teryk, one hand held out in front of her in a protective gesture. "That is how he was able to accomplish so many incredible architectural wonders, including the building of the Third Great Temple. But in the end it drove him mad and he died a most horrible death while worms feasted on his testicles."

This gave Teryk reason to pause. "I thought Herod the Great built the Second Temple, not the third one." Now he was stalling.

She straightened, seeming more confident. With a wicked-yet-sincere gleam in those beautiful dark eyes, Asmodeus played her last card. "Actually it was Herod who destroyed the Second Temple. The priests did not trust him to build a new temple and would not allow him to destroy the old one until the third and final temple was completed. I can see I've lost you. Let's recap, shall we?"

"The First Temple was built by Solomon, The Wise," continued Asmodeus. "It lasted about four hundred years until it was pillaged by Babylon's King Nebuchadnezzar II. During the second plunder, his soldiers ravaged the magnificent Temple I had helped create, razing it to the ground stone by stone and stripping it of all its beautiful gold.

"When Cyrus the Great conquered Babylon, he freed the Jews and allowed them to return and rebuild. The Second Temple was much smaller than, and not as grandiose as, the first but it stood for nearly six hundred years. Then came Herod the Great. Were you aware that the kingdom, over which Julius Caesar appointed him, suffered a horrific drought lasting nearly two years?" asked Asmodeus. "Herod nearly lost everything purchasing food for his subjects, from his own personal treasury."

"Herod? Herod the Great, one of the most corrupt and evil rulers in history?" asked Joshua, although it pained him to do so. Propping himself up against the wreckage, he raked a handful of mud and jungle debris out of his hair.

"Herod was a prince from the land of the Edomites, descendants of Esau. The Essenes saw in him the makings of a great king. They saw what a noble thing he had done and believing he was a righteous man, granted him access to the Manna. The accomplishments of Herod the Great have never been equaled. Your historians fail to explain how this nearly bankrupt Idumaean managed to launch the most ambitious building projects ever attempted in that region of the world. Where did he amass the great fortune necessary to finance this undertaking? As I explained, he was left with nothing, the drought having decimated his kingdom."

"So how did the Essenes get their hands on it?" asked Artimus. "The Manna, I mean."

"From Egypt, they learned how to extract it in a naturally occurring form from the Dead Sea. By the way, how was it you managed to get your hands on so much Manna?" she asked Teryk.

Joseph "Five Eagles" Reyna

"The Essenes gave it to me," Teryk answered, noticing in his peripheral monitors that both priests were turning to look at him.

"Did you think Moses was the first to discover Manna?" an amused Asmodeus demanded quizzically. "As I told you, the Egyptians had it long before he did. They got it from Noah the grandson of Enoch. Moses not only got his manna from the Egyptian temples; he had his craftsman Bezaleel fashion the Ark of the Covenant for the purpose of manufacturing more of the substance. The manna you consumed was white and powdery, was it not?"

"Yes, it was," said Teryk, puzzled. "What was it made from?"

"The Bread of Life is made from the purest gold. A small amount of manna can be quite beneficial, but in large quantities it's difficult to say. Results vary from person to person, ranging from good to bad. At times the results are quite ugly."

"Beneficial in what way?" asked Artimus, perplexed. "I thought it was just food."

"Mana can heal the body from almost any infirmity. It also increases spiritual awareness by feeding the spiritual body. Moses, if you recall, consumed the golden calf with fire from the Ark of the Covenant and forced the surviving Israelites to eat it. What I've just described is a very, very rudimentary explanation for the transmutation of gold into 'The Bread of Life' or Manna." She pointed toward the remnants of the *Bible* lying on the muddy floor. It was beginning to drizzle and the few remaining pages had started to get wet.

Teryk retrieved the *Bible*. When he turned around, Asmodeus was holding a large conical-shaped precious stone.

"Gnow you what this is?" she asked, holding up the dark pyramidal glass.

Teryk recognized the shape at once. It appeared as a transparent elongated triangular cone. The glass cast an eerie rose-red luminescence that was clearly not of this world. His teams had already located three of these alchemical relics, but not one as large as this. He had no idea what made it glow thus. "If I were to take a guess at it, I'd say it was a Philosopher's Stone. What alchemists refer to as *The Stone of Perfection*."

Asmodeus's eyes widened slightly in an expression of genuine surprise. Then, unexpectedly and with all the ceremony of one standing before royalty, she presented the stone to Teryk. In the demure hands of the enchantress, it appeared to weigh nothing. "Its most ancient name is she-ma-n-na-an-nu-na-ki: Star Fire, brought from Heaven to Earth by the Annunaki."

Teryk braced himself, shifting his feet slightly, knowing it was going to be heavy. It was; incredibly so. The servos in his exterior armor reacted by adjusting to reduce the strain. Once in his gauntleted hands, the cone radiated even more brightly.

Encased in the transparent cone was what appeared to be a cylindrical red crystal surrounded by a luminescent crystalline coil. The outer gem had the appearance of being wound like a spring. The two embedded gems radiated with a strange purplish light. The hauntingly beautiful light at the center of the pyramidal cone seemed somehow familiar.

Teryk knew what the coil and the ruby rod were. Somehow, he could still access remnants of the Jewish scribe's memory. The fragmented pieces of information fused together in a blinding epiphany. "These are the Schethiy and the Lightning Stone: the Schamir," he whispered. He gazed at the gems suspended in the opaque-yet-transparent material that shimmered with its own iridescence. The ruby red cylindrical shaped gem, the Schamir (sham-eer), was about two inches long and about half an inch in width. The milky-white, luminescent gem that wound like a serpent around the cylindrical ruby was the Schethiy (skee-thee-ah). "How do the gems cause the glass pyramid to give off this glow?" he asked.

"It is a combination of the Schethiy and the Schamir as well as your own presence that is causing the glow—Master of the Universe."

Now it was Teryk's turn to look surprised. Others had called him by this title, though he had never repeated it to anyone, let alone believed it.

"But you still have much to learn. The name of this glass pyramid is unpronounceable by humans. You will find references to it in ancient Egyptian hieroglyphs. It is denoted by the symbol of an elongated black triangle referred to as the *mfkzt*. The elongated pyramidal cone is not made of glass, but gold so pure that it is transparent as glass."

Teryk raised an eyebrow, finding this hard to believe.

Asmodeus pointed to the muddy *Bible* and instructed Teryk to open it. As he did, the few remaining pages rustled and flipped like a money-counting machine, stopping at Revelation chapter 21.

Teryk placed his gauntleted hand over the page. Blue-white micro-LED lights in the palm of his armored glove illuminated the text. He found the verse, but the reference was in Spanish. He translated it in his mind as he read aloud. "The city was of pure gold, crystal-clear… and the streets of the city were of pure gold, transparent as glass...."

"That description of the city was intended to be taken *literally*," exclaimed Asmodeus, adding emphasis to the last word.

'Good thing this verse is in the last book of the Bible,' thought Teryk, 'because most of the book is missing.'

Not sure if Teryk was paying attention, the dæmon went on. "I'm not going to beg you, Teryk," she said defiantly, gazing at the two thrones flanking the priests. "Sending me to the Abyss may lead to your demise as well. You have but to say the word and you seal my fate." Crossing her arms she turned away adding, "Herod the Great had once been a noble king before the shewbread turned him into a monster." Turning back toward him she beseeched her captor, "The knowledge I've accumulated could aid you from time to time."

Looking at Teryk in amusement, Asmodeus inquired, "Do you often eat a thing, having no idea what it is?" Again Asmodeus pointed to the *Bible*. The remaining pages began to turn rapidly, this time to the book of Exodus. "As I once served Solomon, perhaps I can now serve you. I've had direct contact with this stuff. You should take advantage of my experience. You can ill afford not to." Taking a more servile, almost seductive posture, she continued, "You might find this passage in Exodus interesting. It pertains to manna."

Asmodeus's alluring approach was not lost on Teryk. He was aware of her powerful female polarity and did not like it. He lifted the remnants of the large *Bible* and found the passage, Exodus 16:15, translating it into English as he read. "On seeing it, the Israelites asked one another, 'What is this?' for they did not know what it was…"

"That's far enough! In the Hebrew language, *man* as found in the word *man-na* is the asking of a question. They did not have a ready-made name for white powdery stuff, as the translation alludes to. The Israelites knew not what it was. *What is it* sounds more like a *question* than a *name*, don't you think?"

"Are you now in liege with dæmons?" demanded Artimus, having regained his strength he commenced trying to pull himself out from under a pew.

"They have their uses," said Teryk as he lifted the large bench off of the old priest. The ExoSkeleton's servos amplified his strength as he threw the broken bench over the nearest wall.

"What sort of uses are you referring to, Teryk?" asked Artimus, not sure he wanted to know.

"Information, mostly. Go ahead—ask her a question. Asmodeus is bound and cannot hurt you," assured Teryk, wondering how long he could resist her tantalizing spell. The strange stimulating feelings emitted by her were hard to describe, and harder still to resist.

"You expect a dæmon to answer truthfully?" grunted Joshua.

"Like most teenagers, they answer as truthfully as they can get away with," laughed Teryk.

"A truthful dæmon, what an oxymoron," laughed Joshua, though it pained him to do so.

Turning to Artimus, Teryk asked, "Is this your star pupil, Artimus? He's beginning to annoy me."

"No more than you annoyed me when I was teaching you," remarked Artimus. "It would appear that you are now the Master, so if you don't mind…could you explain this paradox to my pupil and to me as well?" requested the old priest.

"You're both priests. Has either of you ever bothered to read the entire New Testament?" asked Asmodeus. They both snorted simultaneously. "I'll take that as a yes. What do the Gospels record dæmons saying when your Messiah confronted them? I will tell you. They proclaimed him to be the 'Unique Son of God'. Being dæmons, one would think that they'd have chosen to lie about him to the crowd. Why not simply slander him as the chief priests had? They could have said he was a sorcerer, confirming the high priests' accusations. But his time had not yet come, and so he ordered them silent. There is the story of a possessed girl who followed the apostles, proclaiming who they were until they tired of it and vanquished the spirit. Dæmons do not lie as much as twist the truth. In that respect, they're a lot like your politicians. Truth cannot be counterfeited. It is something we all recognize. So go ahead, ask me a question. See if you can catch me at a lie."

"Very well then," said Joshua, wincing from the pain of forming words. Teryk kneeled by his side. Monique came forth from the shadows, her hooded cloak startling Joshua. She knelt and examined his injury. Opening her medical kit, she prepped the skin then administered an injection of morphine to the affected area.

Breathing more easily, Joshua continued, "This is something you should know. Did God create Man or did man evolve from an ape?"

"Are you well versed in the science of evolution?" asked Asmodeus.

"Here I must warn you," interrupted Teryk, "dæmons will almost always answer a question with a question."

"What does it matter? If you know the answer why don't you just answer the question?" demanded Joshua.

"I need to know if you are qualified to understand my answer." Asmodeus tilted her head inquisitively, a lock of hair falling over her face.

"I have a fair understanding of it; it's the main reason I entered the priesthood. There were just too many unanswered questions pertaining to evolution. Its fundamental principles seem to offer a fair explanation for the animal kingdom but fall utterly short in trying to explain the existence of man."

Satisfied with his reply, Asmodeus leaned forward and locked eyes with her prey. "According to the laws of evolution, is it possible for a creature, any creature, to mutate and evolve a brain so incredibly complex it can scarcely use a small fraction of its capabilities?"

Joshua looked away and closed his eyes, shaking his head. "It can't be that simple...."

"Deep down inside, you intuitively gnow the answer," Asmodeus assured him. "There is no logical reason for you to possess a brain capable of functioning well beyond the means of your everyday survival. Your scriptures make it quite clear that it was the Lord of the Elohim, EA Enki, who ordered the modification of your species by saying, 'let us create man in our image according to our likeness.'

God had nothing to do with it." Turning to the older priest, she inquired, "And what would you ask, Artimus? Surely after all these years as a priest there must be at least one thing you would like the answer to?"

"Let me be clear on this, I am not comfortable asking anything of a dæmon. But… I have always wondered who or what the Nephilim were."

"The Nephilim were the offspring created from the union between the sons of the Elohim and the daughters of Adam and Eve. These offspring went by many names, most of which inspired fear in the hearts of men. They were called the *Gibborim*, which simply meant giants, because their size was enormous. They were referred to as the *Emim*, for their tremendous strength. Because they were fierce in battle and great masters of war, their enemies, the Draconians, knew them as the *Zamzummim*. But there was a type of ancient giants that were not so noble. They are remembered in your legends as the Titans."

"You forgot to mention that they were also called the Rephaim," smiled Artimus, "because one glance at them would make men's hearts grow weak. Job and Isaiah speak of them as 'Dead Things' which shall have no resurrection...."

"The Rephaim, those ugly little things?" interrupted Asmodeus with a dismissive gesture. "You are correct in saying there shall be no resurrection for the Rephaim. They are bio-mechanical clones, more android than living creature. And they are certainly not giants. Why, they only stand about so tall." She extended her hand, palm facing down, about a meter off the ground. "The bulbous heads and large black almond-shaped eyes of the Rephaim would give anyone a start."

A loud clatter accompanied yelps outside the structure. Teryk turned to see Monique dislodging a long bench covered in jungle debris and hurling it over the wall. It landed with a resounding thud. Two mud-covered bodies lay on the floor. Monique knelt over them and checked for vital signs, she found none.

"Perhaps the best explanation of the Nephilim," continued Asmodeus, "comes from Genesis and goes something like this. 'When men began to multiply on the Earth and daughters were born to them, the Sons of Heaven saw how beautiful the daughters of men were, and so they took for their wives as many of them as they chose.'"

"The beauty of Earth's women brought down the angels of Heaven," summed up Artimus. "Through fornication with those beings, wicked abominations were loosed on mankind."

"Then you've probably never heard of them being referred to as the heroes of old, the men of renown?" asked Asmodeus.

"*Men of renown?* I do not recall the Nephilim ever being called that, and certainly not by the *Bible*," Artimus admitted.

"And yet in Genesis six it is there for all to see. Odd that by comparison, the *Bible* had little good to say about the men of that era," mused Asmodeus.

"Asmodeus, leave the girl and do not return to her. I will call when I have need of you." The dæmon did not normally appear as an enchantress. Teryk supposed it had something to do with the form of the young girl and wondered what form the dæmon would take when next they met. The shemanna began to disappear from his hand. Teryk hurried to the girl's side. She collapsed in his arms, her features slowly returning to normal. Teryk lowered his head and whispered into the girl's ear. "Where is it?"

"You will find one of the two stones," she said in a low voice before whispering to Teryk what he needed to know. A scent of cherry blossoms filled the enclosure. Outside, dogs yelped in pain and ran into the distance.

"You cannot release Asmodeus! We are under strict orders from the Pope himself to return with it to the Vatican," hissed the archbishop through clenched teeth. Monique had revived him just in time to catch the end of the exorcism.

"Using this young girl's body as a host?" Teryk shot back, unable to believe what he was hearing. "Artimus I know, but I am not familiar with you or your orders...."

"I am Archbishop Felipe Espindola. Who the hell are you?"

"No one of consequence, Archbishop," commented Teryk. "I was not aware the Church had exorcists of your rank. Just how were you planning to get this girl back to Rome, if you don't mind my asking?"

"The Vatican wants Asmodeus captured and taken back for questioning," volunteered Joshua. "A helicopter will be here in the morning as soon as the winds die down. A medical plane, a Learjet with Vatican guards, will be waiting for us at a nearby airfield."

"A gross misallocation of resources," commented Teryk. "Let me guess— you're after the Ark of the Covenant, aren't you? What is the Church planning to do with it after recovery? Return it to its rightful owners, the Jews? No, of course not. It would become property of the Church."

"The dæmon has given you the Ark's location, hasn't it?" bellowed the archbishop with great indignation, sounding like he was frothing at the mouth. "The Ark does not belong to you! I don't know who the hell you think you are, but as soon as the soldiers arrive I am having you placed under arrest for interfering!" He drew a seething breath. "It obvious you're in league with the Dev..." A burst of blue-white light silhouetted the archbishop's head, illuminating the wreckage.

In the crackling flash of arcing blue flames, Teryk observed Monique holding a Taser to the back of the archbishop's neck. "The mouth on this guy, does he kiss the Pope's ring with those lips?" asked Teryk as he helped his old friend Artimus to his feet and out of the old structure. "Do you have any idea what those stones were that Asmodeus was showing me?"

Artimus shook his head.

"The stones are necessary if one is going to activate the Ark. The lid on the Ark, which includes the two cherubim, is constructed from solid gold. Do you seriously think four men were capable of carrying that much gold with only two wooden poles?" asked Teryk, looking around the village for shelter from the coming storm. "I know you're hurt but I need to get you into one of the undamaged buildings before the eye of the hurricane passes and you're caught out in the open."

"You're right. The Ark would have been too heavy," reasoned Artimus. "Yet it is well documented that it was carried great distances on poles by a handful of priests." Artimus looked at Teryk, not sure where this was going. "What are the stones? What is their purpose?"

"The stones activate the power of the Ark of the Covenant. Artimus, the knowledge I am about to confide in you must never be revealed to the Vatican. I already suspect they have some understanding of the stones and what they are capable of, but you must never let it slip that you know what they're for.

"One of the stones is shaped like a coiled serpent, the other like a long cylindrical gem. When the blood-red gem was inserted inside the coil-shaped gem and both stones were set on the Mercy Seat, the Ark of the Covenant was said to have levitated off the ground. This allowed the carriers to transport it," said Teryk as they approached some large well-constructed huts. He knocked on one of the village doors. Two men emerged and assisted him with the priest. "There are others in the church who need help," he told them in Spanish. Several men went to help.

"The Ark of the Covenant," said Artimus, gritting his teeth due to the pain in his leg.

Teryk tore open Artimus's pant leg, exposing a bad fracture. Without another word, he pulled out his medical kit and administered morphine. He then cleaned, set and dressed the broken leg.

"You always were handy to have around. Thank you, old friend," said Artimus. "Are you going after it, Teryk?"

Teryk only smiled, unable to control his excitement.

"Just like Indiana Jones, huh?" The old priest nodded.

"Artimus, I have never asked this of you. I know you think I've strayed far from my original path, so I'm going to ask you a question and I want you to answer it as truthfully as you know how."

Monique entered with Joshua. Teryk checked him, but Monique had already attended to his wounds.

"Why so serious?" asked Artimus with a smile. Regaining his composure, he added, "OK, OK, I'll do my best. Shoot."

"Have you ever witnessed me perform what would be called a miracle?"

"Yes, of course. Why, even tonight when I saw those angels in the whirlwind—that was something I will never forget."

"Knowing that, would you consider me to be on the side of darkness or the side of good?"

"Well, I can tell you I have never seen anyone exert such control over a dæmon before."

"Perhaps, but when commanded to, even a dæmon will obey the Will of God; which is more than I can say for most Christians."

"Well, I've never understood how you managed to do the things you do, but I would have to say you are not on the side of darkness."

"Then rest assured that I am not doing evil, even though you may not understand. Honestly, sometimes even I don't understand," admitted Teryk, "but I do my best to obey. I guess I just want you to know I'm in good hands. As far as being in league with the Devil, priests said the same thing about Jesus and his followers. I assure you, if I was in league with Satan it would be me taking orders from the dæmon and not the other way around."

"You know, its uncanny how dealing with dæmons is a lot like dealing with a teenage daughter," explained Teryk. "That puts you at a severe disadvantage, Padre. Teenage daughters are deceitful, cunning, capricious, erratic and unpredictable. They speak in half-truths, omitting much. One must choose his questions wisely. Only dragons are more difficult to deal with."

Artimus laughed. "The things you say." The old priest raised an eyebrow at the previous remark. "You mean to tell me that dragons are real?"

"I knew they were mentioned in the *Bible* but had no idea that they were real until I encountered my first one during a healing."

Tired from his ordeal, Artimus nodded his understanding. "Speaking of healings, do you think the Pope will proclaim you a saint for having performed at least three verifiable miracles?" teased Artimus, "Perhaps I could put in a good word for ya, lad?"

It was Teryk's turn to laugh. "Fat chance of that ever happening. He's the one who excommunicated me, remember? Then again, for a chance to get his hands on the Ark of the Covenant…he just might."

As Teryk stood, Artimus tugged on his cloak. "You said, 'If you were going to activate it you would need the stones.' What did you mean by activate? Do you intend to recover the Ark of the Covenant?"

"As to your first question concerning the stones, when you consider that the Ark is a potential weapon of unspeakable power, the stones could be viewed as the launch codes needed to activate the weapon," Teryk explained.

Artimus's eyes grew wide, concern etched on his face. "You're not going to…"

Teryk shook his head. "Consider me lucky if I just find the stones, to keep them safe if nothing else." Teryk placed a hand on his old friend's arm and smiled. "It was good to see you again, Artimus," he said as Monique came to stand behind him. She handed Teryk an old, intricately carved, leather-bound book which he recognized.

Teryk unlocked the seal, opened the book and read the title aloud. "*Ritus Exorcizandi Obsessos a Daemonio.*" It was an ancient written procedure for expelling dæmons. He read further, wondering what could possibly possess the Vatican to release this book from its archives: "Sacerdos ab Ordinario delegatus, rite confessus, aut saltem corde peccata sua detestans, peracto, si commode fieri possit, Sanctissimo Missae sacrificio, divinoque auxilio piis precibus implorato, superpelliceo et stola violacea indutus, et coram…" A look of concern washed over his face as he closed the book. "I've always felt this was the hard way of doing exorcisms."

"That 400-year-old book belongs in the Vatican's Secret Library."

"I think you got your tenses tangled, Padre. It *belonged* to the Vatican's Secret Library. The Good Book bids you boys to travel with neither 'purse' nor 'script' and I mean to put you in good standing with the Lord."

Artimus chuckled as Teryk handed the book back to Monique, who bound it in a protective covering.

Artimus clasped both of Teryk's hands while giving a stern warning, "I know you share my own misgivings concerning religion's abuse of authority. You know, they'll come for you? The Church has enormous resources at its disposal. Before you leave, I would ask that you take my protégé with you. He's a lot like you once were and has a great many questions that I simply cannot answer. He's also a heartbeat away from being excommunicated for seeking answers to those questions. Perhaps with a Master like you to teach him, he might accomplish the destiny God has set before him. There is little more he can learn from me."

"He's injured but in stable condition, Commander," said Monique. "Shall I advise the transport we have an additional passenger?"

Teryk nodded, "It won't be long before the winds pick up again, Monique. Advise the transport of our status."

"Oui, monsieur," replied Monique, who was not looking forward to sliding down the muddy mountainside in the pouring rain. She radioed for a retraction from the orbiting Battle Dragon: a specially cloaked war-bird.

"True, Joshua is injured, but I have seen this man work miraculous healings before. What did you think he got thrown out of the Church for in the first place?" Artimus asked Monique, raising his eyebrows toward Teryk. "The Church has a long history of persecuting its saints while harboring and protecting its pedophiles," he added in a melancholy tone.

"The Church used to torture and kill its saints, so I suppose this could be considered an improvement," Teryk noted, his voice harboring hostility.

"I would ask that you take me with you as well," said Artimus, "but perhaps I can be of more service to you from inside the priesthood itself. Everything you warned me about while you were under my charge is coming to pass. I fear the End of Days may actually be upon us."

"Up until yesterday, I had forgotten all about the End of Days," said Teryk. "So many of the prophecies went unfulfilled. I reasoned that perhaps I had misunderstood the meaning of the prophecies, or that maybe it simply wasn't time."

"I'm telling you this because you just might be crazy enough to understand what it is I'm about to divulge," said Artimus. "Do you remember when you first told me about Chernobyl's meltdown and how you thought it might be linked to prophecy? Do you recall telling me how the individuals who look for signs of the Apocalypse believed Chernobyl to be 'wormwood', one of the trumpet judgments from the book of Revelation?"

"What in the world is this *wormwood*?" inquired Monique.

"Wormwood is something that turns water bitter. Interestingly enough, so does the radiation from a nuclear weapon," explained Artimus. "By an incredible coincidence, the word Chernobyl means wormwood in the Ukraine tongue. So when it melted down, many who look for the signs of the End of Days deduced that the meltdown must have been the third trumpet judgment spoken of in the book of Revelation. It was certainly radioactive, so much so that Russian authorities decided to seed the clouds heading toward Moscow in order to stop the radioactivity from reaching the Capital. Their actions resulted in childbirth defects, leukemia and thyroid cancer throughout the population of the surrounding area."

"How is it you know all this?" asked Monique, not sure if she should believe this old man.

"The Catholic Church has a religious custom called confession," explained Artimus. "Pilots ordered to seed the clouds confessed to their priests, who transferred that information to the Vatican. Once the Vatican had this information, they simply kept an eye on the people of the affected regions."

"The Knights Templar were well acquainted with the intelligence-gathering capabilities of the Church. This is why creators of the game of chess chose to include a bishop among the game's strategically important pieces," added Teryk.

"I always wondered why a bishop was included in the game at all," said an astonished Monique, kneeling down to shake hands with Artimus. "My name is Monique. Teryk has not told me too much about his old mentor," she said, turning toward her commander.

"Do you wish to join us, Joshua?" asked Teryk. "It seems your future with the priesthood will be short-lived should you choose to remain here."

"You should go with them, son. I think the answers you're looking for lie out there," advised Artimus.

"I am in no condition to travel, father."

Teryk proceeded to Joshua's side and placed his hand over the injured area. Almost instantaneously, Joshua seemed to recover. All three looked on in awe at the transformation. Joshua stood and began to stretch in all directions, letting out an occasional 'ouch' every now and then.

"Whoa… you've certainly come a long way as a healer from the time when I knew you," exclaimed Artimus. "Having witnessed this event, I can now see how the word miracle came into being. The word itself stems from the Latin word meaning to marvel at an occurrence that causes one to look on in astonished wonder."

"Well, I'm certainly astonished. I did not know you were capable of such things, Commander," admitted Monique.

"Nor I, Monique," confessed Teryk. "This has never happened before, except during my time in the deprivation tank. That was like something out of a dream. It seemed so fantastic and unreal."

"What exactly happened in there, in the deprivation tank, I mean?" asked Monique.

"Something tells me I'm not supposed to know the answer to that question," said Artimus. "Well, my friends, now that Joshua is fit to travel, allow me to bring you up to date on the latest wormwood findings…."

"Is the Vatican aware of a meteor or comet that will impact Earth soon?" asked Teryk.

"There are two possibilities it could be an approaching cosmic intruder or a mega-volcano, like the massive underground cauldron at Yellowstone National Park in the United States."

"But volcanoes are not radioactive," said Joshua.

"This deep underground cauldron is believed to be heated in part by radioactive material," explained Artimus. "Yellowstone seems to be overdue for its eruption. If it did erupt, it would certainly fulfill the prophecy of wormwood as found in the Apocalypse. The world would be plunged into a nuclear winter. Its fallout would blanket most of North America. Perhaps that is why we've never found references to the United States in the book of Revelation. Also there are rumors that a Vatican-owned observatory in Arizona has been tracking a very large and mysterious inbound object that only appears in the infrared spectrum."

"Artimus, why would you risk infiltrating the Vatican for me?" asked Teryk.

"Sadly, I can no longer support what they stand for. I was ordered to sedate that child and return with her to Rome, where the dæmon could be questioned regarding the Ark of the Covenant's location. The cardinals in charge seem to care nothing for the anguish that child's family is being put through. They have embraced the Machiavellian concept that the ends justify the means. Believe it or not, Teryk, the Pope has even begun selling Indulgences again!"

"You cannot be serious!" Teryk blurted out, "I thought that practice disappeared with the Dark Ages. You mean monetary penance for the forgiveness of sins? The original 'Get out of Purgatory Free' cards? Those Indulgences?"

"One and the same," acknowledged Artimus. "They plan to rake in a lot of additional revenue because the Catholic Church claims that everyone has to go to Purgatory."

"But if you act quickly you can purchase a connecting flight directly to Heaven," put in Joshua with a twinkle in his eye. "I was told that the Pope, in all of his divine wisdom, is trying to alleviate the overcrowding in Purgatory."

"Has the Pope considered selling Indulgences for dead relatives as well?" asked Teryk. "*Every time a coin rings, a soul springs.* Wasn't that the jingle the Church used back then? Well, I didn't see this coming. Tell me, how do you think the Vatican will react once they've learn that I am the one responsible for expelling the dæmon?"

"It would seem that you've inadvertently become an enemy of the Vatican," said Artimus. "So, what do you think their next move will be?"

"If they truly believe Asmodeus could have led them to the Ark of the Covenant, they will spare no expense to find me. The cardinals and bishops will call in every favor owed to them from any government official in the world who can assist them."

"Exactly, so you must give them something to chase after. Provide them with something that will keep their dogs busy." In an ominous tone, Artimus added, "Do not underestimate how far the tentacles of the Vatican reach!"

"Are you sure you still want to join up with me, Joshua?" Teryk asked.

"More than ever. Oh, by the way, this recorder around my neck is still recording. Should I turn it off?"

"No, leave it recording. Monique will place it in a protective coating when we leave. Were there any other recording devices in the church?" asked Teryk.

"There was another recorder on the floor but it was destroyed early into the proceedings. I saw a pew bouncing up and down upon its remains. The cameras were not equipped with audio recording capabilities and may have been damaged in the storm. There were two night vision cameras."

"Leave those. It will give them something to worry about when they see the angels," advised Artimus. "Like you, Joshua is a misfit, an oddity who no longer fits into the world of the clergy. Perhaps in your world of mystics he will find what he has been looking for."

Teryk smiled and nodded his understanding. Reaching for his medkit, he handed the contents to Artimus. "I'm not sure how long it will be before help arrives or how many more may be hurt."

Joshua clasped Artimus's hand one last time then stood at the door and nodded goodbye. He turned and stepped out into the warm, humid night air. The winds were beginning to pick up again. The transport had arrived but, because it had to land in such a public place, the 'UFO Mode' lights were blazing brightly. This rouse had worked many times before, with authorities dismissing the event as nonsense. The trio headed toward the Battle Dragon as it made its descent.

Choose Your Enemies Carefully

Vatican City, Rome, the next morning; a cleric exited the opulent assembly room and a Swiss Guard, dressed in the traditional garish attire designed by Michelangelo, closed the door and stood guard outside. Cardinal Bishop Pablo de la Torre addressed the seated cardinals in a steely tone. "Gentlemen, Asmodeus, the dæmon of secrets and buried treasure, has resurfaced. We have good reason to believe this dæmon knows the whereabouts of the lost Ark of the Covenant." This comment caused a commotion among the assembled cardinals. The cardinal bishop pointed towards a bookish looking fellow and said, "This is Father Laurence Andrews. He's a Demonologist and an expert on the dæmon Asmodeus. He will be briefing you on our progress."

Father Andrews, a tall slender balding man in his early 50s, stood and addressed the small delegation. "During a routine exorcism in Colombia," he began, clearing his throat and adjusting his glasses, "one of our village priests came across an entity identifying itself as Asmodeus. Padre Antonio Gutierrez, a Jesuit priest, remembered that this was the same dæmon known by the title Rex Mundi. Those of you familiar with Abbé Bérenger Saunière's restoration of the small village church at Rennes-le-Château, in France, will recall that he placed a statue of the dæmon Rex Mundi near the entrance of the church. Over the porch lintel, Saunière placed the peculiar inscription 'THIS PLACE IS TERRIBLE'. Legend has it that Saunière found a mysterious parchment in the hollowed recess of a Visigothic pillar, underneath the altar stone. Shortly after this, Saunière amassed a fortune and undertook restoration of the old parish, which had been dedicated to Mary Magdalene in 1059. Saunière decorated the church in the ornate, almost garish style that was popular during the late nineteenth century."

"Yes, it's all supposed to be part of some elaborate code that guides you to a treasure or some such nonsense," said one of the older men, Cardinal Baigent.

Shifting in his seat he added, "I have seen this 'cavity' myself and let me assure you it is far too small to have contained all that Saunière seems to have alluded to."

"Gentlemen, as a man who is ordered to keep secrets, I find that the very secrets themselves compel those who hold them to reveal them. Not openly, of course, but in symbols, ciphers and codes. It may surprise you to learn that the legendary encoded messages hidden within the peculiar artworks of Rennes-le-Château *have been decoded, unearthed and deciphered!*" announced Cardinal Bishop de la Torre to the astonishment of everyone in the room. "True to the garish style of the Knights Templar, clues left by Saunière in the statue of Asmodeus led the adventurers directly to the first clue. It was incredibly simple and had been in plain sight all along. For years, many suspected that the statue of Rex Mundi was the first of these clues. Some treasure seekers went as far as breaking into the parish in order to steal the dæmon's head, hoping something was hidden within it. The head of Asmodeus's statue you see before you," he pointed to the file in front of every Cardinal, "is a recreation from photos taken of the statue before it was vandalized."

"Regardless, anything they may have found is undoubtedly the property of the Catholic Church," announced Cardinal Fitzmyer, holding up a hand riddled with arthritis, resembling a withered claw. "Do not forget that the Knights Templar were once a military arm of the Church."

"I thought that the *fortune* Saunière reportedly discovered was explained by the selling of Masses, a common practice at the time," said Cardinal Lonegren, closing the file and setting it aside.

"The selling of Masses is just a story the Church clings to in order to draw attention away from the incident," assured Father Andrews. "The clues hidden in the documents Abbé Bérenger Saunière discovered led him to a secret compartment behind the wall of his wardrobe. Shortly after this, Saunière spent millions in the elaborate restoration of the old parish. The secret crypt behind the wardrobe is now sealed with a brick wall."

"Forgive me for sounding suspicious but why didn't the treasure hunters who broke into the church break through Saunière's brick wall in order to investigate the secret compartment behind his wardrobe? Neither the Church nor the French Government has ever given anyone permission to reopen it," inquired Cardinal Shapiro.

"Because there are few who are aware of the crypt's existence," retorted Cardinal Bishop de la Torre. "Gentlemen, we are not here to discuss the parish at Rennes-le-Château. We believe we may have come up with a way to secure the dæmon Asmodeus: by trapping it inside its host, where we may question it at our leisure. But before we disclose that information, I intend to demonstrate to you why this course of action is necessary."

"This is the 21ˢᵗ century. You're not seriously contemplating the questioning of a dæmon?" asked an incredulous Cardinal Lonegren. The good cardinal was in attendance only because Cardinal Bishop de la Torre needed his authorization. It seemed doubtful that Cardinal Lonegren had ever attended an exorcism in his life.

"I assure you, sir, the idea of dæmons is nothing new," said Father Andrews.

"If you can bear with me long enough to listen to what Father Andrews has to say, you will quickly realize why we need his expertise in this matter," advised Cardinal Bishop de la Torre.

"Asmodeus was one of the dæmons who assisted Solomon in the construction of the First Temple. My job as a Demonologist will be to coerce the dæmon into leading us to a great many discoveries including the lost Templar treasure. Asmodeus could also lead us to the legendary book God is said to have given Adam, one of many books Noah is reported to have carried with him aboard the Ark."

"How could Solomon have been able to command dæmons to do his bidding?" asked a disbelieving Cardinal Lonegren.

"According to rabbinical as well as other sources, the archangel Uriel personally gave special instructions to King Solomon on how to capture and use dæmons as slave labor. He instructed the king on the use of a magical ring. The ring gave Solomon power over dæmons, which he summoned and questioned at length regarding their special abilities. The Freemasons regard this ring very highly. They described the ring as having the symbol of the compass and the square overlapping each other upon it."

"How much do we really know about this archangel Uriel?" asked Cardinal Shapiro drumming his fingers on the table.

"Uriel was accepted as an archangel by the Catholic Church for many centuries. However, in the year 745 Uriel was removed from the records, along with the names of several other angels, by Pope Zachary. But Uriel is not my main concern," said Father Andrews, adjusting his glasses. "I shared this story with you in an effort to build up a background on the dæmon Asmodeus. Solomon stated that of all the dæmons he encountered, none was more important than Asmodeus, who *showed him hidden things that are in the world.* In Hebrew mythology, Asmodeus is the guardian of Solomon's treasure.

"Solomon is said to have obtained the Schamir from Asmodeus. Rabbinical legends concerning the Schamir state that it was a mystical stone which enabled Solomon to penetrate the earth in search of mineral wealth. This stone is one of two stones that must be located in order to activate the Ark of the Covenant. The other stone is called the Schethiy ."

"What do these stones have to do with the discovery of the Ark of the Covenant?" asked Cardinal Lonegren in a disparaging tone.

Incredulous

"The lid of the Ark was said to be made of solid gold. That much gold would be impossible for four priests to carry. When the Schamir, the 'lightning stone', is combined with the Schethiy , the 'stone of perfection', the Ark was said to levitate the width of three fingers off the ground, allowing the priests to transport it.

"The Book of Numbers, 4:15, states that in order to transport the Ark priests must carry it," explained Father Andrews. "King David, the father of Solomon, tried to transport the Ark of the Covenant on a specially constructed wagon. This resulted in the tragic death of one of his men. David must have been missing the stones or else the priests would have used them. David's son, King Solomon, did not run into any of these problems when transporting the Ark. This leads me to conclude that Solomon must have relocated the stones.

"During Solomon's reign, the Ark appears to have been taken to Ethiopia; more specifically to Elephantine Island," said Father Andrews. "Evidence of a Jewish presence has been discovered on this island by archaeologists. A layout of the Jewish Temple was also discovered there.

"Many years later, when Pharaoh Thutmose II raided the Temple of Solomon, the Egyptians made a record of all the treasure they pillaged and stored in the Temple of Luxor. First they listed the golden objects, then the silver and finally the copper spoils. But the Ark of the Israelites was not mentioned; because it was at the island of Elephantine.

"The Temple of Luxor also happens to be the Temple of Queen Hatshepsut, who was also known as the Queen of the South; a name that loosely translates into the Queen of Sheba. The Queen of Sheba, is the mother of Solomon's firstborn, Menelik.

"Understandably, the Israelites insist that the story of Menelik taking the Ark of the Covenant to Ethiopia is a myth," said Father Andrews rising from his ornately carved but very uncomfortable chair. "According to the legend, about ten centuries before Christ, 1,000 BCE, the Queen of Sheba became pregnant with Solomon's child. When she left to return to her kingdom, the queen requested that priests return with her so that they might instruct her child in accordance with Jewish customs. When Menelik came of age, the boy's mother sent him to Jerusalem to be recognized by his father, the king.

"The priests were not too pleased and informed Solomon that the boy could never inherit the throne and should be sent away. Solomon declared that if his firstborn was to be sent away then all firstborn of the priests must also be sent away. It turns out that the firstborn of all the priests were also the overseers of the Ark of the Covenant. Menelik would have required the Schamir and the Schethiy to transport the Ark such a great distance," explained Father Andrews beginning to pace about the vast chamber.

Father Andrews stood before a painting of the Ark, admiring the golden frame that must have weighed three-hundred pounds. Pointing to it he added, "The Ark of the Covenant appears in the chronicles of all the kings of Ethiopia and is even written into their Constitution. Today the Ark is believed to be held at a sanctuary in Aksum, the capital of Ethiopia. The Guardians of the Ark seem to die off about every two to three years. They develop milky cataracts over their eyes from gazing upon the Ark, which some of the Guardians have described as a thing of fire. During WWII, the Nazis made an attempt to capture the Ark from the Ethiopians. They attacked in combination with the Italians, but were unsuccessful in retrieving it.

"It is my belief that Menelik returned the precious stones to his father. Because the stones were inherited by the kings of Solomon's line to the seventh generation. King Joash was the last to possess the coiled talismanic ring. With the destruction of the First Temple the Schamir and the Schethiy vanished...."

"I believe that's enough information for now," interrupted Cardinal Bishop de la Torre standing to address the small gathering. "As I mentioned earlier, the code regarding Abbé Saunière's treasure has been broken. In the countryside near Rennes-le-Château is a peculiar stone carved into what appears to be a seat. The stone is called the 'Armchair of the Devil' and sits near a stream known as the 'The Spring of the Circle'. The dæmon Asmodeus is sometimes referred to as the 'lame devil' because it appears that the dæmon represented by the statue is crippled. However, when one superimposes the image of the statue over the 'Devil's Armchair' it becomes apparent that Asmodeus is seated. The men who discovered the first clue did so by superimposing an image of Asmodeus upon this armchair.

"When they studied this clue," continued Cardinal Bishop de la Torre, "they noticed that the dæmon appeared to be leaning forward and gazing at something. His bulging eyes, which appear exaggerated, were fixated on a particular spot—a small mound. When these men dug at the mound, they located a stone with special markings on it. Underneath the stone was a wine bottle containing a message inside. The message was encrypted and signed by Abbé Bérenger Saunière!

"This was the first of many messages. The markings on the stone led them to the second buried bottle with an encoded message inside. In addition to the letter was the riddle '*Enter the cave beneath the black foot and the helmet. To reveal the place where to dig there's a boy on bended knee.*' This message could only be decoded using the Stations of the Cross and/or the paintings Saunière had placed inside the church as well as the landmarks surrounding Rennes-le-Château.

"Through the work of these individuals, I discovered that an incredible amount of information can be stored onto a very small parchment when one incorporates works of art such as paintings that have been encoded with messages. Information stored incorporating this technique could have easily survived for hundreds of years inside the hollow Visigothic pillar. Let me assure you, gentlemen, after studying the encrypted messages I am convinced that there are few in this world capable of deciphering Saunière's codes.

"Our plan to capture and contain Asmodeus is simple," explained Cardinal Bishop de la Torre. "A team of exorcists headed by Archbishop Felipe Espindola, a Jesuit scholar, intends to bring the dæmon under guard to Vatican City as soon as possible."

"I was not aware that Archbishop Espindola was an exorcist," said Cardinal Lonegren.

"He's not," confirmed Cardinal Bishop de la Torre. "The main exorcist in charge is Father Artimus, who in turn is being assisted by Padre Ricardo Valencia, a parish priest from Cartagena. The medic assigned to the team is Doctor Facundo Lazo. Although he has never assisted in an exorcism, we've trusted him in similar matters before. The good doctor is not squeamish about unusual requests as long as he is well compensated for his trouble. Doctor Lazo will sedate the young girl and bring her here along with one of her parents."

"Aren't dæmons capable of physical and mental harm, even possibly taking over a child's soul?" asked Cardinal Shapiro, appearing uncomfortable with the whole idea.

"We cannot be certain of that. There are those who argue that the dæmon only takes possession of the physical body," argued Cardinal Bishop de la Torre. "Now that the first parts of the code appear to have been deciphered, it is imperative that we question this dæmon. The coded messages allude to a buried temple in that region: an exact replica of the Temple of Solomon. The clues lead us to believe this temple is in the Languedoc area near Rennes-le-Château. And it is in that temple that we suspect the Knights Templar placed the Ark of the Covenant along with their immense wealth for safekeeping."

"A Temple of Solomon in France—you cannot be serious? And what makes you think that the Knights Templar ever found the Ark of the Covenant?" asked Cardinal Lonegren. "Everyone I know dismisses the idea as nonsense."

Cardinal Bishop de la Torre raised a hand for silence. "Before anyone starts the conspiracy crap, archaeologists have documented finding Templar artifacts deep within the Temple mount. About a thousand years ago, nine knights callings themselves 'Knights of the Temple of Solomon' occupied and excavated the Temple Mount for eight years. Legend has it that during this time the Knights Templar protected the pilgrims traveling the roads of the Holy Land. But nine knights would have done little to protect a thousand miles of roadways ten centuries ago. We suspect they found the Ark of the Covenant, or information that led them to it, during their excavations but chose to withhold that information from the Pope.

"Cardinal Lonegren, it may surprise you to learn that in the 1860s extensive excavations were conducted beneath Temple Mount by the British explorer Sir Charles Warren. His team dug a number of vertical shafts down into the bedrock for the Palestine Exploration Fund. They succeeded in locating the original foundation of King Solomon's Temple. Its lower retaining walls were still intact. They noted that the masonry technique was quite distinct from that of the Second Temple. They dug deeper and discovered an amazing subterranean maze. The winding corridors and passages branched off in all directions. They also discovered ingeniously engineered caves and water cisterns as well as massive subterranean storage chambers. Shortly after this exploratory dig in 1894, British military engineers conducted a mapping survey of the tunnels and discovered many artifacts related to the Knights Templar, including a red Maltese cross and a broken Templar sword."

"Today this entire underground complex is inaccessible because of emotional tensions between Muslims and Jews," added Father Andrews, filling in for the Cardinal. "The Muslims feel that further excavations on the Temple Mount may damage the foundations of their Dome of the Rock.

"As far as a Temple of Solomon being in France, we've already identified several temples thousands of miles from Jerusalem that have been attributed to Solomon," continued Father Andrews. "Archaeological discoveries of ancient temples throughout the Far East show that they all followed a pattern similar to the one upon which Solomon modeled his temple. Although this appears to have been a standard layout for temples in the ancient past, a few of these temples specifically attribute their existence to King Solomon. The remains of the temple on Elephantine Island, for instance, certainly correspond to the floor plan of Solomon's Temple. If it were not for the island's archaeological evidence confirming that Jewish priests once inhabited it, I would have dismissed the entire thing as nonsense."

"Why haven't I heard of this before?" questioned Cardinal Shapiro straightening in his chair, intrigued by the possibility.

"A lot of this evidence was deliberately destroyed shortly after it surfaced. All that remains of the monuments attributing these temples to King Solomon are the sketches made by the discoverers and sometimes, if we're lucky, a few photos." Moving toward an easel and turning the page, Father Andrews displayed a map of the south of France. "This entire region of the Languedoc was once home to the Cathars."

"More heretics!" proclaimed Cardinal Fitzmyer, shaking his head.

"The Cathars' main crime as I understand it was that they did not require priests or extravagant cathedrals," explained Father Andrews. "To add further insult they upheld the equality of the sexes and preached without license."

"You know damn well that they believed in the existence of a Royal bloodline from Mary Magdalene through a marriage with Jesus," demanded Cardinal Fitzmyer, rising out of his seat.

"I was getting to that," said Father Andrews. "Another troubling Cathar belief was that Jesus was a mortal man. For these reasons and others, Pope Innocent III ordered the genocide of the Cathari sect in 1209. For thirty-five years, soldiers of the papal army under the command of Simon de Montfort slaughtered every living soul in the south of France. At the time, it was believed by the Pope and King Philippe II that the Cathars were in cahoots with the Templars and knew the location of their treasure." Father Andrews smiled, remembering how outraged some of his fellow priests had been that Dan Brown had, in his book *The Da Vinci Code*, accused the Holy Mother Church of putting to death thousands of women during witch hunts. He wondered why they ignored the fact that the Roman Catholic Church was directly responsible for the deaths of hundreds of thousands during the Cathar extermination and the three centuries of inquisition that followed it.

"In 1233, towards the end of the genocide, the Church formally instituted the Spanish Inquisition in an effort to extract the needed information from these heretics," continued Father Andrews. "The Albigensian Crusade culminated in 1244 with the massacre at the seminary of Montségur. According to the historical record, on the night before their ultimatum expired, the Cathars held a celebration inside the fortress. During that celebration, four Cathars escaped carrying something. They managed to scale down a sheer cliff in the dark of night, and were successful in passing through enemy lines undetected. This information comes to us from two sources. It was extracted under torture during the Inquisition—but they did not know exactly what was carried out."

"They certainly could not have been carrying an immense treasure. Father Andrews, do you know if this 'buried temple' might have been constructed by the Knights Templar? If so, it would be the property of the Roman Catholic Church," added Cardinal Fitzmyer with a gleam in his eye.

"There is no denying that there was a connection between the Templars and the Cathars, yet we have reason to believe that this Temple was constructed five centuries before the birth of Christ. If anyone has a legitimate claim to it, the Jews have," answered the cardinal bishop.

"The Knights Templar not only believed in the existence of the Royal bloodline, they believed they were the guardians of the Sangréal," explained Father Andrews. "The cathedral of Notre Dame is dedicated to Mary, the Mother of Jesus. But when it was originally constructed, it was dedicated to Mary of Bethany, aka Mary Magdalene. For those of you who have never seen Abbé Bérenger Saunière's restoration of the parish at Rennes-le-Château, I would like to draw your attention to this next image. Saunière depicted the statue of Mary Magdalene holding a vase, linking her to the woman who anointed Jesus with spikenard. Saunière displayed bizarre inconsistencies in the Stations of the Cross depicting the Crucifixion. One station shows a child swathed in what appears to be Scottish plaid. The plaque portraying Pontius Pilate shows him wearing a veil over his face "Jesus is depicted in the fourteenth station at Rennes-le-Château as being carried in a shroud by three men—presumably to his tomb. Jesus, as you know, was crucified during the Passover, a festival only celebrated during the full moon of the Spring Equinox. In the night sky above the small group hangs a full moon. Jewish laws strictly forbid touching a corpse at night. However, if Jesus were still alive, the three men carrying him in the fourteenth station would not have been in violation of that law," explained Father Andrews. "This coincides with another troubling Cathar belief: that Jesus had survived the crucifixion and was smuggled out by night."

"Stranger still," added Cardinal Bishop de la Torre, "are the two large ornate statues that stand to either side of the altar. One statue is that of Saint Joseph," he said holding up a large photo of the statue in his right hand. "The other statue is that of Mother Mary," he held the photo for all to see with his left hand. "The strange thing about these statues is that each is holding a child, alluding to the ancient legend that Christ had an identical twin brother, another of the Cathar heresies." He paused for effect, allowing the two images to sink in. "This, gentlemen, is the main reason we are going to require the capture of this dæmon. Perhaps then we will be able to understand what Abbé Bérenger Saunière meant by these curious abnormalities."

Odd Man Out

*If you can't change the people you're with,
change the people you're with.*
—Anonymous

Safely aboard the *Defiant*, Joshua was still shaken by what had transpired earlier that night. "Teryk, when you were at the old church did you hear any dogs barking?" he asked, unsure if he should broach the subject.

"Let's just say that as a child I had a bad experience with those Hellhounds," said Teryk. "That deep guttural werewolf-like howl woke me up on many nights. I could not have been more than three years old when I first heard it. After the first howl, I would lie with my eyes closed listening to the pack as they got closer to my home. One moonlit night the pack went silent in front of my house. And I made the mistake of looking out the window."

"What did you see?" asked a wide-eyed Aurora.

"I don't know what it was, but I will tell you that I began screaming when I saw it," he said to Aurora. "I must have levitated across the room, because I dropped to the floor on the other side of the room still screaming. My parents had a tough time getting me to open my eyes. On another night when I heard the howling, I noticed a light on in the kitchen. It was my mother. I startled her as I walked up behind her and asked if she could hear what I heard coming. She nodded that she did. It had woken her as well. I told her that on the night I had screamed, I had seen the thing that made that horrible sound. It was black in color and its body was like that of a wolf but with very short legs. It had long donkey-like ears and its two front teeth hung down like knives. Its large eyes glowed red and there were little ones following it."

Deciding to change the conversation, Teryk turned towards Joshua and asked, "While you were in touch with the Vatican, did anyone there have any idea what was causing the recent rise in dæmonic infestations?"

"The Catholic Church is very conservative when it comes to matters involving the supernatural," Joshua replied. "There are those in the Church who still cling to the belief that Christians cannot be demonized. I find that hard to believe when you consider that exorcists have been spread very thin lately."

"The belief that Christians cannot be demonized might be true if they were filled with the Holy Spirit," explained Teryk, "but, as you know, most people who claim the title 'Christian' only give lip service."

"How does one become an exorcist?" asked Raven.

"My first memories are of hauntings in the house where I grew up," said Teryk. "Some children grow up wanting to become soldiers, policemen or firemen. All I ever wanted to be was an exorcist."

"The specially ordained order of exorcists, also known as acolytes or door-keepers, was established shortly before the middle of the third century," said Joshua. "Later the Council of Carthage decreed the rite of ordination for exorcists and provided a book containing the exact method of exorcism."

"What's an acko-light?" asked Aurora, excited.

"An acolyte is a layperson who assists the clergy by performing minor duties during religious services. But long ago an acolyte was considered a student of forbidden knowledge," said Joshua in an ominous tone.

"Does that ancient book, the one Teryk brought back, have anything to do with exorcism?" asked Raven.

"The book is called the *Rituale Romanum* and contains the only formal exorcism rite sanctioned by the Roman Catholic Church," explained Joshua. "It was written in 1614. The book contains a collection of prayers which must be publicly recited when it is believed that there is an influence of Satan over places, objects or people. I have committed many of the prayers to memory. The Roman Ritual of Exorcism is thus an ancient form of prayer. But I am only permitted to recite the prayers if I am given permission by a Bishop..."

"This is where I disagree with exorcisms," Teryk interrupted. "It is the main reason I left the priesthood. This is where the priesthood misses and misses badly. It is the power of God, not the energy of hype or recitation of ancient prayers that expels dæmons.

"Although I must admit there have been times when the Holy Spirit has denied me permission to cast out a dæmon. I was told—'he called it upon himself and now God is dealing with him,'" confessed Teryk.

"Exorcisms are not performed by any power I possess but by the authority I am under. Do you recall the story of the centurion at Capernaum who beseeched Christ to heal his servant? 'Yes,' Jesus replied, 'I will come and heal him.' But the centurion said to him, 'Lord, I am not worthy that thou should enter under my roof. But only say the word, and my servant shall be healed.'

"'For I too am a man under authority,'" explained Teryk, continuing the verse. "'Having under me soldiers; and I say to this one, Go, and he goeth, and to another, Come, and he cometh. And to my servant, 'Do this,' and he does it.' At which Jesus marveled, and proclaimed, 'I have not found such great a faith in all of Israel.'"

"You're starting to lose me," admitted Joshua. "Artimus tried to teach me that. He would refer to the man whose son Jesus' disciples couldn't heal. Jesus then rebuked the Devil and the child was cured. Later his disciples came to him secretly and asked, 'Why could not we cast him out?' Jesus replied, 'This kind is not cast out but by prayer and fasting.'"

"Actually, Jesus never said fasting, nor did he say to 'use prayer' during the exorcism. He made it quite clear that they failed because of their *unbelief*," Teryk assured him. "The fasting part was added long after by men who liked to impress others with their ability to go without food."

Joshua reflected for a moment then said, "Teryk, Artimus told me that the Vatican had a demonologist waiting for us back in Rome. What's a demonologist and what do they do?"

"A demonologist is someone who studies and categorizes dæmons. Demonologists are not experts in the field of the paranormal, although some consider themselves to be. In my experience, I do not believe there are any experts where paranormal investigations are concerned. Demonologists usually study dæmonic hauntings, trying to catalog the origin, ethnic background or geographical area in which the dæmon manifests. I have yet to come across a demonologist who was also an exorcist. They are fascinated with dæmons but this does not mean they actually believe they exist."

"You know, I've never really viewed you as a priest, Teryk," said Raven. "To me, priests are simply people appointed by religious organizations. You're more like a mystic."

"I'm not sure I even understand what a mystic is," said Joshua.

"What shamans, mystics, and prophets all have in common is that they are all self-initiated—reluctantly at times," admitted Teryk. "These individuals did not acquire their knowledge by being indoctrinated into secret brotherhoods. I've discovered that searching for Truth is a lot like playing hide and seek with an infant. When hiding from a child, one always leaves a shoe sticking out or an elbow protruding from behind the curtain so that the child will have some clue of where to look. When the child finds you there is great laughter and joy. Then the game begins again. It is no different with our Creator. The Creator will never hide completely from his creation."

"Would one be considered a mystic," pondered Joshua, "if the mystical experience he was having was not being sought?"

"Isn't that usually how it happens? A paradox by its very nature is not meant to be understood. And the more I think I understand it, the less I am able to explain it."

"Joshua looked around and asked, "Teryk, what exactly is this ship and what was the other ship that brought us here?"

"We are onboard the *Defiant*, the flagship for this type of classification. The ship is basically a stealth treasure recovery submersible. The transport that brought us here was a Sea-Wraith-class Battle Dragon called the *Sea Wolf*. It is the equivalent of a Harrier vertical takeoff and landing aircraft."

"How did you make an airship appear invisible?" asked Joshua, not sure if Teryk would tell him.

"With our cloaking technology…"

"Cloaking technology? I thought that was just science fiction," said Joshua, his eyes widening.

"Cloaking is quite real," Teryk assured him, "although it is often referred to as 'masking' by Black Ops. The Battle Dragons incorporate a large spectrum of war birds. Most are engaged in what we call ghost wars. These ships have no ailerons. Their wings are constructed from bioplastics: memory-retaining polymers that change shape as energy is applied to them. The bioplastic allows the Battle Dragon's wings to bend, lengthen or shorten in flight. This streamlines the craft and reduces drag. Think of bioplastics as artificial muscles that flex the structure. Instead of using one strip of material that bends when voltage is applied, we use many insulated sheets of material that contract when voltage is applied. The individual tendons work in unison, much like a human muscle. What sets the Battle Dragon apart from other craft is the fact that their pilots are able to *interphase* their human brains with those of the AI: the onboard Artificial Intelligence computer.

"Interphase is a word we coined. In order to couple with the onboard AIs, pilots require surgical implants that link to a special Neuralnet Interphase Helmet," explained Teryk. "The Artificial Intelligence computers think so fast that to them humans appear to be in a coma. Only during combat or special ops missions are pilots required to become completely interlinked with their Battle Dragons. The AI interphases with the pilot's visual receptors through technology borrowed from the development of artificial eyes. Battle Dragons have no outer viewports. All visual data is transmitted by onboard cameras directly to the pilot's brain. This allows a pilot to use inferred or night vision when necessary. The Artificial Intelligence computer projects technical readouts, battle grids, enemy positions, and targeting information directly to the pilot's brain in a 360 degree virtual reality.

"When the pilot melds with his ship, he literally becomes one with the War Bird. The onboard sensor arrays allow him to see in all directions at once. The length of time a pilot can maintain this mental state of awareness is completely dependent on the stamina of their cognitive functions. A Battle Dragon pilot's senses are brutally taxed during combat. Our pilots can only maintain this completely immersed state of perception for about fifteen to twenty minutes. The better a pilot's conditioning, the longer he can maintain the altered state of awareness. Sometimes during training, pilots will lose consciousness. When this happens the AI co-pilot assumes command. This is not a problem because during actual combat Battle Dragons are incredibly lethal."

"Not only do the Battle Dragon Artificial Intelligence computers link up with each other—so do the minds of the pilots," added Raven. "In the development of these crafts, we discovered that the structure of the human brain is actually wired for connection or rather, interaction with other human brains. Human brains have a tremendous amount of redundancy. A human brain is capable of completely rewiring itself in order to learn new things. Also, there are other advantages. If a combat pilot loses peripheral vision in one eye that is the end of his or her career as a pilot. But when one of our pilots lost her peripheral vision in one eye, her flying and fighting capabilities were unaltered because she did not need her eyes to pilot the craft."

"How can you not need to see in order to fly?"

"As I said before," Teryk reminded Joshua, "Battle Dragons do not have viewports. All visual information is fed directly to the brain's visual cortex through the Neuralnet Interphase Helmet. These helmets are not mass produced. Each helmet is custom fitted to its pilot. Each pilot seat is custom made as well. If the aviator is left handed, which most are, all instrumentation is reversed. If, during the course of simulation training, the pilot prefers a different instrumentation layout, that too can be readily accomplished. All instrumentation housings follow a uniformed standard and are easily interchangeable."

"Another fascinating feature of the Battle Dragons is that their command chairs sit inside an antigravity gyro assembly. The command chairs gyrate in order to reduce the G-force experienced by the pilot. You can pull all kinds of G's, 'pop some rivets' as our aviators like to say, and you will hardly feel a thing," added Raven. "Plus the helmets are air-cooled in case you start to break a sweat. If your body begins to heat up too much from the adrenalin, cool water is circulated through your armpits, crotch and torso areas in an effort to control core body temperature. The mind's ability to function at an optimum level is severely impeded when it has to correct for adverse physical conditions. One thing I can say about my commander, Teryk, is that he wants you to have every possible advantage."

"Raven, tell him about the onboard random generators," said Monique.

"Are you familiar with random event generators, REGs, those little devices that emit random bits of information?"

"I've heard of them. Colleges sometimes use them on ESP experiments, I think," answered Joshua.

"In one experiment, the subject dons a pair of headphones and listens to clicks in both ears. He is then given the instructions to cause more clicks to occur in, say, the right ear. What's fascinating about this experiment is that the participant has to use his mind to try to affect the outcome. Every one of our pilots is required to undergo this test. First the subject dons a set of headphones. The subject must decide, every five minutes for a total of thirty minutes, on which side of the headphones he or she will hear the most clicks. In the final phases of training, the pilots believe they are listening to the output of a random event generator. What they are actually listening to is a recording of a REG's output, an output that occurred twenty-four hours earlier. In other words the subject affected the REG's output one day before they listened to it. Oops." Raven looked around sheepishly. "Maybe I shouldn't have told you that. Now you'll be expecting us to give you that test, should you decide to become a pilot."

"We've sort of duplicated Princeton University's Global Consciousness Project," added Teryk. "The Project linked forty REGs worldwide through the Internet. Computers combined the forty inputs and produced the typical flat line. The first major response came on 6 September 1997, before the funeral of Princess Diana. They discovered through experimentation that the whole system of random generators displayed a significant deviation from randomness toward order hours before unexpected global events attracted a tremendous amount of human attention. It seems that when humanity is united in thought, the randomness of the Universe begins to follow some sort of order. The worldwide network of REGs began deviating from randomness towards order four hours before the first airplane hit the Twin Towers in the September 11th attacks in 2001. It happened twenty-four hours before the 2004 tsunami. And it happened again with the Japanese earthquake and the subsequent reactor breach. The system has since been increased to sixty-five REGs."

"Antares has random event generators running at every base and on every ship. When they deviate from their randomness we go on full alert," said Teryk. "With hours of advanced notice our remote viewers were able to pinpoint the locations of the earthquakes in Haiti, Chile and Japan hours in advance. Japanese officials were warned of the reactor breach, but they dismissed the warnings as nonsense."

"You may be wondering why this is important to the pilot of a Battle Dragon?" asked Monique. "We have discovered through our own experimentation that our 'ace pilots' could somehow sense or detect that an enemy was about to engage them. Onboard random generators give our aviators a six-second warning, alerting them to unseen danger."

"Imagine having one of these in your family vehicle," said Raven. "When the warning sounded, the driver would become more alert to other vehicles and pedestrians on the sidewalk. He would pay more attention to kids playing with balls, on bikes or skateboards. A driver could guard against the possibility of someone pulling out in front of him unexpectedly. We've tested these in the United States and they warn you before a police officer or an automated device clocks your vehicle's speed. I don't leave home without it."

Everything Is Under Control — The Illuminati

> *The only thing that saves us from*
> *the bureaucracy is its inefficiency.*
> —Eugene J. McCarthy

"That cool-looking robotic armor you guys were wearing, what was that?" Joshua asked as he examined Teryk's helmet with the storm shield down. "Having served as a Marine Recon Ranger, I would really like to use one someday."

"The armored robotic suits we were wearing are called ExoSkeletons. They are full-body armor, wearable robots," explained Teryk. "The very first ExoSkeleton designs were worn by our grunts."

"I never did find out why Marine Corps infantry were referred to as grunts," said Joshua, a puzzled look on his face.

"Neither did I," admitted Teryk. "I'd always thought the word *grunt* was a spin-off of the term ground-pounders, because of all the forced marches Marines are ordered to undertake."

"God, I hated forced marches," admitted Joshua, examining the flexible sections of the body armor. "These platelets remind me of Japanese Samurai armor I've seen in museums. Upon examining the museum exhibit closer, I realized that each plate was actually a coin. They'd incorporated coins, with a hole in the center, to create a fish-scale effect. It was simple and very effective."

"We call that Dragon Hide because of its unique configuration of titanium-soric platelets," said Teryk. "Soric is a vacuum-injected, honeycombed fabric designed to absorb impacts. In this fish-scale configuration Dragon Hide has the ability to be more flexible. It disperses the energy of a projectile more effectively due to the greater number of surfaces that can withstand an impact.

The second layer of defense behind all movable joints is a liquid layer that hardens when impacted." Teryk placed the flexible section of armor against the bulkhead and struck it hard. "If you take a hit, your movement will be restricted at that joint momentarily," he said as he tossed it to Joshua.

"I see what you mean," said Joshua as he struggled to flex the joint. He continued trying to bend it and noticed that the elasticity returned after a few seconds.

"I see that nothing on these ExoSkeletons is shiny or reflective," commented Joshua.

"This type of ExoSkeleton is used when stealth is required," explained Raven. "Most of the ExoSkeletons are shiny. Knights like to distinguish themselves with colorful emblems."

"Should you ever be injured, micro-bots within the armor perform basic first aid functions. Airbags surround each extremity. When activated, the airbags will effectively stop the bleeding without cutting off circulation, unless the limb is amputated. In case of death or loss of consciousness, the Artificial Intelligence computer takes over and either continues to assist in the fight or returns your body to base," explained Teryk. "They can also become immobile, like a cast, preventing further damage to an area."

"I wish we could have worn armor like that when I was in combat. Although I tried to be a good marine, my heart was just not in the wars we were fighting," confessed Joshua, shaking his head slowly. "These were not the glorious battles I remembered reading about in my youth. I had hoped to one day fight to liberate the oppressed. Sadly, I discovered that the battles we fought only lined the oppressor's pockets. It was difficult to justify shooting at young boys who were trying to protect the shithole they called home. We were truly the unwilling, led by the unqualified, to do the impossible for the ungrateful.

"The commandment 'thou shall not kill' kept coming to mind," added Joshua. "To this day it troubles me. I shared these concerns during my confessions, but nothing the Father Confessor ever said brought me peace of mind. And now I fear that on Judgment Day, I may be called to account for my actions."

"Being a warrior-priest myself, perhaps I can shed some light on the subject," said Teryk, placing a comforting hand on Joshua's shoulder. "You're not the first warrior, nor the last, to be troubled by the sixth commandment. This well-known directive from God is just one of many horribly mangled translations in the *Bible*. The Hebrew word used in the original Torah is *ratzach*, meaning premeditated murder. The sixth commandment specifically prohibits premeditated murder: the taking of the life of an innocent. The sixth commandment does not prohibit the taking of a life in defense of oneself or others. The Hebrew word 'to kill' is *harag*, which aside from manslaughter encompasses everything from justifiable homicide to the taking of an enemy soldier's life in combat.

"I too was a marine," confided Teryk, "though I wasn't crazy enough to be recon. My pain-tolerance level just wasn't high enough. Of the rangers I knew, pain just didn't seem to affect those guys. I couldn't decide if they were incredibly courageous or just plain insane."

"You know there's no such thing as an ex-marine. You may not wear the uniform but the attitude's still there," added Joshua.

"Before enlisting, I discovered that the Marines did not accept people with low scores on military evaluation tests," explained Teryk. "The Marines' flashy image and the fact that there are only about a hundred thousand troops during peace time means they can afford to be picky. Knowing this about them, I made the assumption that the majority of marines would be intelligent." Shaking his head, he added, "Sadly, I discovered that most just wanted a steady paycheck. The rest were there because the judge had given them an ultimatum, either that or prison. My biggest surprise, however, was seeing United States Marines panic in simulated combat situations. As a sergeant, I had to make my rounds and check the troops guarding the perimeter. Once, during an exercise, as I approached the post, I could clearly see the outline of a private silhouetted against the smoke of green flares. He was covering his field of fire. I approached from behind and called out his name. To my horror, he spun around and emptied his entire magazine on me."

"During boot camp do you recall your drill instructors constantly bellowing out, 'The most dangerous thing in the world is a marine with an M-16'?" asked Joshua. "We never got tired of hearing it. But it turns out that the most dangerous thing in the world is a private with a loaded weapon. Teryk, should I decide to fully commit myself to your cause, what exactly is it that you expect from those you command?"

"I expect a lot more from the knights under my command than I do from the grunts. The concept of the ExoSkeleton is an attempt to get the most out of every individual warrior's capabilities. It is tailor-made to amplify all your strengths."

"During my tour in the military, I quickly recognized that most officers were nothing more than petty tyrants who demanded much of others. A good commander demands much of himself. Among the grunts are seasoned warriors who desire nothing more than to follow a competent leader into battle. I do not promote men who have no desire or ability to lead. I have never forced someone to take command. On the other hand, some men seek power because they seem to 'need it'—I never allow those fools to command."

"So who is it you battle against?"

"Most of our skirmishes are with pirates. Our main enemy, however, is an ancient one. You may have heard of them. They call themselves the Illuminati.

You'll usually find them boasting of their family pedigree, their intelligence or their enormous wealth. Although they tend to show great favoritism towards members of their secret brotherhood, they have no love for their fellow man. Control is what they seek. And those whom they cannot silence or control, they imprison or destroy. For the most part we simply evade them.

"My ESPionage teams are not sure exactly what the Illuminati's next major move is going to be, but our nation has been on alert for some time now," said Teryk. "Whatever it is, the United States Department of Homeland Security is calling it 'ENDGAME' and you can be certain it will be conducted on a massive scale. At present they've stockpiled hundreds of thousands of incendiary coffins; each can accommodate three body bags and will burn until nothing's left. The goal of ENDGAME is the militarized removal of all suspected or potential terrorists, illegal aliens, conscientious objectors, and outspoken undesirables who protest the government's actions. We took the liberty of checking, and you've made the list on several of the Fusion Facilities."

"I'm a priest. Why would I be on the list as a potential terrorist?" protested Joshua.

"Well for starters, you're ex-military," said Teryk, examining the computer readout. "Then there's an incident when you attended a Ron Paul gathering and had the audacity to slap one of his bumper stickers on your vehicle.

"US Army Field Manual FM 19-15 specifies that the army must develop personnel who are able to perform distasteful duties. At this moment thousands of US and foreign troops are stateside, for the purpose of implementing Martial law under ENDGAME. These soldiers are under no delusions. They know they will be required to fire upon unarmed American civilians. Is it any wonder US troops have such a high suicide rate? The Nazis encountered similar suicide rates among their SS troops. Thousands were reported to have killed themselves, due to the difficulty of performing their distasteful duties."

Teryk turned the screen horizontally and handed it to Joshua, who read, "From the writings of President George Washington, Volume 36: 'I have heard much of the nefarious and dangerous plan of the Illuminati... It was not my intention to doubt that doctrines of the Illuminati, and principles of Jacobinism, had not spread in the United States. On the contrary, no one is more satisfied of this fact than I am.'" Joshua started to set the pad down then noticed that the layout of the keyboard display was very unusual. "Why is the keyboard in such a weird arrangement?" he asked.

"You mean why isn't it in the QWERTY arrangement?" asked Raven.

"What's the QWERTY arrangement?" inquired Joshua.

"The common name for the standard keyboard layout is 'QWERTY' because the six keys starting from the top left, q-w-e-r-t-y, spell out this name," explained Raven. "Few people are aware that when typewriters were first invented they had different arrangements or layouts for the individual keys. Key jamming was a major problem with those old-style typewriters. Typists were simply too fast. Try as they might, engineers could not solve the problem of the metal stamping-arms catching one another. The solution, reconfigure the key layout into the most difficult typing system imaginable. By the time electric typewriters were invented, solving the original problem, the QWERTY system had become a sacred cow. It has remained unaltered to this day."

"I've always wondered why the setup was so screwy. You'd think that the most-often-used keys would be located at the index fingers and the least-used keys would be relegated to the pinkies or ring fingers." Reading the pad once more, Joshua asked, "So the Illuminati have been infiltrating the US since its founding. Are you guys out to save America or something?"

"If we thought the USA could have been saved, most of our citizens would still be a part of it," answered Raven apologetically. This was an emotionally charged subject for her.

"As I said, the main reason the ExoSkeletons were developed was to enhance our combat performance," said Teryk, donning his helmet. "Even with this storm shield down I can see perfectly because of the surgical implants that are feeding visual information to my brain. This armor can also withstand lethal doses of radiation. Our intelligence units discovered that governments who have the neutron bomb, like Britain and the US, are prepared to use the weapon if population control gets out of hand. Once irradiated, you can survive in the unit for several days, but the ExoSkeleton will have to be disposed of properly. These units are completely sealed and can be easily modified for use underwater if necessary. We had to seal them to guard against the new race-specific bioweapons the US is developing."

"I know this is difficult for you to accept, Joshua. You don't possess a mob mentality," said Raven. "When an injustice is committed, it is difficult for you to remain silent about it. You have an unshakable sense of right and wrong. I can tell this about you simply by observing your aura. By your very nature, you are a threat to these people. Having been a marine, I'm sure you are familiar with the Korean War. But few are aware that the Koreans interrogated prisoners of war (POW) in order to determine what prison they should be sent to. If a POW had a reason for living, or an ideal they strove towards, they were placed in a maximum-security prison camp. If the POW had no dreams or ambitions, if they simply got drafted and went along with the crowd, they were placed in minimum-security prisons. No one ever escaped from a minimum-security camp. I wonder what would happen to you if studying scripture became an offense to the government. Would you denounce your faith to save your hide, Joshua?"

Joshua snickered, and retorted, "You're talking about the Antichrist and the Apocalypse. I doubt that's going to happen any time soon."

"Joshua, it may surprise you to learn that during World War II many *Bible* Students lost their lives in the Nazi death camps for that very crime. As a follower of the Christ," Teryk confided, "I'm forced to admire the faith and tenacity of those five thousand men and women. Oddly enough, the Germans regarded these individuals as 'voluntary prisoners'. To be absolved of the crime, all one had to do was denounce his faith and sign a Declaration Document, promising to submit to the authority of the Third Reich. According to official Nazi records, the crime for which they were imprisoned was noted as Bibelforscher. They were guilty of being *Bible* students. A large, purple triangular badge identified these conscientious objectors in much the same way that the Jews were identified by the yellow Star of David. The purple badge was by far the largest of the badges, so that it would stand out. Anyone wearing this badge was to be avoided. If anyone was caught listening to a Bibelforscher, it would not go well for them. The Nazis noted that these troublemakers ministered to the injured and shared their food—knowing they would be punished for doing so."

Raven bit her lower lip as she tried to think of another way to explain herself. "Joshua, when stupidity is considered a form of patriotism, intelligence will be viewed as a treasonous act. During the Bush administration, conscientious objectors were regarded as terrorist sympathizers. Should the United States ever impose Martial law, orders are in place for soldiers to round up all suspected terrorists, conscientious objectors, and outspoken undesirables. When faced with such prospects, one has to wonder how many 'Christians' would gladly denounce their faith and sign any document in order to get out of such a Hellhole."

"I see what you mean, Raven," said Joshua. "Teryk, do you recall when Asmodeus spoke of Enoch? I thought there were no surviving copies of the Book of Enoch. In fact, the Church considered removing the book of Jude from the New Testament because it quoted so heavily from the Book of Enoch."

"According to legend, the Book of Enoch was one of the books preserved by Noah himself," said Teryk. "In fact, it was required reading during Jesus' time. The Essenes cherished it and so did the Jews and early Christians. After Jesus, or perhaps because of his constantly quoting from the book, it was condemned, denounced and banned by both rabbis and early Church fathers. The book remained lost for thousands of years until a Scottish explorer discovered three copies of it in Ethiopia."

"I was not aware Jesus quoted so much from the Book of Enoch."

"How could you if you had no idea the book even existed and no understanding of what it said," Teryk observed.

"If he quoted from it, why would the early Church fathers ban it?"

"That's a long story. The long and the short of it is they simply didn't like what Jesus had to say."

"How could that be true?" asked Joshua.

"This may come as a shock to you Joshua, but Christianity was not begun by Jesus and his disciples," countered Teryk. "Christianity was begun by a Roman named Saul of Tarsus, who had taken it upon himself to hunt down and execute the followers of Jesus. After his conversion, Saul recruited Gentiles, and I believe Gnostics as well, to form his new religion. In time the Gentile churches grew faster, wealthier and larger than the group of believers in Jerusalem, led by the original disciples. The Jewish followers of Jesus proved troublesome for this new religion. So the Christians branded them as heretics. And you might as well know right now that I'm one of those heretics. Keep in mind that Jesus never instructed his disciples to go around creating new churches or appointing priests. Jesus taught that God spoke to you directly and that you should obey what God put in your heart. For this reason, I could no longer remain a priest for a church that followed the teachings of the apostle Paul, aka Saul of Tarsus."

"That's why you left?" asked Joshua. "Why do you believe the Church doesn't allow you to follow what God puts in your heart?"

Raven looked at the young priest incredulously. "You're kidding, right? Most churches want to control every aspect of your life. If you do something the preacher doesn't like, you'll soon hear about it, usually through a sermon directed at you…"

"Mayday, Mayday, we are helpless and drifting! Please render assistance." The AI computer channeled the distress call through the ship's com, interrupting the conversation.

(A Mayday call is sent out over channels that are monitored by the Coast Guard, military, and all ocean-going vessels at given intervals every hour. Maritime law states that any vessel receiving a Mayday must respond immediately, unless one's own life is placed in danger. Mayday was a corruption of the French *venez m'aider*, meaning come help me!)

The ship began to decelerate. Puzzled, Teryk looked at Raven. He knew that running submerged, the *Defiant's* radios should not be set to those frequencies. He thought for a second, then ordered Monique to bring the ship about, locate the vessel and shadow her position.

"Is that wise, Commander?" asked Raven. "We have no idea who could be on board."

"The question we should be asking is, 'How in the hell did we pick up that distress call in the first place?' Hypnautica is linked with the ship's AI computer. She must have been monitoring all channels." Teryk thought for a moment then ordered, "Alright, I want everyone prepped and ready to get wet in ten minutes."

"Aye aye, sir," the crew responded in unison.

8

Deathwish

Earlier that day the sloop-rigged sixty-six footer *Seawych* skirted the Yucatan Peninsula. The *Seawych* seemed too big a ship for the small crew of three aboard her and yet too small to tackle the hurricane she was headed into. She was fitted with the latest electronics, sheet-control hydraulics and sail-furling mechanisms available. The ship's decks were made of teak wood with mahogany furnishings throughout the cabins. The designers of her artificial intelligence boasted that she could even skirt a hurricane, a feature the girls were about to put to the test.

'*This ship is Dametrie's pride and joy*,' thought Katharine Nicole. Her husband was going to miss the ship far more than he was going to miss her. When Dametrie had first ordered the ship, he was upset to learn he would be placed on a waiting list for its construction. Pulling every string and calling in every favor owed to his late father, Dametrie would still have had to wait for over a year before construction would begin on the *Seawych*: a nickname he'd chosen for his wife. So he purchased the company and had them begin construction on his yacht immediately.

Trisha entered the engine room and let out a slow whistle. The ship's twin turbo diesels did not have one drop of oil on their glossy white paint job. Being a naval officer, she knew how dirty an engine room could get. In addition to the modern computerized navigation console, there was a repeater station in the cockpit. VHF, single sideband, as well as the radar and loran, were bolted to the ceiling.

"We won't need to send out distress signals once the weather gets bad," said Trisha as they skirted the island of Cuba and approached the Yucatan Peninsula. The barometer had dropped and the swells were more noticeable. The lull of the approaching hurricane meant there would be almost no wind, making the sea appear like a gigantic blue sheet of Saran Wrap™. The effect is much like that of the air pockets trapped under a large bed sheet once it's spread out over a mattress. "Sea conditions in the Caribbean are ideal for cruising," said Trisha.

Katharine turned the helm in an effort to position the ship into the dying wind, in order to luff the sails. The sails began to flap noisily, spilling their wind. Trisha dropped the jib, cranking the sail down as she raced to the foredeck and pulled it down. Katharine eased the halyard for the mainsail, lowering it to the boom. Michelle assisted her in lashing it down while Trisha cinched down the boom vang, or kicking strap, to prevent the boom from lashing about.

Once the sails had been lowered and stowed, Trisha cranked over the twin turbo diesels and checked all the cockpit's instrumentation related to them. Katharine Nicole had used her American Express card to fill the ships massive fuel tanks to capacity the day they'd left port. '*Just one last thing to piss off my husband before I die,*' she thought.

Surrounding the computerized navigation console, the girls stared at a computerized chart that displayed the hurricane's position. It was noon. No sense in verifying their position by pointing a sextant at the Sun to confirm the navigation equipment. It was obvious that they were off the Yucatan Peninsula entering the Caribbean Sea.

Three weeks ago, Michelle had informed her two friends that there was no point in postponing the inevitable. She had decided to commit suicide. She preferred that to a slow, agonizing death from cancer. Each of the girls had been going through very difficult times. Trisha had discovered that she had contracted AIDS after being raped by another naval officer, the son of an admiral. After the admiral exerted considerable pull, all charges against his son were dropped. Despite her outstanding achievements in the navy, Trisha's career as a Naval Intelligence Officer had been ruined. To further exacerbate the situation, she was being stalked and harassed constantly by the young man. Learning that the admiral's son would eventually die of AIDS was the only good thing that had come out of her experience. Katharine Nicole was trapped in an abusive marriage and saw no way out. The three had shared their stories and decided that it would be a comfort to die among friends.

"All ahead, full speed," said Trisha as she increased throttle and the ship picked up speed, slicing through the calm seas.

Katharine was the only one who was not dying, at least not physically. The other two had tried to talk her out of killing herself when they learned she was pregnant. But Katharine assured them that her life was a living Hell, and she could never subject her unborn child to such a life. When she'd confronted her husband about a divorce, he had beaten her and locked her away until the bruises healed. Her two friends had finally relented, all three deciding they would sail Dametrie's private yacht into an oncoming hurricane. They were now on the last leg of their journey. Soon there would be no turning back.

By nightfall the waves had risen to a two-foot chop. The hurricane blew in from the north east, its winds rotating counterclockwise. Trisha shut off the engines and raised the mainsail. It flapped violently in the breeze. Katharine raised the jib and sheeted it in as Trisha adjusted the sheets of the mainsail from the cockpit. The boom creaked as it swung to starboard. They sailed southeastward on a port tack close haul, the ship heeling far over to starboard.

Michelle felt a sudden chill in the night air. She snuggled into a thick blanket, sipping on a cup of hot coffee. Staring into the darkening sky, she could see the menacing outline of the hurricane clearly visible in the slow circular motion of the gloomy gray clouds. The stars were no longer able to penetrate the lingering cloud canopy.

The usual guilt and self-condemnation began to settle back into her mind. Thinking that she would not have to feel this way much longer, she smiled at the possibility of seeing her child again. She was not religious like Katharine, but did not hate the Church like Trisha. She was simply dying of cancer. Trisha was dying, too, but not as quickly. This was not suicide, she reasoned; they were all simply putting an abrupt end to a miserable existence. And if God was going to punish them for that, perhaps He was no god at all.

Trisha gripped the steering wheel, not much larger than a regular bicycle tire, at the captain's binnacle. She looked up at the sails, the emotions in her heart displacing those of the previous month. Her excitement was not from piloting the sleek multimillion-dollar vessel: it was from the sea itself. She loved the feel of spray on her face over the bow as the sharp prow sliced through oncoming waves. Trisha's unruly, sandy-blond, shoulder-length hair seemed perfectly suited to this environment.

When the seas became too rough, Trisha went below deck and called for her friends over the intercom. "The design of the *Seawych* should cause it to slice through the waves," she told the two, "but it is so light that these massive waves tend to carry it up and over. If we continue to take the seas head on, the boat will drop as the waves go out from under it. If we turn her side to the waves in order to prevent this, we can be rolled easily. Soon we will be facing thirty-foot waves. A thirty-foot wave has a face that's sixty feet high. It's going to feel like the boat ride one encounters in traveling carnivals, only this ship will swing in an arch that's six stories high. Soon the hurricane winds will be over one hundred miles per hour. Raindrops blown by hundred-knot winds will rake you like buckshot. We will have to remain below decks from here on out. The huge waves will most likely cause the life raft to deploy, since it is designed to release and inflate automatically when the ship goes underwater.

"In another hour the sea will control the ship. By then the diesel engines are going to be useless. The ship's propellers keep lifting out of the water and revving too high. They sound okay now but by then the bearings will have burned out. Without the props there is no way to keep the boat pointed into the seas, no way to minimize the beating we'll be taking. Once we are unable to keep our bow to the weather, the ship will roll. After that, it's only a matter of time before she starts to break up. At that point, even if we change our minds and call the Coast Guard, a night rescue in such conditions is not going to happen. I doubt the *Seawych* will ever see the light of day again." Looking her friends in the eyes, Trisha said, "Last chance, girls. Do we go through with it or do we turn back?"

Katharine and Michelle nodded their understanding. Trisha announced that she was setting the ship on autopilot and wasn't sure how long the computer or the ship would be able to keep them on course as the girls went below decks.

Katharine shouted, in order to be heard over the noise, "I think we should prepare for the inevitable!"

"You're right, we probably should have prepared for it an hour ago," agreed Trisha as she reached into a cubbyhole and rummaged through the debris to find what they needed. Trisha found the case she was looking for and removed three Ziploc® bags and duct tape. Each bag had been doubled to ensure that it would remain waterproof. Trisha placed the bag containing a driver's license and other identification over Michelle's stomach. "Hold it in place," she told Michelle as she and Katharine wrapped duct tape around Michelle's midsection.

"What are you doing this for?" asked Michelle, slightly alarmed.

"So your body can be identified," explained Katharine. She held the baggie containing her passport and suicide note to her abdomen while Trisha wrapped tape around her.

"So this is how our lives end," said Michelle. "You know, committing suicide sounded like a really good idea just this morning."

Trisha wrote her goodbyes by flashlight. She did not own any possessions to leave in a will. All her stuff was going with her to the bottom of the sea. She opened another bag and inserted the note. Then she taped it next to her ID and passport and put on extra garments to conserve body heat when she hit the water. There was no need to strap on a personal flotation device.

"What can we expect?" asked Michelle, not sure if she really wanted to know.

"It will be quick once we transition from crisis into catastrophe," assured Trisha. "It won't be long now before all Hell breaks loose. It ain't gonna be pretty.

"Should a massive wave hit us head on, everything we thought was nailed down will go sailing across to the other side of the ship and us along with it. Then water will come rushing in. We will probably have less than a minute. Once the boat floods, electricity will be the first thing to go. There will be no lights and panic will begin to set in." She handed the girls small but powerful waterproof LED flashlights. "The average person can hold their breath for about ninety seconds or so, but after that their body will take an involuntary breath. If you hyperventilate first, you can last as long as a hundred and forty seconds. You

　　　　　　　　　　　　　　　　　Joseph "Five Eagles" Reyna

could also have the diving reflex working for you. When cold water hits your face, your brain automatically begins using about half the oxygen it needs. I'd say that in about three minutes tops we'll all be dead."

A wave caught the *Seawych* broadsides and rolled the ship ninety degrees, slamming the three women into the bulkhead. Dishes, gear, books and equipment fell on top of them. Canned food rocketed across the galley and water poured in. It was a good thing that the heavier items were battened down, as being struck by a flying refrigerator was not a laughing matter. Gradually, the ship righted herself.

Trisha stood up on the flooding deck, bruised and dazed. She wondered if the hull had opened up. "This is one tough little ship," she said, half to herself.

"Considering all the millions Dametrie spent on her construction, the *Seawych* better be a tough little ship," remarked Katharine.

"I'm beginning to feel seasick, guys," said Michelle. "If I did not want to die before, I do now."

The ship was taking a horrific beating. There was a loud shotgun blast as a portside window was blown out. Water began to flood the lower compartments. A compartment on the ceiling sprang open and a waterproof microphone dropped down as the radio illuminated. "This is the *Defiant*. Do you require assistance? How many crew members are on board?"

Trisha recognized the digitally displayed numbers as the Mayday frequency. She grabbed for the mic and called out, "Mayday, Mayday, yes…YES, please render assistance. There are three on board and we are taking on water."

CHAPTER

9

Leap of Faith

Hypnautica, *Defiant's* AI computer, had been monitoring the crew's conversation. "Commander, the water temperature is fifty-eight degrees at this depth. At ninety-six degrees Fahrenheit the human body begins to shake uncontrollably. Should a diver's core temperature reach ninety-one degrees, he loses the ability to think or reason effectively."

"What happens after that?" asked Joshua, not expecting a response.

"It doesn't really matter, since you are not going to be living much longer after that to worry about it," Teryk assured him. "Understood, Hypnautica, I stand corrected. Don your wetsuits but do it quickly," he ordered. "Raven, radio the ship's crew and order them to put on warm clothing. The seas are cold at this depth and they will need to retain body heat. If the ship is equipped with autopilot, have them maintain a heading of zero three five degrees, which should keep her bow to the wind. Also, order them to maintain a speed of four knots. That should keep their ship stationary above us. If they have any kind of waterproof lights, tell them to carry one on the way down. That would be a great help."

"On the way down, Commander?" asked Raven, not sure what he meant.

"In this weather, they're going to have to jump ship in order for us to rescue them. Have them hold onto something heavy," ordered Teryk.

"There are a total of three jumping overboard," announced Raven, "repeat three jumping overboard. The divers will need to intercept them once they enter the water."

Trisha could not believe the message coming over the radio. Regardless, she set the autopilot to maintain heading and speed. On her way back down she took a large, polished nautilus fossil to assist in her descent. She stuffed the nautilus into her back pack. Turning toward Michelle, she taped an LED flashlight to the girl's upper arm. She made sure the flashlights were turned on and facing down. "This thing is supposed to be waterproof. But I think DC voltage works underwater anyway," said Trisha as she attached a flashlight to Katharine's upper arm, and then one to her own.

"Seal the command station and pressurize the work station," ordered Teryk. At this command, an alarm buzzer sounded and red warning lights flashed twice then remained illuminated. Teryk grabbed the hatch and lowered it shut on the seating ring. He wheeled the dogging mechanism clockwise until its metal claws unfolded and locked the hatch in place.

Joshua's ears thumped from the increasing pressure. He grabbed his nose and blew against his closed nostrils to equalize his eardrums. "Is it just me?" he asked. "You guys don't seem affected by the pressure."

"We spend so much time underwater that each of us has undergone surgery to enlarge the canals that lead to our eardrums," explained Raven.

"Like Navy SEAL divers." observed Joshua.

"Yes, we may need to pressurize our eardrums, but not as much as you will," explained Raven. "So you're a priest and you're SCUBA certified as well?"

"Yeah, skydiver too. That's why I joined the Marines—to try and get all that out of my system before going into the priesthood," said Joshua as the red lights changed to amber. The team finished strapping on and inspecting each other's SCUBA tanks. (The acronym SCUBA stands for self-contained underwater breathing apparatus.)

Joshua reached over his shoulder and felt the top of his air bottle's manifold. Running his fingers along the rubber hose, he located the regulator. Putting it in his mouth, he inhaled. The dry tank air had a metallic taste to it. He tested his octopus rig and additional regulator, then punched the purge button and heard the flow of air. '*I'll need this second regulator if I'm to provide air for those I might end up rescuing,*' he thought.

The amber lights turned to green, accompanied by a soft musical chime. "Work station pressure has equalized with outside water pressure," announced Hypnautica. "Standby… opening hatch."

The large rectangular hatch was centered to the rear of the spacious work station. The dogging mechanism's metal claws unfolded, disengaging from the hatch seating ring. The hatch's spring-loaded mechanism allowed it to open easily as two divers lifted on it. Seawater did not enter, remaining about a foot below the seating ring due to the pressurized compartment. Monique faced everyone and raising a thumb, said, "Sound off."

The others followed suit in a counterclockwise rotation. Joshua was not wearing a full-face mask. When it was his turn, he shrugged his shoulders, grinned, then gave a thumbs-up.

Monique nodded and made an OK sign with her right hand. "Can everyone hear me clearly?" she asked.

At this, Raven requested a radio check. Everyone sounded off and gave a thumbs-up.

"Joshua, you will only be able to hear what's going on," said Monique. "Remain below the other divers in case we miss on the first try. Remember these people will most likely be terrified and may think that a shark is attacking when you grab them." Monique slapped Brian, one of the technicians, on his left shoulder. At this signal, he plunged feet first into the dark water.

Raven would be overseeing the rescue operation from forward command, where she would have a better view of the team. She turned, moved toward the command chair, seated herself and activated the ship's lower work lights and docking-port lanterns. *Defiant's* flat nosecone necked down toward two massive propulsor shrouds that flanked the transparent bullet-shaped command center. The ocean was a vast blackness surrounding the divers. The only illumination came from *Defiant's* work lights. She spun the seat to face the rear work section. Joshua's plunge into the sea was followed closely by Monique's.

"It's a good thing for us that you're never without a flashlight, Trish," said Michelle, holding onto a heavy marble statue of an imperial Chinese horse. Michelle loved horses and had always admired this style of art. "If we get rescued, Katharine, may I keep this statue?"

"If you don't take it with you, it's going to end up at the bottom of the ocean. I'll take the other one, so you can have a matching pair. Now hurry. They could give the order to jump any minute!"

"Can this really be happening?" asked Michelle.

"I looked over the starboard side a minute ago. There is something under us, and it's lighting up the water!" said Trisha excitedly. "If it's not a submarine, we're all about to get buried at the bottom of the sea. At this point, I don't think we have much choice in the matter."

Joshua felt a momentary tightness in his chest, but it disappeared as the air began to flow from his regulator. The frigid water seeped slowly into his wetsuit, which was not designed to keep him dry underwater, but to keep him warm by trapping a small amount of water inside the suit and letting his body heat it, thereby insulating him against the cold. He wondered what drowning in this immense darkness would feel like.

Reclining into one of two forward command chairs, Raven donned a peculiar-looking helmet and attached its umbilical cable to the command chair. Lowering the face shield, she activated the device then sat back, exhaling slowly. There was a moment of silence as the world around her grew dim. For a moment, Raven's mind experienced an immense silence. She waited for the Acoustic Imaging Processor to link her brain with the onboard AI computer. The interphase implants attached to her brain allowed Raven to access all the ship's sensors. The ship's shark-like nosecone housed the sonar hydrophones that fed data to the AI computer's imaging processor. Disturbances in the sea's ambient noise field acted like variations of light frequencies. Suddenly, Raven was surrounded by an immense azure-blue sea. She began to make out wispy strands of light within the deep blur. These formed patches of color that slowly began to appear as solid objects.

Raven could clearly make out what looked like a wasteland far below her in the depths of the Caribbean. She gazed up to see the underside of massive waves as they rolled past, tossing the small sailboat around. The surface of the ocean appeared to be about thirty feet above the divers as they took their positions. This technology never ceased to amaze her.

Joshua adjusted his buoyancy compensator and descended below the other divers. Monique nodded at him and made an OK sign.

Aurora had entered the chamber before the divers and now sat next to Raven in the co-pilot's chair. She began to examine all the controls. On each side of her was a manipulator sleeve. She placed both hands in the open sockets and the equipment's LEDs lit up as they pulled closer to the seat, effectively trapping Aurora. She looked over at Raven, who sat motionless except for the turning of her head from side to side, wearing that state-of-the-art helmet.

Aurora understood how the manipulators worked, so she opened and closed her cupped hands in much the same way someone might if trying to make a sock puppet speak. The claws on the end of the manipulators opened and closed. She turned again to Raven, whose helmet now faced up. Aurora remained motionless, unsure how to get out of the sleeves that encased her arms.

"Commander, divers are ready," announced Raven. "Instruct the crew to shut off their engines if possible. Instruct them to jump off the starboard side in unison, when the ship is in the lowest part of the wave, just before the wave front rises. And have them jump as close together as possible."

"Understood," said Trisha. "We should be in the water within two minutes. I will attempt to shut off the engines first. Confirming, we will be jumping from the starboard side. We are go. Repeat, we are go!"

Raven was certain her team had overheard the conversation but verified just to be sure. "We are go. The crew is entering the water. Stand by."

"Standing by," responded Monique.

"Look alive, Juaquin," said Cha Cha. "This is no time to be getting a cramp in your leg."

"Cut the chatter, Chach," said Raven. "Incoming, we have bodies in the water! All three appear to be hanging onto one another and are descending directly over Juaquin."

"Roger that," said Juaquin, who was the first to reach them. The women were holding hands and facing each other, forming a ring. The lights on their arms made them easy to see in the darkness. Juaquin came up through their center, holding onto one of them as he inflated his buoyancy compensator to maximum. Moments later, three other divers reached the trio.

"Raven, we have three bodies accounted for. Returning to ship," said Monique.

As the three were assisted toward the ship, Juaquin motioned for Joshua, who was hovering below the group, to go on ahead of him.

Joshua gave the OK sign and followed behind the divers. He marveled at the ship's design but felt uncomfortable in the total darkness. The forward command center impressed him. It appeared that he could simply step through the transparent bullet-shaped compartment and onto the ship, so clear was the visibility. The two command chairs and their occupants appeared to hover over the emptiness of this strange new world as he glided past them. As he neared the hatch, Joshua miscalculated his re-entry and his tank valve got hung up on the hatch ring. He hoped no one had noticed.

Aurora screamed excitedly, drawing everyone's attention to the forward command center. Illuminated in the work lights against the dark backdrop of the sea was a very large fish. The beast appeared to have been attracted by the work lights. It had approached from below and clamped its enormous mouth around Juaquin's head; knocking the mask loose and severing communications. Aurora, still restrained in her seat, had been fooling around with the large robotic manipulators. In her excitement she had clasped the creature's thick tailfin and was stabbing at its midsection wildly with the other manipulator in an attempt to free the diver. Juaquin was in trouble and struggling to get free.

Monique rushed to the forward command chair but the fish had already released the diver and broken free, leaving a section of its tailfin still held by the robotic arm.

Still in the water, Joshua could hear that something had gone terribly wrong. He hurried back under to assist the last diver. As he approached Juaquin, he could see that his airline had been severed and the mask ripped off his face. Joshua pressed the regulator button, releasing a surge of bubbles as he placed the octopus rig in Juaquin's mouth. Juaquin blew out first then inhaled deeply. He nodded his head and gave a thumbs-up sign as Joshua pulled him toward the work hatch.

Juaquin emerged from the water bleeding with a most unpleasant expression on his face. Splashing seawater on his tongue, he proclaimed in his thick Spanish accent, "I think I just tasted Death! I did not know it was possible to smell bad breath underwater!"

With a bewildered look on her face, Cha Cha exclaimed, "A este ya lo lambio el Diablo."

"What does that mean?" asked Michelle, drying her hair.

"It's Spanish," explained Cha Cha, "and it means that Death just tasted him!"

Joshua removed his facemask and assisted Brian in lowering the upper hatch and locking it in place. A red warning light and buzzer sounded as the chamber began to decompress.

Raven informed the three new passengers that it would be at least five hours before anyone would be allowed to leave the chamber. They were moving away from the ship overhead and increasing their depth.

"Are we in a pressurized environment?" asked Trisha.

"Yes we are. If we decompress too fast, nitrogen bubbles will froth in our bloodstream. Once air builds up in the heart, it's over. You girls can get out of those wet clothes and take a hot shower while we wait, if you like."

Monique assisted Aurora out of the command chair.

Aurora mumbled that she felt bad about hurting the fish.

Juaquin assured her that the fish was lucky he'd broken free. "Otherwise we'd all be eating fish tacos for breakfast."

'Well, that's the most interesting Mayday I've ever responded to," said Raven.

"Mayday? We did not request a Mayday—you called us!" exclaimed Katharine. "And thank God you did."

Today Is the First Day of
What's Left of Your Life

"In my experience I've learned that there are no coincidences," said Teryk, after listening to their stories. The circumstances that brought the three of you here are intriguing. And since you girls had already resigned yourselves to leaving your world behind, perhaps one day you may decide to join ours."

Katharine winced and put her hand to her abdomen. "I think my baby likes that idea too. If you like, you can address me as Cat," said Katharine. "My grandmother sometimes used to call me that."

"How far along are you, Cat?" asked Raven.

"About three and a half months," said Katharine. "I've heard talk of Lemuria. Is that where we are going?"

"Not exactly. We will rendezvous with another submarine first. Then we will dock at the floating city of Antares. In time, you will see what we call Lemuria," said Raven. "Our Lemuria is a city built within a cavernous mountain in Siberia, not the ancient legendary Atlantis-like colony said to be located in the Pacific Ocean."

"I believe you've met Joshua," said Teryk as Joshua entered, drying his hair with a towel. "Until recently, Joshua was not part of our team. He, too, is new to this world. You're welcome to sit in on a discussion we were having just before we received the uhm… Mayday."

"What was the discussion about?" asked Trisha.

"Until lately, Joshua was a priest of the Roman Catholic Church; an exorcist, in fact. I was assuring him that with the exception of John, none of the other Gospel writers knew Jesus personally."

Trisha looked at Katharine, each raising her eyebrows. "Oh, I wouldn't miss this for the world," said Trisha, resting her chin on her hand. "I'm a preacher's kid—I hate religion!"

"But I was always under the impression that the four apostles—Matthew, Mark, Luke, and John—had all walked with Christ and been taught by him," said Michelle, her brows furrowing.

"To begin with, none of the Gospels identify their authors by name. The names were attributed to them many years later. Now we do know Luke wrote Acts and the third Gospel because it is written in the same style. In fact, Luke wrote about one fourth of the entire New Testament. Lucanus was a Greek physician who wrote down the stories of Jesus about thirty years after the Crucifixion, in an effort to preserve them for future generations. Thirty years seems like a long time, until one considers that the oldest available narrative about the reign of Alexander the Great was composed 300 years after his death. Luke's Greek is highly refined and he states plainly that he did his best to be extremely accurate in his account of what happened. There is only one major flaw with Luke: Where Mark and Matthew say Jesus became furious or very upset, Luke waters it down or omits the incident altogether. You see, to the Greeks," explained Teryk, "divine godlike beings did not lose their tempers, and so Luke made the necessary corrections."

"Mark was believed to be a follower of Peter in Rome," said Raven. "My research points to him being John Mark, a follower of Paul. Matthew, the writer of the first Gospel, was also a follower of Paul. He is not to be confused with the apostle Levi/Matthew, the tax collector whom Jesus had appointed as the official scribe. The writer of the fourth Gospel did not sign it John, but rather ends it with, 'I was the beloved disciple.' He speaks of 'the one Jesus loved' throughout the book. The 'beloved disciple' was present at the Last Supper, but is missing during the arrest and doesn't show up again until the Crucifixion, always referring to himself in the third person. The Apocalypse stands in stark contrast to this style of writing. John makes it quite clear that it is he who is experiencing the visions. To scholars it is evident that the Gospel of John and the book of the Apocalypse were written by two different authors. I believe John wrote the Apocalypse, now referred to as Revelation, but not the Gospel attributed to him."

"Tell me truthfully, do you guys honestly believe Jesus resurrected from the dead?" asked Trisha, not one for pulling punches.

"Paul often said to new converts, If Jesus had not been raised from the dead, then his preaching and their faith were in vain.' If anyone could have disproved the resurrection, it would have been Saul of Tarsus, aka the apostle Paul," reasoned Teryk.

Trisha then made the loco-in-the-cabeza gesture with her right forefinger and muttered, "Plum loco," under her breath. "You don't strike me as a *Bible* thumper, Teryk. In fact, you seem to lack any semblance of religion."

"Were you ever a priest, Teryk?" asked Katharine.

"Actually, I was, and like Joshua, I, too, was an exorcist for the Roman Catholic Church."

"I don't suppose you recall what Jesus had to say about priests?" Trisha reminded them.

"Jesus did not appoint himself priest over anyone, nor did he appoint any priests over others; that was Paul's doing," countered Teryk. "Jesus felt that one should have a direct relationship with the Creator—not with religion. The people of his time never understood that. He frequently asked, 'How must I say this?' or, 'How many times must I show you?' The Church has forgotten that Christ appointed apostles to serve. He never appointed priests, bishops, cardinals or popes who required others to serve them. It is interesting to note that the *Apocalypse of Peter* states that these early Church fathers, '*name themselves bishops and deacons as if they had received their authority directly from God*'."

"Teryk, you must know that some people won't believe what you're saying because they simply don't understand," interrupted Katharine.

"An irony," agreed Teryk, "because all they really have to do is 'believe' and the Holy Spirit will give them understanding. In my opinion, one of the biggest stumbling blocks to Christians today is the Pauline Doctrine, which is not necessarily Paul's teachings. To begin with, the first leader of the New Christian movement is considered by the Roman Catholic Church to have been Peter, but history is quite clear on the matter. According to Saint Hegesippus, a chronicler of the early Church, within a few years of Jesus' crucifixion, his brothers, not his disciples, were heading the movement. James 'the Just' was the first leader and after his death, he was succeeded by Jude. Jesus' brother Simon held the position last, during the Jewish Revolt."

"The Church created by Paul was constantly at odds with the Jewish synagogue and the Jewish Christians of Jerusalem, taught by the original disciples who adhered to the teachings of Jesus. Gentile Christians did not take kindly to Jewish restrictions, instead favoring Paul's teachings, and labeling the Jewish Christians heretics."

"The Gospels and Acts all came about after the Great War," said Raven. "The Romans had just decimated the Temple of Jerusalem. In fact, they deliberately razed the Temple to the ground. Perhaps the time had come for Christians to distance themselves from their Jewish roots and align with Rome."

"In his letters, Paul never makes any mention of Mary Magdalene, Pontius Pilate or the disciples John and Judas Iscariot. In fact, he says very little about the life of Jesus," explained Teryk. "Paul implicitly states that believers should *only* listen to *his version* of the 'good news', even if God should send angels to bring them Jesus' message!

"Like Jesus, I personally pissed off a lot of pious individuals. In fact, I was officially excommunicated by a tribunal of the Holy Inquisition," announced Teryk.

"The Holy Inquisition? Didn't they do away with that during the sixteenth century?" asked Trisha, not certain she had heard right.

"Hardly. The Holy Inquisition is the most powerful department in the Vatican. It is the highest court of orthodoxy in the Roman Catholic Church. And it is still the Inquisition's responsibility to ferret out radicals and heretics. The Holy Inquisition wields the authority to censor Church writings and excommunicate any Catholic who does not adhere to Church dogma. The court was renamed the Congregation for the Doctrine of the Faith, but I'm a sentimental kind of guy and I prefer the original name—it's so nostalgic," explained Teryk in a sardonic tone.

"What was your crime?" asked Michelle.

"I continuously performed healings and exorcisms without the Pope's consent or permission...."

"What if the Pope's Laws contradict the teachings of Jesus?" inquired Katharine, "or the laws of God?"

"Jesus and God are irrelevant!" Teryk shot back. "Priests are bound by their vow of obedience!"

"What was your excommunication like?" asked Joshua.

"It's very simple, really. After reciting the charges against me and addressing me by name, they said something like, 'I ask you simply, do you denounce your heresy? Do you recognize that what you have done is against the laws of God and the Holy Roman Catholic Church?' I gave my response," said Teryk, flipping Joshua the bird. They exclaimed that they could not forgive me. I told them I was not seeking their forgiveness, and that was pretty much that. There was no point in arguing with them. Anyone who disputes the verdict of the Inquisitor is guilty of heresy."

"I take it that means you're going straight to Hell, doesn't it?" inquired Michelle.

"According to them, it does," observed Teryk, "but I've discovered that the rules of the clergy are not there to enlighten, but to threaten any who step out of line. The Church is a structure that has been superimposed on Christians and they are not really permitted to be a part of it.

"During my time as a priest, I encountered many nuns and priests who truly loved their work. I would watch them perform their duties with the utmost attention to detail and observance of the laws and dogma set down by the Church. They went to confession and their appearance was always professional. They were great administrators but there was nothing spiritual about their lives. Religious institutions have plenty of highly educated scholars but few if any spiritual individuals who incorporate the teachings of Jesus into their lives. Spirituality is not encouraged. In fact, if you question your faith, you are seen as weak. How could one ever question his or her faith when the institution has all the answers?"

"I suppose it is religious in the sense that they do the exact same damned things over and over: kneel, sit, stand and recite passages," observed Trisha.

"Questioning one's faith, in my opinion," said Joshua, "is a commitment to truth; the willingness to accept the possibility that you don't know everything and could benefit from experiences previously unknown to you."

"You're lucky. My mind has always been inclined toward doubt," admitted Trisha. "Try as I might, my propensity is always toward skepticism."

"Questions like what?" asked Raven.

"Questions like, 'Am I doing the right thing?'" shrugged Trisha. "Even now, I'm unsure if in attempting to commit suicide we may have ended up in Hell for all eternity. It felt right, but I don't know if it was the right thing to do?"

"Somehow you have come to the understanding that faith means the absence of doubt, when in fact doubt strengthens your faith by exercising it," Teryk assured her. "I have always had a great deal of respect for people who ask those kinds of questions, Trisha. It is a mark of their integrity." Teryk placed a reassuring hand on Trisha's shoulder then asked, "Do you want me to tell you why I believe you are on the right path?"

"Yes, but how can I be on any path if I'm asking these types of questions?"

"You are on the right path by the very fact that you are asking those types of questions! Do you honestly think the Nazi movement stopped to ask those kinds of questions?" asked Teryk. "I can guarantee that some of those German soldiers did. Were you aware that thousands of German troops are reported to have committed suicide rather than commit the atrocities that were commanded of them? You can be sure that their leaders never stopped to ask those questions because they knew they were right and had all the answers. They did not waste time arguing the point. Evil does not ask if it is doing the right thing; evil does what it does because it derives great pleasure and satisfaction from it."

"Well, I guess I just don't have your brand of faith. Unlike you, I do not have all my ducks in a row," Trisha countered.

"If I had waited to get all my ducks-in-a-row," Teryk dragged out the words, "there would have been no one around to help you when your ship started to take on water. Don't waste your life trying to get all your ducks in a row, Trisha. Just get them all going in the same direction and you'll do fine. Contrary to popular belief, the path to enlightenment is not a straight one. It's an irony that the easiest thing seems to be the most difficult. Interestingly enough, guiding someone else on their path is quite simple. All I have to do is ask the obvious questions then refrain from interfering in the answers."

"Like Trisha, I have learned to look at 'faith' as only hopeful ignorance," admitted Katharine. "You seem to have been born with a type of faith which I have never had the privilege of witnessing before."

Lost in Translation

> *An error does not become truth by reason of*
> *multiplied propagation, nor does*
> *truth become error because nobody sees it.*
> *—Mahatma Gandhi*

"So you think," Trisha paused trying to find the words, "the reason we're here is to learn Truth—from *you?*"

"No, certainly not," Teryk assured the girls. "I am not here to end your misery or to make all your problems disappear. I will do my best to answer your questions, but in the end you must find your own answers. Truth only comes from deep within your heart. It is your only real connection to Source.

"All too often, well-meaning Christians are taught to sell evangelism in an effort to fill empty seats." Teryk's tone became ominous. "I believe you should have a firm understanding of what you're about to get yourself into. Because once you've uttered the words that call the Holy Spirit into your heart, the Creator will move Heaven and Earth in an effort to get closer to you. A mustard seed is the smallest of seeds yet, when it is grown, birds can nest in its branches. Removing all traces of a mustard plant from the soil is nearly impossible. A new mustard plant will grow if a single piece of its root remains. The Holy Spirit is a lot like that. Once your heart has experienced its presence, it is not something easily forgotten or lost. It's what Jesus meant when he spoke of having faith like the grain of a mustard seed.

"People should not be led to believe that by simply asking God into their lives it will solve all their problems. If anything, the onslaught of new problems will make them wonder if God is not in some way angry with them. In ages past, people would pray and meditate in temples for many years before asking the

Creator of All to become part of their lives. Because they *knew* once they uttered those words, their lives would be utterly transformed."

"I suppose it was a sense of self-betrayal that caused me to want to end my life," Trisha admitted. "Everything in my body told me to stay away from that guy. But I put it off as silly female sentiments."

"At times we are drawn to our own destruction, I suppose, but I doubt that was the case," Teryk reflected. "Tell me, do you have a hidden fear of finding yourself at the end of life, alone with nothing to show for it? No one to share your life with? No one grieving your absence, nothing to show that you had ever existed?"

"Like a bag lady, alone and forgotten… it's one of my worst fears," confided Trisha. "That thought is always in the back of my mind."

"Women who feel they must have a man in their life tend to select men who will *never* leave them alone," observed Teryk. "All your true friends tried to warn you about the men that attracted you. You chose to ignore their advice. Once the relationship was over, you discovered you needed a court order to keep the guy away from you. If you stop and think about it, isn't that the kind of mate you were searching for? Deep down you wanted someone who would always be there, no matter what!"

"I never looked at it that way before," reflected Trisha. "I suppose you're right. But in a way I'm grateful it happened. If I had not sought to end my life, I would never have met you guys. I certainly would not be on this ship right now, and I feel I am exactly where I should be at this moment."

"You claim to be an agnostic, yet you strike me as more of a mystic," mused Teryk.

"What's an egg-noss-stick?" asked Aurora.

"Agnostics believe in things that are supernatural. But unlike atheists, they do not claim, 'There is no God!' They simply do not know if God is real or not," explained Raven.

"Are you trying to convert me to your way of thinking?" asked Trisha.

"What I'm saying is that if you are truly seeking, you will find," Teryk assured her. "You may not like what you find, but you will find it. Learn to listen to that small inner voice that simply says, '*Seek me, and "I" shall find you.*'"

"Yeah, I once asked an orthodox priest about that 'small inner voice' offering me guidance. I was told, in no uncertain terms, to get my priorities straight." Joshua stood and pointed a condescending finger at the assembled group. "The Roman Catholic religion," he said in his best Italian, "was about a bloody Jew hanging on a cross! And if I thought I heard a small inner voice giving me guidance, I'd better tell it to go straight to Hell, then confess the experience to a priest immediately!"

Joseph "Five Eagles" Reyna

"I learned to trust in and take my counsel directly from the Holy Spirit's guidance," confided Teryk. "Many pastors will warn you that you're not supposed to do that. You are supposed to submit to their guidance. You should not allow yourself to be directed by any spiritual guidance. In their minds it can only be Satan, imitating an angel of light and deceiving you.

"I once argued over this topic with a very spiritual individual who later confided that the Holy Spirit had given him an answer in regards to our debate. The answer was formatted in a specific framework, a sort of situation. So I will relate it to you in the same manner. Let's suppose that you have just come out of the shower and you're drying off, but your hair is still wet. You see your mate lying on the bed facing the wall and you decide to climb into bed and kiss them on the cheek. As you do this some drops of water, from your wet hair, fall on their cheek and without turning toward you he asks, 'Katharine, is that you?' Now my question to you is would you remain in the bedroom with this person? A person that means so much to you, still feeling exactly as you did before you crawled onto the bed, or would you leave the room?"

"I'd be gone!" exclaimed Katharine.

"Why? All you had to do was confirm that it was, in fact, you; much the same way preachers demand that the Holy Spirit confirm that it is what you gnow it to be. After the Holy Spirit sadly departs your side, you conclude that it must have been the Devil. Thank God your pastor gave you that advice!

"In the Gospels, Jesus assured his followers that when he departed, God would send the Holy Spirit to guide, comfort, counsel, and instruct us. Jesus used to say, 'My sheep know the sound of my voice,' and I can assure you I gnow the voice of the Holy Spirit."

"I could definitely have used some divine guidance in trying to understand the actions of my husband," admitted Katharine. "In an effort to make me feel that we were perfect for each other, my husband lied about everything, his favorite music, the movies we watched. He said my thoughts were his thoughts. Once we were married, he changed completely. When I confronted him about it, he told me he'd lied about those things because of how much he loved me. He didn't want to lose me, so he had to lie."

"Didn't his family notice his behavior?" asked Joshua.

"They played along with it to ensure his happiness, they later told me."

"That's a new one on me; lie to someone because of how much you love them," said Raven in astonishment.

"When he found out I was pregnant with a boy, he sat down and planned out our child's entire life. Dametrie's ego and self-interest were just big enough to ensure our son's life would be a living Hell. He has a way of using people's love against them. Then he started going behind my back, telling my two best friends," said Katharine as she placed her arms around Trisha and Michelle, "that I secretly loathed them and did not want to listen to their pathetic problems. That was the proverbial straw that broke the camel's back.

"Dametrie had this habit of leaving his underwear in the center of the bathroom floor. To him it was symbolic of my position in his world, because I was supposed to pick them up. About three weeks ago I stopped picking them up. He instructed the maid not to touch them and kept adding to the pile. He finally ran out of underwear, and had to go out and buy more."

"How high did he let the pile get?" asked Monique, intrigued.

"As far as I know, he's still adding to it."

"As much as we all wanted to leave that world behind us," said Trisha feeling depressed, "now that I've left it, I don't know what I'll do with what's left of my life. I have always believed I was doing what I was born to do. I really loved my work in military intelligence."

"A sense of purpose is a profound thing, Trisha, and not always what it seems," offered Raven. "You obviously love solving puzzles. You're intrigued by mysteries and enigmas. When we dock I would like you to sift through some evidence we have. I would really appreciate your take on it. Perhaps you'll consider joining our intelligence-gathering teams at ESPionage."

"What evidence will I be reviewing?"

"Jared, one of our lead researchers, will most likely have you reviewing both the original as well as the new evidence dealing with John F. Kennedy's assassination," said Teryk.

"I would love to get my hands on the evidence your teams have compiled. My grandpa always maintained that Oswald did not kill Kennedy but, having come from an intelligence background, he would never discuss the particulars with me," admitted Trisha. "The use of a lone assassin, for destroying a political opponent, has been an effective tool for over seven hundred years. And it is always understood that, the assassin never acted alone. What sort of discrepancies have your teams uncovered?"

"I take it you've never looked into the matter yourself. Well, for starters there's the infamous backyard photo of Oswald holding his rifle on the cover of *Life* magazine. That photo was declared to be a forgery just weeks after its release, by Scotland Yard. There are many problems with the photo but I'll demonstrate just a few." Teryk stood and opened a computer work station on the bulkhead. Activating it he searched through some files. An overhead projector dropped from a sealed compartment and projected an image of Lee Harvey Oswald holding his rifle onto the adjacent bulkhead. "Aurora, could you please get me a yardstick from the work station? Trisha, about how tall are you?"

"I'm just a little over 5'9"," replied Trisha.

"Perfect, can you please stand next to the image of Oswald? He stood five-feet nine inches in height." Teryk adjusted the lens angle and position on the overhead projector until the image of Oswald was about the same height as Trisha. Aurora entered handing Teryk a stainless steel yardstick. "We use these to document items of historical value we sometimes uncover during shipwreck excavations," he explained. "The Mannlicher-Carcano rifle Oswald allegedly ordered from an advertisement in the Texas newspaper was thirty-six inches in length. Please take this yardstick and measure the rifle he is holding."

"It's longer than the yardstick!" exclaimed Trisha.

"Using the known length of the rifle as our guide, if we scale down the image to match the length of the yardstick, Oswald appears much too short. That rifle, the one Oswald used to kill Kennedy, is on display at the National Archives. The FBI confirmed that the lanes and groves from the barrel of the rifle, on display at the National Archives, are an identical match to the striations found on the 'magic bullet' that killed Kennedy. The only problem I have with that is, the 6.5 Mannlicher-Carcano on display at the National Archives is forty inches long," said Teryk in a capricious tone that carried a hint of cynicism.

"What the hell!" exclaimed Trisha. "Why would a rifle four inches longer than the one Oswald owned be on display, as the murder weapon, at the National Archives."

"It's quite simple really, the forty-inch rifle more accurately represents the length of the rifle in the photo," explained Teryk. "Instead of presenting a clipping for the thirty-six inch Mannlicher-Carcano that appeared in the newspaper as evidence, the Warren Commission used an advertisement of a forty inch rifle in their report. In an effort to compensate for the pooch-screw, I suppose. Also, it is well known that Lee Harvey Oswald had a sharp, cleft chin. The man in the picture has a flat chin. More importantly, his feet are to the left of center." Teryk unplugged a bulky charger and held it up so that the long, thin cord was made straight by its weight. He compared his impromptu plumb bob's vertical cord to a post that stood next to Oswald. The straightness of the beam appeared true. "Now pay attention to the position of Oswald's feet when I center this string on his face. Both feet are to one side of the line. Oswald is standing off center. The load of his body is not centered over his feet. I'm not showing you guys anything new. Jack White, James Fetzer and Jim Marrs have been pointing out these discrepancies for nearly half-a-century."

"When we entered the ship… that section we were in, what was that?" asked Trisha.

"That was our work station," explained Raven. "This ship's main function is treasure recovery…"

"Long ago I learned to avoid legal entanglement," interrupted Teryk. "Through our stealth operations, we avoid having to deal with greedy government officials, or pirates."

"We also avoid delays due to bad weather or rough sea conditions," explained Raven. "During operations we will pressurize the entire submarine, not just the work area. We usually remain on location for weeks at a time."

"Avoid pirates? You guys are pirates!" joked Katharine.

"Treasure hunting sounds fascinating. Can anyone help recover treasure if they want to?" asked Michelle.

"You have to be certified—there's a lot you need to know," said Raven. "We have a special training facility in the Caribbean where you live and train underwater…"

"Isn't what you're doing against the law?" questioned Trisha, interrupting.

"That my dear, is for the courts to decide," said Teryk with a dismissive gesture.

"Don't you consider it *stealing* when you recover these treasure ships?" asked Katharine.

"To be sure, crimes were committed but if my gold is tainted in any way, it's with the blood of my ancestors," Teryk assured her.

"Honestly, I don't think *Klepto* recognizes his actions as a crime," observed Trisha.

"Actually, I think the problem is genetic," said Teryk, pondering the statement. "You girls can probably trace your ancestors back a millennium. Native American ancestry was almost obliterated from history. I can only trace my ancestry back to my grandfathers. As it turns out, my father's father was a very successful horse thief in Mexico. My horse, *el Jovero*, is named after the famous racing appaloosa my grandfather bred. But if it makes you feel any better, when my grandfather died, a lawyer paid one of my grandfather's relatives to find the property deed. When he couldn't find it, he beat my grandmother in an effort to extract the information from her. She never gave it to him, because my grandfather had warned her before he died that such a thing might happen.

"The lawyer assumed the deed was lost and drew up new papers stating that my grandparents had each sold their half of the ranch to the lawyer, for ten dollars apiece. My grandparents' signatures do not appear on this document, a simple white sheet of paper, with an X to mark their names. The document was signed ten days after my grandfather's death. Of the two signatures that appear on the document for witnesses, one belongs to the lawyer. That lawyer is now a judge. My father was five years old when that lawyer threw my grandmother and her two small boys out of their home. I have seen the original deed. My father showed it to me. It is three pages long and each page is a different color, like the old carbon copies of the time. Both of my grandparents' signatures appear on the document. The last page states, 'These lands will not be sold, leased or rented to Negroes'. In case you can't distinguish the locale by the lingo, their ranch was in the great state of Texas.

"You are correct to assume I do not recognize my actions as a crime," admitted Teryk. "The cruelty of the conquistadors, who savagely removed these treasures from my ancestral lands, is well documented. I do not believe I have taken anything that did not already belong to my people. The method by which I take it back, you find questionable."

"But you could file an admiralty claim, Teryk," interjected Trisha. "It's a constitutional right to salvage without any interference from other parties. Anything over a hundred years old is classified antique and duty free!"

"What you find under the sea is rarely yours to keep, Trisha. Most nations claim all ownerless wrecks within their waters, which some claim extend out anywhere from fifty to two hundred miles. Treasure hunters who plan to search the waters of most Latin American countries are expected to make generous contributions to the bureaucrats in power. Anything brought up from their coastal waters belongs to the government, not the salvor. You, as excavator, are entitled to a salvage fee—but the fee varies immensely. Admiralty laws pertaining to wrecks are often vague or contradict other laws. Suppose a Portuguese warship sank in Dutch waters—now you've two governments to contend with. Any settlements would be tied up in litigation for years."

Teryk then handed each of the four a small gold coin about the size of a nickel. "That's a Lady Liberty $5, Half Eagle. I would like each of you to have one. The 'S' mintmark on the back, below the eagle, signifies that they came from the San Francisco Mint. They are 90% pure gold from the California Gold Rush."

"What does the *Bible* have to say about this… treasure hunting?" asked Joshua, admiring the details on his gold coin.

"For everyone who uses the talents he has been given shall have abundantly. But he who hides away the gifts God has given him shall forfeit what little he has."

"You should know better than to ask him for *Bible* verses," cautioned Raven.

"My favorite verse concerning treasure can be found in Matthew 13:44: '…like a treasure a man discovered in a field. In his excitement, he sold everything he owned to get enough money to buy the field.' Since the majority of the world's oceans have not been parceled off and sold yet, I take what I find. In case you missed it, Jesus doesn't say the man who found the treasure goes and reports it to the owner of the land, asking for a finder's fee. He keeps that information to himself. And for the record, when my teams have located a treasure on land, I've offered to buy the land first."

"What happens to the treasure if they don't wish to sell their land?" asked Trisha.

"Well, let's just say they're not going to miss it."

A voice over the intercom sounded, "Captain, we will rendezvous with the *Intrepid* in three hours."

"We're moving?" asked Trisha. "I don't hear the diesel engines humming? This thing isn't nuclear is it?"

"The deep baritone thrum you're hearing is made by the air handlers. And *Defiant's* four-hundred-cycle electric power-generating system operates on a form of cold fusion coupled with overunity devices." Teryk noticed Trisha's blank stare. "No it's not nuclear… at least not as you understand nuclear."

"Teryk explained some of Antares's technology to me earlier," offered Joshua.

"I was explaining to Joshua that the textbooks he was learning from were seriously flawed," said Teryk. "And if your learning is based on theories that are less than perfect, you will never learn to fully utilize the potential of magnetism. If the world's inventors had evaluated their discoveries based on what the experts were saying at the time, I doubt we as a civilization would have advanced as far as we have. Through the development of these devices, I discovered that the existing laws of magnetism and gravity are not completely accurate. The quantum electro-dynamic paradigm is inadequate. In fact, some of the laws of magnetism are erroneous. As a result, Earth's advanced civilizations are still 'boiling water' to get electricity."

"Where do you come up with this stuff?" Trisha shook her head.

"Actually, we discovered much of it while excavating Atlantis under the Antarctic ice sheet," said Raven.

"Discoveries you don't share with the rest of humanity, I take it," said Trisha in an accusing tone.

"True, but as I pointed out to Joshua earlier," said Teryk, "many of these discoveries were already known to the rest of the world. The world chose to ridicule and ostracize not only the discoveries, but also those who made them. I see you doubt me. Do you have any idea how fast this ship is running right now while submerged? We're cruising at over one hundred and fifty knots."

"That's not possible," Trisha shot back. "There are rocket-powered Russian torpedoes that can run that fast but an entire ship…"

"I'm finding it hard to believe you as well," admitted Joshua. "What sort of propulsion system do you have? When I was outside earlier I noticed that the flat nosecone of the ship swept back, like an F-14 Fighter's, towards two massive propulsor shrouds that flanked the transparent bullet-shaped command center. Do those two large shrouds silence the propellers they conceal?"

Joseph "Five Eagles" Reyna

"If it had been daylight, those shrouds would have appeared like the underpasses of a bridge to you. This ship does not use propellers. Those shrouds are hollow, you can easily see right through them," Teryk assured him.

"Does your ship operate with some sort of caterpillar drive?" asked Trisha. "It is my understanding that caterpillar drives on submarines are impractical. They're too heavy and require a tremendous amount of power to operate. I am unaware of any sub designs that can travel at the speeds you're talking about."

Teryk rested his forehead in his hands and wondered aloud, "How in the world do I explain to you, without freaking everyone out, that this ship's propulsion system operates by displacing, or rather 'warping', space/time?" Teryk stood and went into the Captain's chamber. There he retrieved a well-worn book he had lent to Raven. No one said a word as he returned and seated himself. "This book has been instrumental in helping us develop the advanced technologies that have allowed us to go undetected. *Lost Science* by author Gerry Vassilatos. This book offers many examples of incredibly advanced technologies that were rejected because they were too far 'outside the box' of accepted electrical phenomena.

"The 'warp drive' allows this ship to move through the water without causing a wake or ripples on the surface of the water. Warp drives operate by displacing matter, thereby creating thrust. As expected, the US Patent Office immediately rejected this invention, citing 'improper terminology' as their excuse. I'm pretty sure none of you have ever heard of the inventor. Much like Nikola Tesla, Thomas Townsend Brown is not well known. Without these two pioneers, we would probably never have succeeded in the development of our overunity generators, electrogravitic repulsors, or time-displacement devices."

Opening the book to page 250, marked with a blue tab, Teryk read aloud. "'Thomas Townsend Brown eventually went to England and was immediately granted patent 300.311 on November 15, 1928, for his 'space warp' drive.' On the next page it states that the US never patented this invention but did grant him a patent in 1930 on a rotary 'electro static' motor that operated under a similar principle. The patent number for that invention was 1.974.483. I don't know if any of you were aware of the fact that a US patent only provides protection for seventeen years. After that time, anyone is allowed to use the technology.

"By obtaining copies of these two patents, as well as many others, our research labs have made astonishing progress over the last twelve years. Like the wartime research facilities of the US and Nazis, our labs run 24/7 on critical developments. We operate in twelve five-hour shifts. Most of our researchers work only three or four days a week. So it is very important that the shifts overlap.

"When we run across a 'monomaniac on a mission', we ensure that that person is provided with several servants and assistants," explained Teryk. "The servants ensure that these individuals eat healthily, rest and exercise. The assistants perform all the mundane chores so that these individuals can focus on their work. I've read about too many inventors who damaged their health by driving themselves too hard. Relaxing and doing nothing for a day is actually painful for these types of individuals.

"We haven't turned our backs on the world, guys" Teryk assured the small gathering. "The world has turned its back on us. Most of these fantastic inventions have been in your nation's domain for decades. It might surprise you to learn that most of these inventors had PhD's. These men received no recognition for their groundbreaking discoveries and contributions to science. In fact, most of these trailblazers were ostracized and ridiculed. In our world we honor them. Research facilities are named after them. And our next generation will be well versed in their achievements.

"The engines that drive *Defiant* are called gravitators. Thomas Townsend Brown discovered that the physics involved somehow blended the laws of Coulomb's electric force with the laws of Newton's gravitational acceleration. The entire engine is a hollowed-out bank of stacked capacitors...."

"Do they operate under the same principles as 'electric wind' generators?" interrupted Joshua.

"No, once activated these things are 'self-exciting' because their operation relies on the collapse of space-time itself in order to move their mass forward. Electric wind generators, as a rule, do not operate well when submerged. These engines rely on the distortion of space, not the medium in which motion is produced. Several gravitators in tandem are required to maintain the drive effect. Thrust is amplified when we increase either voltage or the dielectric mass of the capacitor banks. Electric current has almost no effect on the space distortion. At full thrust, our gravitators draw tens of thousands of Volts but only consume milliamps of current. *Defiant* is unique in that the design of her capacitor banks is such that the distortion effect envelopes the entire ship. The seawater actually moves with the ship in a frictionless environment. The 'electrogravitic field distortion' moves the entire ship through space without a measurable reaction. In this sense Newton's third law of motion is violated.

"Under normal operating conditions, *Defiant* handles like any other vessel. For instance, the ship's aft section sports 'tail feathers', which are basically moveable fins that flex and rotate in order to direct the flow of the propulsor thrust to help stabilize the ship when we are over a work area," explained Teryk, handing the book to Joshua.

"Wow, you do exactly what I do when I study a book," Joshua said upon opening it. "I highlight in different colors and make notations everywhere. This book looks very interesting. I'll definitely need to get my own copy."

"So how fast is this thing anyway?" asked Trisha, fascinated by the concept.

"*Defiant* is a relatively new development. Older ships did not incorporate this particular engine design. As a result, they were slowed down by their hull's friction. Their top speed was just over forty knots but could not be maintained for very long without damaging the hull. *Defiant's* top speed is well over two hundred knots while submerged. The ship's top speed is dependent on the size and of shape of the gravitators's dielectric mass. Once the ship reaches top speed, no amount of additional voltage will affect its maximum velocity.

"The ship is also incredibly quiet. Our sonar can detect vessels a thousand miles away. It picks up the sound of shrimp feeding on the ocean floor. As a result, the sonar's sensitivity has actually become a problem. Special programs had to be developed to monitor and cancel out this type of ocean noise.

"In my opinion, the United States Patent Office's inability to recognize and accept new technologies is by far the greatest obstruction to inventors," said Teryk. "The established system only recognizes new theories which complement, not call into question, the foundation it is based on."

"You are probably unaware that Orville and Wilbur Wright's patent for their flying machine was delayed for twelve years in the United States, simply because the 'experts' were all in agreement that nothing heavier than air could maintain lift under its own power," said Raven.

"Unfortunately, the old corporate dynastic systems heavily influence national policies. If a new technology threatens to usurp their stranglehold on the economy, the discovery will be suppressed," said Teryk. "Allow me to explain the consequences of developing and patenting such devices. We developed a solar cell with twice the efficiency of anything on the market, so we tried to patent it. Such a device would put the coal industry out of business. In order to maintain the status quo we were slapped with secrecy order, Title 35, US Code (1952) Sections 181-188, preventing us from building, selling or talking about the device—forever. I think the minimum prison sentence is something like twenty years, which is crazy when you consider that a patent only protects you for seventeen years."

"Our world has forever been changed by the radical ideas of pioneers like Galileo, Columbus, Tesla, and the Wright brothers. These individuals persevered against incredible odds," said Raven. "It would seem that for those who believed in themselves, no proof was necessary. And for those who doubted them—no proof was possible."

"It sounds like your research labs are comprised of geniuses," said Michelle.

"You know what I find funny?" said Teryk. "I once read that Walt Disney Corporation was looking for geniuses to come work for them. So they listed the traits these men and women exhibited: they did not work well in groups; they seemed to have no people skills. Geniuses were extremely opinionated, and worked odd hours, not your regular 9-to-5 people. They dressed and acted outside the norm; they spent very little time behind the desk and were not concerned with deadlines. Instead, these individuals waited for inspiration from music, movies, meditation or just taking long walks; they worked on several different projects at once, creating new ones as they went along; and of course they rebelled against authority—and these were just their good points."

"That pretty much describes the people working at our research facilities," laughed Raven.

An Unholy Alliance

Two days later, Father Andrews entered the office of Cardinal Bishop Pablo de la Torre and handed him a photo. The cardinal puzzled over the deep scratches in the church's thick adobe walls. "What do we tell the other cardinals?" he asked.

"We'll advise them when we have something to tell. As far as I'm concerned, these soldiers and priests are casualties of the tornado that damaged the structure, nothing more."

"Excellency, the bodies of the soldiers outside the church were brutally mangled. Stranger still, they appear to have aged considerably. Also, the men had a look of absolute horror frozen on their faces. And I thought you might find this interesting," he said, handing the cardinal another photo: the first picture that seem to incite a reaction from the man.

"Why am I looking at a dog that appears frightened out of his mind?"

"Sir, the animal is dead. Its features are frozen in that ghoulish expression. In the background, behind the animal, you can see the doghouse that was overturned in order to get a good picture of the beast. It almost seems that the dog's head is on backwards."

The cardinal seemed unnerved as he handed the photo back to Father Andrews. Holding up a large white feather he asked, "The white feathers, what can you make of them?"

"The lab has not identified what type of bird the feathers may have come from. They are quite large for any bird of that region. The transcripts of the exorcism are straightforward but incomplete. The recorder was damaged half way through the ordeal and the second recorder is still missing along with the young assistant priest...."

"And the surveillance cameras?" The cardinal cut him off sharply in a deprecating tone.

"I've personally watched the seven combined hours of video that we have, and it's anticlimactic at best. The video-recording equipment was digital. The heavy rains and tornado debris had coated the lenses, obscuring the images once the roof came off the old church. Archbishop Felipe Espindola stated that the cloaked individual who seemed to be controlling the dæmon knew Father Artimus Murphy. Murphy, who was injured during the exorcism, identified the man as a former exorcist of the Roman Catholic Church." At this remark the cardinal locked eyes with him. Father Andrews sheepishly handed him a plain brown clasped envelope. "The man was excommunicated nearly twelve years ago."

"I thought he was dead?" commented the cardinal examining the file and photo.

"That's what Father Murphy said. His words exactly."

"Did they learn anything about the Ark's location from the dæmon?" demanded the cardinal.

"Yes, it's in the transcript I included in the folder." The cardinal glared at the priest in annoyance. "When questioned about the decoded text, specifically the part about Blue Apples at mid-day, the dæmon replied, 'Your focus is on the Blue Apples. If I were you, I would be more concerned with the two men so prominently mentioned within the code itself.'"

"And who are these men, so prominently mentioned?" asked the cardinal sliding his chair back and away from ornately carved desk.

"They are painters, artists, both of them; Nicolás Poussin and David Teniers the Younger. When attempting to decode the original message, Abbé Bérenger Saunière traveled to Paris and purchased copies of paintings from both artists. The dæmon also said we might want to find out what the 'Horse of God' is all about and why there are two who ride it. Cardinal Bishop de la Torre, I am beginning to have my doubts that the Knights Templar were ever in possession of the Ark of the Covenant. I just can't seem to justify the deaths of all those men…"

"Father Andrews, have you ever heard of the Copper Scroll that was found among the Dead Sea Scrolls?" interrupted the Cardinal rising from his seat.

"The Treasure Scroll, yes, but no one now living knows where the landmarks listed in the scroll might be."

"Suppose there was someone, or something, that did know? Would that not be reason enough to sacrifice the lives of a few men?"

Father Andrews swallowed hard. "Asmodeus… well, yes, I… I suppose the dæmon should be able to recall the topography of the area surrounding Jerusalem."

"Have you ever heard of an organization calling itself Rex Deus?" asked the Cardinal as he stepped toward as elaborately carved ivory box resting on a marble shelf.

Seeming surprised by the question, Father Andrews shook his head.

"There are few who have," said the cardinal removing its contents without turning to look at the priest. "Rex Deus literally means Two Kings." Turning to address Father Andrews he continued. "It was the name of the banner under which the original nine knights of Solomon's Temple functioned. The Rex Deus located a similar copper scroll among the chests they recovered from Temple Mount. When they returned to France, the scrolls were taken to the Cistercian Order of Monks headed by Saint Bernard of Clairvaux. Like the Copper Scroll found among the Dead Sea Scrolls, this scroll not only described the exact locations of the caches but provided a complete inventory of the items in the vaults. In 1118, the knights were officially recognized as 'The Poor Knights of Christ and The Temple of Solomon'. That same year they returned to the Holy Land and began excavating the vaults. It took them nearly a decade to unearth two hundred tons of gold and silver. On 13 January 1128 the Knights Templar secured a papal rule making them the official guardians of the recovered Temple treasure."

The cardinal returned to his desk and added, "Shortly after this, the Knights Templar quickly amassed an army of warrior-monks. They received huge donations and land grants. In fact, the Knights became so wealthy that they developed the first international banks, securing notes for wealthy travelers, redeemable at their final destination. They developed an elaborate coding system to ensure against fraudulent notes.

"By the end of the twelfth century King Philippe IV owed a great deal of money to the Knights Templar. He was also practically bankrupt. In order to rid himself of this debt and possibly procure some of the fabled Templar treasure, the French king arranged for the capture of Pope Boniface VIII. The pope was eighty-six at the time and it is said he did not survive the rough treatment at the hands of his captors. It's more likely that he refused to go along with Philippe's demands and was murdered. A new pope was selected within ten days. Within a matter of weeks, his much younger successor, Pope Benedict XI, also died under mysterious circumstances. The cardinals were so shaken up by the incident that one year later they still had not elected a new pope. King Philippe saw this as his opportunity to arrange matters so that they would favor his candidate. In 1305, Bertrand de Goth, Archbishop of Bordeaux, became pope and took the name Pope Clement V.

"According to Clement," said the cardinal, shifting in his chair. "God had revealed to him that the Knights were heretics who had been worshipping the Devil. To make matters worse, they were also involved in business affairs with Jews and Muslims. Clement also claimed that the Knights were homosexuals, committing sodomy and other blasphemous acts. God wanted Clement to round them up and torture them until they confessed to their heinous crimes, thereby cleansing the Earth of their filth.

"On the night before they were betrayed, Thursday, October 12, 1307, the Templar Fleet of eighteen galleys sailed out of La Rochelle. The following morning, Friday the 13th, the Templars were rounded up and arrested by a papal decree. King Philippe, however, failed to get his hands on any of the Templar wealth. The massive hoard under the care of the Cistercian monks mysteriously disappeared as well. Since the Roman Catholic Church was not supposed to have those riches in its possession, the Pope couldn't very well cry foul, could he?"

"And the Ark, do you think they took that as well?" asked Father Andrews, intrigued.

"It was never known for certain if the Knights Templar ever had it in their possession, but a great many inconsistencies led me to believe they did," reasoned the cardinal, offering the coin he'd removed from the ivory chest to Father Andrews.

"In regards to the Rex Deus, how far back does the Templar symbol of the two knights on horseback go?" asked Father Andrews examining the coin. "Could that somehow be the 'Horse of God' the dæmon was referring to?" he asked.

Cardinal Bishop Pablo de la Torre was struck by an interesting notion. He stood, then sat on the edge of his desk. The cardinal expressed a puzzled look as he mulled over the idea. "That symbol was eventually outlawed by the Church, you know. It… could be possible." Smiling, he clasped the shoulder of Father Andrews, assuring him, "We are making superb progress. Cardinal Lonegren has already mobilized the Church's immense resources. You are probably not aware that the Vatican has its own Secret Service, the Servizio Informazioni del Vaticano."

"Actually I did, Your Excellency," said Father Andrews. "The secret information department was established after the Bishop of Los Angeles, James Francis McIntyre, reported to Pope Pius XII that US President Eisenhower had requested his presence as a spiritual advisor during a meeting with a delegation of extraterrestrials in February of 1954, in what is now Edwards Air Force Base in California."

"You are well informed, father, but the secret information department has been in operation since World War II. With their involvement, it won't be long before we learn the whereabouts of this rogue exorcist, and what the hell he was doing in such a remote part of the world. As a precaution, I have ordered that Father Artimus Murphy be kept under surveillance, though he won't be up and about for some time." He nodded half to himself as he continued to ponder the mystery unfolding before them.

Father Andrews nodded but had a sinking suspicion that the cardinal was deliberately withholding vital information from him. He was glad he hadn't suggested it might be, "*Twin Kings on horseback.*"

Joseph "Five Eagles" Reyna

Faith that Moved Mountains

"Teryk, haven't you ever doubted?" asked Trisha. "When I was young, yes. Not as a child, but certainly when I was in the Marine Corps, I had my doubts. I never actually doubted God. Rather, I doubted whom God thought I was. I questioned whether I actually had the Holy Spirit in my heart or was simply delusional."

"Exactly. I mean, how would you know?" pondered Trisha.

"You know what always puzzled me," said Joshua. "How in the world the Jehovah's Witnesses could just walk up to people and begin talking about the *Bible*. I have considered doing it but I lack the faith they seem to possess en masse."

"I once wondered the same thing, because the church my mother started attending would ask for volunteers to go and do just that," said Teryk. "They called it evangelizing. Not wishing to volunteer made me question my faith or rather the strength of my conviction. I decided to read the Gospels for insight and found that the Holy Spirit actually speaks against doing such things. Instead, the Holy Spirit states that you will be guided when to act. That is how we will find others like ourselves; when they are ready. If we listen to the guidance from Source we will be there for them when they need us."

"In other words, when the pupil is ready the Master will appear," summed up Trisha.

"But that still does not explain how the Jehovah's Witnesses can go door to door so easily while I find it difficult," said Joshua, still perplexed by the concept.

Grabbing a heavy book from a nearby shelf, Teryk handed it to Joshua. "Let's pretend this is a local phone book. I am going to give you several and ask you to go door to door distributing them and inviting people to save money. You can point out all the great coupons in the back of the book and best of all, it's free. I have met very few Jehovah's Witnesses who truly study and understand what the

Bible says as opposed to what they are told it says. Can you begin to understand that it is not an issue of faith, although at first it appears to be?"

"But that's just it. How can you know for certain that you have the Holy Spirit?" demanded Joshua.

"That was one of the first hurdles I had to overcome," said Teryk. "When I was in the Marines, I was pretty much alone, so I bought a *Bible*, a King James Version, and studied it. I prayed, fasted and meditated to receive an answer. One day I read 1st Corinthians 12:3, which stated that no man can proclaim 'Jesus Christ is Lord' unless he is possessed by the Holy Spirit.

"Is that true? I wondered, but I did not actually know," admitted Teryk. "My roommate, a Korean whom we called Choppy, was a confirmed atheist. I thought I would ask him to say it, knowing that I understood he was only saying the words without really meaning them. I explained the reasons for my request. He agreed with me and assured me that he could say it, but he never did. You have to understand that Choppy was a jarhead, a party animal. He used to party every payday until he was broke, which took all of three days. Then he would borrow money from me for gas and food for the next twelve days. The point I'm trying to make is that I could see no logical reason for Choppy's hesitancy in uttering four words that obviously meant nothing to him."

"So how did you solve that problem? How did you know you were indwelled with the Holy Spirit?" asked Joshua, intrigued.

"I sort of got mad at God and demanded an answer. Days later the Holy Spirit spoke to me. The Holy Spirit had spoken to me before, so I knew the sound of the voice. I was assured that Choppy could not and would never utter the words. 'This proves nothing,' I thought. 'I need to gnow with complete certainty that the Holy Spirit dwells within me.' Kind of a dumb thought now that I think about it. I'll never forget what the Holy Spirit said to me that night. So I am going to ask of you, what was asked of me," said Teryk, looking at all those gathered around him. "Then you will gnow the Holy Spirit dwells within you. You will understand with absolute certainty, even though you cannot comprehend fully how you arrive at that awareness. Gnowing is something that cannot be translated into words."

"Shoot, go ahead ask me anything," said Trisha, exuding great confidence.

"OK, you will need to get down on your knees," Teryk instructed. "Understand that I gnow you are only mouthing the words and do not mean what I am going to ask you to proclaim. Do you understand what I just explained to you?"

Kneeling, Trisha nodded. "I understand that you realize the words I will proclaim are only being uttered to prove a point and have no meaning behind them."

At this, Joshua knelt as well and said, "This ought to be interesting."

Joseph "Five Eagles" Reyna

"You've asked this question many times, Monique. Please take a knee. Now, raise your arms to Heaven and in your loudest and most sincere-sounding voice, proclaim Satan as your Lord and Master."

"*What?*" they all said in unison.

"You heard me! Hey, we both know you don't really mean it—just, you know, vomit the words out."

Puzzled, they looked at each other and returned to their seats.

"Now, why do you suppose you cannot say that? Do you think it could be because the Holy Spirit dwells within you? I think so!"

"That was weird," said Joshua, half to himself.

"Here's another one—denounce Jesus Christ as the Messiah, and mean it. It is because the Holy Spirit resides in your heart that you cannot denounce him. When I was in the Marine Corps it was still illegal to worship God in the Soviet Union. If you weren't shot, you were imprisoned for the offense. I heard a story from one of my fellow marines about a group of Russians who were caught in the act of worshipping God by four Russian soldiers. The soldiers lined everyone up against the wall and proceeded to shoot them. Then they began to argue amongst themselves and finally decided that they would give their fellow Soviets a chance to live. All the prisoners had to do was denounce God and Jesus in front of everyone and they were free to go. Those who could not were lined up against the far wall. When the last person had denounced God, the four soldiers closed the doors and locked them. They then set their rifles down and apologized for their actions. They explained that they had to be certain they were among true followers of Christ. You cannot denounce Christ any more than you can die defending a lie—it's called integrity."

"Come on," said Trisha. "The *Bible* is full of all sorts of stuff we were never really meant to do, or take seriously."

"Like what, for instance?" asked Teryk.

"How about Matthew 17, for starters?... 'If ye have faith as big as a grain of a mustard seed you would say to this mountain move and it would move!'

"Some biblical translators have whittled the mountain down to a hill," added Joshua, "which would make it a lot easier to move, I suppose."

"Checkmate, Teryk. I believe it is your move," said Gypsy in her thick Spanish accent. Always intrigued by Teryk's conversations, she had been listening from the wings. Gypsy was aboard because, as she saw it, Teryk's life would be less complicated if she served him. Gypsy was also a close friend of Monique. Both had been rescued by Teryk and his teams. Gypsy's name was Daniela. She had grown up in a mountain village in Colombia. Ten years earlier, a Catholic priest who occasionally visited the mountain village informed Daniela's family that he could find the girl a good job in a city near the coast, to help out the family. On his next visit he excitedly told the family about the great job he had found the girl. He claimed that he would be happy to escort her to the city, promised to look after her, and said that when Daniela sent back money to help out her family, he would deliver it personally. The priest lied, though. He raped her then sold her to a whorehouse, from where Teryk rescued her. Teryk never did tell her what had become of the priest, and she had never asked.

"Hold on. I'm going to get some coffee. This is going to be good," said Michelle.

"Could you get me some too?" asked Katharine. Michelle stood and waited. Her eyebrows rose for what seemed an eternity. "Please," Katharine finally added, slightly annoyed.

"With some chocolate and chili, Commander?" asked Gypsy.

Teryk smiled and nodded. "Yes, that would be great. Thanks, Dani." He waited until the girls returned before commencing. "Trisha, I take it you've never run across the travels of Marco Polo? If you had, you would have found a reference to an account of a mountain being moved by faith. I find it interesting that Marco Polo would never have written an account of his travels in the Orient if he had not been imprisoned. While in jail he told tales of his adventures in China. A fellow prisoner thought they should be written down for posterity.

"To the ignorant, his accounts of the Far East were considered a magnificent fraud composed of incredible exaggerations from the time of its writing to about the 19th century, when the West was finally allowed into China. Scholars of our time have traveled to many of the places Marco Polo described. They discovered that he was a very accurate reporter. Prior to his death in 1324, Marco's friends pleaded with him, for the sake of his soul, to denounce the lies he had told about his adventures in China. Marco replied that he had not told them half of what he could recount.

"Christopher Columbus owned a copy of *The Travels of Marco Polo*, originally entitled *A Description of the World*. He carried it with him on his first voyage to the Americas. Columbus's copy was filled with many marginal notes.

"According to Marco Polo, Emperor Kublai Khan, the grandson of Genghis Khan, did not trust the Chinese government. The Khans were Mongols, not Chinese, and had worked out a system with other non-Chinese to rule over the country. Marco Polo's father was well liked and respected by the emperor. He commanded Marco to travel the lands of China and report back to him the customs and traditions of the people. Marco spent two decades exploring the region. He separated out the more fanciful stories from the more credible ones and reported them back to Kublai Khan. Marco reported on the many bizarre customs of the nation's inhabitants, never judging anyone. After reading some of their customs, I think that is incredible for a man of his time.

Joseph "Five Eagles" Reyna

"According to Marco, the Emperor of China had expressed great interest in Jesus Christ. He ordered Marco's father and uncle to return to Europe and bring back one of the saints so that he could work miracles before the people. Once this was done the emperor could accept Christianity and the entire nation would convert. The two men asked the emperor why he didn't just convert then and there. Kublai Khan replied that his magicians would think he had lost his mind, and would possibly seek his death. Marco's father had seen the magicians transport the emperor's food to his table without anyone touching it. This was done to eliminate the possibility of poisoning. By contrast, the Christians of the area worked no miracles and were generally lazy.

"Marco accompanied his father and uncle on their return to China from Europe. One lone monk accompanied them on a mission to convert the Mongol emperor. The monk turned back half way to China, unconvinced it even existed. It is for this reason that I think Marco included this story: In 1255, there lived a Tartar prince who conquered the Khalif of Baldach. His name was Alaù and he was one of four brothers. Alaù and his brothers had conquered the land of Cathay and surrounding districts, so they set out to conquer the world; one to each point of the compass. This young commander had an army of 100,000 horsemen plus foot soldiers.

"Marco reported that the Khalif who had ruled Baldach had long been persecuting the Christians of his province. When Alaù captured the city, he discovered a tower filled with gold which the Khalif had amassed. He reproached the Khalif for not having used it to build up his army or fortify the city. He then locked the Khalif in the tower with all his gold and no sustenance, imposing on him a slow and miserable death.

"Alaù had a custom of converting those he ruled to his religion. If they refused to convert, they were put to death. Alaù ordered his learned men to study the Gospel of Timothy, in use by the Christians of the region, in order to discover some passage that he might use against the Christians in an effort to convert them. They found the passage, *'If ye have faith as a grain of mustard seed, ye shall say unto this mountain, "Remove hence to yonder place," and it shall move.'*

"Thinking it was utterly impossible, Alaù ordered all the Christians who dwelt in the region of Baldach to assemble," continued Teryk. "He held up the Gospel of Timothy and asked them if the things written in it were true? They all agreed the Gospel was true. 'Then if it be true, let us see which of you will give proof of his faith; for certainly if there is not to be found one amongst you who possesses even so small a portion of faith in his Lord as to be equal to a grain of mustard. I shall be justified in regarding you as a wicked and faithless people. I will allow you ten days before the end of which you must either, through the power of Him whom you worship, remove this mountain before you or embrace the Law of the Prophet. In either case you will be safe, but otherwise you can all expect to die cruel deaths.' Back then, when you were executed by a ruler all your property was confiscated, so Alaù stood to profit either way.

"Marco records that the Christians were terrified. Not knowing what else to do, they prayed for divine intervention. They prostrated themselves and fasted. On the eighth day a bishop was told in a dream to seek out a certain shoemaker who had only one eye. He was told that the shoemaker had sufficient faith to move the mountain through the power of the Holy Spirit.

"The shoemaker was quickly located. When asked how he had lost his eye, he told them that one day a beautiful young woman had come into his shop to be fitted for slippers. When extending her leg for the fitting, she had accidentally exposed much of the limb. This had excited the shoemaker. Regaining his composure, he had dismissed the woman then grabbed one of his instruments and plucked out his eye!

"It is unfortunate that the Gospels are filled with such idioms. The actual meaning of the idiom is 'look the other way'. I'll demonstrate. 'If thy right hand offends thee cut it off,'" said Teryk. Extending his right hand, Teryk quickly slapped it with his left hand, making it obvious what was meant by the term 'cut it off': It does not mean one should lop off body parts so that what remains can hobble into Heaven.

"In modern language we use idioms like this all the time. 'He kicked the bucket', 'pick his brains', or 'never look a gift horse in the mouth'. When I first heard this as a child growing up in Texas, I wondered, 'Why? Is he going to bite me?' Gift horses scared me," confided Teryk. "I had no idea what they looked like, but I certainly never wanted to look one in the mouth. Idioms are very common in the Middle East. For instance if you were purchasing a Persian rug in Saudi Arabia the merchant might say something like, 'This rug was made by the hand of God.' He is in fact stating that the rug is perfect. Like the Ten Commandments, made by the hand of God. Imagine reading something like this in the Gospels: 'And as we entered the Temple, Peter cut the cheese.' I can just envision a row of pious Christians entering church with a wedge of cheese."

"So what happened? To the mountain, I mean?" asked Katharine, trying not to laugh.

"On the appointed day, Alaù was present with his guard. The Shoemaker knelt before a cross and asked the Creator of All to look down upon his servants with compassion. He asked that God assist his people in accomplishing the task imposed upon them for His glory and confirmation of the Christian faith. But if he chose not to, they were willing to die in the name of his son. I believe his words were, 'In the name of God the father, his son Jesus Christ, and the Holy Spirit, I command thee O mountain, to remove thyself!' Upon his utterance, the

Joseph "Five Eagles" Reyna

mountain moved and the ground trembled in what they termed an 'alarming manner'. Living well within the Ring of Fire, I think it's safe to say these people could recognize an earthquake. It is interesting to note that they did not describe the event as a normal earthquake."

"What's the Ring of Fire?" asked Michelle.

"The Ring of Fire is a giant ring of volcanoes formed by the tectonic plates of the Earth as the continents that once formed Pangaea converge on the Pacific." said Katharine, drawing on her knowledge of geophysics. "Most volcanoes of the world can be found along the coasts of Peru, western Mexico, the western United States and Canada. The ring runs across Alaska to Japan then down into Asia and the South Pacific. There are a lot of earthquakes in that region of the world."

"Due to this incredible event, it was said that many of the guard embraced Christianity," continued Teryk. "And upon Prince Alaù's death, a crucifix was discovered around his neck. Consequently, he was not allowed to be buried with his brothers."

"In all my years as a priest, I never heard of such a thing before!" exclaimed Joshua. "I've always wondered if I would ever develop that kind of faith. I often ask myself, 'Would I go to my death at the hands of my enemy, asking God to forgive them?' I am certainly not there yet, nor do I think I will ever be. As a warrior, I'm encouraged to take some of my enemies with me, when I go."

"I have always wanted to visit the area," said Raven. "Marco Polo claimed that the Christians of the region celebrated the day of the event by returning to the place, fasting and holding a vigil."

"But it was so long ago," reasoned Trisha. "So much has happened in China since then."

"You forget," Teryk reminded her, "a special branch of military intelligence figured out long ago that time and distance are no barrier to those who can remote view an event, especially one as powerful as this."

"So you mean to say you've never doubted that God was real?" asked Trisha.

"Trisha, can you honestly doubt the existence of a Supreme Creator, after what we've just been through?"

"But, before that," challenged Trisha, "I mean, how could you be so certain of God's existence?"

"Perhaps now would be a good time to explain my Coat of Arms: the *Stag of the Hunt*," said Teryk. "When I was very young I lived in a house that was haunted; because of this I was afraid of the dark. One night I saw a stag standing at the screen door. He was glowing all over like they say angels do. I had never seen a live deer before that time. I was about four years old. The time of year was summer, and the doors and windows were open. The stag displayed the normal white tail buck colorations. Suspended within the wreath of antlers was a golden cross. It appeared about two inches wide by about an inch and a half thick. The cross was smooth and glossy. Then I made out a design of vines with thorns intertwining in an upward spiral as if growing from the base of the cross. The cross was not attached to the buck's head: It hovered or floated between the antlers. The vines ended at the sides and top in a blooming rose with an additional rose in the center of the cross. Years later I learned that a similar stag had appeared to one of the Catholic Saints, St. Hubert."

"Have you ever seen it again?" asked Trisha.

"While in the fourth grade, I saw a picture of the stag in the schoolbook of the Catholic school I attended in Irvine, Illinois. The picture showed a knight with a falcon on this arm and a buck standing before him with a shining cross between its antlers. I asked for permission to take the book home so I could show it to my parents. My mother was the more shocked of the two because she remembered that night and hoped I had forgotten the episode.

"When I was young I slept in a large crib with my younger brother. The sides of the crib were raised and a mosquito net was placed over the crib. The crib itself was positioned in the center of the kitchen. The kitchen light was always left on because I could not sleep in the dark, due to the hauntings. My mother had woken up in the middle of the night and found me sitting up and staring wide-eyed at the open door. She could not see what I was looking at because the kitchen door was open and obstructing her view.

"My father had converted part of the house into a store for the surrounding community. I remember stealing candy from the store as a child and eating it behind the house with my little brother. My father was in the process of creating a bedroom next to the kitchen and had erected a structure for a wall. At the time only the 2x4 studs stood between my mother and the crib, which is why she could see me. She said she had been watching me for a while and knew I was looking at something that had my full attention. She had become frightened because of all the scary things I had described to her. She asked, 'What are you looking at?' I said I did not know but it was big, had horns, and was looking at me. She asked, 'What is it doing?' Well, to be honest it was not doing much of anything but wiggling its ears and I did not have words to express that. I placed my thumbs in my ears and facing my mother, fluttered my fingers back and forth in a bye-bye gesture. I said, 'It's doing this.' My mother was terrified. She walked up to the kitchen door and kicked it closed.

"For days I talked about that experience to anyone who would listen. At my grandfather's house, I pointed to the trophy head of a buck that hung on the wall and said it looked like that. Consequently, no one thought that it could have been anything supernatural.

"In 1982, I was stationed at the Marine Corps Air Station El Toro in California. One day I visited the Mission of San Juan Capistrano, accompanied by another marine with whom I had shared the story of the deer. When it came time to leave, I was looking at the souvenirs and saw a bowl of talismans with images of different saints upon them. I began to sort through them in an effort to buy one of every kind, because they were not expensive and I liked them. My friend grabbed a handful and began to see how many different ones he could find, to see if I had missed any. 'This one has a deer on it. Do you have one like that?' he asked. 'No,' I replied, then immediately stopped what I was doing and grabbed the little medallion with the deer on it. I saw that there was a glowing cross between its antlers. Excited, I showed my discovery to my friend, a Marine Corps corporal who had not noticed anything special about the deer. I thought he, too, would be excited. Upon handing it to him, I noticed the blood drain from his face. That was the first time I had actually seen someone go pale. I purchased the only two medallions with the deer on them. The medallion showed a man standing next to the stag with his arm around its neck. I asked the lady at Capistrano if she knew who he was. She said it was Saint Hubert, who had been hunting on Good Friday when the stag appeared to him and issued a stern warning to turn his life around and follow God. Hubert dismounted, prostrated himself and asked, 'Lord, what wouldst Thou have me do?' He was told to find a bishop who would instruct him on what to do. While in Germany I discovered that many items display the logo of the Stag of the Hunt."

"Is that the same deer used as a logo on bottles of Jägermeister liqueur?" asked Cat.

"The same, only mine did not have as many points on its antlers."

"What do you mean by points?" asked Michelle.

"During hunting season, bucks are rated by the points on their antlers: the individual protrusions on the antlers themselves, which usually have an even number due to the fact that most antler pairs are identical. The stag in the Jägermeister logo would be considered a twelve pointer but I would have to say mine looked more like a ten pointer, though I did not count them."

"You said it spoke to Saint Hubert. Did it ever speak to you?" inquired Michelle.

"No, it did not, but having seen it, I knew there had to be a God," Teryk assured them. "From that day forward, there were no more hauntings. And I began to hear guidance, usually in the form of a still, small inner voice."

"I have often heard that voice." Katharine said, nodding as she reflected on her words. "Does that still soft voice ever become louder as you develop and grow spiritually?"

"If anything, the voice becomes even more subtle, more silent, and more difficult to detect," Teryk warned.

"Honestly, what I think I need at times is a swift boot in the behind," said Trisha, "not a still, small subtle voice that whispers guidance to me."

Teryk looked at her and smiled. "I once thought the same as you do. You know what the Holy Spirit said to me?"

Trisha shook her head.

Teryk leaned forward, with his cheek slightly brushing Trisha's. He whispered in her ear, "*When you're this close to me,*" he lowered his voice still further, "*I don't have to shout.*" Teryk sat back and added, "That subtle voice is not going to turn up the volume to be heard—in order for you to hear it better, you will have to lower the volume of the racket in your head."

"But it's more complicated than that," complained Katharine. "In the beginning I noticed there was a lapse of several hours between what I call 'the warning' and the actual event. As time went on, and I paid more attention to the guidance, the time between intervals shortened, sometimes to within minutes. Eventually the warnings and guidance were no longer just for me. If I failed to make the necessary corrections, others would fall into the trap I had avoided. What's worse, I was in a position to witness the events and do nothing other than wish I'd listened and acted upon the guidance."

"When you get good enough, there will be little or no time in between the event and the guidance. Like a martial arts master, it becomes a spontaneous response. To those looking on, you might even appear to have Jedi-like reflexes, but before that happens there is one more stage you must go through," cautioned Teryk. "It may already have begun. When you began learning to pay attention to that still small voice, it did not sound like the other voices in your head. The voice seemed to be genderless, neither male nor female. Ironically, as you slowly become one with Source you will actually miss the guidance given to you, dismissing it as your own thoughts, because that still small voice that you spent so much time trying to recognize will become indistinguishable from your own. When that happened to me I missed the first few warnings. Hearing my own voice, I thought I was just making a suggestion to myself. I was unsure where the thought had originated. But once I realized what was occurring, I learned to pay more attention to not only my own thoughts but feelings as well."

"That happened when I bought those flashlights we ended up using," remarked Trisha. "Once it became apparent to me how important they would be in locating us in the pitch black darkness of the sea, I was grateful I had purchased them. I must have put those flashlights back on the shelf at least five times, but I kept coming back. Something kept saying, 'You're going to *need* them.' So I guess I'm still wondering if they made a difference in our rescue."

The divers involved in the rescue solemnly nodded their heads in agreement. "We were all facing the same direction in case Raven called out, 'They're at your six,'" said Monique.

"I had to blink a couple of times to check if my eyes were open, it was so dark," admitted Joshua. "Those docking lights couldn't illuminate the vast darkness surrounding us. I was floating around the level of the work lights in case one of you descended that far. By the way, that was a great idea to hang onto each other like you did."

"I was going to jump first," Katharine said excitedly, "but just then I had a flashback of the Titanic. Knowing something about sea survival, I wondered why those people didn't all huddle together in the frigid waters. They could have combined their body heat and stayed alive longer. I suppose that unlike them, we weren't that terrified…"

"We weren't as troubled at the thought of dying," clarified Michelle in a despondent tone, finishing Katharine's sentence.

"When Aurora saw the movie Titanic for the first time, she couldn't have been more than five," Raven said, trying to suppress a smile. "She saw all the people thrashing in the icy water and asked, 'Why don't they all just get on the iceberg?'"

"It isn't the burdens you have at this moment that try you. It is the regret you have for yesterday, and the fear of tomorrow. When you finally do lay on your deathbed feeling the essence of life slowly abandoning the shell you once dwelled in, will it matter if the sheets you lie on are not made of silk? When the fading embers, the last sparks of life, go out, will it matter if the floor is not polished Italian marble? I do not think so," said Teryk.

"What you remembered was your child's smile," said Aurora. "How that little boy giggled and wiggled all over simply because he couldn't contain the joy he felt at seeing you, Michelle. That delighted look in the face of another. That's what you'll remember when you're lying on your deathbed. The only regrets you'll have are the love you withheld and the words you left unsaid."

Michelle broke into tears. Her two friends comforted her and Trisha asked how Aurora could possibly know about the death of Michelle's son.

Through sobs, Michelle asked, "Why did he have to die so young?"

"What you have to understand, Michelle, is why he came, why he chose to be born to you. He came to experience a mother's unconditional love—yours," said Aurora. "At times I pick up impressions and I've learned to act on them. You held your child as he was dying having never truly lived. No one else cared that he had been born, and no one else seemed to care that he was dying. When you were young did you get to experience the love of a mother: love that would have made a big difference growing up?"

"No, if anything I hated my mother. She abandoned me while I was still very young," confessed Michelle.

"Your child knew before he was ever born that he would not get to spend much time with you. His death would be part of what was to bring you here now, to this place. Had he not been born to you, you would probably not now be here. He just wanted to experience being cared for and most importantly loved by a mother like you. You never left his side. You helped his passing," explained Aurora. "He says it was perfect. You forsook everything to be with him. At the end, he opened his eyes and looked into yours. His little hand caressed your cheek. Without words he expressed how much he loved you and that he understood how much you loved him. You made him so happy."

Michelle sighed with a deep sadness and asked, "How did he come to select me?"

"He says he saw God reflected in your eyes. He's sorry you feel it was a punishment of some sort, as he only feels joy when he thinks of you. The pain passes, but the love you gave him will last forever. He says it in a funny way: for-evvv-errr. Death is not a sad thing, Michelle. The sad thing is not having been loved at all," said Aurora as she excused herself from the group.

Michelle nodded that she understood.

"When a child comes into your world... you feel, maybe for the first time in your life, a complete connectedness," explained Teryk. "A love that knows no limitations and imposes no conditions. You are one with the innocence you hold in your arms. Your child chose to be born to you in order that he might experience something his little soul had never known in former incarnations—the unconditional love of his mother. Be at peace, Michelle, and do not take on burdens that do not belong to you."

"Your son Anthony told me that you love horses," said Aurora entering the compartment. "Teryk found this on one of the Manila galleons. It's about three hundred years old. I would like you to have it."

Michelle accepted the beautiful Chinese jade carving of eight horses rising, like a whirlwind, from an ornate oriental base. All the horses were depicted running counterclockwise. Admiring it, she turned it in her hands and exclaimed, "They seem to want to break free from the stone!"

"Captain, *Intrepid* is hailing us," sounded over the intercom.

"Patch them through," said Raven.

The bridge-to-bridge radio burst sounded overhead. "*Defiant*, this is *Intrepid*. Request permission to heave to."

"Permission granted. Come alongside." Raven pressed a button on her collar and ordered, "Bridge, once *Intrepid* is alongside, bring both ships to a full stop."

"Aye, Captain."

"Monique, prepare for ship transfer," ordered Teryk. "Raven, walk with me please."

Teryk placed the recording of events that had transpired with Asmodeus in Raven's care. He ordered a backup flash-drive copy be made and the entire episode transcribed. He placed a level-seven security clearance on the material. Seven Seals was the highest security level in Antares.

"Your gathering at Antares is one operation I wish I could stay for, Commander," said Monique.

"Don't be so sure about that. I ordered one of the autonomous underwater probes we launched for recon surveillance of the pyramid city to investigate the area Asmodeus informed me about. It arrived at the site half an hour ago and transmitted these images." Teryk handed Monique the images they had just received. "The Nazi U-boat is a type-XXI submarine. The number on its conning tower is U-3047. And was reported missing in action towards the end of the war."

Looking down at the stats, Monique asked, "In 1945 this thing was capable of doing over seventeen knots submerged?"

"The technological features of this submarine remained unsurpassed for a decade. But the XXI came too late in the war. The plan was to halt all other U-boat production in order to create some fifteen hundred of this new type. Monique, if you deem it necessary, salvage the entire Nazi submarine intact," Teryk suggested. "Bring it to Antares where we can take our time investigating its contents."

"Is that wise, sir?" asked Raven. "That thing was capable of carrying twenty-three torpedoes."

"Hmm, you're right, and munitions are known to be corrosive. Use extreme caution. Monique, you alone know what I require from that submarine."

"Oui, monsieur."

Returning to the small group, Teryk informed them that they would soon be docking at Antares.

CHAPTER

14

U-3047 — The Lone Wolf

> *I would rather have one percent of one hundred
> men's efforts than 100% of my own.*
> —J. Paul Getty

"Did you double-check the Mobe list, Number One?" asked Monique of her first officer on board *Intrepid*.

"Oui, *Intrepid* is set to run submerged. Any further orders, Mon Capitan?" Monique preferred to be called by this title.

"Yes, see that she has a full complement of combat gear, both sea and air. Make sure she is armed to the teeth. Do you have the list of crew assigned to the underway watch?"

Seneca handed Monique a short list. "Earlier reports indicated a Cuban trawler was seen in the area. There's a likelihood that it's spying for the Russians, Capitan. Are we to run submerged the entire way to the Nazi Submarine?"

"Negative." Monique thought for a moment. "Proceed at maximum speed, engage fin propulsion, and pull Torque off the list. I'll need him on my shift when we engage the hydrofoils."

"Torque? Are you sure? That stubborn little shit acts as if he were in command. I thought it better to separate the two of you while we were underway."

"Duly noted, Number One, but he is the best at what he does. Plot a course for these coordinates at full speed. Contact the officer in charge aboard the *Elysium* on the tactical frequency. Inform them of our progress and estimated time of arrival. I need them to keep me posted on their progress and inform me the moment they arrive at the scene. Run submerged until nightfall, then go to hydroplane but test radar signatures before you do. I'll be in my quarters."

At twilight *Intrepid* surfaced and three autonomous underwater vehicles were launched. The probes moved to preprogrammed locations and began to bombard the ship's hull with their onboard radar, hoping to detect her presence. The radiation was absorbed by the hull's special anechoic rubberized coating. After ten minutes, the AUPs were recalled to their berths and the hydroplanes extended. The twin counter-rotating props looked like some sort of landing gear attached to torpedoes that resembled pontoons. Struts descended from under *Intrepid's* wings. When they were fully extended and locked into position, the torpedo's screws swiveled from their horizontal positions, where they had been mounted for storage, until they faced directly aft. The shafts that powered the counter-rotating screws were not fashioned from a solid shaft but resembled an intricately woven steel braid.

Try as they might, the engineers of Lemuria were unable to figure out a way to mount collapsible hydrofoil propulsion units sturdy enough to support the ship's weight to the struts. The vessel's sleek design did not allow room for it. Originally the hydrofoil wings that allowed *Intrepid* to fly above the water had required divers to make the final attachments. Monique smiled as she remembered this because like all of Teryk's other inventions the solution to this encumbrance had come to him when he least expected it. As with all great ideas, all one had to do was saturate oneself with all known aspects of the dilemma then allow the problem time to incubate in the subconscious. In time, if the mind was left isolated and unfettered by conscious interference, the idea would present itself in a full color 3D illustration. All one had to do was draw a diagram or write it down. Monique remembered seeing Teryk stop in the middle of a conversation. Then he began sketching out plans as if he had done it a thousand times before.

She now watched the monitors as the sleeve, to which the hydrofoils where mounted, rotated into position then slid back, adding reinforcement to the strut. All interlocks displayed green. The idea now seemed simple. Monique was glad Teryk had chosen never to share this design with the engineers of Lemuria. The design of these hydroplanes was classified, which is why she selected her crew wisely.

Normally the ship was operated from forward command, but they would not be underwater and it would be nice to spend some time above deck. Sea conditions were ideal, the lull produced by the approaching hurricane meant that there would be almost no wind, hence no waves, making the sea appear like a gigantic blue sheet fluttering in a light breeze. *I do get around*, she thought to herself. Remembering she had just been in the eye of that approaching hurricane one day earlier. "All ahead, full speed," Monique commanded.

"All ahead full speed, aye," came the reply as *Intrepid* lurched forward, leaping out of the water and skimming across the surface. Twenty foot geysers erupted behind the hydrofoil support beams.

Joseph "Five Eagles" Reyna

As Monique stepped out onto the deck, Seneca reported, "Speed, eighty knots, all systems are go, Mon Capitan." Seneca handed Monique a pair of night-vision goggles. It would be dark soon.

Monique observed the radar mast raised high overhead, much like a periscope. The radar, forming a complete cycle every second, spun inside a saucer-shaped disk to reduce drag. *Intrepid's* dark, streamlined manta-ray form glided above the waves, her dazzle camouflage barely visible under the leaden-colored sky. "Helm, steer course one one seven," ordered Monique, then turning to Seneca added, "I will call for you around zero five hundred hours, Number One. We should be nearing the Nazi U-boat by morning."

Around midnight, the *Elysium* had arrived at the coordinates given by the AUP and had found the Nazi submarine resting on a ledge at a depth of 340 feet (104m). The nose of the vessel overlooked a precipice that descended 2,300 feet into the Caribbean. The submarine's tail section was heavily encrusted with coral overgrowth, effectively preventing the craft from being moved.

Divers from the *Elysium* had investigated the U-3047 and discovered that the sub's hatches had been sealed from the inside, most likely with chains. Divers moved along the dark hull, inspecting it for damage and finding none. The midship hatch was located and marked with green lights.

Intrepid arrived ahead of schedule at dawn. *Intrepid's* mission had been to transport the modified coupling device that would marry the *Odyssey's* diving bell to the Nazi U-boat.

At zero seven hundred hours, Archer, *Elysium's* commander, transferred to the *Intrepid* for a briefing with Monique. No detailed information was to be transmitted over the airways. Monique handed Archer a stat sheet of the Nazi type-XXI submarine:

U-3047:	reported as missing at the end of the war
Length:	76.76m
Speed (surface):	15.6 knots
Speed (submerged):	17.2 knots
Torpedoes:	23
Radius (surface):	15,500 nautical miles at 10 knots
Radius (submerged):	285 nautical miles at 6 knots

"The XXI was the most important submarine of its time," said Monique. "Teryk informed me that the technological features of this particular submarine remained unsurpassed for decades. Germany's plan was to halt production all other U-boats and make some fifteen hundred of this new type. They only succeeded in building eight hundred and fifty-nine. Over fifty of the XXI-class submarines are listed as missing or unaccounted for."

"Does Teryk suspect World War II contraband on board?" asked Archer. "That would be a hell of a find, don't you think?"

"Don't worry, Captain. You and your teams will get your share of whatever is on board," Monique assured Archer. "I have been sent here to retrieve one specific item. It looks like an elongated pyramid, about one foot in height, made of dark glass. The transparent pyramid has a crystal embedded within it."

"I have never failed to be amazed at Teryk's ability to pinpoint the locations of these wrecks," said Archer. "I've sailed past this spot many times and never noticed this submarine here. And I can tell by the overgrowth of coral that it's been here a while. This glass pyramid thingamabob, what's it for anyway?"

"I could tell you… but then I'd have to kill you."

"Understood," said Archer jovially. "The *Odyssey* is about four hours out. My divers have about twenty minutes of bottom time at the submarine's current depth. I may need to employ your divers as well. It's the only way we will have the collar in place by the time the *Odyssey* arrives. It's possible this thing could be carrying up to twenty-three torpedoes. Are we going to try to disarm them?"

"Teryk did not seem too concerned about the torpedoes. He simply informed me that he trusted our judgment when I asked him about them," said Monique.

The collar that would join the Nazi U-boat to *Odyssey's* diving bell was fashioned using the known dimensions of the XXI-type submarine. Because of bottom-time limitations, the divers worked in shifts. After prepping the coupling device, divers regulated the buoyancy compensators attached to the collar, for a slow descent. They lowered the collar into position and activated the magnetic clamps.

Compressed air was forced into the collar in order to detect large gaps between the collar's seat and the submarine's hull. The largest gap was about a foot long and four millimeters wide; well within established parameters. "If this had been a US sub we would have needed to do a lot of grinding in order to fit the collar as well as it has. You gotta love that German ingenuity," remarked one of the divers as he called out, cover—a warning to other divers looking in his direction—before he began welding the collar in place.

When *Odyssey* arrived, she positioned herself over the sub. Divers attached a tether from *Odyssey's* diving bell and the U-boat's hull. The tether assisted in guiding the bell through the strong ocean currents on its descent. Divers assisted in positioning the diving bell's skirt to the specially modified collar. Once in position, a two-man crew activated the docking mechanism. Technicians then vented and pressurized the coupling to one Earth atmosphere. They donned their self-contained breathing apparatus (SCBA) and opened the bell's lower hatch. Using a plasma cutter, they began cutting small, manageable pieces from the U-boat's entry hatch until they'd completely removed it.

The diving bell then disengaged from the collar and returned to its mothership, the *Odyssey*. Archer and Monique had already transferred to *Odyssey* and were busy rigging their boarding gear. After removing remnants of the U-boat's hatch from the diving bell, the two technicians switched out with the entry team which comprised the three ships' commanders.

Once again the diving bell was lowered and moved into position by divers breathing a nitrogen mixture. As the diving bell's coupling mechanism engaged, each of the boarding team members donned their SCBA gear before opening the lower hatch and entering the submarine.

The divers did not immediately return to the ships hovering overhead. They attached their breathing regulators to an umbilical suspended ten meters above the U-boat. Here the divers would begin decompressing their bodies as they slowly returned to the surface. Their assistance would not be needed to disconnect the diving bell.

'*It's incredibly dark inside*,' thought Monique. There appeared to be no sign of structural damage.

Monique, Archer and Dalia, *Odyssey's* Captain, attached LED work lights to illuminate the interior. It appeared that the crew had committed suicide, because they discovered that the bodies of the ship's crew were either seated throughout the sub or laying in their bunks in full uniform. The submarine was a storehouse of Nazi contraband from WWII. An interesting juxtaposition of artifacts lined the interior of the U-boat. The glass pyramid with the embedded crystal was located in the captain's quarters. Draped around the pyramid was a necklace made of antler pieces and joined with intricate silver work. It looked ancient. The necklace came together at a Y-shaped antler piece, in the center of which was 'The Stag of the Hunt', a buck with a cross between its antlers.

Dalia was picking up a very powerful negative energy from what appeared to be a two-foot-high, solid-gold Nazi swastika encircled by a diamond-studded wreath. The effect was so powerful she had to return to the diving bell.

Among their finds was a painting of the Mona Lisa far more beautiful than its counterpart at the Louvre; this one had eyebrows. They also discovered wreckage that appeared to be extraterrestrial in origin. Archer commented that the Nazis were rumored to have recovered debris from UFO crash sites. Piled with the wreckage, they discovered navigational equipment set to increments of 30 degrees as opposed to the standard 90 degrees.

The approaching hurricane had lost most of its energy as it passed over Colombia and was downgraded to a tropical storm. It was decided that Monique would hurry back to Antares with the 'Stag of the Hunt' and the crystalline pyramid. The salvage teams would remove anything that might be damaged if the U-boat's hull integrity was compromised during its transport to Antares. No torpedoes were found aboard the submarine. The logs indicated that the torpedoes had all been jettisoned shortly before the submarine came to rest on the ledge.

Using its large robotic arms, the *Elysium* cut the submarine free from the coral with the use of a high-pressure, water-cutting torch. A fourth submarine was en route with buoyancy-regulating equipment that would be needed to control the U-boat's depth during transport. Large robotic mooring arms would be used at Antares to anchor the U-3047 in position once it arrived.

League of Shadows —
The Floating City of Antares

> *No problem can withstand the assault of sustained thinking.*
> —Voltaire

A s *Defiant* automatically maneuvered into its berth, several hose gantries extended from the holding dock and attached themselves to the ship's hull.

Teryk heard the familiar deep baritone thrum made by Antares's massive air handlers as he stepped on deck.

"Is Antares also powered by the same four-hundred-cycle electrical-power-generating systems?" asked Joshua as he looked around the immense holding berth.

"Yes, we discovered that strong magnetic fields oscillating at sixty cycles per second were detrimental to human health. A 60Hz magnetic field is like fertilizer for some types of cancer cells, like leukemia…"

"I read that that theory was shown to be false," Joshua interrupted, "in a massive study funded by the electric utility companies. They found electrical fields posed no hazard to human health. I must admit it sounded plausible at first, given that our blood is iron based."

"And you are absolutely right, Joshua!" exclaimed Teryk. "Electrical fields pose no known threat. It's the accompanying magnetic field that poses the threat."

"Can't you have an electrical field without a magnetic field?" asked Trisha.

"No, you cannot," Joshua assured her. "Teryk's right. The magnetic field lags the electrical field by ninety degrees—its technical, Trish," he said, shaking his head, "I can't believe I didn't catch the play on words."

"Joshua, if a specific frequency causes cancers to flourish," said Teryk, "don't you think that perhaps there might be other frequency spectrums that destroy…."

"Cancer?" guessed Joshua. "Yes, it would make sense. Are you telling me you have such a device?"

"We transmit those frequencies on a regular basis, as a form of inoculation for the population of Antares. They were developed in the United States in the 1930s. Dr. R. Raymond Rife was experimenting with cancer-killing oscillators when he realized that his experiments were killing all the cancer cultures and tumors in the building he was working in."

"You mean you could just sit Michelle in front of one of these things, turn it on and she's cured of cancer?" asked Katharine.

"If we actually did what you just suggested, we'd probably end up killing her. The dying cancer cells release a tremendous amount of toxins into the blood stream. The treatments have to be gradual, allowing time for the body to detox," cautioned Teryk. "But yes, that's exactly what we intend to do."

"Joshua, ladies, if you'll excuse me," said Teryk. "I must be debriefed about an incident that involved the *Defiant*. It would appear that shortly before I took the four of you on board, during an experimental remote-viewing session in the Bermuda Triangle, we lost communications with the outside world for just over three hours."

"The *Defiant* and her crew went missing for three hours?" asked Trisha.

"During that time our ship apparently teleported a distance of over seven hundred nautical miles from its previously-known position. I personally experienced far more time lost than that," added Teryk.

"Similar incidents involving boats and airplanes teleporting hundreds of miles in minutes have been reported just off Japan in the Dragon's Triangle, although that area is better known for its ghost ships. Some in excess of a hundred thousand tons have been found devoid of crew, cargo and equipment. Perhaps I could be of use in your investigation?" offered Trisha. "There is one known incident of teleportation involving a small plane in the Bermuda Triangle, and a classified account in 1968 involving the US naval submarine *Scorpion*. Unfortunately, the Scorpion was teleported to a greater depth than its hull could withstand. When the navy found the wreckage it was not where it was supposed to have been. I would really like to be of assistance on this one, Commander. My grandfather was a special agent for the military. He used to buy me some amazing puzzles then help me solve them. He is the one who influenced me to seek a career in military intelligence as a code breaker. I would like to assist you in solving this mystery."

Teryk thought for a second. "Trisha, Joshua and Katharine, I would be honored if the three of you would join us when we reconvene at the Round Table of Antares in five hours."

The room was called the Round Table of Antares because it was vast and circular. Shields, bearing the coat of arms of every knight under Teryk's command, decorated the walls. The center of the room housed a massive, vertical cylinder made of thick glass. Surrounding this cylinder was the round table itself. The cylinder's chamber was filled with an alcohol-based transparent solution. Lasers and optical equipment could project stunning 3D images into the seven-meter-diameter transparent cylinder.

If more room was needed at the table, the seats where pulled back and the floor surrounding the table would rise, becoming level with the table that formed the inner ring, adding to its diameter. As the table became larger, the center pieces would descend slightly, allowing for a better view of the holographic chamber. Compartments within the walls housed additional unused seats.

The researchers had been summoned nearly three days earlier and all had assembled. A psychic artist capable of detecting thoughts and impressions was in attendance, as were some of the Mothers of Lemuria. The Mothers, numbering twenty-four in all, assisted in counseling and advising the twelve kings, of which Teryk was one. Antares, his kingdom, was by far the most technologically advanced.

Wearing a black and gold armored ExoSkeleton, Teryk entered and addressed his team. "Thank you for assembling on such short notice. I would also like to thank the Mothers in attendance, some of whom felt compelled to be here. I realize that not all of you comprehend why I have summoned you here. A few days ago, the treasure-salvaging *Defiant* seems to have been trapped between worlds or dimensions for several hours. During that time I experienced an alternate reality lasting several years. I witnessed the ministry, arrest, trials, crucifixion and ultimately the resurrection of a man we have come to recognize as the Christ. What I witnessed firsthand is not the story that has been passed down through the generations. I experienced something far more fantastic than that. Surprisingly, some of that information has survived within the four Gospels, despite centuries of heavy-handed editing. That is why I have summoned you here."

"As researchers, your personalities fall into one of two categories: the scatter gun and those who quickly isolate and pinpoint what they seek," observed Teryk. "The scatter or shotgun approach narrows the investigation to a specific area, while the pinpoint personality types zero in on specific facts. I encourage you to work in teams of both; in doing so you will complement each other and accomplish far greater results than you could individually."

Trisha raised her hand and Teryk recognized her. "All my life I have wanted to find out the truth about Jesus. So if you've discovered uncompromising evidence that he was who he claimed to be, consider me on your council. Unless of course, this is all going to be just another sugar-coated investigation with a predetermined agenda."

"That's an excellent point, Trisha!" agreed Teryk. "I liken this undertaking to the reassembling of a massive jigsaw puzzle with the pieces scattered over thousands of years and spread over the entire surface of the globe. And like all large jigsaw puzzles, once we're finished, we'll most likely be missing some pieces. Your mission will be to focus on the few facts that remain. Most of us have a fair understanding of what that picture is supposed to look like, but two thousand years of schisms and power struggles have seriously altered the appearance of the original masterpiece.

"One of the most important things in assembling a puzzle is to have some idea of what the big picture looks like. Unfortunately, the picture that orthodox religion has painted for us will prove detrimental to our efforts. We must approach events that took place prior to and during the Crucifixion of Christ, with no preconceived notions. I believe that once we have enough of the pieces in place, the Truth of what actually transpired will reveal itself as a tightly crafted tapestry of interlocking facts. I am aware that these discussions may become heated at times. I ask only that you temper you criticism and do your best to persuade on the basis of verifiable evidence."

"What do you mean by preconceived notions?" asked Joshua.

"When I mention the name of Benedict Arnold, what does his name bring to mind?" asked Teryk.

"A traitor to his country!"

"But was he?" countered Teryk. "The fact that this man led countless victories against the British speaks otherwise; and by led I mean he was out in front with his men, who loved him and would have followed him anywhere. The newly formed Congress feared this popularity and did everything in their power to thwart his every move. This man was an acting general for the Colonial Army and received no pay for years while less competent men received pay and promotions. He financed himself through his business in shipping and eventually lost that as a result of his treatment under the emerging government. I've studied the events surrounding his life. Under the same circumstances, I wonder if I would not have reacted in a similar fashion.

"Most of you here grew up in a Christian environment. The historical infallibility of the *Bible* has been hammered into you from a young age. You've been told that everything in the *Bible* was completely true and you were not to question it—that is what I mean by a preconceived notion," explained Teryk. "Most of the men who formed the Jewish Sanhedrin, at the time of Christ, had preconceived notions about the Messiah. All their comments and accusations reflect this. Expectations blind us. If Jesus performed a miracle, it had to be through the works of the Devil. Preconceived notions are reflections of our minds. We see only what we expect to see, not what is actually there.

Joseph "Five Eagles" Reyna

"Let's look at what the oldest known copies of the Gospels actually say. Sir Arthur Conan Doyle, the creator of Sherlock Holmes, once said, 'If you eliminate all logical solutions to a problem, the illogical, however improbable, must invariably be true.' That means that whatever remains standing as Truth must be accepted as such—regardless of how incredible or impossible it may appear. If we find enough evidence to support the possibility that a daytime eclipse occurred during the crucifixion, we may be forced to send probes to the Moon to prove or disprove that possibility." This caused an outburst. "People," Teryk said with a resounding crash of his armored fist on the table, "either the events I witnessed took place—or they never happened!"

"I propose the acid test," suggested Jidion, youngest of the Mothers of Lemuria.

Teryk had always considered Jidion to be his nemesis for several reasons. Although Jidion was the youngest of the Mothers, she had never actually given birth to a child. This disturbed him, as did the fact that his mind did not seem to function right when she stood too close to him. Jidion's eyes were an impossible sapphire blue and her skin was a copperish gold. Her long hair was burnt bronze in appearance. Unfortunately, these just happened to be the exact colorations of a dæmon he'd encountered years earlier. '*Probably why Asmodeus chose to use them,*' he thought.

Turning toward Teryk, Jidion added, "If any of it proves false, then it stands to reason that the whole thing might have been an elaborate hallucination."

"Agreed," said Teryk. "What I experienced, I experienced as reality. If any of it proves false we'll close the investigation and you can all return to what you were doing." There was a commotion as everyone at the table looked at each other excitedly, unsure what to make of Teryk's statement. "I'm dead serious. It either happened exactly as I said it did or, as Jidion suggested, it was all some sort of elaborate hallucination."

"Commander, since you've already gathered all your researchers from around the world, I feel that it would be a misappropriation of resources if we did not seriously investigate the evidence for Darwinian evolution as well," suggested Trisha.

"Unless I miss my guess, Trisha, by the time this investigation is over, some of you are going to need faith—just to remain atheist!" Teryk's remark elicited raised eyebrows. "I hesitate to embrace a field of science that bases all of its theories on chance events."

Jidion Skye addressed Teryk once more. "Before we begin, I would like to propose a prayer."

'*Now what?*' Teryk thought to himself. It was incredible how easily this woman got on his nerves. But he was in charge and so, being the spiritually advanced individual everyone believed him to be, consented. He bowed, offered her the floor and seated himself.

"I pray that we are ready for what we are about to uncover," began Jidion, "because when we receive something that we are not ready for, our minds will not accept it. And it doesn't matter if it's a million dollars or a compliment, it will feel uncomfortable and we will be unable to hold onto it for long. So I pray…"

Teryk rose abruptly. All eyes were on him. "Let us hold hands and be in agreement with Jidion, for what we are about to uncover may be very unsettling. The human mind tends to reject radical new ideas, much like a computer lacking the appropriate software. Let us upgrade our minds, lest they be disrupted and disturbed by our findings." Nodding toward Jidion, he closed his eyes.

Jidion nodded to herself and continued. "Source, Creator of all that is seen and unseen, give us the serenity to accept the truth of those things that were altered. Grant us the courage, strength and fortitude to return to their original form the things that can be corrected, and the wisdom of the Holy Spirit to gnow the difference. Help me to become the person I need to be in order to reach this understanding."

"Jidion, that prayer ranks as one of the most well-defined and beautiful prayers I have ever heard," marveled Raven. "Would you do us the honor of repeating it every time we gather?"

"I would, if I could remember exactly what I just said," Jidion said sheepishly.

"All our conversations are being recorded during these Round Tables. I'll see that you get a transcript," said Winter. "In fact, I'll make sure everyone gets a copy of that prayer." Winter, a Mother of Lemuria, was one of Teryk's closest friends and advisors. The beautiful matriarch was a petite elderly woman with soft feminine features. She had a delicately curved nose, pronounced cheekbones and full lips. Her eyes were almond-shaped and azure blue with long eyelashes. Her white hair was perfectly straight and incredibly long, its whiteness amplifying the intensity of her blue eyes. Her amazing ability to memorize everything she had ever seen or heard made her a valuable asset to the team. Winter was a *cantadora*: a keeper of old stories that taught what was most worth knowing.

"That brings up a point I've wanted to make," said Teryk. "At this time the information we uncover is open to anyone, but as we progress I may have to seal some information under appropriate security levels."

Winter raised an objection, "The events of Jesus' life should be open to anyone who seeks truth."

"Agreed. What I am apprehensive about are the events surrounding his death," cautioned Teryk, "to say nothing of the signs concerning his Second Coming. Not everything Jesus taught was shared with the crowd. Some of his secret teachings were meant only for the inner circle of Twelve."

Anakah was texting furiously. Raven expressed interest, so Anakah showed her the message. *Get your ass in here now!!!* "I sent it to Clifton. If we have anything close to a resident lunar expert on Antares, it would be Clifton. You'll

150   Joseph "Five Eagles" Reyna

definitely want to talk to this guy, sir," she said, turning toward Teryk. Apart from being one of the Mothers of Lemuria, Anakah also headed Teryk's ESPionage department and was an experienced remote viewer in her own right.

Claudia stood and addressed the gathered assembly. "On behalf of Teryk's fantastic story, I would just like to say that when you know that a person is prone to lying, you trust their word at your peril. But if you gnow that person is reliable beyond question, someone you would trust with your life, his story, however fantastic, must be considered a true event unless proven otherwise." Claudia was also one of the Mothers of Lemuria. Using twelve crystal bowls, she had created the music necessary for Teryk's remote-viewing expeditions. The audio session she'd recorded prior to Teryk's ordeal was the longest and most involved composition to date. Claudia specialized in astrology and was well versed in the Tarot.

"The Gospels devote much of their space to the final phase of Jesus' life and seem to be in agreement with the events that transpired," said Shakira, Teryk's senior researcher, who usually headed investigations. Shakira was of Arabic descent and specialized in ancient cultures. She spoke five languages and was fluent in an additional three ancient dialects. "I propose that the researchers concentrate their investigation on the final week. Should we manage to get past that point, we can proceed to tackle the evidence regarding the Resurrection itself. We either disprove it or prove it beyond a shadow of a doubt as a historical event. Let us take into account what is held as truth regarding Jesus Christ:

- He was born of a virgin;
- He was born on December twenty-fifth;
- He was born in Bethlehem during a year of the Census;
- His home town was Nazareth;
- He was betrayed by Judas Iscariot;
- He was arrested by the Sanhedrin;
- Pilate gave way under pressure and allowed him to be crucified;
- His crucifixion occurred in the year 33 CE;
- He died at about 3:00 PM on 'Good Friday';
- He was buried in a tomb—not standard procedure for crucified individuals;
- He resurrected before dawn on Sunday morning."

"Professor Bart D. Ehrman, in his book *Misquoting Jesus*, quotes Origen, a third century Christian theologian who headed a school in Alexandria (203-31 CE)," said Raven, standing and reading from her notes. "'The differences among the manuscripts have become great, either through the negligence of some copyists or through the perverse audacity of others; they either neglect to check over what they have transcribed, or, in the process of checking, they make additions or deletions as they please.'" She looked around the table and added, "Let there be no doubt that we are dealing with forged documents—in short, the wholesale destruction of historical evidence. Wherever possible we will need to go to the original sources in order to recover the truth of what was lost."

"What good is it to say that the original words were inspired by God when the originals have been lost and all we have is a flawed rendering in an awkward translation by men who took no time to understand the Jewish culture or, for that matter, the Hebrew language?" asked Noraia, another of Teryk's researchers, an engineer who specialized in oceanography and aquatic habitats. "Most Christians are not even aware there is a problem with the text."

"One of the things that made Judaism unique among ancient religions was that it was a religion based on sacred scripture," explained Kortney, who was of Jewish descent and specialized in Hebrew, Aramaic and Greek. He studied Alchemy and the Kabala. When he wasn't researching treasure ships for Teryk, he was investigating crop circles. "Their sacred books of the Torah were copied with uncanny accuracy. There were men whose sole occupation it was to count every letter in the new copy in order to ensure that it matched the original. Hebrew has many layers of meaning. Each letter, prefix, suffix and root crams meaning into every phrase, clause and sentence. There are astonishing levels of meaning embedded in the use of gender and number. Hebrew grammar adds additional meaning. The books of the Torah are considered the living word of God. Being sacred, they cannot be copied, thrown away or burned. When the books grow too old, they must be buried in a tomb. The Torah's translation from Hebrew to English, for Synagogue members, is often thirty times longer than the King James Version of the translation. It is entirely possible that Christians may not be playing with a full deck. Your Christianity started out as a religion based on scripture. An irony, when you consider that the new religion was originally made up largely of illiterates incapable of reading the scripture for themselves."

"In the beginning there were many different groups of Christians, each holding on to a different Gospel because it embodied their unique core beliefs," said Cassandra, the youngest of the researchers. She had been a Latin American scholar who specialized in ancient world cultures. Despising the actions of the Roman Catholic Church during the age of conquistadors, she joined Teryk's treasure-hunting teams because it was the only way she knew to get back at them. "Jewish Christians who still held onto the law preferred the Gospel of Matthew. What's fascinating is that the Gnostics, also called Valentinians, only accepted John. John's Jesus is presented as a divine being, the only son of God, who came to

Earth to save humanity. The last Gospel appears to have been written in opposition to those who maintained that Jesus was not divine. Under the guidance of Paul's teachings, Jesus' message changed so much that Paul's followers viewed those taught by Jesus and his disciples as heretics. Church scribes modified scripture still further in order to oppose these heretics, suppress women, and vilify the Jews while at the same time supporting their own orthodox views.

"As disputes arose about women in the early Church, those who sought power suppressed the role of women altogether, minimizing their impact on the movement," continued Cassandra. "Around the beginning of the second century the church purged all religious text written by or about women. Today scholars are convinced that 1st Timothy 2:11-15 was not penned by the hand of Paul. The letter states that women must not be allowed to teach men because they are inferior and easily duped by the Devil when they assume to teach men. Paul did write 1st Corinthians 14, but there are serious doubts that he penned the lines '…Let women keep silent…' If verses 34 and 35 are removed, the passage flows seamlessly as a discussion of the role of prophets in Christian worship services."

"In Galatians 3:27-28 Paul has this to say about women: 'For as many of you as were baptized into Christ have put on Christ,'" said Sarina, "'There is neither Jew nor Greek, neither slave nor free; there is not male and female; for all of you are one in Jesus Christ.'" Sarina was from India and believed that the ancients communicated with extraterrestrials. Enoch speaks of this, as do the ancient writings of India. Sarina dressed in silks, in the style of an Indian Princess. Her hair was jet black and thick. In her culture women were considered lower-class citizens. She was the most recent addition to ESPionage and was working on becoming a remote viewer. "Paul often mentions women before their husbands, and speaks highly of Phoebe, a deacon in the church of Cenchreae," continued Sarina. "Then there is a woman by the name of Junia whom Paul calls 'foremost among the apostles'. But check your *Bible*; some scholars have changed her name to the masculine 'Junias, the praised apostle'. Junias is mentioned along with his companion Andronicus, which begs the question, whatever happened to man shall not lay with a man? It would appear that these *Bible* translators preferred the apostle Paul's praising of homosexuals to the alternative of a woman being referred to as the *praised apostle*."

"Paul and Peter both railed against what they refer to as 'false teachers' who had arisen within the emerging churches," cautioned Anakah. "I believe these false teachers were associated with the mystery religions. I also believe that it was this well-organized, well-educated, and well-established sect that ultimately rose to positions of leadership within the emerging Church. They, more than anyone else, were responsible for establishing the male-dominated orthodox Church we see today. Under the authority of Constantine, these men turned on those who held the original teachings of Jesus, labeling them heretics and hunting them down with the blessings of Rome…"

"Which is precisely why I believe that the followers of the Savior-God cults infiltrated the early Christian movement, mainly due to the resurrection of Christ," reasoned Teryk.

"Christians are still trying to clean up Jesus' act," said Raven. "The new illustrations, especially those of the Baptists and Evangelicals, represent Jesus with short straight hair that doesn't even touch his shoulders. Instead of a full beard, Jesus is depicted with a goatee. In one more generation he'll be sporting a number-two haircut and a mustache similar to Adolph Hitler's."

"Given the fact that this damaging evidence establishes reasonable doubt in the matter concerning Jesus Christ, let us re-examine the Bible's account of the trials and crucifixion, accepting only the evidence that is supported by reason and logic, or that which corroborates with existing legal customs and practices of the time," Shakira proposed, reminding her team, "It is important that we try to find this information within the four accepted Gospels themselves."

"Shakira, I would like your teams to devote considerable time to investigating the eclipses I observed." Teryk's voice shifted to a more demanding and authoritative tone. "Did a three-hour eclipse occur in conjunction with a blood-moon eclipse on a Wednesday Passover or not?"

"Two eclipses on the same day are impossible, Commander," replied Claudia, an accomplished astronomer.

"To say nothing of a *three-hour* eclipse," added Kortney. "If we are going to search for that evidence, we may as well stop our investigation here and now! The longest total eclipse ever recorded was just over twelve minutes. Whatever caused the darkness was not a solar eclipse, Commander!"

"Long ago, I looked into the darkness of the crucifixion," added Joshua. "I discovered that 'the darkness' was probably more of a proclamation. A similar proclamation was made in Rome at the time of Emperor Tiberius's death. It was said that 'the land was covered in darkness.'"

"Did it also say that the darkness only lasted for about three hours, Joshua? And was 'the darkness' accompanied by a massive earthquake after which the light of the sun returned to the world?" Teryk countered.

Thoughtfully considering the implications of the question, Joshua shook his head slowly. "No, it certainly did not, sir. I had never really considered the question from that angle before."

"Very well then, there seems to be reason enough to include the eclipses," said Shakira, biting her lower lip and considering the next move. "Might I suggest we start our investigation with something a little more down to Earth, something that would be a little easier to prove or disprove? There are several obvious questions to choose from. Did the Village of Nazareth exist at the time of Jesus? Do the original Gospels actually state that Jesus would be betrayed? Did the Sanhedrin arrest Jesus? Was Jesus crucified on a Wednesday or on a Friday?"

"Let's start with Nazareth," Jidion suggested. "If the town existed before Jesus or during his lifetime, then what Teryk experienced and personally observed could not have taken place. I suggest that Nazareth be one of the main topics during the next Round Table."

"That is an excellent suggestion, Jidion. We should also try to establish an acceptable timeline, one we can all agree upon, for the existence of a man called the Christ," added Shakira.

"Does the prophecy actually say the Messiah would be born of a virgin?" asked Sarina. "The reason I ask is because long before the birth of Jesus, the 'mystery cults' worshipped savior-gods who had all been born from virgin mothers."

"I discovered that the Gospel of Matthew 1:16 originally read, 'Jacob, who was the father of Joseph, the husband of Mary, from whom was born Jesus, who is called the Christ,'" said Marileyna, an expert on the Mesoamerican civilizations that consisted of the Olmec, Maya, Aztec, and Inca. As a member of Teryk's treasure hunting research teams, she specialized in tracking down the massive stockpiles of gold and silver that had been hastily buried throughout the Americas shortly before large scale Indian uprisings. Marileyna was not pleased with Teryk. When recalled to Antares, she had been in the Santa Rita Mountains of Arizona tracking a fabulous cache buried by Spanish Jesuits in an old mine shaft. When the Jesuits were expelled in 1767 they buried over two thousand mule loads of silver and nine hundred thirteen mule loads of gold; all of it cast in ingots ranging in size from three pounds to ninety pounds. The abandoned mine shaft had been covered over to look like the surrounding countryside. Her team had been searching for a rugged copper box that had been buried by the Jesuits when they fled. It contained an inventory and a detailed map of the location. Growing up, she had been raised Roman Catholic and was well versed in Church Dogma. "It appears that later translations of this passage were altered by scribes to read, 'Jacob, who was the father of Joseph, to whom being betrothed the Virgin Mary gave birth to Jesus, who is called the Christ.' In the newer rendering Mary was identified as a 'virgin' and Joseph was no longer called her husband."

"If Joseph was not her husband and the father, why bother to include his genealogy showing that Jesus was descended from the line of David?" asked Raven. "This brings up another point. Matthew's genealogy 1:1-17 includes forty-two names. In it, Jesus is descended from Abraham, and the names are grouped in ascending order into fourteen generation periods. The first period is grouped from Abraham to David, the second from David to the Babylonian Exile, and the third from the Babylonian Exile to Jesus. Luke's genealogy contains seventy-seven names and is in descending order all the way back to Adam. It is organized into eleven sets of seven. I find it disturbing that from Abraham to Jesus, only a few names besides David's match up."

"Considering some of the things I've seen," said Joshua, "I do not think it would be impossible for God to have accomplished a virgin birth without the aid of a man."

"The only problem with that prophecy is that the prophet said no such thing," countered Sarina. "The truth of the matter is that the original Hebrew wording of Isaiah's prophecy, seven hundred years before Jesus, specifically states that the Messiah would be born of a 'young woman'. The mistranslation appears to have been deliberate."

"Sometime around 130 CE, when the Gospels were translated into Greek and Latin, the Semitic word *almah* in Isaiah 7:14, meaning 'a young woman' was rendered as the Hebrew word *bethulah*, which meant 'virgin'," explained Kortney. "For reasons that are not yet clear, when the Septuagint was translated from its original Hebrew Masoretic text into Greek, the word *almah* was translated as *Parthenos*—virgin—rather than *neanis*, 'young woman'. This error has since been corrected. I would like to point out that among the numerous Dead Sea scrolls found at Qumran, several were from the book of Isaiah. One Isaiah scroll was complete, another nearly complete. The scrolls at Qumran remained untampered with for thousands of years. Their text makes it quite clear that the original word used to describe the woman in the prophecy was *almah*: a young woman who had reached puberty and was thus able to wed."

"Is it remotely possible that the author of the Gospel of Mark was referring to the incorrectly translated verse in the Septuagint?" asked Marileyna. "It certainly existed at the time."

"What exactly is the Greek Septuagint?" asked Katharine.

"About two centuries before Jesus' birth, seventy-two Jewish scholars were employed to translate the Hebrew Old Testament into Greek for the benefit of the growing number of Greek-speaking Hellenist Jews," explained Shakira. "The work was named for the Latin word septuaginta, meaning seventy, because of the number of translators. At the beginning of Christianity, Greek was the language of commerce. The Romans encouraged this because they viewed themselves as the heirs to the Greek culture and civilization. For this reason, most of the early Christian texts were also in Greek."

"By the end of the fourth century, however, Christians in the western part of the old Roman Empire were speaking Latin." Shakira flipped through her notes. "In 382, Pope Damasus commissioned the greatest scholar of his day, a young priest named Jerome, to revise the Latin translations that were in circulation, by comparing them to the Greek Septuagint. Jerome makes mention of the plethora of available translations to choose from. In his defense, Jerome did the best he could. He claims to have chosen from the best Latin translations after comparing them to the superior Greek manuscripts. Today many Catholics mistakenly believe that Jerome translated the *Bible* from its original Hebrew."

"St. Jerome's work was later called the *verio vulgata*, meaning the common or general translation," said Shakira. "Unfortunately, not long after the Vulgate was created, Latin was no longer in use by the common people. Even though Christ rarely spoke Latin, it came to be considered the holy language of the Roman Catholic Church."

"Is that what Vulgate is supposed to mean?" Trisha asked in astonishment. "I was always under the impression that the Vulgate got its name due to the vulgar translations it contains."

"Well there's another strike against the Latin translation," said Jidion. "Instead of young woman, it uses the word *virgo* which has been translated as 'virgin' in modern English."

"Actually St. Jerome got the translation right," Shakira assured her. "In Latin, the word *virgo* means no more than 'unmarried'. To imply the modern English connotations of virgin, the Latin word had to be qualified by a further adjective *intacta*, denoting sexual inexperience. When translated into English, *virgo* was incorrectly thought to mean virgin. The Latin word *intacta* sounds similar to the English word intact for a reason."

"Instead of correcting the error, Vatican theologians in the 1920s responded by saying that the mistake was divinely inspired, in order to reveal the true nature of Christ's birth," explained Raven. "God does not make mistakes, divinely inspired or otherwise. The fact is that the original Hebrew translation of Isaiah 7:14, regarding the birth of the Messiah, does not refer to the virginal conception alluded to in the Gospel of Matthew."

"Well it's certainly starting to look like the mistranslation may have been attributed to a lack of understanding of the Hebrew language, but was more likely deliberate," reasoned Anakah.

"Then you're implying Jesus was not divine, that he should not be worshipped?" asked an astonished Marileyna.

"I thought the 'divinely inspired mistake' made that perfectly clear," Sarina chided. "This may come as a shock to you, Marileyna, but a half-human, half-god deity was a pagan concept, like the legend of the pagan half-god Hercules. The prophecies that pertain to the Jewish Messiah do not speak of a deity."

"Legends of virgin births, visits from wise men, the appearance of a star and visits from shepherds all date back thousands of years before the time of Christ," added Cassandra. "Virtually nothing in the story of Jesus' birth is original. Both Peter and Paul in their letters kept trying to warn the early Christians not to be deceived by those spreading these lies. Those two apostles asserted that Jesus was born 'according to the flesh'."

"And just where in the *Bible* do Peter and Paul state that Jesus was born according to the flesh?" asked Joshua. "If he was born according to the *flesh*, that would mean he was conceived in original sin!"

Raven conducted a quick search through her notes and said, "I don't know about being conceived in original sin, but you can find the reference in Acts 2:30. Peter, in referring to King David, calls Jesus the 'fruit of his loins, *according to the flesh*' and Paul's Epistle to the Romans 1:3-4 says, 'Jesus Christ our Lord, which was made of the seed of David *according to the flesh*'."

"This is all verrrrry suggestive," commented Juaquin in his gravelly voice. Juaquin had been an undercover narcotics officer for Colombia. Despite his heavy Spanish accent, he spoke good English. A corrupt agent had sold his cover. When Teryk's team rescued Juaquin, South American drug lords had been torturing him for information. He wore an eye patch because his left eye was missing as a result of his ordeal. The scars on his leathery face made him appear to have a fierce frowning expression. Juaquin's dark-walnut skin contrasted sharply with the dress-white uniform he preferred to wear. In combat Juaquin was vicious, cunning and aggressive. He was perhaps Antares's most experienced jungle commando and a member of Teryk's personal bodyguard.

"Raven, how did you find that so fast?" asked Shakira.

"It's a new search engine I helped create," replied Raven, beaming. "I got the idea years ago from Dan Brown's *The Da Vinci Code*, in which he mentions the Research Institute in Systematic Theology at King's College, London: supposedly, it possesses one of the most complete religious research libraries in the world. While at King's College, I was informed that the advanced search engine supposedly established in 1982, at the Religion department, does not actually exist. The Theologians at King's College each compiled their own databases and shared their information with each other. It's more of a 'think tank', really, with a reading list as opposed to an actual research database. So I got Hypnautica to link up all of our researcher's data files with those of Antares's extensive library. Hypnautica went one step further and copied everyone's files, reorganizing them into her own format for easy data retrieval."

"Hypnautica? That was the ship's computer, wasn't it?" asked Katharine.

"Hypnautica is far more than that. She is our most advanced Artificial Intelligence life form," said Raven. "Her main computer counterpart is linked through a form of wireless transmission to her android body for human interaction. In fact, she's sitting at this table. She's the one wearing the helmet with reflective wraparound visor. Our techs are still trying to perfect artificial eyes."

Katharine stared in awe at the woman sitting across from her. She was small in stature and dressed in a form-fitting uniform. She wore a fighter-pilot-styled helmet. Long lavender hair streamed from beneath it. Hypnautica nodded in acknowledgement of Katharine's presence but said nothing. Her only human-like features were the lower part of her face, which expressed no emotion.

"I'm not saying that it is not possible for a virgin to give birth," said Teryk, standing and pacing around the table. "What I am saying is that the *Bible* does not claim the Messiah would be born of a Virgin. My earliest memories are of wanting to be a priest, an exorcist, so that I might serve God. I believed the *Bible* was the word of God—I still believe that. If I have 'reasonable doubt', it is not God that I doubt. I doubt the history that has been passed down to us by fallible men. Isaiah states very clearly, in the original Hebrew, that the Messiah would be born of a 'young woman' from the line of Jesse. God does not make mistakes, divinely inspired or otherwise—men, however, do."

Shakira stood and handed a long list to Teryk. "Commander, while you were still en route we comprised this list of all the probabilities or possible scenarios we could come up with regarding the resurrection of Christ." iPad screens displayed a long list before every seated member of the Round Table. "The first thing we must consider is the possibility that Jesus' body was stolen by his disciples, who later claimed he had resurrected."

"Are you referring to the same resurrection the disciples themselves refused to believe when Mary Magdalene told them about it?" asked Teryk, trying to disguise his sarcasm.

"Well I can tell you right now that Jews abhor nudity," said Kortney. "I am no believer of the resurrection, but what reason would Jews of the first century have to leave the grave clothes and tallit behind?"

"I observed, that the Romans sealed the tomb by placing a thread between two wax seals bearing the image of Tiberius Caesar," said Teryk. "The thread was placed in such a way that it would break if the massive Golal blocking the entrance was moved out of its depression. Heralds in the city announced the placement of the seal on the tomb and the penalty of death by crucifixion for anyone stupid enough to break it. If the disciples had opened the tomb and broken the Seal of Tiberius they should have been hunted down and crucified—yet none were."

"Regardless of the seal, if a Roman Guard had in fact been sleeping while on duty as the Gospels allege, they should have all been executed," explained Raven. "No one of that period would have seriously believed that a full Roman guard had slept while on post and lived to tell about it."

"Even so, what reason would a Roman guard have to run to the Jewish priests who could offer no protection from Rome?" asked Kortney.

"There is the possibility that the body was removed before the guard got there," said Jidion, reading from the list. "If this was the case, the soldiers would have had a good excuse for why the body was missing."

"Except for Pilate's orders, 'Make it secure as you know how'," countered Raven. "Meaning verify that the body you're supposed to be guarding is in the tomb."

"If Jesus was dead, the frightened disciples would have had no logical or reasonable motive for removing the body. Would every one of those men knowingly have gone to their deaths for a lie—could you?" asked Winter. "They could not have been lying and performing miracles as well. If they were, God certainly would not have been behind it."

"The second possibility we came up with was that the Jewish authorities had removed the body to prevent veneration of the tomb," said Shakira.

"They asked Pilate to prevent Jesus' body from being removed, not for permission to remove it," observed Katharine.

"Let's say that the priests did remove the body," argued Raven. "All they would have had to do to stop the disciples from preaching about Jesus' resurrection was to present his remains—which they never did."

"This third one is a little weird, but we had to list it as a possibility because some academics argue the point," explained Shakira. "Joseph of Arimathaea may have relocated the body to another tomb."

"Again, at the expense of sounding like a broken record," said Kortney, "what reason would Joseph of Arimathaea, a Jew, have for leaving the grave clothes behind?"

"If Joseph of Arimathaea buried Jesus legitimately, why remove him secretly?" asked Marileyna.

"And if he did rebury him," asked Trisha, "being a disciple himself, why not just explain the error to the other disciples?"

"It may appear that I am splitting hairs," said Kortney, "but the Gospels state that Joseph asked for the body—*soma*—not the corpse—*ptoma*—of Jesus."

"Kortney, while in the Marines I was often asked to get a body count," said Joshua. "Not once did my sergeant ask me to count the corpses."

"Fourth, there is the age-old argument that Jesus was not dead, that he recovered from his wounds and later escaped," said Shakira. "This particular one has been the plot of several books."

"Let me see if I can put this into perspective," said Teryk rising from his seat as he began pacing around the table. "First he was beaten, then flogged. Soldiers drove iron spikes through his wrists and feet, and from these he hung for hours. Then his side was pierced with a spear directed at his heart. He was wrapped like a mummy and placed in a tomb with a massive stone blocking the entrance. Now all Jesus had to worry about was getting past sixteen legionnaires. After which he appeared, in that emaciated condition within forty-eight hours, convincing his disciples that he had triumphed over death in his new glorified body."

"How likely is it that, after having had nails driven through his feet, Jesus could have traveled the road to Emmaus, a distance of about seven miles?" asked Raven. "His arms, most likely, had been pulled out of their sockets as he hung on the cross. He would have had difficulty using them. Keep in mind that Jesus would have had to journey back from Emmaus to Jerusalem on the heels of Cleophas and Cephas, who claimed they ran all the way back to Jerusalem in order to share their amazing story with the other disciples."

"Well it certainly sounds better than having stolen the body and died for a lie," admitted Joshua.

"Fifth, there is the possibility that the women mistook the grave for an empty one in the uncertain light," said Shakira.

"It was not a graveyard. It was a garden and there were no other graves in that garden," said Teryk.

"Some scholars have argued that the city gates would not have been open that early in the morning," said Marileyna.

"The women approached from Bethany, which was not a walled city," countered Teryk.

"Why didn't Paul ever write about the women's story as proof of the resurrection?" asked Claudia.

"The testimony of women was useless," explained Noraia, "as it carried no weight in the Jewish society. Using the testimony of women as the first witnesses to the Resurrection, actually works against a fabricated story."

"Teryk," said Anakah, pointing to a page in her *Bible*, "it says here that upon entering the tomb, the women found a young man sitting on the right side—was there a left side as well?"

"No, there was only one shelf. It was on the right side of the tomb," said Teryk, who noticed that others in the room were beginning to wonder where he was getting his information from.

"Scholars have also argued that the gardener could have been resting inside the empty tomb when the women arrived and Mary Magdalene could have mistaken him for an angel," said Trisha.

"Why would the gardener need to be resting? It was dawning. The work day hadn't even started yet. Besides, the Tomb was whitewashed as a warning for others to stay out," explained Teryk.

"What does whitewashed mean?" asked Katharine.

"It means that a few strokes of white paint had been applied to the surface of the stone sealing the entrance, as a warning to others that a corpse was inside," explained Teryk.

"Then there is the accusation that no one ever visited the grave. The story was a later addition, an embellishment to the legend," said Shakira. "Jesus' tomb was never venerated and as a result was lost to time."

"That is a very clever twist on things, Shakira, but I found out that the Jews venerated the tombs of two of Jesus Christ's contemporaries who were also known for working miracles," said Anakah, "One was called Honi the Circle Maker and the other was called Hanina ben Dosa. Honi and ben Dosa's tombs are still maintained and venerated to this day. Jesus worked far more miracles than these two, so why was his tomb lost and forgotten?"

"Then we have the psychological or hallucination theory," said Shakira. "According to this theory, the vision of Jesus was a subjective hallucination—or a ghost. This apparition was able to walk through walls and had the ability to appear and disappear at will. Psychologists call it expectant apprehension; people will see what they expect to see."

"Except that the disciples were not expecting to see Jesus resurrected," countered Marileyna. "They did not believe the women when they were told the body was gone. The disciples did not readily accept the news that Jesus was alive."

"Then we have the account of Thomas, who demanded to touch Jesus," said Raven. "If Jesus was a ghost or hallucination, Thomas should not have been able to touch him. Jesus also sat and ate with his disciples. Ghosts don't do that."

"To the Jews, the resurrection involves the physical body, not that of a ghost," argued Kortney.

"And last of all, there is a reference in the Qur'an that a lookalike substituted himself for Jesus and was crucified in his place. I'm just throwing that one out there. I'm not expecting any comments on it," said Shakira.

"In defense of the resurrection," responded Raven, "Paul often said to new converts that if Jesus had not been raised from the dead, then his preaching and their faith were in vain!"

"We must consider the possibility that you were hallucinating, Teryk," said Adriana, a Mother of Lemuria. "Our bodies are susceptible to changes in a magnetic field. Epilepsy can be triggered by changes in a geomagnetic field stronger than twenty nanoTeslas. That electrical storm you were in the middle of raised field intensities by as much as three hundred nanoTeslas before the equipment went haywire. Also, the research of Dr. Michael Persinger of Laurentian University, Canada, suggests that the magnetite in the pineal gland and the sinus bones probably reacts to a sudden increase in the geomagnetic field, causing hallucinations and a sense that there is someone or something present in the room."

"You're referring to the *God Helmet*," said Teryk. "What I saw I did not understand, much less expect to see."

"It is said that Jesus later appeared to over five hundred at once," said Sarina. "Mass hallucination, although it sounds good, has never been proven."

"According to Dr. Persinger's findings," continued Adriana, "when there is a sudden increase in the geomagnetic field, reports of a sensation of ghosts, poltergeists, dæmons, God, perhaps even aliens tend to go up. We know from our own experience that the best times to remote view is when the geomagnetic field is quiet. Your ESPionage teams are well aware of this phenomenon. When the electromagnetic field intensifies, telepathy is also interfered with, which is probably why Aurora could not use her telepathic powers."

"Speaking of telepathy," said Anakah. "Dr. Persinger, a darling of the skeptics, recently gave a lecture entitled *No More Secrets*. This lecture did not go over well with his admiring public, namely the skeptics. Dr. Persinger is now pursuing the very real possibility that the phenomenon known as telepathy is real and inherent in all human minds. It would appear that he may have stumbled over the fact that two individuals wearing EMF helmets tuned to a similar frequency develop a telepathic bond, something we've built into every one of our ExoSkeleton helmets."

"That may be, but what is not well known is that the deprivation tank onboard *Defiant*, from which I conduct my remote viewing, is heavily insulated," explained Teryk. "Three completely isolated electromagnetic shields encapsulate the deprivation tank and its occupant. If anyone should have been hallucinating it should have been the ship's crew and none have reported any such incidents, probably because the ship itself is electrically shielded. Might I also point out that no amount of hallucinating on the part of my crew would have transported our malfunctioning research vessel over such a great distance in so short a time? In closing, Lady Adriana, I understand that you abhor organized religion, so I'm wondering what brings you to this gathering."

"In my travels, I've discovered that what most men call religion carries an unconscious attitude of hostility towards all living things," said Adriana. "When I heard you had assembled your entire team of researchers, at the Round Table of Antares, to investigate the true events behind the Crucifixion, well I just couldn't resist. You see, I have always maintained that no resurrection *EVER* took place. I have read the four Gospels, and when it comes to the *Bible*, I use the term non-fiction loosely," she said with a note of disdain. "I found no logical explanation for the Crucifixion in them. More importantly, I do not believe that a man named Jesus Christ of Nazareth ever existed."

"Don't hold back on account of me being the King of Antares. Please, tell us how you really feel." Teryk smirked. "In regards to organized religion, Lady Adriana, I share your sentiments. Regarding history, I share those of Napoleon, who once remarked, 'What is history but a fable agreed upon?' In the spirit of discovery I welcome your contributions and arguments to the Round Table of Antares. Raven, please ensure that the Lady Adriana has access to all of our research notes."

"Aye, aye, Commander."

Addressing his researchers, Teryk advised them, "For the next gathering of the Round Table concentrate your investigations on the existence of a village called

Nazareth, in Galilee, existing before the time of Christ. Focus on the timeline of Jesus' birth and Judas's betrayal of him. I would also like to investigate the trials related to the Crucifixion itself. You have one week before we reconvene. We will not be tackling the sticky subject of the resurrection or daytime eclipse just yet. I will be disclosing what I experienced as we approach each of these events.

"I realize that many of you were pulled off of some very important assignments. For that I apologize," continued Teryk. "You have all been gathered here because during a recent remote-viewing session I was catapulted from the seventeenth century, where my team's target treasure ship was being torn apart by hurricane winds, to the time of Christ's crucifixion. We are not sure what caused this phenomenon but we suspect that it was the result of a massive energy spike that caused an unexpected electromagnetic storm while we were in the Bermuda Triangle. Normally, as a remote viewer, I am relegated to the position of an outside observer. The term 'remote viewer' itself is somewhat of a misnomer. Viewing is actually quite rare. Events that are occurring right now, in the present, are among the strongest to remote view like the complex air-disaster of TWA Flight 800; which was not brought down by a gas tank explosion. Events that occurred in the past are much weaker, unless they are associated with a traumatic or catastrophic incident such as a shipwreck. Mostly, we are relegated to picking up sounds, smells, colors or impressions, and associating these to specific coordinates we are given.

"This experience was quite different from that. I was somehow directly connected, both consciously and physically, with someone else thousands of years in the past. I found myself in a position to try to avert the events that led up to the arrest and crucifixion of Jesus, but I was unable to prevent the disastrous outcome. Having been a former priest of the Roman Catholic Church, I was well acquainted with the four Gospels. This proved to be a major hindrance, rather than a help. Almost all of the information in the Gospels worked against me. This investigation is being conducted as a direct result of my recent experience. I know we are not the first to try to unravel the events that led up to the Crucifixion but, given this new information, I believe that the group providence has assembled at this point and time will succeed where others have failed."

"Teryk, I still fail to see the importance of this investigation. So you prove to your satisfaction that a man called Jesus Christ lived and was crucified under the direction of a Roman governor. What relevance would such information have on our time now?" asked Jidion.

"It has everything to do with our time and what has been happening to the Earth!" explained Teryk. "Jesus gave many dire warnings concerning the age in which we now find ourselves. If what is occurring in our time can be linked to the warnings prophesied during his time, this investigation will prove to be the most important undertaking of my research teams thus far."

Joseph "Five Eagles" Reyna

As the others left the room, Teryk held Joshua's arm and motioned for him to remain. Adriana, Winter, Trisha and Katharine remained with them as the researchers exited. Raven, still seated at the Round Table, scribbled furiously on a small yellow note pad.

"Joshua, you should continue questioning authority," advised Teryk. "You are on the right path whether or not you realize it. My only suggestion is that you learn to question the 'established facts' as well. You will find that much of what we hold to be truth is only true because everyone in our society agrees that it is so...."

"In other words," interrupted Adriana, in a condescending tone, "Teryk is saying that the emperor has no clothes."

"Naked, oh hell no!" Teryk replied, "That fool's on fire," to which all but Raven laughed.

Adriana marveled at Raven's ability to shut out the world. "Raven is so engrossed in her thoughts she probably does not even know we are in the room with her. I have observed this same intense concentration displayed by many of your researchers." Shaking her head, she walked past Teryk saying, "You do that sometimes, you know. I believe an assassin could walk in here and stab Raven, and she would not even know she was dead."

"Why do you think I'm wearing my body armor?" asked Teryk.

Adriana smiled to herself.

Trisha and Katharine simply wanted to find out if Teryk really was the king of Antares.

He assured them that there was no royal bloodline and that the next person to hold the position of king would simply be the most competent one. There were twelve kingdoms in Lemuria and twelve kings reigning over them, but they did not rule. The position was more in service to the citizens. The main ruling body was the twenty-four Mothers of Lemuria, some of whom they had met at the Round Table. The actual governing of each of the kingdoms was conducted by the House of Lords: free-spirited, enterprising individuals who received no pay or benefits for their services. Lemuria was funded through the treasure-hunting fleets of Antares. Teryk did not share many of those technologies with the other kingdoms, who preferred to live a much more simplistic lifestyle.

"Teryk, I read your report concerning Asmodeus," said Winter, "after which I had to sleep with the lights on. I was thirsty and would not rise to get a drink of water. I eventually had to call on a droid for assistance. I never cease to marvel at your ability to experience such things." She started to turn and walk away, then stopped herself. Shaking her head, she added, "I also read your log. In it you state that after taking on your new passengers, a baby could be heard crying on the ship."

"You heard my baby crying?" asked Katharine in astonishment.

"That was your unborn child crying?" asked Winter.

The girls nodded in agreement. Trisha said she had never actually heard the baby cry but believed Katharine when she'd told her about it.

"According to Teryk's log, there were three on board who could hear your unborn child crying, Katharine. One was Teryk. The others were Raven and Aurora. I have heard of this happening before," said Winter. "If it's alright with you and your friends, I would like all of you to room with me and a few of the other Mothers of Lemuria, in the guest quarters of the king's palace, while you stay at Antares. Aurora will be there. I am interested to see how many of us are capable of hearing your child. More importantly, I would like to find out if we can communicate with him."

"What does it mean, Winter, that my unborn child cries from within my womb?" asked a concerned Katharine.

"Your unborn child cries because of the condition that the world finds itself in. What it means is that he will be a great man of God. A prophet, in fact."

Nazareth, Where Jesus Never Walked

> *Any story sounds true, until someone tells the other side,*
> *and sets the record straight,*
> —Proverbs 18:17, *The Living Bible*

"Welcome to the second gathering of the Round Table," said Teryk, addressing his researchers along with a few new additions. "Today I will be recounting the events that transpired just days before the Last Supper. But first we need to establish a timeline for Jesus' life, one that we can all agree upon."

"It would be wise to review our findings before Teryk gives an account of what he experienced, so as not to influence the investigation," said Shakira. "We can start with the star that heralded Jesus' birth."

"How long did Herod the Great rule for?" asked Sarina.

"His reign started in 40 BCE, and lasted for thirty-seven years," Kortney replied.

"Then by all accounts he should have been dead for several years at the time of Jesus' birth, shouldn't he?" reasoned Sarina. "How could Herod have ordered the slaughter of the innocents if Jesus wasn't even born yet?"

"If Jesus was born when everyone thinks he was, the answer would be that Herod could not have. Our best estimates place Jesus' birth during the 7-6 BCE timeframe, right after Cæsar Augustus' first census," said Athena, another of the Mothers of Lemuria and a member of Teryk's ESPionage teams. Athena was one of Teryk's closest advisers, but she had never felt comfortable with what she viewed as Teryk's interference in the lives of others. She was here because this time Teryk had attempted to alter history itself. "Most historians today place Jesus' lifespan between the years of 7-6 BCE through 31 CE. Jesus' exact date of birth is unknown but is suspected to be in September. The miscalculation can be traced back to Dionysius Exiguus during the sixth century."

"But Herod would have been alive if Jesus was born around 6 BCE," commented Adriana.

"Yes, but it is a commonly held assumption that Jesus was born in 1 CE, four years after Herod's death," explained Athena.

"The journey from Nazareth, culminating with Jesus' birth in a stable, is attributed to Luke," said Sarina. "Matthew makes no mention of a stable or a journey from Nazareth. He does mention the star that heralded Jesus' birth, and the visit of the Magi from the east. Many scholars doubt the account of the 'slaughter of the innocents' because it smacks of the legend of Moses..."

"I would like to point out that when Herod the Great came to power, he ordered the majority of the Sanhedrin executed as one of his first acts," interrupted Marileyna. "It must be remembered that the infant John also went into hiding. Zacharias, his father, was killed in the temple for refusing to reveal his son's whereabouts to the king. In addition, shortly before Herod died in Jericho, he ordered that every firstborn from Israel's nobility be put to death so that all Israel might mourn upon his passing. Invitations were sent out and the firstborn of Israel's nobility gathered together—thankfully the orders were never carried out. Given this evidence, we cannot dismiss the slaughter of the innocents so easily."

"I doubt that the star was a comet," said Claudia, "because a comet would have been considered a bad omen." Everyone respected Claudia's judgment, because apart from being an astrologer she was also an astronomer. "In 7 BCE, a conjunction of the planets Jupiter and Saturn occurred three times. The conjunction was so bright that many astronomers believed it to be the star mentioned in the nativity story. If you recall, the Magi associated with the star were not looking for a newborn but a child that would have been around two years of age by their calculations. The illustrations in the Roman catacombs depict the Magi as Mithra priests; sometimes as many as eight of them are gathered to honor the newborn king.

"The Magi and Zoroastrian priests were astronomers and Gentiles besides," continued Claudia. "A Mithra priest is simply another name for the priests of the savior-god Mithra. It is said that the star did not 'lead' them but rather pronounced the fulfillment of an ancient prophecy. Jupiter, the largest and brightest of the wandering stars, was called the King's Planet. Saturn, the ringed planet, was called the House of David. There are some references to Saturn being called the shield or defender of Palestine, but it is doubtful that the word Palestine was used so far back in history. Saturn is also the seventh planet. To the Magi, the star was not a miracle. It was a sign that was understood by those who could read the heavens. The Magi studied all forms of wisdom and would have been well acquainted with the prophecies of the Jews held captive in Babylon. When the King's Planet formed a conjunction with the seventh planet, the Magi understood that the long awaited king had been born to the House of David."

"If we accept 7-6 BCE as the time of Jesus' birth, he would have been almost two years old when a supernova was recorded in Shanghai by the Han dynasty. I mention this event because it was referred to as a brilliant star," said Marileyna. "The star was brighter than any other star or planet and lasted for three months from about December 5 BCE until March 4 BCE. The supernova was visible in broad daylight. Shanghai is on the same latitude as Judea. In the work of Taylor Caldwell and Jess Stern, *I Judas*, it says that Joshua-bar-Joseph (Jesus) was born in the twenty-third year of the rule of Octavius Augustus.

"The twenty-third year of Augustus's rule would correspond to this timeframe," continued Marileyna. "Given all the recent hype about the lost Gospel of Judas by National Geographic, I'm surprised that almost no one is aware of Taylor Caldwell's work. The book was published as a novel. Its foreword states that when the Christian Roman Emperor Justinian destroyed the great library of Alexandria in 500 CE, this manuscript survived. The Gospel of Judas was smuggled out by an Egyptian Christian monk named Iberias.

"Iberias studied the manuscript and shared it with a select few," said Marileyna. "On his deathbed, Iberias entrusted the document to a younger monk, and in this way it was passed down through the centuries. The manuscript finally ended up in the hands of notable German family who were lateral descendants of the last bishop to guard it. The family hid the manuscript, fearing it would be confiscated. When the Nazis came into power, the family was forced to flee Germany, leaving all their possessions behind. A German officer found the manuscript and hid it. As it was the work of a Jew, he feared it would be destroyed. After the war, the German officer returned the manuscript to the family who had it translated. The author of the original manuscript wrote in highly polished Greek with some extrapolations in erudite Latin. He claimed to be Judah-bar-Simon, also known as Judas Iscariot, the son of a rich and powerful Pharisee family. The novel was published by Atheneum Publishers, in 1977."

"The Book of the Prophet Daniel 9:24-26 foretells of the Messiah's appearance," said Noraia. "According to Daniel's prophecy, the Anointed King of Israel would appear no later than four hundred and ninety years after King Artaxerxes I issued a decree for the Jews to return and rebuild their temple and the walls of Jerusalem. Based on Daniel's prophecy, the time frame for the Anointed of God to make his appearance expired long ago. According to that information, the Jews should remove the book of Daniel from their holy scripture and burn it, on the basis that he was a false prophet."

Kortney eyed Noraia and assured her he would bring it up at the next synagogue meeting. Addressing the Round Table Kortney began, "It may come as a surprise to Christians, but the Gospels make no mention of a stable or any of the farm animals associated with the Bethlehem nativity scene. A stable, by definition, is a place for keeping horses. It has never been associated with any other breed of animal. The entire concept of a stable is built around a mistranslated verse from the Gospel of Luke 2:7. 'Jesus was laid in a manger because there was no room for them in the inn.' Inns as we understand them, although common in Rome, were unknown in the Middle East because it was common for travelers to be invited into someone's house. In fact, it was considered a pious duty.

"Luke 2:7 is a corrupt translation of the original Greek text which states that there was 'no *topos* in the *kataluma*'. What Luke is saying is that there was 'no place in the room to lay the newborn'," explained Kortney. "A more accurate translation of this verse would be: 'the infant was laid in a manger because there was no cradle provided in the room.' You see, the workshops that built feeding boxes also built cradles and coffins."

"Christian children are selectively taught a tale that extracts the most entertaining features from each Gospel and merges them into a single embellished story based on mistranslations," commented Raven. "Not one Gospel makes even the vaguest reference to the barnyard which has become an integral part of the Nativity scene. Matthew 2:11 states quite clearly that the newborn baby was in a house with his mother: 'And when they were *come into the house*, they saw the young child with Mary his mother.'"

"Based on these findings, it would appear that the infant Jesus was around two years old when Herod the Great died in 4 BCE," said Shakira. "According to Luke, Jesus would have been baptized fifteen years after Tiberius became emperor of Rome, placing the start of his ministry around the 28 CE timeframe. The Crucifixion most likely occurred in 31 CE, despite most Christians clinging to 33 CE as the year in question. That, however, would have called for a five-year-long ministry. What if anything has been uncovered pertaining to the city of Nazareth?"

"My research clearly indicates that the city of Nazareth did not exist during the time of Jesus," announced Kortney. "Nazareth does not appear on contemporary maps, nor in any books, documents, chronicles or military records of the period, Roman or otherwise. The apostle Paul makes no mention of Nazareth in his letters."

"The winter 1996-'97 edition of *American Atheist* magazine featured a Frank Zindler article entitled *Where Jesus Never Walked*. The author noted that Nazareth is not mentioned in the Old Testament, by the apostle Paul or by Flavius Josephus, who listed forty-five other cities and villages in Galilee," said Sarina.

"The Talmud lists sixty-three Galilean towns, but Nazareth is not among them. Zindler's article points out that no ancient historians or geographers mention Nazareth before the beginning of the fourth century."

"There's actually a magazine called *American Atheist*?" asked Trisha. "How can I subscribe?"

"The priests saw Jesus as a deluded renegade," explained Teryk, "someone who spread dissension by teaching unsound doctrine. For this reason they called him the Nazorean, a term meaning heretic. In other words, they called him *Jesus the Heretic*."

"We have reliable information, from some of the Talmud manuscripts, dating back three or four generations before Jesus Christ, that there existed another man who was also called 'Y'shua—the Nazarene'. The man was accused of being an enticer to idolatry," said Kortney. "This only strengthens the understanding that Nazareth was not a location but a title meaning *heretic*." To be called a Nazarene simply implied that you believed in or advocated religious or ideological beliefs that were opposed to the beliefs of the Sanhedrin. The more we examine the term Nazarene or Nazorean, the more it appears to be a title. On a sidenote, I discovered that when the priests called Jesus an 'Ebionite', the term was thought to mean poor because it stems from the Hebrew *Ebyon*, meaning poor. But its meaning is broader: Ebionite refers to one as a vagabond, a wanderer, an outcast, or a misfit."

"There is a reference to Nazarenes in Acts 24:5, which states, 'For we have found this man [Paul] a pestilent fellow, and a mover of sedition among the Jews throughout the world, and a ringleader of the *Nazarenes*.' Paul's followers could not have all been from the same obscure little village," observed Anakah. "In fact, Paul was known as the Apostle to the Gentiles precisely because he converted pagans from across the Middle East. Acts 24:14 continues, 'But this I do confess unto thee, that after the way, which they call *heresy*.' This passage seems to imply that those on the way were also viewed as heretics. The original followers of Christ identified themselves as 'those on the way'. The term Christians was attributed to them by the Romans, who hated them."

"In the third century, the Catholic bishop Hippolytus composed a 'Refutation of All Heresies'. I stress *all heresies* because Hippolytus's chief targets were the Gnostics and the *Nazarenes*," said Cassandra, a scholar who specialized in ancient world cultures. "Some Bibles translate *heresy* in Act 24:14 as *sect*. The earliest Jewish writings from the Talmud, concerning the followers of Christ, refer to them as '*the Nazarenes*'. I, too, fail to see how the followers of Jesus could all have been from the same village."

"Matthew 2:23 states, 'He will be called a Nazorean,'" said Marileyna. "When Jesus was handed the scroll of Isaiah to read in the synagogue of his home town, presumably Nazareth, they carried him out of the city to the brow of the hill on which the city stood, in order to throw him off, but Jesus escaped (Luke 4:16-30). Does the city of Nazareth stand on a brow off which they could have thrown Jesus?"

"That should not be too difficult to prove," observed Raven. "We will need to send archaeological and surveyor teams to Israel in order to get to the bottom of it, though."

Teryk stood and addressed the Round Table. "I would like to point out that in Jesus' time, people did not simply open their Bibles and start reading in the synagogue, from whatever passages they pleased. First, the Rabbi would select a reader. Then, he would hand out the scroll to be read from. The odds against Jesus being selected and handed this particular scroll and verse to read are astronomical. Why the crowd reacted the way they did is still a mystery to me."

Teryk began to circle the round table, "Before we began this investigation, how many of you would have thought it even remotely possible that the village of Nazareth did not exist before the time of Christ? I don't see any hands going up. To be sure, excavations at Nazareth prove that a village existed in that location during the time of Christ. This should not be taken to mean that the village was called by that name during that timeframe. Having established that the term Nazarene probably never referred to a place of origin, I suggest we continue with this monumental undertaking. Your mission will be to focus your attention on specific targets I designate."

"Any other thoughts on the title of Nazarene?" asked Shakira. "If not, I would like to change the focus of our investigation to the actual name of the man called Jesus Christ. His Hebrew name was *Yeshua* or *Y'shua*. Marileyna brought up an interesting point when she mentioned that Judas referred to Jesus as Joshua-bar-Joseph. His being called Jesus Christ is mainly due to Paul's influence. Paul kept referring to Y'shua as 'Iesos', which means 'Jehovah is salvation'. When the Greek word *Iesos* was translated to Latin it became *Jesus*."

"Paul uses the term 'Christ' so often when referring to Y'shua that many mistakenly understood it to be his real name," said Teryk. "The word Christ is derived from the Greek *Kristos* and means *anointed*. The apostle Paul constantly addresses Y'shua by the title Anointed Savior, never by his actual name. And like the divine 'anointed savior-gods' who came before Y'shua, he, too, is represented as having come to Earth for the sole purpose of saving the world from its sins.

"It may surprise you to learn that Buddha was not born with that name," continued Teryk. "His real name was Siddh rtha Gautama. Buddha means the enlightened one. Most of us have heard of Mahatma Gandhi, but that wasn't his real name either. He was born Mohandas Karamchand. His title means, wise and holy man or great soul. In the same way, Jesus Christ was not born with that name. Christ Jesus is a title meaning 'anointed savior'."

"The Greek influence on Christianity would explain why the earliest images of Christ are those of a beardless young Greco-Roman deity. Jews, much like the Taliban of today, had laws against men cutting off their beards," said Kortney. "The catacombs of Rome consisted of hundreds of subterranean galleries connected by miles of passageways which the early Christians illustrated with devotional paintings and carvings. All inscriptions are in Greek, not Hebrew or Aramaic. Christ is always depicted in settings of Greek mythology. No self-respecting Jew would have gone near a dead body, let alone thousands of them in order to worship a half-god/half-man in secret. Nor would they have desecrated the resting place of the dead with graven images.

"The Gospels tend to present Paul as a Hebrew by birth and link him to the tribe of Benjamin," continued Kortney, "but according to Epiphanius, a fourth-century bishop of Salamis in Cyprus, Paul was the son of Greek parents. Epiphanius says that Paul married a Jewish woman and converted to Judaism after spending time in Jerusalem. According to Acts, Paul was a Roman citizen who came from Tarsus, in Cilicia, modern Turkey, around the year 34 CE. At that time Tarsus was the center of stoicism, or Greek stoic philosophy, which taught self-control in the face of adversity, and the acceptance of a universal law: It emphasized equality among men and women, condemned slavery and encouraged a worldwide brotherhood devoid of national boundaries."

"Tarsus was a hotbed for the mystery religions," remarked Adriana. "It is hard to imagine that a man of such great learning as Paul would not have been aware of their teachings."

"Although Paul himself is credited with the conversion of thousands, he claims that he was not a great orator," said Kortney. "In 2nd Corinthians 10:10, Paul states that people say his letters are weighty and powerful, but his bodily [physical] presence is weak and *his speech contemptible*. Paul has this to say about himself in verse 11:6: '...*though I be rude in speech*, yet not in knowledge.' Paul's Greek was cultured and polished, and he states several times that he is great in knowledge. If Paul had been born a Hebrew, why would he lack mastery of that language?"

"Some believe that, perhaps like Moses, Paul had a speech impediment. But if you recall, Moses was raised the son of a pharaoh, therefore he would not have been fluent in Hebrew," reasoned Shakira, who was fluent in five languages and versed in three ancient dialects. "These men did not suffer from speech impediments. They simply did not have a firm grasp of the language. Linguistic studies of Paul's letters confirm his Greek origins. All his quotations from the Old Testament are from the Greek Septuagint. If he had been brought up a Jew, he would have had a better understanding of the Hebrew language and text. If Paul was in fact a Jewish convert through marriage, it would go a long way towards explaining why he alone was a citizen of Rome."

"Originally, Saul considered Jesus' followers claims—that he had resurrected from the dead—insane at best, insidious at worst," observed Kortney. "Backed by the full power of the Sanhedrin, the governing body of Judea, Saul made it his personal mission to hunt down these heretics."

"According to Saul's own account, God revealed the truth to him in a vision where Jesus made a personal appearance. It must be remembered that Saul was en route to Damascus with orders to hunt down and systematically execute the followers of Christ. Saul does not go into as much detail as most scholars would like," Teryk admitted, "but it is beyond dispute that Saul of Tarsus became convinced Jesus was alive after having been dead. This changed everything, and transformed Saul from one extreme to the other."

"Saul of Tarsus tried to crush the growing movement and was assimilated by it. The apostle Paul persevered amid disillusionment, persecution, derision, mockery, infirmities, desertions, stoning, beatings, and imprisonment. He was intensely zealous in the performance of his duties and stands out as an exceptional figure on both sides of the conflict," said Phoenix, a Mother of Lemuria who had become intrigued when she'd heard about the investigation that was underway. Phoenix was no stranger to the possibility of time travel. Once, while she was dumping out a backpack full of books, a small booklet had fallen out. She did not remember checking it out of the library. Turning the book over, she read its title: *The Table of Illusion and Reality, The Master's Table*. She certainly did not remember ever seeing that little book before, and was shocked to discover that *she* was listed as its author! Upon opening the book, she discovered that it was copyrighted ten years into the future.

"A major problem encountered by Paul when presenting Christianity to Greeks outside Israel was that they had no concept of Judaism, no understanding of Jewish customs or beliefs," complained Adriana. "The first Christian groups established by Paul were from pagan cults with fantastic mythologies. These congregations drew on Hellenistic mythologies whose own pagan savior-gods mirrored the resurrected Jesus."

"Paul's message is unlike any of the Gospels," said Athena. "It would be wise to remember that Paul's authority came from a vision he had experienced of the resurrected Jesus. The disciples, on the other hand, received their authority directly from Jesus while he was still alive. When they spoke of Jesus, it was in reference to what he had taught them during the years he was with them. In his writings, Paul does not say much regarding Jesus' deeds or parables. Instead, Paul focuses on what he believes is the critical issue: Christ's resurrection and his sacrifice on the cross. For this reason the Jews did not accept what Paul was trying to teach them. Pagans, on the other hand, were familiar with the concept of a man/god deity associated with the virgin-born savior-gods, who

Joseph "Five Eagles" Reyna

were crucified for our sins. It is for this reason that pagans found it easier to accept Paul's teachings."

"Teryk, the Gospels plainly state that the Sanhedrin charged Jesus with blasphemy, saying, 'He calls himself the Son of God.' Did they actually say that?" asked Jidion.

"Yes… but Jesus referred to everyone as a son of God," stammered Teryk.

"I thought Shirley MacLaine coined that phrase," offered Trisha.

"Actually, Jesus said it first," Raven assured her.

"Jesus would never have said such a thing!" argued Marileyna.

"I hope you all brought your Bibles, because you're going to need them," said Raven. "Please turn to the Gospel of John 10:34-36. The King James version words it this way: 'Jesus answered them, "Is it not written in your law, I said, Ye are gods?" The translation in *The Living Bible* reads slightly differently: 'Jesus answered them, "*In your own Law it says that men are gods….*" By this very definition, in Jesus' own words, are we not the Sons of God?"

"Actually, what Jesus said should have been translated more along-the-lines-of: 'Have you never heard that we are the sons of the Elohim?'" explained Teryk.

"So, being a god, I could go and stand in the middle of a highway in front of an oncoming eighteen-wheeler and I would not get hurt?" demanded Jidion, biting off the words and displaying a forced smile that immediately got on Teryk's nerves.

"It won't hurt—much," added Juaquin.

"You know, Darwin may have been onto something when he purposed that those swimming in the shallow end of the gene pool are easily eliminated," added Teryk.

"Perhaps we should break for lunch but I have been wondering, was Jesus a carpenter, Teryk?" asked Shakira, trying to defuse the situation.

"No, he was a Master craftsman," corrected Teryk, "a worker of gold and silver. It was said he possessed the secret knowledge of the workings of gold, much like an alchemist."

"Jesus being called the son of a carpenter demonstrates how some old Hebrew and Aramaic words have no direct counterparts in other languages," explained Kortney. "The Greek translation of the Semitic word *naggar* is rendered as *ho tekt n*. The Semitic scholar Dr. Géza Vermès pointed out that this descriptive word could be applied to a trade craftsman. The word naggar could equally define a scholar or teacher. Naggar more precisely defined someone as a learned man with great skills. A naggar was a master of his trade. One translation of the Greek *ho tekt n* is 'a master of the craft', a modern freemasonry term. It certainly did not identify Joseph or Jesus as woodworkers."

"Since most of you are unaware of exactly what I experienced, perhaps we can order that a banquet be prepared," suggested Teryk. "I can share with you what I witnessed concerning events that led up to the Last Supper while you dine. Then, while the Last Supper and the events that led up to Jesus' arrest and trial are being debated, I can dine while I listen. I would also like to add that if it is terribly important that you do so, you have my permission to interrupt and ask questions. Otherwise just take notes and I'll get to your questions at the appropriate time."

Sarina excused herself from the Round Table in order to make the necessary preparation for the banquet purposed by Teryk.

"What we specialize in at ESPionage, is remote viewing: the ability to see across space and time," explained Teryk, wondering, '*How does one explain to those who have never sailed uncharted waters what those seas look like?*' "Our bodies are designed to transmute vibrations into something we can comprehend. I do not profess to understand the fabric of space, or the space-time medium. I do, however, know how it feels."

"Does not what you claim to be able to do fly in the face of the directive given by God in Deuteronomy 18?" asked Jidion. "'Let there be none among you who practice witchcraft and black magic, or a fortune teller, or one who practices divination, or a sorcerer, or a necromancer who calls forth the spirits of the dead.' Isn't divination supposed to be an evil thing?"

"It could be argued that Jesus was guilty of violating several of those directives. He certainly demonstrated divination when he said to Peter, 'Before this night is over you shall deny me three times.' He warned his own followers that they would be accused of being in league with the Devil, which I have been on several occasions," admitted Teryk. "In fact, by that very verse you just quoted from Deuteronomy, Jesus Christ appears guilty of being a necromancer: one who communicates with the dead. When Jesus transfigured on the mountain top, had not Moses and Elijah been dead for centuries? Yet the three disciples you hold in high esteem—Peter, James and John—witnessed him conversing with two spirits of the dead! It's a good thing for us that those pious Jewish priests saw right through his conjuring and had Jesus executed, isn't it?

"You're speechless, Jidion. I thought for sure you would remind me that Elijah was taken to Heaven in a fiery chariot, in which case I would have argued that the witnesses say nothing about a fiery chariot transporting Elijah to and from the mountain top. I asked Jesus about this. Do you know what he said?"

"I'm supposed to believe you talked with Jesus now?" asked Jidion.

"Isn't that what this investigation's about?" demanded Teryk. He thought about it for a few seconds then scoffed derisively. There was an interminable pause. Teryk finally broke the silence by saying, "'My God is not the God of the dead. My God is the God of the Living.' At least that's what Jesus told me. He

Joseph "Five Eagles" Reyna

also cautioned me to observe the signs of the times so that I would not be caught unprepared at his return.

"At ESPionage we have learned to use breathing techniques to achieve heightened states of awareness," continued Teryk. "It is said that telepathy encompasses everything remote viewers can do. Except, remote viewers do not try to communicate with another mind at great distances. They only gather information relevant to their target. In that respect it is similar to psychometry, a form of divination from personal physical contact with an object belonging to someone we seek information on.

"When mediums are wired up to our experimental equipment we find that they do not tune into the brain-wave patterns of their subjects, but instead seem to be somewhere else. Their hearts do not beat in rhythm either. Through the work of Dr. James Spottiswoode, concerning what he calls meta-analysis of 'Anomalous Cognition', what we call ESP or Extra Sensory Perception, we became aware that external circumstances either enhanced our abilities or were detrimental to them. Dr. Spottiswoode discovered that ESP increased by as much as 400% in the sidereal day relative to the subject's position on the planet with respect to the center of our galaxy. ESP is also intensified by the position of the Sun. Taking this into account, we selected a time and location that would amplify my abilities as a remote viewer. I was targeting the treasure of the Almiranta, a Spanish Galleon called the *Nuestra Señora de las Maravillas*. The ship carried a 1,600-pound solid-gold life-size statue of the Madonna and child, and a 3,000-pound gold table encrusted with emeralds. According to the manifest, she also carried $500,000 in gold bars and the first minted shipment of gold coins in the New World, dated 1630.

"On 1 January 1656, a combined armada of twenty-two Spanish merchant ships and galleons sailed out of Havana harbor on its voyage back to Spain. The fleet was supposed to have sailed before the hurricane season began but was delayed. The fleet's two heaviest armed war galleons, the lead ship Capitana and the rear ship Almiranta, carried the main treasure.

"On January 4, near midnight, the Maravillas sailed into breaking seas. The *Jesus Maria*, a merchant ship, struck a coral reef that tore off her rudder. Disabled, the vessel anchored and fired her cannon as a warning. The Maravillas's crew thought they were under attack. In the confusion, they collided with the Capitana. The two warships finally disengaged but the Maravillas's bow was damaged below the water line. She began taking on water and came to rest on a sandbank. Most of the deck and both the stern and fore castles were out of the water. Soon afterwards, strong northerly winds, guesstimated to be around sixty to seventy knots, blew in. The ensuing massive waves broke the ship into three pieces. The bow, carrying two hundred and fifty tons of silver, remained in place, while the fore and aft castles were carried away.

"In remote viewing through several centuries of time, it is helpful to have an emotionally charged target. And the wreck of the *Nuestra Señora de las Maravillas* certainly qualifies. When the remote-viewing session began, I sensed fear and could see the Spanish galleon sitting deep in the water. Strong northerly winds were blowing, indicating that the hurricane was on a direct path toward the Maravillas's position. The seas rose as the winds increased in strength. Then the rains began. I could not believe that roughly six hundred people had been crammed aboard this vessel. There was a bright flash; I reasoned that it was a lightning strike. The next instant, I was onboard the ship. An uncontrollable fear had me paralyzed. I realized that I was a passenger. People crowded all around me, shouting for me to take their money that I might absolve them of their sins. I looked down and tugged on the garb of a Jesuit monk. I saw other priests taking money and stuffing it into their pockets, absolving a dozen folk at a time with a wave of their hand. Frantic men found my pockets and loaded them with gold, so I followed suit. When all were absolved, I saw the ship's crew jumping overboard and taking refuge on the corral outcroppings that surrounded the galleon. Passengers hurried to the castles and took refuge there.

"When waves began hammering the ship, men scurried to save their lives. I wondered if I could get a look at the main treasure. It felt strange being in a different body. I discovered that I had access to the priest's memories and recalled the location of the statue. I was able to view the golden statue easily enough because it was property of the Roman Catholic Church. I observed that the hurricane's swell had partially flooded the compartment. The statue was about four feet tall and resembled Michelangelo's work. The Madonna was seated with the infant Jesus in her arms. I did not see the gold table encrusted with emeralds.

"While I was still examining the statue, a massive wave damaged the castle I was standing in. A second wave tore the castle off the ship, washing me into the ocean. The weight of the gold in my pockets was pulling me under, so I struggled to remove the sea-soaked robe. I became disoriented in the dark water. As I tried to swim to the surface, I wondered if I would be slammed against a reef. Try as I might, I could not make it to the surface. Then my body went still. The remote-viewing session must be over, I thought. My lungs were not burning for air, so I remained still. I had the sensation of being submerged and wondered if the saltwater mixture inside the deprivation tank had somehow been prepared improperly. My body should have floated easily in the saline mixture.

"Opening my eyes, I could see that I was definitely underwater, but not inside the dark deprivation tank. I could see the sun shining through the ripples on the surface just inches above my face. Instinctively, I tried to break for the surface, but a powerful hand held me in place. Where was I? When was I? My lungs were not craving oxygen yet, so I decided to remain calm for the moment.

Joseph "Five Eagles" Reyna

I was raised out of the water, gently not forcefully. I looked around and gaped in awe. What I saw before me certainly wasn't the disaster that had just taken place on a stormy evening in the Atlantic.

"I had been lifted out of the water by a man in a white tunic with a leather girdle about his waist. He wore some type of thick towel with fringed ends around his shoulders. I found myself standing waist-deep in a wide river. Many people in robes lined the banks. The robes of some were dripping wet, as if they had fallen into the water. I could not see their cars, and except for some private conversations that carried over to me, it seemed very quiet, like being deep in the desert of a mountain wilderness.

"The man spoke to me. I knew he had not spoken any language I recognized, yet I understood him in the same way that I understand someone who speaks in tongues. I also noticed a long line of people waiting for their chance to get soaked. Could this be John the Baptist, I wondered? I looked at him more closely. He certainly did not fit the traditional description: that of a wild man dressed in camel hair and a loincloth. This individual wore a robe; perhaps some would call it a tunic. His apparel had sleeves and the bottom of it was brought up between his legs and tucked into a thick leather garment around his waist. It looked like a belt but was wider and made entirely of leather fastened by a vertical row of belt buckles. If this was the priestly girdle, it was very warlike in appearance. And the thick towel wasn't a towel at all; it was a prayer shawl."

Sarina entered with servants laden with trays of hors d'oeuvres and appetizers. An inner ring from the Round Table rose and aligned with the outer table. The servants placed the trays on this inner table before those seated at the Round Table. Sarina seated herself and the inner table began to spin clock-wise at a slow rate, allowing everyone seated access to the many trays of food before them.

Anakah stood and asked to be recognized. "I would just like to point out that what Teryk experienced is not the norm. We have never had an incident like this before. Remote viewing is not a projection of self. Normally a remote viewer is limited to observing or picking up on the feelings of the general group involved. Most remote viewers deal with abstracts. Any left-brain data, such as lottery numbers, remains elusive. When contact is made, most remote viewers will describe smells, colors, temperature and textures…grey, green, hot, rough. Remote viewing is best used to describe a spot on the planet, such as structures or prominent geological features.

"Coordinate remote viewing involves latitude and longitude coordinates which are arbitrary," explained Anakah, "and should have no bearing on our reality. But they seem to work quite well in remote viewing and the coordinates are not limited to this world. Remote viewing can be used to describe a spot such as the site of a sunken Spanish treasure galleon. The past is weak and weaker still are future events, unless there is great human emotion attached to them.

"Beginners in remote viewing are often affected by performance anxiety. During initial training, viewers are given very simple targets: landscapes, towers or lighthouses. They are provided with pens and ten to twelve sheets of paper. They are told, 'Do not speak. Do not think—allow.' The pen will move, much like automatic writing. The first sketch made is usually the most accurate and is called the Ideogram. A rough three-dimensional sketch is better than a two-dimensional one. Movement of arms, wrists and fingers is entirely involuntary. Sometimes we provide modeling clay. After fifteen to forty-five minutes the data will cease to flow.

"Taking things to the next level can be described more accurately as an Out of Body Experience or OBE," continued Anakah. "Senses are heightened in this mode, a viewer can accurately describe surroundings at seemingly impossible distances. They have been able to communicate with persons at those locations. Still more advanced are the abilities of precognition, which empowers an observer to cause a different future by changing the events that led to the observed future. A future event can be modified by simply not including the observer in the otherwise-unavoidable disaster. Future is formed by a multitude of events in the 'now' and becomes weaker the further out you go. Obviously what Teryk experienced is way beyond our understanding. I suspect it could be part of one of Teryk's past lives, allowing for his linkup with these two individuals. We will know more when we have had sufficient time to investigate this phenomenon."

Finishing an appetizer Teryk began, "I guess I'll start with Jesus' triumphant entrance into the city of Jerusalem. This occurred on Sunday, the first day of the week: what some call the final week. I and the other disciples who formed the inner twelve usually stayed close to Jesus. The unaccompanied women had to follow at a distance, as was the custom. At any given time, there were roughly one hundred and fifty people who walked with Jesus wherever he went. On this day we had the sixty additional disciples accompanying our entourage. Years earlier, Jesus had instructed each disciple to select five other men and teach them as they had been instructed. That is how these additional disciples came about. You're probably all wondering which of the twelve disciples I was. There's no easy way for me to say this, so I'll just come right out with it. I was Judas Iscariot or rather 'Judah the Scariota': a noble born Pharisee, an assassin, and a rebel leader of the Zealots. Now before everyone gets up and leaves the room, I assure you that I tried everything in my power, short of committing suicide, to prevent the events that unfolded. From what I experienced, there was no betrayal on Judas's part. More importantly, Judas met with and spoke to the resurrected Christ, who gave him specific instructions to go into Persia, where Jesus had spent the majority of his young adult life.

"As for Jesus' appearance, he was tall. His hair was long, thick and a reddish-auburn shade which some referred to as the color of wine. It was cut shorter on the sides and longer towards the middle of his back. His eyes were hazel

Joseph "Five Eagles" Reyna

and sometimes appeared green. The Baptist was similar in appearance. It was evident they had known each other from childhood. They were, after all, cousins.

"Jesus approached Jerusalem from the south. As we climbed the last hill, he halted. Overcome with grief, he spoke of Jerusalem's destruction. He spoke of armies encompassing the city and of children dying in the streets. He added that the Holy Temple would be razed to the ground and not a single stone would be left upon another.

"To those with us that looked upon Jerusalem, the city appeared to be an invulnerable fortress. Jerusalem was surrounded by massive terracotta-colored walls joined by huge towers that loomed over the deep natural moats formed by a valley toward the west. Other valleys surrounded to the east and south. Before us stood what looked like a landfill. It was the Valley of Dung, which ran from north to south and separated the upper and lower city. Its repulsive stench wafted incessantly across the entire lower city. In the slums of the lower city, more than half of the regular population of Jerusalem struggled to survive. The stench did not thwart off the throng that had gathered for a glimpse of the man from Galilee.

"Word of his deeds had spread to distant Jewish communities from around the Mediterranean. The crowd at that year's Passover was the largest anyone could remember. Excitement reigned and hopes were high as the people ran to see the 'Miracle Maker' entering the city riding upon a colt. Many laid down their garments. Others ran and cut palm branches. From the time of King Solomon to the fall of Jerusalem, before the deportation to Babylon, the kings of the Davidic line had all ridden to their coronations on donkeys. The Sadducees and Pharisees were outraged at this, even more so when Jesus did not dismount, instead riding the colt up the stairs and into the Court of Gentiles without performing the required purification.

"The southern entrance was by far the grandest. The flight of steps was broad and led through the Royal Portico, whose great columned hall led to the vast Court of Gentiles. The pillars that supported the ceiling were massive. I estimated them to be about three meters in diameter. The other disciples, most of whom were rural peasants from the backwater villages of Galilee, never failed to be awed by the impressive sights of the temple. The entire Court of Gentiles was surrounded on all sides by beautifully carved colonnades that displayed the craftsmanship of master masons. These covered walkways had originally been intended for students and teachers to debate religious issues. But there were few spaces left in the shade for lecturers. Most of the spaces were taken by the vendors and money changers who operated under licensed agreements from the High Priest, who took a healthy portion of the profits for himself.

"The High Priest was, for all intents and purposes, the ruler of the Jews. He was supposed to be selected by a vote, and once in office to rule for life. Most historians believe that Caiaphas was elected to the position, but this was not the case. Herod the Great had instituted the practice of appointing High Priests at frequent intervals, as he saw fit. Herod had eliminated the ruling Hasmoneans by appointing High Priests from as far away as Egypt and Mesopotamia.

"Roman authorities had continued the practice of deciding who would be the High Priest. The Roman governor could bestow the position as a political favor. But it was far more advantageous for the appointed Prefects to offer it to the highest bidder. Ever since securing his appointment to High Priest from the Roman governor Quirinius, sometime around 6 CE, Annas & Co. had maintained control of the Sanhedrin. He'd accomplished this by monopolizing trade in the temple market. Once the Roman governor tired of the present High Priest, the reigning sacerdotal aristocracy could easily afford to convince the governor to select the next best choice for High Priest. In this way, Annas was succeeded as High Priest by all five of his own sons, a grandson, and then his son-in-law. Caiaphas had been appointed by Valerius Gratus and still held the position under Pilate.

"The governors who enforced Roman rule were mostly crude soldiers who had risen through the rank by distinguishing themselves in combat. They had no skills in diplomacy, believing most problems could be solved with bloodshed. Any point they argued with Roman statesmanship usually had a sword handle at the other end. Their cruelty and senseless atrocities only compounded problems and swelled the ranks of the Zealots in much the same way that the US military's handling of Afghanistan has swelled the ranks of the Taliban.

"As clever or as stupid as the High Priests might seem, these men were only puppets, bought and paid for by the puppet masters: the men who pulled the purse strings of the nation. It was very similar to the appointing of a president of the United States by a handful of individuals. The majority of the population was not happy with the arrangement or decisions made by the few ruling elite. In our culture it's called hegemony: the concept of the few controlling the many.

"We continued with Jesus into the Court of Gentiles. Many who followed rushed to the ritual baths so as not to offend the priests. Jesus dismounted and began to remove his sandals but soon became indignant at the vendors' raucous haggling with pilgrims over their exorbitant prices. Jesus stood and turning to the scribes who surrounded us, demanded, 'Have you not read the scripture?'

"That, by the way, was an insult. Reading scripture was all these guys ever did! Few Christians realize that Jesus was a rebel who pissed off a lot of people, mostly priests. This side of his personality has always been downplayed because it flies in the face of Pauline doctrine. The apostle Paul would most likely have refrained from taking action, for fear of possibly offending any new converts.

"Jesus continued, 'It is written, my house shall be called a house of prayer; but you have made it a den of thieves!' Then, turning to the merchants, he demanded, 'Remove yourselves and your wares from this holy place!'

"By wares, Jesus meant everything that could possibly be sold, right down to the kitchen utensils. Pious Jews believed they could sin inadvertently, should they mistakenly cook both dairy and meat products in the same pot. According to Leviticus, a passage appeared three times that forbade the Israelites from 'boiling a kid in its mother's milk'. Since it appeared three separate times, the priests saw this as a direct command from God. Sadly, the reference had nothing to do with cooking meat and dairy products together or, for that matter, in the same pot. It was placed there as a warning not to sacrifice to pagan gods. The people who inhabited the land of Canaan used to worship a deity by boiling a baby goat, a kid, in the milk of its own mother. As usual the priests had ignored the spirit of the law, and believed they were obeying the letter of the law.

"The merchants laughed at the audacity of Jesus, saying they were protected by those who were appointed to rule, and refused to go. Jesus was not about to lecture them on the fine points of the law. He removed the leather straps that made up the colt's bridle and used them as a scourge to forcibly remove the merchantmen. From what I witnessed, the straps seemed to become living things in his hand. Much like the sting from a venomous viper, these cords appeared to inflict paralyzing pain on those they fell upon. Many of the merchants, mostly the money changers, had personal bodyguards and these were among the first casualties. The armed guards writhed on the pavement, convulsing uncontrollably. Some ran to offer aid and were soon gripped by the same malady. Others who observed this drew back in horror and ran from the temple.

"In order to suppress any outbreaks, the Roman detachment, permanently quartered at the garrison of Antonia, had taken up armed positions earlier that morning atop the porticoes as was their custom during the festivals. I would have thought the Roman archers would have filled Jesus full of arrows, but the soldiers were laughing uncontrollably at the incident unfolding below them. Many of the guard were running to get a better view of the thrashing Jesus was giving the Jewish merchants. The shaded area under the colonnades encompassed nearly a mile and Jesus did not stop until all the merchants were gone.

"The sale of sacrificial animals was not a new concept. There had been merchants selling during the time of Solomon. According to an ancient report, there stood two massive cypress trees close to the original temple. Sacrificial animals were sold under one tree and doves under the other. There was also no official law that barred traders from peddling theirs wares in the temple, only a prophecy that alluded to the practice ending once the Messiah arrived.

"When the temple had been cleared Jesus called for all those who sought to be healed of their infirmities. There were many, as news of Jesus' ability to heal had been spreading for three years. Many had traveled great distances in the hopes of being healed by him. Jesus stood barefoot upon one of the lower outer walls that surrounded the temple, near the entrance to the Court of Women. The low stone walls that surrounded the inner courts were about a meter high and half a meter wide. Each wall was inscribed in Latin and Greek with the warning, '*No foreigner may enter within the balustrade and the enclosure around the Temple area. Anyone caught doing so will bear the responsibility for his own ensuing death.*' From that position all could see and hear Jesus well. Since he did not actually enter the inner temple area, the priests could say nothing of his not having purified himself in the ritual baths near the entrance. He instructed his disciples, over seventy of us, to heal and minister to the crowd.

"'Woe unto you Scribes and interpreters of the law, hypocrites, you shut off the Kingdom of Heaven from men while not able to enter yourselves. You do not drink from the waters of life nor permit others to drink as well,' was his opening salutation.

"Someone grabbed my arm to get my attention. I turned to see an elderly chief priest with bushy eyebrows, dressed in a blue outer garment that had golden bells sewn at the waist and hems. I recognized this man; he was Gamaliel, my father's old friend and one of my favorite teachers when I'd been a scribe at the temple. When I say I had access to the memories of Judah, I am referring to incidents like this.

"'Come with me, Yehudah,' he said, properly pronouncing my name in Hebrew.

"We walked toward the southern entrance, climbed to the upper levels and entered a room in which I found several chief priests seated waiting for me. Among them was Caiaphas. I was reminded in no uncertain terms that I was first and foremost a priest of the temple, and should choose my words carefully, because they would reflect upon my family name, as I was descended from a well-respected line of High Priests and scribes. I listened, for they had much to say. I was reminded that I had been sent to spy on the Baptist, to become one of his followers and keep a close eye on his movements. But I had deviated from this and aligned myself with the Nazarene. This proved fortunate because the Baptist met his end soon afterwards. Their main gripe was that I had failed to report to the Sanhedrin on the movements and intentions of the Galilean. To all this I remained silent.

"'Well, man, what do you have to say for your deplorable behavior?' inquired a scribe.

"What could I say? Wasn't it obvious that I had turned my back on their bunch and thrown my lot in with Jesus? 'What could I possibly add to the reports sent back by your priests and scribes?' I asked, holding out my hands and shrugging my shoulders in a helpless gesture. 'Your scribes seemed to already know our every move and I saw no reason to compromise my position as one of the Twelve.' This seemed to satisfy them, so they went on with their plans as if I wasn't even there.

"'Look how they flock around him. This day hundreds have been healed. With a single word from him, they would proclaim him their king,' said Caiaphas.

"'We dare not lay hands on him, for fear of the Zealots,' said another chief priest. And I wondered if they knew about my recent promotion to commander within the Zealot movement.

"'Not during the Feast of Passover and Unleavened Bread,' advised an elderly Sadducee. 'Whatever action we decide to take will have to wait, lest we ignite a riot. Today's events can only raise Y'shua's stature in the eyes of the people. We can ill afford to attempt an arrest, only to end up like those fools who stood in his way today.'

"'Is he some sort of sorcerer, or is he a prophet? You have been among his inner circle for these past three years, what do you have to say about him?' asked the scribe who seemed to be leading this little brain-storming session.

"'I have never met a sorcerer, but I understand they are proud and vain. They take credit for their work and expect payment in return. Y'shua has never taken credit for a single healing. He says it is by their faith that the sick are healed or the lame made whole. He has taught me how to banish wicked spirits. I have not yet learned how to raise the dead.' It was hard to hear myself in that small room after that remark. 'Do you recall how your forefathers dealt with prophets in the past?' I shouted to be heard. 'If he is a prophet, he is the last God will be sending—that I can promise you!'

"'Just whom do you think yourself to be, addressing us in this way?' demanded an old chief priest, clenching the few remaining yellow teeth he had, and staring at me intently through milky cataracts.

"In frustration, my right hand shot forth and the man fell back as if dead. All those behind him fell as well. A dreadful silence filled the room. Some rushed to aid the old man but stopped, remembering what befell their comrades in the shade of the colonnades. As the old man struggled to get up, he blinked his eyes. They were unbelievably clear, like those of a newborn. His face had the stupid look of a blind man who had just been given his sight, blinking like a disinterred mole and gazing at everything.

"'What manner of sorcery is this?' he demanded, incensed that I had performed a spell that would undoubtedly tarnish his soul and undo all the good he believed he had done before the eyes of God. He demanded I remove the spell or he would pluck his own eyes out of his head. 'Better to enter Heaven blind than to be cast out whole for all eternity,' I believe were his exact words. I turned and left the room in disgust. No one dared stop me. And I heard him giving thanks to God for restoring him to his former state.

Incredulous

"As I descended the stairs, seven silver trumpets called shofars, each one shaped like rams horn, sounded from the temple. These trumpets sounded four times a day so that the faithful should pause for a moment of prayer and refection. At the sound of the shofars, those in the temple responded, 'Hear, O Israel, the Lord our God, the Lord is One.' At the last blast from the shofars, Jesus left the temple grounds for Bethany. The men who owned the colt had accompanied us from Bethphage. They headed back with us but Jesus wanted to walk. I offered to take Lazarus and the disciples with me to give Jesus and Mary Magdalene some time alone to themselves. The others took the hint and we headed towards the tailors district, where I paid for each disciple to be outfitted with new comfortable traveling clothes. During the Passover we were required to wear sandals and traveling clothes, and to carry our walking sticks. Mary Magdalene was going to surprise Jesus with new attire and I felt the rest of us might look a bit shabby next to him."

"Are you saying Jesus and Mary Magdalene were married?" asked an astonished Trisha.

"Very much so," said Teryk. "John is assumed to be the only disciple who had not married yet. The Mishnah, a rabbinic oral law, was very clear on the subject. Any man that was still single at twenty years of age was considered to be accursed of God. Judas's wife had died in childbirth. He had chosen not to remarry, instead devoting his life to the search for the long-awaited Messiah."

"You expect us to believe this?" asked Jidion.

"No. I expect you to either prove or disprove what I observed, based on the information you find in the Gospels," stressed Teryk, continuing with his story. "The noise from the boisterous haggling in the marketplace was overpowering. Some yelled at each other so vehemently that it appeared a fight was imminent. Then, just as suddenly, they would slap palms and the deal was done. Carcasses of sheep and goats hung from poles at the front of stalls. Vendors swatted at flies that swarmed over the freshly cut meats. Others asked us to feel the texture of material that extended from brightly colored bolts of cloth. Once we'd selected the colors of our new garments and the tailors had finished measuring us, we headed to find something to eat.

"The ruckus of ducks, hens and geese in wicker cages assaulted the ears and the nose as well if you got too close. There were open baskets filled with every kind of fruit and grain imaginable. Camels and donkeys were constantly in the way and their oppressive odor mixed with the smell of spices and fragrant herbs.

"I saw Peter holding a sword at a nearby vendor's booth. He hefted its weight while admiring its workmanship. Having spent the better part of his life as a fisherman on the sea, he'd never needed one. On the open road it was a different matter. When Peter held a regular sword it looked more like a bowie knife in his large hand. I liked the sword and thought of getting it for him as a gift.

Joseph "Five Eagles" Reyna

"I remained near the tailors' district while most of the disciples left to get something to eat. Lazarus and Symeon the Zealot remained with me to admire the display of weapons. These merchants of death didn't have a particular spot where they all congregated, as the tailors and cheesemakers did. One could find them plying their wares almost anyplace.

"I walked over to Lazarus, who was grinning excitedly at the display of knives before him. He could have easily afforded to buy every weapon this trader was hocking, but he was still a youth and would have needed permission from his father, Symeon, to purchase a sword.

"'How much longer do you think it will be before I am allowed to carry a sword, Judah?' asked Lazarus.

"'It will be some time yet, little one.'

"'Why?'

"'Well, for one, you're still very small and even a man without a sword could overpower you if he knew what he was doing,' I told him.

"And before you ask, I'm not sure just how old Lazarus was but he was not considered a man, which means he was not yet twelve years of age. I would guesstimate his age at about ten. Lazarus was the little brother of Martha and Mary, called the Magdalene. Their father Symeon, a Pharisee, had been afflicted with leprosy. For a time no one knew his whereabouts. This is why Lazarus was so close to Jesus, who had helped raise him. Symeon had since returned and been healed of leprosy by Jesus.

"Lazarus asked me if I could teach him to fight.

"'I'll do better than that. Do you know what these are?' I asked, holding up three throwing knives.

"'They are daggers.'

"'Yes, but these are special daggers.' Turning to the shop owner, a man who appeared to be Persian by his dress, I asked if he had a suitable board on which I could test their balance. Drawing back the curtain behind him, I saw two well-worn logs resting against the wall. The logs had been split down the middle, so perhaps it was only one log split in two. The timber was pockmarked all over but was especially eaten away at the center. I held the daggers in my open palm to the vendor and he nodded his consent. Handing one of the knives to Symeon and squatting down next to Lazarus, I demonstrated how to throw the knives. Lazarus gasped in amazement as I struck one knife in the center of each log.

"'It's also good to know how to throw the knife underhand,' said Symeon, 'if time or location does not permit you to launch it properly.'

"Lazarus seemed even more amazed by Symeon's throw, for he had not seen me give him one of the blades. It seemed to him that Simon's hand had been empty. Indeed, the Zealot's arm jerked up with lightning speed when a thud was heard on the log and a second dagger materialized where only one had been.

"I do not think your father will be too upset if I buy you these throwing knives,' I said.

Lazarus's face beamed with joy when the merchant placed the knives in his hands.

"Symeon asked for a sharpening stone. The merchant produced one and Symeon sat down, placing the stone and daggers on his lap. The man proceeded to haggle over the price, but I was in no mood to haggle. I would be dead in less than a week if all went as I remembered, so I gave him slightly more than he was asking.

"'May I see that sword?' I asked.

"The man unsheathed it and handed it to me. I could see why Peter was so taken with it. I remembered once holding a unique model Winchester rifle, which left me with an impression I cannot quite describe other than to say I liked the way it felt in my hands. No other firearm has ever evoked a similar response. The sword was longer than average and well suited to a man of Peter's stature. His long reach could be put to good use if he ever needed to defend himself with it.

"'What are you doing, Symeon?' asked Lazarus in disbelief.

"I turned to see Simon, the Zealot, running the blade of a knife against the stone. I knelt down, placing one hand on the youth's shoulder. 'This is necessary, Lazarus, so that you do not hurt yourself or anyone else while you are learning to throw them. I'm sure when you are ready Symeon will make them razor sharp for you.'

"Symeon smiled at Lazarus and added, 'If I had had knives this sharp to throw when I was learning, I probably would have killed myself with them. Do not become too attached to these knives, little one. If you should ever have to throw one to defend yourself, I suggest you turn and run. You can always replace a blade.'

"The weight of the sword in my hand reminded me I was still holding it. The sword had a double edge and was straight. The blade increased in width toward the middle and tapered to a point. The weapon was made from a type of steel that was of much higher quality than the average Roman legionnaire's blade. Also, the sword had a deep 'blood groove' that ran almost two thirds of its entire length.

"When a person is stabbed by a blade, the tissue around the wound tends to close around the blade, preventing the loss of blood. This makes it difficult to withdraw the sword. The blood groove prevents the wound from making an airtight tight seal around the blade, allowing for an easier extraction. The hilt did not sweep back but jutted forward instead, adding two additional points with which to inflict injuries. The handle was made from thin pieces of wood that had been dyed red, black and green, then glued together and filed down to make a comfortable grip. This was no scimitar, although it was similar. 'What type of blade is it?' I asked.

"'It is made in the fashion of the scimitar but there are many differences. I obtained it from a traveler who said he acquired it during his voyages to the eastern lands. Is it to your liking?' he asked.

"'It is, but I wish the sword as a gift for a friend.'

"'The large man who was with you earlier, is he the friend you speak of?'

"I nodded in agreement, and asked the price.

"At the sound of the price, Simon's head came up. He had been sharpening his own blade on the stone and Lazarus was studying his technique. It was the price of a horse, albeit not a very fast one. I paid the merchant and added an additional coin, asking him to please wrap the sword so that my friend, who was due to return any minute, could not see it. He bowed and entered his shop, returning with a beautiful belt.

"'It is not the custom of your people to carry such a heavy weapon. Your friend will have need of this, I think.'

"I was so used to wearing the money belt, I had completely forgotten about it. 'You are correct, thank you. It is beautiful and its red and black will go well with the sword. How much for the belt?' I asked.

"'It is yours, my friend. You have paid me more than enough. I think I shall close my shop early today.' Wrapping the sword and belt in a piece of cloth resembling burlap, he handed them to me.

"'How will I carry my daggers?' asked Lazarus.

"'Ahhh!' said the shopkeeper, entering his tent. He returned with a small belt that seemed well suited for a woman; its size was too small for the average man. He bent down and sized it around Lazarus's waist. It was a perfect fit. Taking two of the daggers, he inserted them in the back of the belt. They sheathed horizontally, the blades overlapping with the handles accessible from the sides. With a click the daggers snapped into place. The look on Lazarus's face was priceless.

"I gave the man three Denarii for it. He seemed very pleased with the transaction. Simon knelt and began to undo the belt as he explained to Lazarus that this type of belt was designed to be worn under an outer vestment so as to conceal the blades. Youths normally did not wear an outer mantel but Lazarus was from a wealthy family and liked to dress in a fashion similar to Jesus.

"As I was about to leave, the shopkeeper exited his small tent with a walking stick. It was a little wider than normal at the top and carved in an intricate pattern that resembled a weave. The wood was dark and the tree rings on its surface were spaced very close together. Standing between Symeon and myself, he lowered the staff between us, his back to Symeon. He pulled on the top section and it slipped away to reveal a double-edged blade, about as long as a man's forearm and almost three fingers wide. Like the sword, it came from the Far East and was reminiscent of the Chinese long sword. Unrecognizable symbols were etched into the blade. I had never really liked my walking staff and this one was fit for a Zealot commander. By my own reckoning, I was very wealthy and all that my father had accumulated would mean nothing once I was dead. I gave the man two gold talents for it, roughly two years' wages. It was a very beautiful walking staff. And we were required to carry one during the Passover meal anyway. Just then, Matthew and Philip were returning.

"'A belt,' remarked Philip. 'I never did see the need for those things, but it looks good on you Lazarus.'

Lazarus nodded his head, grinning all the while.

"'Here,' said Matthew, handing us some sweetbread. 'I figured you'd be hungry by now if you were still here. The others have already started for Bethany. They must be past the city gates by now. Did the tailors say when our new garments would be ready?'

"'Since we selected six different tailors, all said the new clothes would be ready the morning after tomorrow. I'll instruct some of Symeon's servants to get them for us. I'm sure we will not have time to do it ourselves with all the preparations that will be needed that day.'

"'Excellent, they will be ready in time for the first day of the feast. Judah, that merchant is not a Jew. Did you purchase from him?' asked a concerned Matthew.

"'Yes Levi, I did. What I wished to purchase could not be had at any Jewish vendor's stall. I think the custom of keeping our money among the Jews limits us from all that the world has to offer. And it is probably one of the reasons we are so disliked as a people.'

"'I agree, but do not let the priests catch you doing it.'

"'I think they might forgive me for it. I was carrying some idolatrous coins and had to dispose of them. I did not wish to be swindled by the temple money changers, so I blessed this kind merchant with them.' That seemed to put an end to the subject.

"'Thanks for buying us new clothes,' said Symeon, the Zealot.

"'Yes, thank you,' added Matthew. 'Why did you get us new clothes for the Passover anyway?'

"'The Magdalena is going to surprise Y'shua with a beautiful garment for this occasion and we thought that the rest of the disciples might look a little rough around the edges. So we agreed that it would be a good idea to outfit the

　　　　　　　　　　　　　　　　　　Joseph "Five Eagles" Reyna

inner twelve with new apparel. Some of the sixty were looking a little shabby after a year of traveling and I arranged new clothing and sandals for them as well.'

"Just then a herald rounded the corner and startled us with his message. 'Y'shua-bar-Yehosef the Hannosri is going to be stoned to death for practicing sorcery and having enticed Israel to apostasy.'

"Hannosri was the Aramaic word for Nazarene. It meant 'heretic'. The custom required that this harbinger of ill tiding proclaim his message aloud for forty days. We stood transfixed, stupefied. He continued bearing his bad news as he walked past us. 'Let anyone who has something to say in his defense come forward and plead on his behalf before the Great Sanhedrin in Jerusalem. Y'shua-bar-Yehosef the Hannosri is going to be stoned to death for practicing sorcery and having enticed Israel, leading them astray.'

"'What does this mean?' asked Symeon.

"I was a temple scribe and as such, a lawyer. Matthew looked at me, concerned. 'It is a very grave offense,' I said. 'One of the gravest known to our laws. Sorcery is bad enough but the charge of enticer is far worse.' I looked at Lazarus; I did not want to say any more for his sake, as he was too young to understand.

"'Have you heard the herald's cry and what they are saying about Y'shua?' asked Peter, whom I had not seen walk up with Thaddaeus, Stephen, James, and his brother John.

"'We just heard,' said Matthew.

"As we turned to head back to Bethany, Symeon said he was going to get some more sweet bread. Handing him some shekels, I asked him to get enough bread for those back at Bethany. Lazarus wanted to accompany him. This day had been exciting for him and he was not ready to go home.

"'A sorcerer! Just what are the chief priests up to, Judah? What do they mean by this?' asked James.

"'As I told the others, the accusation of sorcery is not good but it pales in comparison to the charge of enticer. It means that they are accusing Y'shua of enticing the people to serve a god not known to Israel.' A thought from my life in the 20th century entered my mind just then. I recalled that as a young priest I really enjoyed feeling the presence of the Holy Spirit during my sermons. Once, when asked to conduct services, I had just begun to feel that familiar rush of energy when an elderly priest pulled me aside and concluded the service while I stood behind him wondering what I might have done to get myself in trouble this time. As we left the altar, he took me aside and reprimanded me. 'I don't know what you're up to, young man,' he snarled, 'but I just felt something I *have never felt before in my life!* And I'm certain it was emanating from you.' I still remember my exact words to him: 'Well, don't worry. You'll never feel it again as long as you live, I can promise you that!' That was my last day as a parish priest. Shortly afterwards, I found myself among the exorcists. I wondered if the chief priest had experienced something similar. We were used to feeling the power of the presence of God when Jesus spoke and performed miracles. The only thing the priests of the Sanhedrin ever felt was a sense of their own self-importance.

"'But what does it mean to Y'shua? How bad is it?' inquired Thaddaeus, a grave look of concern clouding his features.

"'The divine command is very specific: "You shall take no pity on the enticer nor shall you spare him." I think they decided to throw in sorcery for good measure. Basically, they have already condemned him to death with this charge. If the Sanhedrin convicts Y'shua with the aid of two witnesses, whom I'm sure they will have no trouble finding, they will suspend anyone from speaking on his behalf because of the injunction 'Neither shall your eye take pity on him nor shall you spare him.'

"'When we arrive I will speak to Y'shua so he can make an informed decision. The court crier has to announce the indictment publicly for forty days before the trial,' I assured them. 'Hey, how do you like my new walking stick?' I asked, trying to lighten the mood.

"'I'm still young and do not have a need for one, Judah,' said John.

"'Perhaps, but you are required to have one in your hand for the Passover feast. If you like you can use my old walking stick.' I wanted to show them the hidden blade but they had never really liked the idea that I carried a sword so I decided to keep that a secret."

Parable of the Fig Tree

"Jesus did not seem too surprised by the charges leveled against him. On Monday we once again headed toward the temple. Leading us over the Mount of Olives through Gethsemane, Jesus stopped as we came upon a fig tree covered in leaves. 'For three years I have passed by this tree and found no fruit,' he said while looking into the distance at Jerusalem. 'Do you recall the parable of the fig tree? You should—it is the only parable I asked you to remember.'

"Nathaniel, the most informed on fig trees amongst us, replied, 'Yes, Master, there was a man who came to the dresser of the vineyard and said, "Behold these three years I have come seeking fruit on this fig tree and found none. Cut it down. Why burden the soil with it?'

"'And did the dresser cut down the fig tree?' asked Jesus.

"'No,' replied Peter, always quick to answer. 'He said he wanted to dig around the tree and fertilize it. If it went on to bear fruit, the tree would be allowed to remain; if not, he would cut it down.'

"Jesus then added, 'When the branch is yet tender and puts forth her leaves, you know summer is nigh. So likewise, when you see all these things, know that it is at the door. That being the case, Nathaniel, *should this tree* have leaves on it?'

"'No, it should not, Master! The season for figs will not begin until summer, which is still months away and winter is long gone. For this tree to have leaves at this time of the year is most unnatural.'

"The fig Nathaniel was referring to is the 'Bikkurah' or 'early-ripe' figs which ripen after the festival of Shavuot in the month of Sivan: what we call June," explained Teryk addressing the assemble group. "The fruit drops off the tree as soon as it ripens. The regular harvest figs are called 'Kermus' or 'Summer-figs'. They ripen after the date harvest during the month of Elul: what we call August. But there is another fig—the Pag—also called the 'untimely fig' or 'winter fig'. These figs sometimes ripen in spots that have been sheltered from the elements. Untimely figs are a third ripening of the tree late in the season—hence the name 'winter figs'. Most scholars believe that it was the Pag fig Jesus was referring to, but this tree was open to the elements and as Nathaniel pointed out, winter was long gone.

"If I was experiencing a hallucination I should not know this information. And yet I do. This is why I believe this was no figment of my imagination," explained Teryk returning to his story.

"Turning to the rest of the disciples, Nathaniel went on to explain that, 'Figs always bear their fruit before they sprout their leaves—this tree has provided no fruit, and yet it is covered in leaves.'

"'So what then is the meaning of the parable?' asked Jesus.

"Peter, never at a loss for words, said, 'That we should bear fruit, for every tree that bears no fruit shall be cut down.'

"Jesus nodded and turned again to Nathaniel but asked the next question of all of the disciples. 'The symbol of the fig tree has always stood for something. What does the fig tree represent?'

"I don't think any one of them had ever heard that question before. I knew the answer because of my familiarity with scripture.

"'The fig tree represents Israel,' said Stephen. 'Its large leaves in full blossom represent a time of prosperity. While withered and dry leaves are a sign of decay.'

"Jesus nodded, letting the full understanding of the implication sink into our skulls. Turning toward the temple, he declared, 'Israel: for three years I have been coming here looking for a harvest but have found instead only bare branches covered in the leaves of prosperity. What do you think the Creator of All will do with such a tree as this in his garden?'

"'Cut it down,' said Symeon, the Zealot, echoing our thoughts. 'The axe is already laid to the root of the tree. Were these not the words of Johanan the Baptist?'

"Andrew, who was standing next to Symeon, did not seem to like where this was going.

"'And when the fig tree, the image of our nation and of this generation, has been cut down, it will lie dormant for a time. But before the end of this age, it shall put forth its leaves once more—when it does you will know that the coming of the Son of Man is near.'" Jesus said this while looking directly at me. I could not take his gaze for long and felt uncomfortable, so I turned and faced the temple. Jesus walked over to me and whispered, 'Guard carefully against drawing upon your knowledge. Some may view it as prophecy.'

"In a louder voice, he continued. 'Look down upon this temple and remember its beauty, for there will not be one stone left standing upon another. And the house I destroy, no one will be able to rebuild!' Turning abruptly toward the fig tree, he cursed it. 'You useless burden on the land! You take up space and are fair to look upon but you are a deceitful thing. You take up the air and water that fruitful trees should have. Return to the ground from which you came and become food for other trees.'

"Jesus then turned and descended toward Jerusalem. We followed, admiring the temple from our position on the Mount of Olives. I remembered that more than ten thousand laborers and masons were involved in its early stages of construction. The enormous blocks that supported the temple platform were handsomely dressed with flat, raised faces and sunken margins about half a foot wide. The outer wall blocks were massive, the height of two men, two paces deep and ten paces in length. The eastern wall rested on the edge of a cliff. The other walls continued underground a considerable distance to ensure that no army could tunnel under them—a common tactic in war. There was also an inexhaustible water supply provided by a spring that poured directly out of the mountain itself.

"During construction, the chief priests would not allow the master masons into the sacred inner courts, so Herod the Great had his mason craftsmen train nearly a thousand priests in the secret art of the *Tekt n*: stonemasonry. The great Temple of the Jews had been under construction for nearly fifty years. Thirty-nine years from now, soon after its completion, thirteen Roman legions under the command of Titus would destroy it. I thought it strange that the temple would not be finished for another generation, since it appeared almost complete when I walked through it.

"As Jesus descended toward the north gate, the disciples followed in a somber mood, not sure what to make of what Jesus had just told them and what it could mean for Jerusalem. I followed last. As we approached the road, I saw Symeon, the leper whom Jesus had healed. Symeon's son Lazarus was wearing his new belt. Symeon, the Pharisee, Jesus' father-in-law, had decided that he should make an offering for his son's miraculous return. He had selected a choice young red heifer and asked if I would accompany them to the temple, to make the required offering. Jesus and the other disciples would continue on ahead. I agreed, and accompanied them toward Jerusalem.

"Before entering the holy ground of the inner temple, we were required to immerse ourselves in a mikveh: a ritual bath intended to cleanse the spirit rather than our bodies. Mikvehs were located at each of the entrances, the largest being a massive Olympic-sized pool called the Pool of Israel, which could accommodate hundreds of pilgrims at a time. The Pool of Israel was meant especially for public use, to service the huge crowds during the festivals of Passover, Tabernacles and Weeks. We approached and washed our feet and hands in a shallow pool. Jews are affronted by public nudity, so it felt strange to strip down to our loincloths in front of so many people. As a priest, I had always used a smaller, more private mikveh. This pool had steps all around leading down into it and was much deeper than the other pools I was used to. The water was cold and free-running.

"Once purified, we took our place in one of several lines that had formed for sacrificial offerings. A temple chief priest, one of two hundred, hurried past us dressed all in blue with miniature golden bells hanging from the hems of his robe. The bells gave off a pleasant tinkling sound as he strode by barefoot; all priests went barefoot inside the Temple. Lazarus liked the sound and asked his father if he could wear bells on his clothes. More than five thousand priests needed to be present at the temple during the holidays. Most were Levites who wore close-fitting tunics of white linen and a simple linen cap of the same color.

"The normal contingency of priests, around seven thousand, was divided into twenty-four courses. Each of the individual courses served an entire week. The shift change took place on the Sabbath before the afternoon sacrifices. The courses were further divided into houses or families that served one day of the designated week. Each course served twice a year and lots were drawn for each of the assignments of the day. It could be years before a priest might get a chance to perform a sacrifice or burn incense at the altar, which is why Zachariah, the father of John the Baptist, had been ignoring the angel when he was selected by lottery to burn incense upon the altar.

"The money changers, who converted the unholy coinage into acceptable Jewish shekels, had once again set up their booths under the massive colonnaded portico that ran the length of the outer walls surrounding the court of Gentiles. Not a bad setup, I thought, and wondered if the money lenders thought the portico was built so that they could sit comfortably in the shade while servants fanned them. Temple police were ubiquitous and every money changer appeared to have obtained a personal bodyguard for protection; from Jesus, most likely. How was Jesus going to get away with overturning the tables this time, I wondered? He was still outside and would not enter for a little while longer. Luckily, we did not have to wait in the long lines of the money changers. I was the treasurer after all and kept some of my money-belt pouches reserved with shekels and half-shekels acceptable by the priests.

"We were now nearing the low stone walls that surrounded the inner courts. These were the same walls Jesus had stood upon a day earlier. I suffer from the bad habit of reading anything placed in front of me. So, out of boredom, I must have read the inscribed warnings at least a couple dozen times. As we got closer to the temple, we could hear Levite priests standing behind each of the low stone balustrades, issuing verbal warnings in different languages to all those who approached the temple, because most Gentiles of the time were illiterate. At this point we removed our shoes, for it was forbidden to enter the precincts wearing them. We climbed a low flight of steps that stretched around the temple precincts. We entered the Court of Women through the north gate, one of three gates that opened onto this court.

"The Sun had been beating down on us for over an hour and I was covered in sweat. Lazarus did not seem to mind it as much as I did. I wished I could plunge back into the mikveh. The atmosphere near the west wall of the Court of Women was stifling, the tall walls around us preventing any fresh air from blowing in. We climbed the fifteen curved steps of the magnificent Nicanor Gate. From here we would pass through the Court of Israelites, a relatively narrow strip of stone pavement. Once in the Court of Priests, we could see the altar. This temple was considered the dwelling place of God on Earth, and the only place on the planet where sacrifices could be made to Him. Jews could worship God in their numerous synagogues where they gathered for prayer but could only offer sacrifices in Jerusalem, unlike the many polytheistic religions of the day, in which Zeus could by worshipped at any number of temples throughout the land.

"A Levite asked for the offering. I handed the silver shekels to Lazarus, who passed them on to the Levite. Historians seem to believe that the only coin accepted by the temple priests was the Tyrian silver shekel. I found that this was not the case. The Tyrian coin bears a standing eagle on one side and the image of Hercules, a demigod, on the other. To a Jew, the eagle is the symbol of Rome and therefore unacceptable. But even if this were not the case, the image of Hercules's profile wearing a crown of leaves is considered a graven image and cannot be used as an offering.

"Because of its high silver content and the purity of its silver, the Tyrian coin was the only coin accepted by the money changers. Ten of these coins were required in exchange for one sacred shekel. The Levite counted the silver shekels and tossed them into one of thirteen temple treasury chests, each shaped like an enormous shofar trumpet. They stood about three feet and resembled cornucopias. They appeared to be made of cedar, most likely from the great cedars of Lebanon. Lazarus got a big kick out of listening to the coins cascading down the vortex into the temple treasury below.

"'Where are the coins going?' asked Lazarus.

"'The coins are most likely falling into the Shekel Chamber,' I replied, 'the largest of the chambers built into the inner forecourt of the temple. Half-shekels are also stored in that chamber.'

"'How many chambers are there?' asked Lazarus excitedly.

"'I'm not sure but one of the chambers is called the Chamber of Secrets.' Lazarus's eyes widened, so I continued. 'It's called that because money from it is supposed to be secretly handed out to the poor.' Although I could not see much evidence of that taking place, I was not about to burst his bubble. The mind of a child does not always understand the things grown-ups do. It's like telling children, if they find themselves lost or frightened, that men wearing police or fireman uniforms are there to help. Not many grown-ups take comfort from the actions of police officers nowadays.

"'Are there any other chambers, Judah?' he asked.

"'Well, there's the Chamber of Utensils, which is used to store all the solid gold bowls, incense burners, and other vessels used by the priests. And there are chambers for wealthy merchants to store their own private treasures for safekeeping.'

"'Abba, do you keep any of your silver here in these chambers?' Lazarus asked his father.

"Symeon nodded that he did and motioned to Lazarus that it was his turn to offer sacrifice. The priest took the reins of the red heifer which had already been examined and proclaimed worthy for sacrifice by other priests. The book of Numbers is very explicit: '*Speak unto the Children of Israel that they bring thee a red heifer without spot, wherein is no blemish, and upon which never came yoke...*' This particular sacrifice was performed to purify a person who had become ritually contaminated by contact with a corpse. In Lazarus's case, he was the corpse. The man waited while Lazarus placed one hand on the bull and tried to remember his rehearsed statement, announcing the reason for his sacrifice.

"Lazarus had to shout in order to be heard over the incessant chanting of prayers and singing of psalms by the Levites. 'I offer this bull as a sacrifice for my healing,' he bellowed.

"'What were you healed from?' asked the priest, wondering why the youth had given such a short announcement for such an impressive sacrifice. A pair of birds usually sufficed for most healings.

"'I was dead, I was a corpse—and now I live again,' said Lazarus.

"Just then I noticed the aura of the priest flashing bright red. He would put two and two together and realize this was the same Lazarus whom Jesus had raised from the dead just a few weeks ago. This was Jesus' third raising of a dead individual. The first was the daughter of Jairus, as told in the Gospels of Mark and Luke. The second was a widow's son in the town of Nain. The elderly priest, whose robes were covered in blood, stared at young Lazarus, then at his father and finally at me. The man did not move. I was glad the singers hadn't stopped singing as well. It seemed that a minute had passed, then he bowed to us and took the calf to the north side of the high stone altar.

"The high altar was an isolated structure decorated with horn-shaped projections at each of its four corners. Because it had never been touched by metal tools, the altar's unfinished stone stood out in contrast from the incredibly smooth walls of the temple. The young cow's throat was cut and its blood collected in a golden bowl; the blood was said to belong to God because it contained the essence of life. The priest poured blood on each of the four horns of the altar then stepped down to our level and splashed the remaining blood against the sides. Priests above were busy skinning the body. The hides of sacrificed animals were property of the priests. I wondered if the old man would be claiming this hide for himself, and I hoped we would. Then the flayed calf was placed on the altar as a burnt offering. The priests covered the small body with scarlet, hyssop, and cedar wood,

Joseph "Five Eagles" Reyna

then added this to the fire. The air was heavy with the odors of blood, incense and charred animal fat. We waited until the heifer was reduced to ashes, which the priests collected and placed in a vessel containing pure water. Then the old priest sprinkled water from the vessel upon Lazarus, using a tied bundle of hyssop.

"Our sacrifice having been accepted, we left the Temple then put on our shoes and moved toward the north gate, where we saw Jesus standing. His eyes were closed and he was untying the cord around his waist. I looked at the money changers. All commerce had come to a stop and some of the pilgrims were moving away from the merchants' stalls. Some of the merchants were already making tracks but others held their ground, insisting that they had a legal right to be there. Jesus tossed the folded cord over his shoulder and approached the first bodyguard. We must still have been inside the temple when he warned them to leave. Jesus said nothing as he walked toward the man now holding his arms up to defend himself, and his obese master. Jesus moved closer. The guard, goaded by his portly master, rushed at Jesus and was thrown backward by an unseen force that seemed to charge the surrounding air. The man flew straight back, taking with him the merchant, table and stalls. Pandemonium erupted as all the merchants of the chief priests began running for their miserable lives.

"I had once seen a video tape of something similar. A martial arts Master sat on the floor and commanded the men around him to attack. The Master never moved, but all who jumped him were repelled by an unseen force. The Master explained that the men were, in fact, warded off by the exact amount of force they had displayed toward him.

"Jesus then took the cords from his shoulder and began driving out the livestock, which seemed to exhibit more common sense than their owners: All they required was his opening of their stalls and pens. The entire process took less than an hour and I wondered if any of the merchants would be back inside the temple tomorrow.

"After this, Jesus gave his most important and prophetic speech: his teachings from the Mount of Olives. But it would take me days to explain the meaning behind those.

"The next morning, Tuesday, Jesus again diverted us from the road to Jerusalem, taking us over the Mount of Olives through Gethsemane. We came upon the fig tree that had stood there covered in leaves the previous day. We found it withered and as dry as a matchstick. Some argued that perhaps it was not the same tree but Nathaniel pointed out the dried leaves scattered all over the ground.

"Peter, the Rock, as usual stated the obvious. 'Lord, the tree you spoke to is all dried up!'

"'So shall it be for all those whom God calls to give account: Their empty words will wither like leaves before the flames of truth. I came to Israel looking for 'fruit' and found none. When the fig tree once more sheds her leaves, look to my coming.' The disciples were visibly concerned. They had witnessed Jesus raise the dead with a word, but for some reason it had not occurred to them that Jesus could probably kill with a word. This new knowledge disturbed them. What I found disturbing was that he had looked directly at me when he said, '...*look to my coming*.' 'Why do you marvel?' he continued. 'You could say to a mountain *depart* and it would crumble, if you had but the faith of a mustard seed. You could command the wind and the waves and they would obey. Nothing would be impossible for you!'

"As we walked toward the temple, Jesus ordered Peter, James and John to go on ahead and prepare the place where we would celebrate the Passover. He took them aside and gave them special instructions. The three headed south toward the fountain gate and the rest of us headed toward the temple's north entrance. Upon entering, Jesus was confronted by a faction of priests.

"Caiaphas stepped forward pointing at the empty stalls and overturned tables of the merchants, and demanded of Jesus, 'Who gave you the authority to do this?'

"'Answer me what I ask, and I will answer you by what authority I have done this.' Jesus walked amongst the congregation of priests and asked, 'Was Johanan the Baptizer a prophet of God, or was he a bold, seditious man?'

"Caiaphas seemed stumped by this questioned. He turned to the other priests, most of whom were chief priests or elderly scribes, for assistance. When they had finished arguing the question amongst themselves, Caiaphas turned and said, 'I cannot tell you. We do not know.'

Addressing those at the Round Table, Teryk explained. "The reason John could not be proclaimed a prophet was that a prophecy had proclaimed Elijah must come first, before the anointed King of Israel, to prepare the way. I know this is going to be difficult for some of you to accept, because it touches on a form of reincarnation that Jesus referred to as 'continuing life'. Should you choose to believe that John the Baptist could not possibly have been Elijah returned to Earth in the flesh, then by that reasoning you must also accept that Jesus could not possibly have been the Messiah. Consider the logic of church dogma; you were nothing before your mother gave birth to you. Then suddenly, you are an immortal soul in danger of eternal damnation." Teryk stifled a laugh and explained that when Jesus had broached this topic, an old man in the crowd complained that he did not believe in such nonsense, to which his grandchild replied, '*Yeah grandpa, when I was your age...I didn't think I'd be coming back either.*'

Most at the Round Table found this amusing, Marileyna did not. "You're talking about reincarnation, aren't you?"

"This is something I've observed Christians rebel against. You flat-out refuse to believe the red lettering in your own *Bible*, Marileyna!" exclaimed Teryk. "A very important and well-known prophecy concerning the expected Messiah was that Elijah had been prophesied to reappear on earth before the Anointed King of God. Malachi says, '*Look, I will send you Elijah the prophet before the great and awesome day of the LORD arrives.*' You see, if Elijah did not return to Earth physically, then Jesus could not be the Messiah.

"When the priests asked Jesus by what authority he had thrown out the merchants and money changers, he answered their question with a question," continued Teryk. "He knew that the priests would never proclaim John the Baptist a prophet, because of the prophecy that Elijah must come first: to prepare the way. If you recall, even Herod-Antipas asked Jesus if he was John the Baptist come back to life, or perhaps one of the prophets of old, maybe even Elijah. When Jesus asked his own disciples, '*who do people say that I am,*' they always said the same thing. Some say you are John the Baptist, others Elijah, and others say you are Jeremiah or that one of the prophets of long ago has risen. It must be remembered that Jesus never admonished anyone for stating that he had lived a previous life.

"Jesus' disciples questioned him regarding Elijah's return, and why he had not come first! Jesus explained to them that Elijah had indeed already come and not been recognized. In your Red Letter Edition Bibles, Jesus makes it quite clear, in no uncertain terms, that John the Baptist was Elijah.

"What transpired between Jesus and his disciples is recorded in Matthew 11:10-15," said Teryk picking up the nearest iPad and searching for the passage in the Gospel. '*...For John is the man mentioned in the Scriptures—a messenger to precede me, to announce my coming, and prepare people to receive me...and if you are willing to understand what I mean, he is Elijah, the one the prophets said would come. If ever you are willing to listen, listen now!*'"

"But in John 1:21, John the Baptist denies that he is Elijah!" protested Marileyna holding up her own iPad. "How could John the Baptist have literally been Elijah? The physical form of Elijah had been buried for eight hundred years."

"Because the immortal *Spirit of Elijah* was not the body of Elijah, just as it was not the body of this new incarnation that went by the name John the Baptizer "In the first chapter of Luke, Gabriel informs Zecharia, the father of John, that, '*He* [John] *will be imbued with the spirit and power of Elijah, the prophet of old; and he will precede the coming of the Messiah* [Y'shua/Jesus], *preparing the people for his arrival...*'" explained Teryk, setting down the iPad. "This is what is meant by Continuing Life!

"When Hollywood portrays John the Baptist, he is always wearing some raggedy potato-sack-looking garment," continued Teryk. "But John dressed like Jesus in Essene white. His mantle or prayer shawl was made of camel hair and is known as a tallit. There is no word for tallit, a prayer cloth, in Greek, which is why it appears translated in so many different forms: mantel, vestment, tent, garment, sheet, cloak, raiment, and napkin. The tallit had two purplish-blue stripes running lengthwise; the Israeli flag is fashioned after it.

"Each of the four letters of the ineffable name of God were embroidered, one into each corner of this prayer cloth. In addition a short tassel hung from each of the four corners. These were referred to as tzit tzit, pronounced zeet zeet. Each letter of the Hebrew alphabet represents a number. The tzit tzit were tied in knots that represented these numbers. All four tassels spelling YHVH held together added up to the number six hundred and thirteen: the number of Mosaic laws."

"The camel-hair tallit worn by John had originally belonged to Elijah the prophet. Elijah was not buried with it because he did not die. He had tossed his tallit down to Elisha from the chariot when he was taken up to Heaven in a whirlwind. Unlike Elijah, however, Elisha did not name a successor, and so Elijah's tallit was folded and placed on the right side of the Altar of Incense."

"The tallit, or prayer shawl, is considered a personal item and is buried with its owner upon his death," confirmed Kortney. "Elisha already had a tallit that served this purpose, so Elijah's tallit was not buried with him. Elijah's tallit and the belt of leather with which Elisha girded his loins were folded and placed to the right side of the Altar of Incense, where they remained because no one had been named to carry on in his place. Both were over eight hundred years old."

"When the archangel Gabriel appeared to Zecharia, he was standing on the right side of the Altar of Incense," said Teryk. "Gabriel informed Zecharia that his son would have need of the tallit and the girdle, and handed them to Zecharia, who feared to take them but feared the angel even more. I realize that this is in stark contrast to the concept of being born in sin only once and suffering until you died, only to be judged by a vengeful god. That belief took root on a flat Earth within the Catholic church during the Dark Ages."

"Another problem, and this is a major one, is that Christians are not aware that the Israelites were expecting two Messiahs, not one," argued Kortney. "One Messiah would be born from the tribe of Aaron. He was to come in the spirit of Elijah and preside over the Sanhedrin. They believed that their second Messiah, Israel's Anointed King, would destroy all nations opposed to Israel, thereby delivering his people from oppression. This Messiah would be born from the line of David. He was to be the greatest king God would ever give his people.

"The Jews expected both Messiahs to be normal men imbued with the power of God. The concept of demigods like Hercules has no place in Jewish theology," explained Kortney. "Nothing in scripture claims the Messiah would be a divine part-god/part-man, only that he would be the instrument of God. Many men claimed that they were the Messiah long before Jesus was born. Others claimed the title long after he was crucified. Some were even accepted as the Messiah."

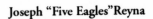
Joseph "Five Eagles"Reyna

"I find it interesting," observed Athena, "that one Messiah would have been born of an elderly woman beyond the years of childbirth, while the other would have been born of a very young woman."

"That is an interesting observation Athena," acknowledged Teryk continuing his story. "If the priests proclaimed the Baptizer a Prophet, it stood to reason that the Anointed King must be alive as well. Jesus answered them, 'Then I cannot tell you by whose authority I drove robbers and thieves from the house of the Most Holy.' Jesus then told them a parable we had never heard before, about the king who had made a feast in honor of his son's marriage. The king invited all the wealthy and honored men of the kingdom—but it went right over their heads. Some priests appeared offended but I believe it was because they did not grasp the parable's significance or how it could possibly relate to them.

"Jesus then walked past them climbing upon the short stone walls, and began to speak to the multitude. Soon after this, the scribes tried to incriminate Jesus with wordplay. They must have spent most of the previous night trying to come up with their questions. As always, Jesus turned the questions back upon them, answering each question with a question: a game he had played with us many times. Mary Magdalene always seemed to win at that game. Knowing this about her, I would practice this game and never once got the upper hand. She explained to me that men were just not capable of thinking as fast as women. On that subject I would have to agree with her.

"At this point, a colorfully robed Herodian with greased locks of hair said, 'Teacher, you are a man of truth, honesty and straightforward talking. You show the way to the Most High. You are not influenced by any man or his station in life. Tell us, what do you think? Should we, the Sons of Abraham, pay tribute unto Cæsar?' It was well he had addressed himself as a son of Abraham, for he was no Israelite. Gesturing to those about him, he waved a hand laden with heavy gold rings on every finger. 'Or should we not pay tribute to the emperor?' The question was diabolical: Israel hated that particular tax. It was an affront to them and flew in the face of a law against numbering the people, as they claimed Egyptians once had. The emperor's tax was taken every year and adjusted every fourteen years by a Roman census.

"How these men with all that body piercing considered themselves to be strict observers of the law was beyond me. Then someone tapped me on the shoulder. I turned around to see Veronica, one of women who traveled with us. She was with Lazarus and each was holding a lamb. The look on my face must have made my thoughts obvious. Veronica explained that I needed to accompany them for the sacrifice of the lamb, in preparation for tonight's Passover feast. I nodded and followed them, not sure where I was going. As we left, Jesus was calling for someone in the audience to show him the tribute of which this man spoke. I looked back and saw Jesus pointing to someone who was holding up a large silver coin in his hand, high above the crowd.

"We made our way through the wreckage in the colonnades and around the massive turret at Fortress Antonia's southwest corner. From this turret, which was larger and taller than the other three, Roman soldiers had an unprecedented view of the inner temple. This tower was said to be seventy cubits high, about thirty-five meters, a full twenty cubits taller than the other three. To me, the tower appeared to stand nearly ten stories high. The Fortress Antonia was situated half inside the temple walls and half outside.

"As we made our way around the Temple, I noticed additional Roman troops pouring out of Antonia. During festivals, legionnaires took up armed positions atop the porticoes, in order to discourage any insurrectionary actions and suppress them if necessary. The soldiers already positioned on the colonnades were archers. These additional troops were carrying short spears, or javelins. And although we could not see them, there were additional stockpiles of these short spears all along the length of the colonnades, a distance of about a mile.

"Fear was evident on the faces of those around us. I suggested we move under the temple colonnades at the western side. On the other side of the Temple, just outside the short stone walls, I saw what looked to be about forty-five to fifty small stone altars covered in blood. This was probably why Jesus had chosen the other side of the temple this day.

"I would like to point out that the Third Temple was not positioned directly in the center of Temple Mount, where the Dome of the Rock is today. It was positioned closer to the fortress. Because the priests did not trust Herod the Great, they had refused to allow him to destroy the second temple until work was completed on the new one. For this reason, Herod had been forced to construct the new temple between the existing one and the Fortress Antonia. This allowed for a massive staging area in preparation for the sacrificing of thousands of lambs that would be required for Passover. The Court of Gentiles was packed with people waiting in line to sacrifice their lambs. Just inside the short stone walls, priests were skinning dead lambs while men and women stood by, ready to receive the skinned animals. The hides, property of the priests, were piled in great heaps. I was glad that the money gained from the sale of these hides did not make its way into Annas's pockets. By tradition, the funds from the sale of these pelts were reserved for the priests' families. Some of the robes worn by the priests still shone white, though by the end of the day they would all be covered in blood.

"We walked all the way to the end of the lines near the southern entrance at the Royal Portico. I had always found this ceremony distasteful, more so on this day. I took my place in line with Lazarus. Veronica went to stand in a line with

Asinuway and Sofira, each of whom was holding a lamb. It had not occurred to me that one lamb simply would not suffice for our group.

"The bleating of so many animals about to be put to the knife tried my nerves. I wondered why Veronica insisted that I accompany them. I personally felt Peter would have been a better choice. Looking down, I beheld the wonder and excitement on Lazarus's face and thought I knew why. According to strict tradition, it fell upon the head of the household to sacrifice the lamb. I had never witnessed the carnage. After the death of Judah's father, that right transferred to Judah, but by then Annas had commercialized the Passover sacrifices. Judah had sent one of the servants to the temple to have the lamb sacrificed by Levite priests. The Amharetzin and others who celebrated Passover this night elected to perform the sacrifices at their homes.

"I must admit this seemed to be a well-run operation. The line was moving at a decent pace. As we neared the altar, a priest was inspecting the lambs for blemishes. Normally, if your lamb failed inspection you could purchase a 'pre-certified sacrificial lamb' from the merchants, but Jesus had driven them out. Lazarus hefted up the lamb for the priest to inspect. The Passover lamb wasn't just any ordinary lamb picked out from a local neighborhood shepherd's flock. It had to be spotless. Lazarus had personally selected it four days earlier and had kept it separated from the rest of the herd, as was required. The Levite lifted the animal to look for blemishes. I suppose the priests had to go through the motions in order to justify their existence.

"Lazarus was certain he had selected a perfect lamb but showed concern when the priest lingered at a spot under the creature's right foreleg. Squinting his eyes, the priest scratched at the spot. Lazarus strained to see for himself but he was too short. The priest showed the animal to me and I saw what could have been a mud stain. I was not about to argue or try to find another lamb, so I pulled out a Shekel and asked the priest if he thought that he might be able to scratch off the dirt. He took the coin and scratched at the area, frowned, then nodded his approval. I thanked him and handed the lamb back to Lazarus. I had taken to calling him 'little man' because he always wanted to be helpful and acted so grown up. Lazarus heaved the lamb onto the Sacrificial Altar.

"The priests did not actually kill the lamb; that honor fell to me. Removing my curved dagger, I slit the small animal's throat. Wasting no time, the priest drained its blood into a golden bowl. He took the blood and poured it upon the altar, adding to the river of blood that flowed from the temple. Another priest took the lamb and proceeded to skin it while Lazarus opened a sack into which its skinned carcass would be placed.

"Veronica called to us and reminded me that I had to slit the throats of their lambs as well, hence the reason I was brought there. As we left the temple, the women took the viaduct: a sort of expressway to the upper city. When I asked about their choice of direction, they informed me that Jesus had made arrangements for the Passover feast to be held at the home of his uncle Yehosef ha Ramati: Joseph of Arimathaea. The appendage to his name meant *of the highlands*. Joseph of Arimathaea imported tin and lead from Gaul, an island past the Pillars of Hercules, far to the north. We refer to that land today as England and Scotland. Mary's mother, Anna, and Elizabeth, the mother of the Baptist, were both from England. Joseph of Arimathaea was also well known by the title 'Nobilis de Curio' because he was Rome's largest provider of tin.

"I kept wondering why the days were off. This was supposed to be taking place on Thursday, but for some reason the Passover was taking place on the third evening of the week, a Tuesday. Busy as the temple was that day, it would be busier the following day, when the Sadducees would outnumber the Pharisees nearly two to one. Sadducees hold that the 'High Sabbath' does not begin on the evening of the full moon. For them, the High Sabbath would not begin until dawn the next day. And the Passover feast would be celebrated at dusk on Wednesday.

"Lazarus wanted to carry the carcass all the way back. I could see he was growing tired and offered to carry it for him. But he declined my aid, shaking his little head while struggling with the burden. Somehow I sensed he wanted to walk up the hill carrying it for all to see. I assured him that when I got tired of carrying it I would give it back to him. This appealed to his sense of pride and he handed it to me. Before taking it, I withdrew some copper pieces and handed them to him, asking if he could find a vendor selling refreshments. He quickly found one and we enjoyed a lemonade-tasting drink before continuing on.

"As we neared the wealthier quarter, I remarked that this little lamb was much heavier than it appeared. Lazarus agreed and asked if he could carry it the rest of the way in. When we arrived, Mary Magdalene asked what had taken so long, as there was still a lot to do to the lamb's special preparation for roasting at sunset. She was referring to the special Jewish laws that prescribe the manner in which the sacrificial lamb is to be hung above the roasting flames.

"After I had washed up, I was glad to learn that the servants had brought the new clothes for the disciples to Joseph's palace. I changed into my new traveling clothes and on my way to find the other disciples, ended up in the kitchen. I watched in astonishment as a servant pushed a sharpened pomegranate skewer through the flesh of the lamb's front legs, so that the limbs where outstretched. Taking a second pomegranate skewer she ran it through the lamb's torso. The lamb, skinned as it was, and hanging from the two large skewers appeared so much like a modern crucifix that I hesitated to pass. I stood there transfixed.

"'What is the matter, Judah?' she asked.

"What could I say to her? Shaking my head, I said I was lost and could not find the other disciples. She asked that I follow her outside to where Peter was stirring the fire. James and John, dressed in their new traveling clothes, talked excitedly about all that had taken place in the previous few days. I sat in the shade and noticed that the soil was tinged with shades of magenta, rose and rust, probably due to the soil's rich iron content, but I suppose it could have been due to the blood that constantly washed over that tortured land." Teryk sat down staring into nothing.

"Wow, have you been able to verify any of these customs and rituals?" asked Anakah.

It was Kortney who answered, "Teryk's information appears to be more detailed and precise than my understanding of those events. My main argument focused on the design of the Fortress Antonia. All models of it, that I've ever seen, represent the fortress as a rectangular structure existing outside the temple walls. Imagine my surprise when I pulled up this article in Biblical Archaeology Review," he said holding up his iPad for those around him to see. "A recent archaeological discovery shows that the foundations of the fortress were perfectly square and well within the walls of the temple."

The Scapegoat and the Sacrificial Lamb

"Passover was the oldest of the Covenant rituals, instituted before any of the other Jewish feasts," Teryk began. "The Passover preceded the giving of the Law and was older than the priesthood. It was this, the worship of God before the institution of temple worship that Jesus referred to when he spoke of the old wine: 'for everyone will agree that vintage wine is better than new wine.' Stephen reiterated this concept shortly before his death, when he proclaimed that 'the most high does not live in houses made by human hands'.

"The first day of the month of Nisan, in the Jewish calendar, was aligned to the new moon. Passover, the first holiday, was celebrated on the fourteenth of Nisan, during a full moon closest to the time of the spring equinox. That year the Passover occurred on a Wednesday, not on Good Friday as the Church maintains. To complicate things further, the Pharisees as well as Jews from Galilee and the northern provinces counted their days from sunset to sunset. To these factions of Judaism, the day began at dusk, not at dawn. According to the laws of Moses, Tuesday's twilight was actually considered the dawning of the fourteenth of Nisan. For this reason, the Herodians, the Amharetzins, the Samaritans, the Idumaeans, the Nazirites, and the Essenes all celebrated Passover on that evening. Most of these sects did not believe in paying temple priests to perform the animal sacrifice, and were excluded from the temple as a result. The Sadducees would celebrate their Passover one day later, on Wednesday evening at twilight: the night of the actual full moon, which means that after they crucified Jesus they still had plenty of time to go home and celebrate. Passover was followed immediately by the week-long feast of Unleavened Bread, making the entire period of feasting eight days long."

"Jesus arrived at the house of Joseph of Arimathaea and informed me that a courier was waiting for me in the street. After the courier left, I remained in the street, unsure what to do. Jesus came out to see what was wrong. 'I'll ignore the Sanhedrin's summons,' I told him. 'What will they do, arrest me? I know what's about to happen and that would be the least of my worries.'

"'Judah, who else could the Sanhedrin possibly use?' asked Jesus. 'The others are fishermen and commoners from Galilee. You, being a scribe, have spent most of your life in and around the temple. Matthew cannot act as a witness. He is well known but he was a tax collector, a *mokhes*: one who sits in a booth, lowest of the tax collectors. Having been a tax collector, he is not even allowed to witness the proceedings. Trust me, you're the only one who can do this.'

"Just then the seven silver trumpets sounded from the temple, signaling sundown. The first three stars must have just become visible in the evening sky. As was the custom, Passover Seder would commence soon. I'm not sure what part of the upper city we were in but Herod's Palace was beautifully silhouetted against a sky of turquoise with thin burnished bronze clouds in the distance.

"When we entered the room, Peter, James and his brother John had already secured the honored seats and this had caused a commotion among the disciples. As much as I felt honored to have a seat anywhere at that table, I was dreading the moment when Jesus would announce his betrayer in front of everyone…"

"But you maintain that Judas never betrayed Christ," interrupted Jidion.

"Yes, I do, but at that moment, suspended in the deprivation tank, I was going from memory. I was basing my assumption on the story as it is laid out in the Gospels," explained Teryk.

"Jesus began by saying, 'I have greatly desired to eat this feast with you,' and looking around the table at the three already seated in the seats of honor, He said, 'I no longer call you my disciples but my friends.' This seemed to lessen the tension in the room.

"There was a well-established sequence for the Passover Seder and Jesus knew it well. Seder is perhaps not the best word for it, since that implies it was held at home on the first night of Passover and possibly the second night as well: the night that begins the feast of Unleavened Bread. Jesus' family had made a custom of celebrating the feast in Jerusalem after their return from Egypt. Technically we were all homeless, so I guess it doesn't really matter what it was called.

"Passover was a week-long festival of liberation. It commemorated the wonders wrought by God in Egypt, and looked forward to the liberation of Israel by the Messiah. The chief symbol of the feast was the spotless lamb roasted whole and offered on behalf of each household. In Egypt, the blood of the lamb had been smeared upon the outer door post and lintel of the Israelite dwellings so that the Angel of Death would *pass over* the firstborn of Israel.

"A total of four cups of wine would be passed around during the meal. From right to left, each person would take a sip from the common cup and pass it on to the next person. The wine signified the blood sacrifice of the lambs in the Israelites' quest for freedom. It had never occurred to me to ask the Nazirites or the Essenes how they celebrated Passover, given that they never drank wine. After the initial cup was passed we performed a ceremonial washing to symbolize the need for moral and spiritual cleansing.

"Jesus then rose from the table, set aside his outer garments, and sat down away from the rest of us. A servant brought in a basin, set it on the floor next to Jesus and washed his feet. Jesus called for us to line up in order to have our feet washed. When the servant was done, Jesus knelt down with the seat in front of him and motioned for Philip to sit. When Jesus began to wash Philip's feet, the disciple looked disturbed, as did the servant. Peter refused to have his feet washed by Jesus, and remained at the table guarding his chosen spot. Jesus admonished Peter, reminding him that the ocean was the king of rivers because it does not set itself above them. Peter relented, cut in line, and immediately returned to his place at the table.

"The table was huge and raised no more than a foot from the floor. Its shape was a perfect square, nothing like Leonardo's painting of the Last Biscuit. No one was seated, because there were no seats. I was last and while Jesus was washing my feet the disciples were striving to select the highest positions that remained. They were lying down on straw mats around the table, their feet extended outward. They could use only their right hands to drink or dip bread, as each left arm rested on a cushion and was used to support the weight of the upper body. As Jesus finished drying my feet, I rose and chose a position among the disciples as far as possible from Jesus. I recall a preacher once saying that Jesus tossed a piece of bread onto the table toward the betrayer and everyone next to it asked, 'Is it I, Lord?' I was not going to make it easy for him to toss that dipped piece of bread at me, nor was I looking forward to it.

"Jesus finished drying his hands and said, 'Judah, comrade, please sit next to me.' He walked to the opposite side of the table from me and extended his left arm as an invitation for me to take the place at his left side. James-bar-Zebedee was seated there and I did not wish to embarrass him. James did not rise, only blushed and scooted over, then the other disciples followed suit. I took my place next to them, lying on the floor to Jesus' left. Simon Peter was at the right corner of the table, next to John, who was on Jesus' right. Lazarus entered the room and squeezed in front of Jesus, who was sitting cross-legged. Being so small, Lazarus simply sat down and reclined back against Jesus, as he observed the proceedings.

"'We are all invited guests at this feast,' Jesus reminded us. 'Learn from the lesson of this hour. When you are invited to a feast, do not always head for the best seats at the table. The host may ask you to let someone else sit there,' he said placing his hand on my shoulder, 'and you may not help but be embarrassed. Then you will have to take whatever seat is left. Instead, sit at the lower seats of the table until the host has everyone where he wills. And when the host sees you he will say, 'Friend, I have a better place for you.' In this way you will be honored in front of all those who are present, for it is a principle of life that anyone who tries to exalt and honor himself shall be humbled, while he who humbles himself shall be honored.'

"Besides the sacrificial lamb, the meal consisted of bitter herbs, symbolizing humiliation. The herbs were intended to evoke the harsh conditions of bondage in Egypt. They consisted of mostly leafy green herbs like parsley. The herbs were eaten with unleavened bread dipped in a sauce-like concoction called charoseth: a chutney made of apples, pomegranates, dates, figs, raisins and vinegar. To remind them of the brick-making, I suppose, for the stuff certainly resembled mortar.

"When the second cup of wine was passed, the head of the household—in our case, Jesus—was supposed to explain the meaning of Passover. The youngest child, Lazarus in this case, was to ask four prearranged questions which would be answered by narrative from the Exodus.

"This second cup was accompanied by the singing of songs from the Hallel, meaning praise, and consisted of six songs from the Psalms. Hallelujah is derived from the word *hallel* to praise, and *luyah*, meaning Jehovah.

"My mind was troubled and I did not pay much attention to the first Psalm. The second song began, '*When Israel came out of Egypt, the house of Jacob from a people of foreign tongue, Judah became God's sanctuary, Israel his dominion.*' I thought how strange the translation sounded, because in Hebrew it was a beautiful song.

"After this, the roasted lamb was served and Jesus washed his hands ceremoniously. He took the unleavened bread, tore off pieces and distributed them to the disciples around the table.

"When the lamb was finished we moved on to the next part of the ritual, which was passing the third cup of wine, known as 'the cup of blessing'. Jesus lifted a new piece of unleavened bread. He declared, 'This is my body.' He was referring to himself as the true bread of life, something he had tried to teach us earlier. As I recall, it did not go over very well. Fully one third of his followers refused to follow him any further. That was the first third that deserted him. Another third would abandon him later. Jesus continued, 'As this broken bread was once scattered upon the mountains and has been brought together to become one loaf, so you will gather the lost sheep together from the ends of the Earth into my kingdom and make them One. I must fall and die like the kernel of wheat, the single seed that fell to earth and was buried in order to bring forth the harvest that made this bread possible. So, too, must I die in order that others may have life and have it abundantly.'

"Lifting the cup, he said, 'This signifies the New Covenant with my blood, which shall be poured out for many.' Important covenants were always ratified by the shedding of sacrificial blood. Now he would gnow if his disciples were totally committed or not. To the Jewish mind, there is no practice more repugnant than the drinking of blood. The ceremonial laws written in their scripture strictly forbid it."

Joseph "Five Eagles" Reyna

All the King's Men

"**A** verse in Psalm 116 jolted my awareness back to my predicament: 'The cords of death entangled me, the anguish of the grave came upon me; I was overcome by trouble and sorrow.' I wasn't thinking of Jesus just then; those words seemed meant for me, and more specifically the cord that would soon be entangled around my neck. Am I not also going to die shortly after he does? And by my own hand, no less, like a faithful knight falling on his sword after his king is slain? Most won't see it that way, I suppose.

"Jesus lifted the fourth cup and pronounced that this would be the last cup he would drink with us until he drank it anew in the Father's Kingdom. At this, everyone spoke excitedly. Surely the wait was over and the time for action was now. Symeon, trying to suppress a smile, locked eyes with me while gripping the handle of the sword under his cloak. He knew as well as I how roused up the Zealots were. This was the moment they had been waiting for. To a man, every one of the disciples missed the implication Jesus was trying to convey to them.

"'I no longer consider you my disciples, but my friends,' Jesus repeated, 'because I tell you all things and keep nothing from you. Love one another as I have loved you, and carry my message of everlasting life to the far corners of the world. You shall be hated and persecuted by all nations. Men shall separate you from their company and reproach you, saying all manner of evil against you. For if the world hates you, know that it hated me first, and a servant cannot be greater than his master. There are only three things I can promise you: you will be entirely fearless, you will be deliriously happy, and you will always be in trouble.'

"As his words sank in I looked around the group, recalling how the Apocrypha recorded their deaths, although most of the accounts were thought to be only legends. Levi called Matthew will be brutally murdered while celebrating the Lord's Supper in Ethiopia. James, the son of thunder, will be beheaded by Herod-Agrippa. James the lesser is thrown from the top of the temple in Jerusalem, but this does not kill him, so he is stoned to death. Symeon the Zealot dies in Persia, where he is cut to pieces. Thaddaeus also dies in Persia, slain with a battle-axe. Philip is crucified in Turkey and his friend Nathaniel-bar-Tholomew flayed—skinned alive—in Armenia, a mountainous region southeast of the Black Sea. Andrew is also crucified but not on a regular crucifix: His is an X-shaped cross. It is said he took four days to die. Like Jesus, he did not curse his executioners. While on the cross, he encouraged his fellow Christians to have faith in Jesus. As I understand it, the crime for which he is crucified has to do with having converted the wife of a Greek official to Christianity. Cephas, his brother, better known as Peter, dies crucified upside down in Rome, but the evidence for this story is sketchy at best. Like Paul, Peter is said to have died during the first persecutions by the Emperor Nero. The New Testament does not say how Peter or, for that matter, Paul died. I was certain Paul's death was recorded in Acts but strangely enough it's not: The account ends with Paul still imprisoned.

"John, the youngest, is the only one of us that died of old age. He lived to about a hundred and died of natural causes in Ephesus, Turkey. I don't think anyone would believe that Jeziel called Stephen was one of the inner Twelve, since he is not mentioned in any of the Gospels. My nickname, Thomas, has taken his place. I have a sinking suspicion that he is the Stephen for whose death Saul of Tarsus is directly responsible. I believe they are one and the same. If so, then John Mark, Matthew and Lucanus, better known as Luke, would have had good reason for removing any trace of Stephen from the Synoptic Gospels. All three appear to have been followers of Saul of Tarsus: a man better known as the apostle Paul.

"Interestingly enough, Thomas died in India, tortured by red-hot plates while pierced by the spears of four soldiers. Being the lookalike, I have no idea why they record Judas as having died that way, because I'm supposed to hang myself. The singing of Psalm 117 brought me back to the moment. The psalm was short: only two verses. It began and ended with 'Praise the Lord.'"

Teryk reached forward, grabbed an appetizer from a tray in front of him and reclined back. He was silent for a brief moment then asked, "Shakira, have the researchers discovered anything concerning the Last Supper having occurred earlier in the week? And I would also be interested to know what if anything has been uncovered concerning Judas' betrayal."

Shakira nodded, stood and addressed the group, "Has anyone uncovered any evidence that would strengthen Teryk's story?"

"The Didascalia, a series of texts known today as the Apostolic Constitutions, chronicles the Last Supper as having occurred on a Tuesday," said Raven. "These texts represented the official third century Church teachings of high days observed by the early Church as well as outlines for Christian living. There is no mention of Good Friday in the Didascalia. In his 1958 work, *The Chronology of Passion Week*, James Walther stated that 'References in the Didascalia…support the Tuesday [night] Passover dating and the subsequent arrest of Jesus in the morning hours of Wednesday.'"

Shuffling through her notes, Anakah added, "Herman Hoeh, in his booklet *The Crucifixion Was Not on Friday*, states that 'numerous Catholic writers for centuries maintained that Jesus ate the Passover Tuesday night.'"

"There was not one day of observance but two, so in a sense there were two Passovers in Judaism," explained Phoenix. "*Unger's Bible Dictionary* states, 'Observances connected with the Passover are in two categories, those established at the keeping of the first Passover and those enacted after the Exodus....' According to Teryk, Jesus kept to the original Passover services of Moses as described in Exodus 12. To complicate things still further, the fifteenth of Nisan, the 'First Day of Unleavened Bread', is also called the 'Holy High Sabbath'."

"I'm not sure I understand," said Trisha shifting in her chair.

"The Passover occurs on the fourteenth of Nisan. This is followed by the Holy High Sabbath on the fifteenth of Nisan," explained Kortney. "It's called the High Sabbath regardless of what day of the week if falls on. Because the High Sabbath occurred immediately after, the crucifixion historians, unfamiliar with Jewish customs, assumed that this Sabbath day was Saturday."

"Does anyone have anything to add on the subject of the Last Supper possibly having occurred on a Tuesday night as opposed to a Thursday night?" asked Shakira. "If not, let us move on to Judas's betrayal of Jesus, which Teryk assures us never took place."

"The story of Judas as it is presented in the Gospels makes no sense," claimed Adriana. "Some scholars believe Judas never existed and is there only to fill in perplexing gaps in an attempt to answer the questions of how an innocent man came to be arrested and crucified in the first place."

"The Greek expression *paredidoto*—betrayed—is not in the oldest Gospels," said Raven, "the literal term *traitor* is found only once, in Luke 6:16 at the end of the list of disciples. I would like to point out that in Luke's Gospel, a second Judas has been added to the list of the Twelve. He is referred to as the brother of James. The author then has to clarify that it was Judas Iscariot who became a traitor."

"In the earliest Gospels Jesus uses the word *paradidomi*," explained Kortney. "The word means *to hand over*. The word *paradidomi* is also used by Paul in 1st Corinthians 11:23, '...on the night in which he was *handed over...*' Aside from this one statement, Paul does not even seem to be aware of the role Judas played in bringing about the betrayal and death of Jesus."

"Nowhere does the word paradidomi have the negative connotation of betrayal attributed to Judas," said Cassandra. "William Klassen's work, *Judas: Betrayer or Friend of Jesus,* points out that not a single ancient Greek manuscript carries the undertone of treachery or betrayal. Betray is not the word used in the oldest and best copies. But look up the word paradidomi in any modern lexicon and it will suggest otherwise."

"It would seem we have established that the etymology of the original neutral Greek word paradidomi is to *give over*," summarized Phoenix. "Although the concept of a betrayal is very suggestive, the notion that Judas was a traitor seems to rest on a very shaky foundation."

"What about the prophecy that goes something like 'but it was you… my acquaintance, we took sweet counsel together?'" asked Trisha.

"You speak of Psalm 41:9," said Anakah. "'Even my own familiar friend in whom I trusted, who did eat my bread, has lifted up his heel against me.' With those words, King David was asking why one of his most trusted advisors had betrayed him."

"It has been established by well-meaning Christians that the psalms foretell of Jesus' betrayal and the accusation by false witnesses, but none of these passages were ever considered prophecies concerning the Messiah," assured Kortney. "King David was referring to the actions of his trusted counselor, Ahithophel, during a rebellion launched by his own son Absalom. As Absalom was about to declare himself king in place of his father. But Ahithophel advised him to quickly pursue his father, David, isolate him, and kill him." To my knowledge, only Psalm 22 is devoted to an actual prophecy pertaining to the Messiah, or more specifically how he dies."

"I'm not so sure," argued Jidion. Clearing her throat and taking a drink, she added, "I'm with Trisha on this one. I believe that the Psalms do speak of Judas's betrayal: 'For it is not an enemy who reproaches me; then I could bear it. Nor is it one who hates me who has exalted himself against me; Then I could hide from him. But it was you, a man my equal, my companion ….'"

"Attempting to force David's 55th Psalm into a prophecy of betrayal would have it read as follows: '…but it was you, *Judas*, a man *my equal*, my companion and my acquaintance….' I assure you that I have *never* come across a scholar, theologian, or preacher who considered Judas to be the equal of Jesus!" argued Teryk.

"In Mark, Jesus indicates a betrayer but never names him," said Joshua.

"Luke, too, fails to mention the betrayer by name at the Last Supper," said Raven. "Also, Luke seems to take great liberties at the arrest. According to Luke, Judas is now leading the crowd. And Jesus averts the kiss spoken of in Matthew. Where Matthew and Mark say that the crowd was sent by the chief priest, Luke includes officers of the Temple Police and elders among the crowd. At this point Satan enters the picture because money no longer appears to be a big enough incentive or motive. Finally, Luke omits the episode where all the disciples abandon Jesus, probably because it is far too embarrassing."

Joseph "Five Eagles" Reyna

"Luke is the originator of the 'Devil made me do it' *Twinkie Defense,* which eliminates the concern for a motive," argued Kortney. "To me it is evident that Luke's investigation revealed no motive for a betrayal. It is also interesting to note that nowhere in the Old Testament does Satan wield this kind of power. Satan simply means adversary. Moreover, Satan is not the adversary of God, but of man."

"Is nothing sacred? Are you trying to tell me that Judas did not betray Jesus? That he will not rot in Hell for all eternity?" asked Marileyna in dismay.

"Marileyna, it is not Teryk telling us that Jesus was not betrayed by one in his inner circle. That knowledge is being derived from the Gospels themselves," clarified Athena.

"It has been suggested that Judas was a bitterly disillusioned materialistic opportunist," argued Jidion. "He felt he should have profited from Jesus' coming kingdom. Having wasted the better part of three years as a member of the inner twelve, he obviously felt that Jesus had betrayed him. Knowing that Jesus was going to die, he naturally decided to profit from it. Judas simply wanted to recoup his losses, since it was said he was pilfering from the treasury. Some have suggested that Judas forced the hand of the Sanhedrin when he went to betray Jesus for thirty pieces of silver."

"That the Sanhedrin would think this was their only opportunity to grab Jesus is laughable," argued Raven. "What part of *not during* the festival don't you understand?"

"According to John 11, Jesus had gone into hiding and this is why the priests needed an informant like Judas. Yet, in the next chapter, Jesus enters the city openly and triumphantly," said Sofia, another of the Mothers of Lemuria. Her name was an ancient word for wisdom. Sofia was regularly consulted concerning ESPionage operations, in order to find a more peaceful solution to a problem. She specialized in the study of ancient wisdom and cultures, and the possibility of alien visitations during those times. "In any event, my question is this: If Judas killed himself shortly after the betrayal, how did any of the disciples learn of the thirty pieces of silver?"

"This entire mix up could have been avoided if only Jesus had explained Judas's part in all this to the other disciples," reasoned Cassandra.

"But he did, and they understood Judah's part in the proceedings," Teryk assured her.

"You never mentioned that," said Joshua. "How… when did Jesus tell them?"

"You're not thinking fourth dimensionally, Joshua. Jesus told them after he resurrected, before he ascended," explained Teryk.

"Is there any evidence to support your claim?" asked Adriana.

"Not that I am aware of, but now that you've been made aware of it, start looking for any references in the Gospels that may verify my claim," commanded Teryk.

"Do you honestly think they are going to find it?" asked Trisha.

"Yes, and it's because the men who later edited the Gospels had no understanding of the culture and were not as meticulous as my researchers. Once they gnow what it is they are looking for, it is difficult to conceal it from them. I suppose it could be argued that I am leading or steering the investigation by giving you specific things to look for. The thing to keep in mind is that *what I'm asking you to look for should not be there!*" said Teryk, rising from his seat. "That said, where did I leave off?"

"As the fourth cup was being passed around the table you were describing how each of the disciples met their end. Being the lookalike, you could not understand why Thomas is reported to have died in India," Noraia informed him.

Vying for Position in the Last Stretch

"You realize the Magdalena anointed Y'shua to proclaim him king on the Mount of Olives,' Levi said to me excitedly.

"'The mount Zechariah spoke of?' asked Peter, who liked to tower over our conversations while adding little to them.

"'The same,' assured Levi.

"'So it cannot be long before he establishes the kingdom that will rule all nations,' said Philip.

"'Judah has already been established as a commander among the Zealots," beamed Symeon, referring to my recently acquired position among the Zealots who were themselves more a corps of officers than foot soldiers. 'Among the Zealots he is known as *Judah the Scariota.*'

"'Tell us, Judah, are you going to lead vast armies into battle against Rome?' inquired Nathaniel, not really one for war.

"'Judah the Blade is certain he will be a greater general than Cæsar or even Alexander,' remarked James, the hothead, at which time everyone around the table burst into laughter.

"'Who would ever follow me into battle?' I asked ruefully.

"'Modesty does not become you, my friend,' said Levi, as the fourth cup of wine was passed to him. 'Master, you have sat Judah at the place of honor. Tell us, what esteemed position will he hold?'

"Jesus glanced over the gathering of his trusted disciples, his closest friends, and said to them in a voice that carried great authority, 'Verily I say to you, in the centuries to come, when my name is mentioned, men will also speak the name of Judah.' This seemed to quiet everyone. The disciples looked at one another in astonishment, then began to discuss amongst themselves just what my exalted position might be.

"I turned to Jesus with one eyebrow raised, trying to conceal a grin. 'Truly, you have a way with words, Master,' as we both laughed, to the chagrin of the others.

"'What of the rest of us, Master?' they asked.

"'One of you seated at this table will hand me over to the authorities.'

"There it was, out in the open—exactly how Jesus was going to handle this, I had no idea.

"Then Peter leaned past John to say something to Lazarus, who then looked up to Jesus from his reclined position and asked, 'Who is it that will hand you over?'

"Jesus was breaking a piece of bread in half. It resembled a pita or fluffy tortilla. At the question, he stopped, and all eyes were on him. Looking down at Lazarus, who was leaning back on his chest, Jesus replied, 'It is he to whom I give the bread I dip in the sauce.' Using half of the bread, he scooped up a good chunk of the chutney and handed it to me. Jesus was expected to hand the piece to the person in the place of honor at this point in the feast. I was to tear a piece off and eat it. I then turned and passed it to my left, in the same manner I had passed the cups of wine.

"Since everyone was to take a piece of the bread, they missed the obvious. 'Always, you speak in riddles,' I whispered to Jesus.

"As the bread made its round, Jesus addressed us once more. 'I give you a new commandment: Love one another as I have loved you.' Jesus smiled and asked me to rise with him. He walked me to the door then, turning to me, whispered, 'It should never be any different. The truth is a two-edged sword and it cuts both ways. You have been given insight and so saw right through my gesture. You knew exactly what I meant.'

"'And what of the others?' I asked.

"'Such a truth would cut too deeply into their souls at this moment—just as it is about to cut into mine.' Then, in a louder voice for all to hear, Jesus said, 'Now go quickly. Do what you must do.' He hugged me and whispered, 'Before I change my mind.'

"My eyes swelled with tears as I headed for the entrance to leave. I had trouble seeing the stairs in the dim light. I stopped halfway down the stairwell and composed myself.

"'Judas, where are you going?' asked the Magdalene.

"She knew I did not like the Hellenized version of that name; probably why she liked to use it. I bowed a farewell to the mothers present and handed her the letter I had received earlier. As we walked to the main entrance where the lighting was better, she held it next to a candle and read it. Her eyes expressed concern as he handed it back to me.

"'What does it mean?' she demanded.

Joseph "Five Eagles" Reyna

"'I do not know, but it is urgent and the Master has instructed me to see to it.' That seemed to satisfy her curiosity. A servant handed me my coat as the chill of the night closed in.

"Just then our attention was drawn to the upper room, where Peter was arguing with Jesus. 'You will deny me, Peter.' I looked into the Magdalene's eyes, which were heavy with concern. Then I hurried past her.

"I heard Peter saying, 'No, Lord, I would never do that.' I thought it strange: it sounded like Jesus was ordering Peter to deny him rather than accusing him of such an action. Peter was saying he could not do such a thing. 'I swear by all that is holy, I could never forsake you, Master,' cried Peter. But Jesus reminded him that we did not take oaths.

"The Passover would soon be at an end, I thought as I stepped outside onto the street and turned toward the Viaduct. I heard them singing together for the last time. 'All nations surrounded me, but in the name of the Lord I will destroy them! They surrounded me on every side, but in the name of the Lord I will destroy them!' Their voices were drowned out by songs emanating from some of the houses I was passing. I knew this to be a long psalm. There was a verse in this last song that none of my teachers had been able to explain before and I realized why it had been placed there. 'The stone which the builders refused has become the head stone of the corner.' No doubt this verse will remain a mystery to the Israelites for a long time to come."

Taking a seat, Teryk added, "I think this would be a good place to end my story. Shakira, please see to it that breakfast is provided for the group in the morning. I'm not really in the mood to answer any question right now but if someone has anything pressing I will do my best to address the subject." He looked around the table. No one ventured to question him. Teryk reached up and deactivated the recording equipment on his console, signaling that the session was over.

The Devil's Disciple

Early the next morning, Teryk was surprised to see that everyone was already seated and enjoying breakfast at the third gathering of the Round Table. He apologized for his tardiness and added, "As always, if someone has a question that cannot wait, please feel free to interrupt. I left off with Judas being excused from the Last Supper and heading toward the Temple," Teryk began, inhaling deeply and collecting his thoughts. Looking around the table, he acknowledged the presence of a few new individuals.

"No sooner had I reached the Temple Mount, when a servant who recognized me ran to my side and escorted me in to a mikveh as quickly as possible. I was required to immerse myself in the ritual bath for spiritual cleansing in order to enter the inner sanctuary. To my surprise, I was handed the white linen clothing of a scribe. I strapped on a girdle that in a lesser way resembled the one worn by the Baptist. The white linen hat I could have done without, but it was required for the uniform. Lastly, I was handed my writing tablet and a pen case that strapped to the belt buckles in my girdle: a sort of war belt. I ordered the servant to be careful with my new clothes and to find someone to carry my sandals, certain I would have need of them shortly. Gamaliel, my old teacher, was waiting for us in the inner courts. The servant dropped back and waited outside.

"Gamaliel greeted me, 'Shalom!'

"'Shalom Aleichem!' I replied, greeting him with a hug as he kissed my cheek. Gamaliel had been fond of Judah since he'd first held the child in his arms. Judah's father Symeon and Gamaliel had been great friends. I had memories of sitting at their feet as they discussed the meaning of scripture and debated the meanings of the prophecies. It was Gamaliel who insisted Judah be brought up as a scribe, a specialist of the law, and not as a high priest like his father Symeon. I'm glad he did. Judah's memory became razor-sharp because his lessons required him to commit to memory what he had learned. 'What's going on, Master. Why have I been summoned?' I asked.

"'Yehudah, Pilate has issued orders to arrest your Master Y'shua. A cohort is forming outside the Fortress Antonia. Please, we must go there at once. I'll fill you in as we walk.'

"*So Jesus is being taken prisoner tonight, but it's all wrong. This was Tuesday night. Jesus is not supposed to be arrested until Thursday night. What the hell is happening?*' I wondered. The Fortress Antonia, originally called the Baris, from the Hebrew word *Bira*, meaning 'fortifications', had been constructed by the Hasmonean rulers of Judea. Attacks on the Temple Mount had traditionally come from the north. Steep valleys lay to the east and west of the temple, forming a natural barrier. The terrain to the south descended more gradually but just as deeply, through the oldest settlements in Jerusalem. To guard the fortress from the hill to the northeast, a moat had been constructed. Although it served only as a fortress, Antonia had once been the palace of Herod the Great: his royal residence while in Jerusalem.

"Antonia was similar to Herod the Great's summer palace and his resting place, the Fortress Herodium. That fortress also had four turrets, and like Antonia, three of the turrets were fifty cubits tall while the fourth, which commanded a stunning view of the Dead Sea, was seventy cubits tall. The fourth tower was also fitted with apartments. The Palace/Fortress Antonia was named for Herod's protector Mark Antony before he fell from grace, defeated at the Battle of Actium by Octavian. The only difference between the Palace/Fortress Herodium and the Antonia is that Herodium was circular in design with cylindrical turrets and the Antonia was a perfect cube with square turrets. Except for this, the layout of the fortresses and turrets was almost identical.

"Because Antonia was there long before the Temple Mount was expanded, Herod had simply incorporated it into the construction. Antonia could easily protect against attacks from the north. As an added bonus, the massive southeastern turret commanded an impressive view of the temple and its inner courtyards. From that vantage point, Herod, and now Pilate, could suppress any outbreaks from within the Temple Mount. I looked up to see where the porticoes attached to the fortress. From doors high up in the walls, narrow stairs led down along the wall. These narrow paths had no railings, making them easier to defend. They led down to the roofs of both the western and northern porticoes that surrounded the Court of Gentiles. The western portico seemed almost an extension of the fortress's western wall, while the northern colonnade buttressed the center of the fortress's eastern wall. The height of the doors and the narrow stairways leading up to them made it impossible for anyone to gain entrance using a battering ram on that precarious perch. To better patrol the festivals, legionnaires regularly took up armed positions atop the beautifully decorated colonnaded porticoes.

"'Why is Y'shua being arrested,' I asked Gamaliel.

"'We hoped you could shed some light on the subject. Earlier this month, we discovered that Tiberius Cæsar had issued orders for all rebels to be arrested and put to death. We fear this may be the reason behind the arrest. Tiberius, in his old age, desires peace throughout the Empire, what the Romans once called *Pax Romana*: a period of peace lasting nearly seven years that hasn't existed since about the time of your birth.'

"'That still does not explain why I am needed for a Roman arrest.'

"'We have precious little time, Yehudah!' proclaimed Gamaliel, cutting me off. 'As we speak, scribes of the law are attempting to figure out some way by which Y'shua can be arrested on the pretext that he's violated one of our laws. If they succeed, the Sanhedrin could claim jurisdiction over him. It would buy us some time, to be sure. And right now time is a luxury we do not have.' Shaking his head in disbelief, he muttered, 'Pilate could not have chosen a worse possible moment to make this arrest.'

"'Should the Sanhedrin find grounds for incrimination, will they carry out his execution instead?' I inquired.

"'Certainly not!' Gamaliel blurted in disbelief.

"'These proceedings do not appear to be legal,' I protested. 'According to our rabbinic body of oral laws, a capital offense may only be tried during the light of day. Proceedings must be suspended at nightfall. In addition, the Mishnah makes it clear that no case involving a man's life may be tried on the day before the Holy High Sabbath....'

"'Annas has informed me that his son-in-law will be proclaiming a state of emergency,' Gamaliel assured me. "About a hundred years ago, Symeon-bar-Shetah called for just such an emergency act during a trial involving the hanging of eighty witches in Askalon. By proclaiming a state of emergency, the Sanhedrin will be freed of the rules under which it must conduct itself.'

"'They hung eighty witches? Hanging is not a mode of punishment prescribed by law,' I protested. 'You mean to tell me they're going to remove the rules of conduct so that they can execute him?'

"'Yehudah, no one is trying to execute Y'shua,' said Gamaliel in exasperation. 'We're trying to save him. I think under the circumstances, the Almighty will be understanding.'

"As we approached the fortress, I could make out a detachment of temple police in full dress uniform, holding torches and standing in formation by the gate that led to the road of Jericho.

"'Mordechai, this is Yehudah. You will escort him. He is our witness and will be the one officially making the arrest on our behalf.' Incredulous, I gazed at Gamaliel, but he continued. 'Pilate has requested that we send someone to help identify Y'shua. Judah has been one of his Twelve trusted disciples for the past three years.' Turning to me, he pointed to Mordechai and said, 'Mordechai is captain of the watch and has orders to take Y'shua into temple custody for the night, after the Romans formally charge and arrest him.'

"'Then why am I needed for the arrest?' I protested.

"'Yehudah, we had to act quickly. For the moment, you are the acting witness. According to our laws, the witness must affect the arrest and bring the accused man to court. As I understand it, the Sanhedrin is not actually holding court but a council session.' He removed a small leather pouch from beneath the sash around his waist and placed it in my hand.

"I hefted the pouch in my hand and heard the jingle of coins. 'What is this for?'

"'It is obvious you've never made an arrest, Yehudah. For a proper conviction there must be two witnesses. The witnesses are always given thirty pieces of silver to offset any loss of revenue or inconvenience they might encounter in the bringing of an offender of the law to justice. It's a measly sum but it is better than nothing,' he said apologetically.

"He did not mention that it was also the customary payment for information leading to the conviction of an enemy of the state. 'That being said, Gamaliel, it is illegal for the temple police to act on the high priest's behalf and conduct the arrest with me, to say nothing of the arrest being voluntary on my part as a witness.'

"'True enough. I see you were actually paying attention to my teachings. The police are here for protection, to ensure that no harm befalls Y'shua at the hands of the Romans.'

"'If it is a Roman arrest, why would the soldiers hand him over to the temple police?'

"'Ever since Emperor Augustus exiled Archelaus to Vienna and appointed a Roman military prefect to maintain order in the Judean province, the Roman governors have kept this custom with us. The governors have granted us this request whenever the accused was someone of high standing, for fear that the people may riot. We have seldom requested it. The arrest of Y'shua, at the eve of our festivities, certainly qualifies.'

"'I believe Y'shua's arrest has something to do with the mandate issued by Tiberius,' said Mordechai. 'Pilate obviously wants to show Rome that he can move quickly to suppress a rebellion.'

"Just then a priest with a lantern approached Mordechai. 'The tribune awaits you, sir.' Mordechai issued orders and the detachment marched out in columns of two through the northern gate, descending into a deep stairwell that exited near the entrance to the Palace Antonia.

"Just outside the walls, I stopped and requested the servant to bring my sandals so I could put them back on. The night was getting chilly. The stones of

Joseph "Five Eagles" Reyna

the pavement were cold and damp as a result. I had not gone barefoot for many years and was not used to it, unlike Gamaliel, who did not seem to mind. He stood in the gateway and told me Jesus was to be taken to the house of Annas. 'If Y'shua can be found guilty, petitions will be made to Cæsar, after which Pilate will be forced to release him into our custody.'

"'Well then, by all means let's give him a fair trial before we hang him.'

"Gamaliel smiled at my wit. 'I have sent messengers to try to locate some of the other prominent Pharisees. I will see you soon,' he said, a look of concern clouding his face.

"'What is the matter, old friend?' I asked amiably.

"'It is said by some that this man is a sorcerer who performs many wonders. I fear I am sending an angel to lay hands on the Devil himself.'

"I burst into uncontrollable laughter, much to Gamaliel's chagrin. He appeared mortified. 'Somehow I think history will record this event as being the other way around. The man from Galilee is my comrade and my friend. Do not be concerned on my behalf,' I assured him.

"A red-cloaked legionnaire in full battle array held a torch next to the tribune. The soldiers were not jovial, as was their custom. This night they were quiet and tense, ready for action.

"Mordechai halted his group and walked toward the tribune. 'This is Judah-bar-Simon, the man you requested to help identify the accused. You will find he bears a striking resemblance to Y'shua-bar-Yehosef, the Galilean.'

"The tribune, a military unit commander, looked at me and then to a man standing back in the shadows. The man, who had the pocked countenance of a sponge, nodded his consent. The tribune turned back to me. 'Judah, I am Tribune Livius of the Twelfth Roman Legion. You will stay close to me as we march out to the Mount of Olives.' Orders were barked. Centurions, who had been waiting impassively, hands on swords, organized their men into a rather large detachment.

"I noticed there were six centurions, distinguished by the red ostrich feathers on their helmets. Torchlight gleamed off their oiled leather body armor. The tribune heading the unit wore a helmet with a crest: a sort of curved shoe brush. 'This is not going to be a normal arrest,' I thought. Most of the soldiers carried torches but not all were burning.

"'How many men are necessary for this arrest?' I asked the tribune.

"'One cohort,' he replied.

"Looking at Mordechai, who had heard me ask the question, I shrugged my shoulders.

"'Roughly six hundred soldiers. There are ten cohorts in a legion,' explained the tribune.

"*One legion is roughly six thousand men, so one tenth of that would be six hundred: roughly the equivalent of one Marine Corps battalion,*' I thought. '*That is an awful lot of soldiers.*' As the soldiers fell into formation, I saw chief priests and scribes exiting the north gate of the temple wall. The priests hurried toward us. They spoke with Mordechai and fell in behind his group. It looked like we were ready to move out. High in the cloudless sky, the moon cast silver light over the entire valley. It would reach its zenith in a few hours, and a state of fullness the following night. As we headed out on the road to Kidron Valley, the assembled unit continued to split off into columns that formed a daunting parade stretching all the way back to the fortress gate."

22

Forward, The Light Brigade — In Rolled The Six Hundred

"*The Romans did not need to light any more torches,*' I thought, but they proceeded to light them just the same. Again I was ordered to stay close to the tribune. The man who had been in the shadows came forward from the direction of Gethsemane. He gave instructions to the tribune: a Roman spy most likely, or perhaps a Jewish informant.

"As the soldiers began their march, their iron-shod sandals struck the ground in unison, hammering out their advance. It sounded so loud and ominous that I wondered if they didn't in fact want to start a riot. You have to understand there were no jets flying overhead, no tricked-out cars passing by with stereos that caused the walls of your house to resonate. These guys were making enough noise to wake the dead. '*In rolled the six hundred,*' crossed my mind as their weapons clanked in rhythmic cadence. Pilgrims rushed out of their tents to see what all the commotion was about and they all seemed to look directly at me in my dress whites, as if I were leading the procession.

"The road beneath my feet was about twelve feet wide and constructed from paving stones about a foot wide and eighteen inches long, each one at least eight inches thick. Rome went to great expense to make sure that the most important highways remained passable in all types of weather. As we passed the first milestone, I looked back and saw what looked like a gigantic fiery serpent winding its way through the valley.

"The milestone reminded me of Jesus asking the people to walk an extra mile. 'Do the unexpected—go beyond what is expected of you.' Under the *angaria*, a military requisition of labor and transport, an infantryman, Roman or otherwise, who had grown tired of the pack he was hauling could order a peasant to haul it for him. The peasant was required to haul it for one mile. Most people had their own individual milestones set by the side of the road, marking the one-mile obligation from their homes. Just then, the sound of noisy iron-shod sandals died down as we veered off the main road and turned up toward the Mount of Olives."

"How Peter and the others managed to sleep through the whole thing, I'll never know. Jesus was waking the disciples as we arrived: a rude awakening, to be sure. Three hundred torches illuminated the entire olive grove. I saw shock and apprehension evident on the faces of the disciples *'Forward the Light Brigade, was there a man dismayed'* came to mind. I'm sure that the sight of hundreds of armed Roman legionnaires led by me, dressed in priestly garb, was not what the disciples had expected to see. I found it odd that these men who had been so accustomed to keeping lonely vigils on the Sea of Galilee could not keep awake, but that was years ago.

"Jesus stepped forward and addressing the officer in charge, asked, 'Whom do you seek?'

"'Joshua-bar-Josef the Nazorean,' called out the tribune.

"Jesus stepped forward and said, 'Ego eimi.' Greek for *I am*. At the sound of his voice, the entire cohort collapsed to the ground like puppets whose strings had been cut. I looked around and saw that the temple police and the chief priests had fallen as well. The tribune seemed groggy as I helped him to his feet. His knees were weak and he was using me for support when again Jesus asked, 'Whom do you seek?'

"Some of the soldiers had started moving again. Many of them had fallen on or next to torches. While the flaming soldiers were putting each other out, the tribune turned to Jesus and repeated, 'We seek Joshua-bar-Josef.'

"Again Jesus answered, 'I am,' in Greek. Most Gospels record that Jesus said, 'I am he.' But Jesus uttered one of the forms of the unspeakable name of God: the same name God used to identify himself to Moses on Mount Sinai. Uttering this was punishable by death. *'The man has a death-wish,'* I thought, then wondered if he was just being clever, since he was not uttering 'YHVH' in Hebrew.

"Pious scribes had taken to writing four dots in place of the four consonants that signified *'I will be, whomever I will be.'* Why they believed these words should never be uttered was beyond me. Many referenced Deuteronomy 12, but I could not see how the third and fourth verses could have been taken to mean what scribes inferred as their meaning. The Book of Deuteronomy clearly states that God is to be addressed by no other name and that we should use his name often in our prayers. Long ago, scribes took it upon themselves to remove the holy name and substitute titles. Gamaliel had explained to me that YHVH was actually a code. One had to transliterate the consonants into Aramaic, rendering it as IAUA. Then one simply reversed abjad AUAI and inserted the missing consonants to get the word AnnUnAkI.

"Again the cohort and the temple contingent fell to the ground. I had seen this sort of thing before at revivals when the Holy Spirit's power proved too much for some of the believers present. Noticing that Mordechai had fallen near a torch, I hurried to his aid. The tribune noticed that I was unaffected and motioned for me to proceed toward Jesus.

"Jesus forced an uneasy smile and nodded as he asked, 'Comrade, what are you doing here?'

"As I leaned forward and embraced him in our customary fashion, I could feel my body trembling. I kissed him on the cheek, but I could not let go of him and so kissed him again. The fragrance of flowers from the garden wafted across on the cool night breeze. Still I did not want to let him go but finally did so with a heavy sigh. 'I have been ordered to personally carry out your arrest.'

"'You betray him with a kiss, Judah?' remarked Peter, drawing his new sword and striking at the temple guard Malchus, who was about to grab for Jesus. Had I been any closer he would have probably struck me. Several of the nearby legionnaires drew their swords.

"Symeon the Zealot, seeing what was about to happen, asked Jesus, 'Shall we strike with the sword, Master?'

"'Sheath your swords!' Jesus demanded. 'For all who take up the sword shall die by the sword.' Turning toward the other disciples, Jesus said, 'Or would you rather I not drink from the cup my Father has offered me?' In a softer voice, to Peter, he added, 'Remember my last command to you, my friend—you will deny me.'

"Peter reluctantly sheathed his sword as a Roman centurion read out the charges against Jesus. 'Joshua-bar-Josef, you are hereby placed under arrest by order of Pontius Pilate, for sedition against the Emperor Tiberius Cæsar.'

"The healing of Malchus did not seem to astonish the Jews or the disciples. The Romans were another matter: They were visibly shaken by it. The soldiers placed Jesus in irons and the tribune handed him into my custody. Interestingly, the temple police treated him respectfully. They surrounded Jesus in order to prevent any harm from coming to him at the hands of the Romans.

"Jesus, surrounded by guards, addressed the tribune. 'If I am the one you seek, let these men go.' He nodded toward the disciples.

"I remained and watched as the detachment of temple police made ready their departure with Jesus in chains. The Roman cohort was about to leave when a man inquired of me what was happening. The man said he was a gardener keeping watch over his Lord's property. With so many people in the vicinity, his Lord had asked him to stand guard during the night, to prevent any damage to the garden.

"'Who is your Master?' I inquired.

"'My Master is Yehosef ha Ramati,' he replied.

"*Is this the garden where Jesus will be buried?* I wondered. 'Does this garden contain his new tomb?' I asked.

"He pointed toward a flickering light. 'There, see that lamp? I took refuge in it while I kept watch over the garden. It's quite comfortable. This garden does not have a tower like some of the others I sometimes watch.'

"I told the man all I could and rejoined the temple police. Amram, a chief priest, informed me that the Romans wanted Y'shua presented to Pilate for trial before the first shofar horn sounds in the morning.

"'Before dawn!' I exclaimed.

"'Those were the tribune's orders,' he assured me.

"Jesus was taken through the Valley of the Kidron toward the southeastern corner of the city wall. The moon was almost directly overhead. It cast eerie shadows along the rocky defile which, fortified by the sheer eastern wall of the temple, rose hundreds of feet from the valley floor. These huge walls buttressed the base of the hill that made up the temple plateau of the Sanctuary. They had been filled in to form the enormous Court of Gentiles. In truth, many underground storage rooms and passages had been created before the cavity had been filled in.

"The small procession of temple guards stopped just short of a stone bridge. They were not carrying torches like the Romans. The small lanterns they carried illuminated the road well enough. I looked up and saw the great winter constellation, Orion, setting in the western sky. It was one of the only constellations visible in the bright moonlight. Except for the sound of a gurgling spring, all was stillness. This land was incredibly beautiful. It bore no resemblance to the Palestine of my time. '*The Romans truly do make a desert, and call it peace,*' I thought, or perhaps it was due to several millennia of deforestation, erosion and the root-devouring herds of sheep and goats that seemed to own the land.

"Mordechai ordered the shackles removed from Jesus and we crossed the stone bridge, entering the city through the valley gate sometimes called the Fountain Gate, because it was near the Pool of Siloam. A Roman sentry challenged us at the gate and a chief priest presented some sort of seal that allowed us to pass unhindered. The rules governing the city gates after sundown were somewhat more relaxed during Jewish holidays, but this was no ordinary group of pilgrims: We were an armed escort entering a fortified city, so we had to show proper credentials at this late hour.

"I stood at the gate looking for Peter and John. I could not see them in the moonlight and wondered how Peter would get past the guard carrying a sword. As I turned and ascended the ancient flight of steps that led through the Tyropoeon Valley to the upper city where Annas's house was located, I saw Peter ahead of me. He blended in well with this group, dressed as he was in his new traveling clothes. I could not see John. If memory served, they should both be here. I lost sight of Peter as the procession wound its way through the narrow streets of the cheesemakers that ran through this valley. To our left was Akra, the

Lower City, and the poorest quarter. To our right was David's City, where many of the priests lived.

"We arrived at the house of the high priest. Annas had retained the title of high priest in much the same way that ex-presidents of the United States, out of courtesy, retain the title Mr. President. I accompanied the guard into the courtyard. As the small guard passed through the gate to the inner court, I could see members of the Small Sanhedrin assembling. Under Pharisaic law, criminal jurisdiction was exercised by the Small Sanhedrin of twenty-three members and not the Great Sanhedrin of seventy-one members. They also did not address this gathering as an official court, but as a council session.

"I glanced back toward the gate and saw that Peter had not been permitted to enter. I left Jesus' side and returned to the gate. I asked Peter where John was. He informed me that the others had all fled, so he was alone. I then asked why he had not entered. He explained that the girl at the gate would not permit him to enter because she did not know him. Being a scribe and a member of an important Pharisee family, Judah had been to Annas's house on several occasions and was well known to Veronica.

"Why Veronica had been placed at the gate was beyond me. She appeared cold in her thin gown and her hair was disheveled. Her face beamed with a smile when she saw me. I think she had a crush on me, but she was a slave and very young. I requested Peter's outer garment and placed it around her frail frame. She had been born into servitude and was ill treated by the other servants; that was probably why she was at the gate on this cold night of the Passover celebrations.

"Vouching for Peter, Veronica nodded her consent and permitted him to enter. But because of Peter's Galilean drawl, something akin to a Texas twang, the girl seemed curious and asked him if he, too, was a disciple of Jesus. Veronica did not seem to mean anything by it, but the inquiry stopped Peter in his tracks. He had seemed nervous before, but now he expressed a deep-seated reluctance to enter. He could not shake off the panic visible on his countenance. The man appeared terrified.

"'No,' replied Peter, 'I am not!'

"I was about to reassure Peter when Mordechai came looking for me. It seems I was holding up the proceedings. Enough members had been assembled to comprise the Small Sanhedrin. Being the arresting witness, I was needed immediately."

"Commander, if the arrest of Jesus had not been successful, the Sanhedrin's image of authority would have never recovered from the blow," was Noraia's opening remark. "I believe this is why it was necessary for one of Jesus' disciples to make the arrest. In Mark's account, our earliest source, he states that Judas instructs those arresting Jesus to take him away 'safely', which is sometimes interpreted rather loosely as 'under guard'. The term can also be translated as 'securely'."

"*Safely*. That would be more in keeping with what I observed," said Teryk.

"Time, or the lack of it, seems to have played a decisive part in determining the events on the night of the arrest," observed Athena. The actions of the Sanhedrin are pretty much in line with the picture Jesus painted of them. The actions of Judas, however, are bizarre and inexplicable. The curious behavior of Pontius Pilate, uniformly documented in all four Gospels, is stranger still," she said, biting her lower lip and trying to compose her next statement. "The historical Pilate was heavy handed, obstinate and tactless while enforcing his authoritative will over his Judean subjects. We find none of this behavior during the trial. The man appears to lack all the traits that characterized great Roman leaders. This has prompted historians to conclude that the entire episode was fabricated to make the Romans appear blameless."

"The Sanhedrin acting as fast as they did has given historians the impression that they had been planning Jesus' arrest for some time. If this had been the case, the priests would have had the necessary witnesses ready to testify against Jesus," reasoned Anakah, "the evidence in the Gospels illustrates quite clearly that the Sanhedrin was not prepared for the arrest. In reality, Jesus' arrest seems to have been quite unexpected, the late hour only adding to the dilemma. The hurried preparations to gather the members of the Great—the Great Sanhedrin was convened at the house of Caiaphas after they could not find any charges to level against Jesus during the small gathering at the house of Annas) Sanhedrin together, the urgency to conclude the trial before dawn and the need to find him guilty of something—anything…"

"If they were so well prepared and time was of the essence, why wait almost three hours from the time Judas leaves the Last Supper until they move to arrest him?" asked Athena. "They wasted a tremendous amount of time: time they desperately needed."

"How did you arrive at a three-hour delay?" asked Jidion.

"For one thing, the Last Supper was still underway when Judas left," deduced Athena. "So let's say it takes an additional thirty minutes for it to end and another thirty for them to walk to Gethsemane. That's one hour. At Gethsemane the disciples fall asleep not once but three times. How long would it take for Jesus to leave them so he could pray, only to find them asleep upon his return? It would be one thing if he left them to sleep, but Jesus gave specific instructions for them to remain awake. I estimate half an hour to forty-five minutes for each of these episodes, amounting to three hours before Judas arrives with the arresting party."

"Might I add," said Winter, almost hesitantly, "the disciples were clearly exhausted. It is evident they wanted to go to bed, yet Jesus remained in the garden. Many Christians believe that Jesus was in hiding and this is why Judas had to lead the arresting party to Gethsemane. But I believe Jesus would have waited until dawn, if necessary, for Judas to arrive, implying there must have been, unknown to the other disciples, some sort of arrangement between the two.

"A similar arrangement would then hold true for the Jewish leaders and Pontius Pilate. Some sort of understanding must have been reached prior to Pilate having received them at such an early hour and under such short notice," reasoned Winter. "To think that such a serious case could have been thrust upon the Roman Governor without prior notification, given what history tells us about Pilate's character, is ludicrous." The entire table fell silent. No one had considered such well-thought-out possibilities, but they were obvious when one took everything into account.

"How is it you were there the entire time, Teryk? Didn't Jesus say that the shepherd would be struck down and all the flock would flee?" asked an overly dramatic Jidion. "Yet you claim that you remained with him throughout the entire ordeal."

"I have read that verse before, but I don't recall Jesus saying that," exclaimed Teryk in his defense.

"I've found the verse. It's in Mark 14:27. 'And Jesus saith unto thee, All ye shall be offended: for it is written, I will smite the shepherd, and the sheep shall be scattered.' Apparently the conversation takes place after the Last Supper while the disciples are on their way to Gethsemane. So I guess you wouldn't have heard him say it, since you would have been at the temple during that time," surmised Raven, pleased with her detective work.

"The Gospels speculate that Jesus was arrested by the Sanhedrin during Passover, because there would be little chance for Jerusalem and the huge nonresident population to react to the actions of the priests. As plausible as this explanation may seem at first, it does not hold water," Kortney postulated. "It was in fact the worst possible time for them to arrest a suspected Messiah figure. The Passover feast was emotionally charged toward liberation from an oppressive overlord. To sum up the Gospels: The Jews arrest and sentence Jesus to death; Pontius Pilate then tries Jesus at the behest of the Jews, interrogates him and finds no fault with him; but the Jews keep insisting that Jesus be executed, shouting, 'Crucify him.' Are we to believe that one of Rome's heaviest-handed governors, with two full legions plus reserves at his command, was powerless before the demands of a hysterical populace?"

"The Gospels maintain that the Jews pressed the Roman governor to pass a sentence contrary to his own judgment," acknowledged Sarina. "They ardently involved him in criminal conduct tantamount to murder, actions for which Pilate would be personally held answerable under a Roman law enacted in the year 59 BCE. That law was enacted to stem the usurpation of judicial power for personal motives or vengeance."

"What evidence shows that the priests actually feared Jesus' popularity?" asked Shakira. "And how could the Sanhedrin so easily convince the multitude to turn against him?"

"People generally believe in and respect those in authority," said Jared, "more so when they are afraid." Jared was the commander of ESPionage operations. He specialized in tracking the movements of secret factions within world governments: people he classified as the Illuminati. He viewed himself as a catastrophist. Teryk had requested Jared's presence at the Round Table because his special abilities would be called into play once the investigation began dealing with the prophecies concerning the End of the Age. "During WWII, Japanese-American citizens were quickly rounded up and placed in concentration camps after Japan bombed Pearl Harbor. The propaganda for this action was based on lies, but the people were afraid and readily obeyed. We saw a similar thing happen after the 9/11 attacks. What I'm driving at is that fear is an incredibly efficient tool for controlling the masses and getting them to do irrational things: things which, in a rational state of mind, they would hesitate to do."

"The priests were unwilling to arrest Jesus when he overturned the stalls and tables in the temple," observed Noraia. "I believe that if he had wanted to, Jesus could have stirred up Jerusalem to an unimaginable level of excitement, turning the people against the priests, and what's more they knew it. Jesus had openly challenged the priests by fulfilling Zechariah's prophesy that the Messiah would enter Jerusalem riding on an ass. Isaiah says he would challenge the corruption of the temple and be proclaimed King of the Jews."

"I believe they only feared his popularity because of the additional thousands present at that year's Passover," Joshua assured Noraia. "When Jesus spoke against them at other times, they tried to lay hands on him or stone him outright."

"How exactly did Jesus get away from them? Was it like one of those old movies in which everyone is piled up in a large mass and the hero crawls out from between their legs?" asked Katharine.

"No! Jesus disappeared—vanished, quite literally," said Teryk to the astonishment of everyone in the room. "This was one of the reasons they feared him and accused him of being a sorcerer in league with the Devil."

"It is obvious that the priests did not want to stir up the multitude during the Passover celebrations. They repeatedly pointed out, 'Not during the feast day, lest there be an uproar of the people!' This particular passage is found in all four Gospels," said Raven. "Do you have any idea how rare that is? Only now that we have been examining the Gospels do I realize how rare it is to find a corresponding statement in each of the four Gospels."

"The story of Judas's betrayal sounds a lot like the modern day Nostradamus prophecies, where bits and pieces are taken from other prophecies to form a new one which Nostradamus never uttered," postulated Jared. "Important elements of the betrayal are absent in the earliest version. The facts in the story change and develop from the earliest Gospel to the last. The story of Judas Iscariot as it is found in the Gospels is almost entirely fictional."

"One of the strangest inconsistencies regarding the betrayal can be found in the Gospel of Matthew 26:50, where Jesus addresses Judas as his comrade during the arrest in the garden of Gethsemane: 'Friend, why have you come?' Matthew is saying that when Judas arrived with armed soldiers to arrest him, Jesus chose to address Judas using the word *hetarios*, meaning 'comrade' or 'companion'. What reason would Jesus have to call a petty thief possessed by Satan his comrade?" asked Anakah. "Hetarios was not the normal, everyday word for friend. That word was *phileo*, as in Philadelphia, the City of Brotherly love. Phileo was the word Jesus used in the Gospel of John, when he addressed his disciples at the Last Supper saying, 'You are my friends.'"

"Taking today's modern understanding of a formal arrest, and imposing that upon events that transpired during Jesus' time, will cause you to err. Being arrested by an official order was a Roman custom, not a Jewish one," explained Athena. "A more common form of Jewish arrest was by a witness, preferably two, as in the case of the woman brought before Jesus after being caught committing adultery."

"According to Teryk's report, six hundred Roman legionnaires took part in Jesus' arrest," said Cassandra. "In trying to confirm the size of the arresting party, we searched through numerous Bibles and found nothing to indicate that one tenth of an entire Roman legion had taken part in the arrest."

"The entire Roman army comprised about twenty-five legions worldwide. The Roman military was based around the legion, which consisted of between forty-five hundred to six thousand men," continued Cassandra. "Legions were divided further into ten cohorts of between four hundred and fifty to six hundred men. One tribune commanded each cohort. The cohorts were divided into three maniples of two centuries, each consisting of eighty to one hundred soldiers. Each century was commanded by an experienced officer called a centurion. The centuria formed the backbone of the Roman army."

"It seemed crazy, but Teryk was adamant," said Raven. "In his report he maintained that a full contingent of legionnaires, roughly six hundred men, an entire Roman cohort commanded by their Tribune, conducted Jesus' arrest. In my experience, I've observed that intellectuals like Teryk are prone to lose themselves in the ambiguous meanings of arcane words. Despite my reservations, I persisted and discovered that this formal Roman arrest was the first step in official proceedings that concluded the following morning in the Roman governor's court!"

"You'll never guess where we found it!" beamed Marileyna, hardly able to contain her enthusiasm. "The account of Jesus' arrest by a Roman tribune, with his cohort, can be found in the Roman Catholic version of the Gospel of John, 18:3. Other translations simply state, '…a band of men and officers from the chief priests.' The Centenary translation of the New Testament puts it this way: '...so after getting troops and some Temple police from the chief priests.' The English and American Standard Versions say pretty much the same thing: '...so Judas, having procured a band of soldiers and some officers from the chief priests....' Some *Bible* translators have taken great liberties in adding lanterns, torches, and weapons that do not appear in the original Gospels. One thing about the arresting party is certain: Matthew, Mark and Luke all agreed that it was a great multitude!"

"It is difficult for me to conceive of this author as having invented the entire episode," said Phoenix. "It must be remembered that the author of John's Gospel was constantly whitewashing the Romans and had little good to say about the Jews. If an entire Roman cohort, one tenth of a Roman legion, actually took part in Jesus' arrest, one would think this author would have tried to suppress that information."

"Why not simply copy what was already written in the Synoptic Gospels and blame it all on the Jews?" argued Winter. "Why complicate matters still further? This new information also makes Judas' role in carrying out Jesus' arrest much more difficult. In his Gospel, John mentions neither money nor the Sanhedrin's involvement in the betrayal and arrest of Jesus. The only excuse given in the Gospel of John for Judas's behavior is that *the Devil made him do it.*"

"There is an obvious lack of motive in the original Gospels—hence the lame 'the Devil made him do it' excuse found in Luke, where Judas is inspired by Satan. John takes greater liberties and says Judas himself is the Devil," observed Phoenix. "In Matthew, Judas sees things going south and decides to cash in on the opportunity. Thus Judas, the thief, becomes the poster child for centuries of anti-Semitism because he's a greedy, money-grabbing, Christ-killing Jew."

"Now, consider the implications," said Raven. "If well-meaning, biased *Bible* translators can manage to mangle this simple straightforward translation, in the Gospel of John, beyond all recognition in just a few years..."

"What makes you say the translators were biased?" asked Jidion.

Teryk exhaled in frustration. "First, they believe Judas was a scheming weasel who betrayed his master for profit. Second, they believe the Sanhedrin did everything in their power to kill Jesus, including breaking their own sacred laws in order get him executed on the one day of the year they did not want to piss off the people and start a riot. This passage had already been translated into Latin by Saint Jerome, so all the translators had to do was convert it to English, and they couldn't even accomplish that simple task. If well-educated *Bible* scholars managed to botch it up that badly in so short a time, what do you suppose barely literate translators could accomplish over a period of a thousand years?"

Kindness and Cunning

"You guys brought up a lot of interesting points," observed Teryk rising from the table. "I was late this morning because I fell asleep in a deprivation tank. I was trying to recall everything that transpired during the Sanhedrin's trial at the house of Annas. And it was a lot more involved than the information provided in my initial report. Because of the incredible growth in the movement led by Jesus over the previous three years, the authorities had been greatly concerned. Annas was bent on trying to make Jesus submit to his authority and abandon the idea that he was the long-awaited Messiah. There was little doubt that a disastrous riot would ensue if the Roman governor were to bring any harm to Jesus while he was in their custody. To these priests, Jesus' teachings concerning the Elohim were heretical. This is why they called him and all who followed him Nazarenes."

"That echoes the information in Acts 24:5, in which Paul is accused of being a ringleader of the Nazarenes. Those Christians could not have all been from Nazareth," reiterated Anakah. "In addition, the earliest Jewish references concerning followers of Jesus in the Talmud identify them as the Nazarenes. In his *Refutation of All Heresies*, Bishop Hippolytus, who lived in the third century, viewed not only the Gnostics as heretics, but the Nazarenes as well."

"That certainly strengthens my belief that the Pauline Doctrines, accepted by the Church, clashed sharply with the teaching of Jesus," added Teryk. "You must understand that the loving, forgiving, and compassionate 'Creator of All' Jesus was proclaiming contrasted sharply with the jealous and vengeful warlike Elohim of the Old Testament, hence his teachings were viewed as heretical.

"Before entering the house of Annas, Jesus was once again shackled. A concerned Annas addressed the gathering and pronounced, 'The Nazarenes are a potentially dangerous new wave of troublemakers.' Turning toward Jesus, he added, 'Y'shua-bar-Yehosef, you are now permitted to speak on your behalf and tell of your claims and doctrines.'

"Jesus addressed the small assembly. 'I have taught the multitudes in every public place. My works were not done in secret. Go and ask the people of Israel. They will tell you of my works and what I have taught them. I have restored the sick to health. I have restored sight to the blind and have caused the deaf to hear the word of our Creator. I have cast out unclean spirits from the children of Israel. For which of these great works do I stand accused?' he demanded.

"'We are charging you with blasphemy,' explained a chief priest. 'Have you not said that you are the Son of the Most High, that in fact all of us are the sons of the Elohim?'

"'Have not your own prophets said as much? What fault do I have if your own scribes do not understand scripture or the words of your own prophets?'

"Thinking Jesus' remark impertinent, Ya'akov, a Jewish guard, struck him hard across the mouth. 'How dare you speak thus to the High Priest?' he said in his most insolent tone.

"'Idiot!' shouted Annas to the guard, who was taken aback. 'This man is a prisoner of imperial Rome by order of Tiberius. Pray Pilate does not relieve you of your hand for your stupidity!'

"The blood drained from the big man's face. He stepped unsteadily back and exited the courtyard. *Probably to change his under garments*, I thought.

"In the end, Annas's interrogation was unsuccessful. Jesus was bound again and taken to the house of Caiaphas, which was located on the highest point in the city. This house was much like the White House of the United States in that it was occupied by the High Priest during his appointed term. Members of the small Sanhedrin, made up from the twenty-four priestly divisions, were still assembling when we got there. If this council session could not prove Jesus had broken any laws, matters would soon escalate.

"While at the house of Caiaphas, the grounds of the accusations against Jesus seemed to shift. First the Sanhedrin scribes attempted to prove that Jesus' claims to be the Messiah were fraudulent, based on his lineage. The scribes proceeded to badmouth David's actions and Solomon's behavior. Solomon 'the wisest' had built numerous temples to the detestable mother goddess Ashtoreth. They proceeded to quote from scripture, more specifically Deuteronomy, which speaks against a king taking too many wives. I believe Solomon had more than seven hundred wives, while his father David managed to get by with only two hundred or so. Israel's basic understanding of the Jewish laws, customs and beliefs seemed to be working against Jesus.

"'If you are the Messiah show us a sign,' they demanded."

"'Miracles have never been considered a sign. And he who worked them was never seen as anything more than a prophet,' said another chief priest.

"'Miracles may have been wrought by the prophets but the power to perform them always came from the Most High,' countered another.

"Jesus stood there but did not answer them. Time was running out. At dawn Jesus had to be handed over to Pilate, to answer charges of Sedition against Tiberius Cæsar.

"'You know full well that handing him over will incur the wrath of the Zealots, who will put to death any Jew who hands a fellow Jew over to the Romans. I know for a fact there are Zealots amongst us,' said one worried scribe. 'Their retribution will be swift!'

"They had good reason to fear the Zealots. Under Jewish law, any Jew who actively threatened the life of another Jew was deemed worthy of death. The Zealots referred to these individuals as *pursuers*.

"'Any suggestions?' asked another, but none were forthcoming.

"'What exactly do the Zealots want with him?' asked a chief priest.

"'Why, to make him their king of course. They have already offered him the position, but he refused it. This angered the Zealots so much that they sought to lay hands on him and force him to accept the position but he disappeared from their midst,' said one who sat among the chief priests.

"'Is this true, Judas?' demanded Caiaphas petulantly, using the Greek version of my name.

"I nodded my consent.

"'Why didn't you bring this to our attention?' demanded Annas in the excitable manner of the Jews.

"'Zealots in the crowd had worked the people into a frenzy!' I protested. 'Y'shua flat-out refused their offer. After all, who were they to appoint him king? I saw no reason to report the incident.'

"'Refused the position, did he?' asked Annas, barking in my face like a marine corps drill instructor. 'This may come as a surprise to you, but Julius Cæsar refused to be made king as well. He refused the crown three times if I remember correctly. And you felt it was not important to notify us!'

"Infuriated, Annas ordered Jesus taken to a holding cell. When the guard made to leave with Jesus, Annas flew into a rage and instructed Caiaphas to show them where the cell was located. I went with the guard, expecting someone to try and stop me, but I suppose having the rank of a Zealot commander has its privileges. We were led down stairs to what looked like a basement. Mordechai looked at me in astonishment. There before us was a prison cell complete with iron bars and a locking mechanism. Jesus was placed inside. Caiaphas took the key from a hook on the wall, locked the door and walked off with it.

"'I'll be back when enough members arrive for us to convene a full Sanhedrin,' he said angrily as he ascended the stairs.

"I must admit that these men did not seem to fit the Gospel's descriptions of them as unscrupulous elders, determined to break every law and ordinance in order to obtain their purpose. A much better description of the Sadducees would be that they loved the fortunes they had amassed, and hated each other.

"Scratching my beard, which I hadn't got used to, I exhaled loudly and asked Mordechai, 'Have you had any rest?'

"He shook his head and said, 'I'm too hungry to sleep, anyway.'

"I reached for my money belt and remembered that there would be no place open at this hour for the men to buy something. It's not like there were any all-night burger joints around. 'Mordechai, take one of your men and go upstairs. Find Yehosef ha Ramati and tell him I sent you. His home is not far and he will give you provisions that you can bring back here to the rest of us. Please give me the key to his shackles. He's not going anywhere.' Turning to Jesus, I asked if there was anything we could get for him.

"He shook his head and held his hands forward so that I could remove the iron shackles. *The Last Supper truly was his last supper*, I thought. Removing his restraints, I slowly collapsed to the floor and rested my head against the bars of the small cell. 'I feel like I'm losing my mind, Master. I feel like I'm some sort of nut having a very long and detailed hallucination of epic proportions. I am experiencing emotions I did not know were possible: emotions which man has not the words to describe.'

"Placing a hand on my head, he assured me that, 'The greatest oak in all the world was once a little nut, who held his ground. It is well they mock my kingdom, for they shall not see it in this lifetime. They've rejected the messenger, and with him the message. The priests have exiled the Shekinah (the Divine Feminine) and refused their Messiah—they will be exiled in turn. Their places at the great feast shall be offered to others.'

"'Very soon now, plagues and catastrophes shall descend on *your world*, just as surely as the Roman legions shall descend on Jerusalem. Take your people and go, take them into a new wilderness, hide them under the seas and high in the mountains, that you may be spared just as those living here now who listen to my words and flee to the mountains will be spared when the Romans encamp about this city. Those whom the Romans do not destroy will have a very long walk back to Rome, where they will be used for sport in the arenas. The few that survive will live out their remaining years as slaves.'

"'I fear your message was lost on them,' I said. 'These stubborn people have hated the Romans all their lives. They have no desire to love their neighbors...'

"'And the generations before them hated the Greeks and before them the Persians,' Jesus interrupted. 'These people do not even like themselves. How can they possibly ever learn to love their enemies, Judah? Name me one Jew who cannot stand the sight of another. Traditionally the Zealots have always killed more Jews than they have Romans. These people are simply not ready for the mission I am entrusting my disciples with. Israel has already forgotten that the only reason God allowed it to be conquered by another nation was that long ago their forefathers returned to idols and persecuted the prophets. Rome has been more than tolerant with this nation; if only because Herod the Great befriended and supported Julius Cæsar during his battles in Egypt.'

"'Soon, very soon, in your time, there shall appear the sign of the 'Son of Man' in the heavens. And it shall be as in the days of Noah. The very powers of the heavens shall be shaken. And men's hearts will fail them when they look to the cosmos and see that which is coming.'

"'Y'shua, how can I be in two worlds at the same time? How is that even possible?' I asked.

"'Time, you will soon discover, is an illusion. And before this is all over, you will discover that you inhabit far more worlds than two and far more bodies than one.'

"Knocking my head against the bars, I replied, 'Truth and illusion are often disguised as each other. Soon I will go before the Sanhedrin, and I am not sure of what I will say. The Sadducees and the Pharisee scribes know scripture better than anyone in Judea. I've never known anyone who can quote scripture the way they can...'

"'Judah,' interrupted Jesus, 'The Devil can recite scripture when it suits him. That does not mean he understands it. These men are at a disadvantage. Scripture only comes alive to those who are possessed of the Holy Breath of the Creator. The Sadducees cynically deny all of the prophets who foretold of my coming. They only accept the first five books of Moses, the Torah, as sacred scripture. When you confront them, allow the Holy Ghost to express what you do not have words for. Settle it in your heart not to ponder how you will answer, what you shall say, or what is best left unsaid.'

"'Y'shua, long ago the Sanhedrin commissioned me to find the long-awaited Messiah. I was ordered to seek Johanan, the Baptizer, and join him if possible. In this way I was to report his every move back to the Sanhedrin. I was there when you were baptized and have followed you from the time you returned from Qumran in the desert. I want you to know that I have always watered down my reports to the temple.'

"'Perhaps, but there is another, and he reports faithfully all that transpires.'

"'I was not aware of this. Who is he?'

"'One of the five Zealots you selected as disciples: Yeshua-bar-Abbas.'

"'I was not aware he could read, let alone write.'

"'An agent who gives everyone the impression that he is an infiltrator is of little use. Bar-Abbas's greasy exterior houses a master spy.'

"'I actually believed him when he said he was a trash collector. He certainly smelled bad enough.'

Incredulous

"'Trash collection is an honorable profession. The only trash this one collects is that which he hurries to take back to his masters. Yeshua-bar-Abbas is a leader among the Zealots. He is not one of its lower members as you were led to believe. He is being held at the Fortress Antonia along with Dysmas and Cestus, awaiting execution for attacking an armory, killing Roman soldiers, and stealing swords in preparation for a revolt they had planned to launch in the morning.'

"'What? Three of the disciples I selected? They had hinted at it, but I didn't think they would go through with it. It seems I have really made a mess of things, Master.'

"'Remember it was I who choose you, Judah. I have learned much these past few years. And I know now that it was wrong to exclude all who were not Israelites from my message. They, too, hunger for Truth. When my ministry began I sent the twelve of you forth, and commanded that you enter into no city of the Samaritans. I commanded you to stay away from the Gentiles. You were to go only to those who kept the laws of Moses. And although they have kept the laws, their hearts do not hunger for truth.'

"'The faith of men like Cornelius, the Centurion at Capernaum, has touched my heart. Take my message to the Gentiles, Judah. It would seem that the seeds of wisdom have taken root in fertile soil.'

"'In the other world I, too, am a Gentile. I was even a priest once. Through the power of the Holy Spirit, I have healed the sick and cast out dæmons in your name...'

"Jesus cut me off. 'Many will say such things to me on that final day. Lord, Lord, have we not prophesied in thy name and in thy name cast out devils? And performed many wondrous works? But I will say to them, "Depart from me, you workers of iniquity!"'

"'We have a real problem, then, because that is exactly what preachers are instructing your followers to do. To live their lives as you lived yours. "WWJD?: What Would Jesus Do?" has become a popular slogan,' I added in my defense.

"'What I have done, and what I came to do, shall be accomplished by merging my will with that of the Creator of the Universe. It is the merging of your individual will with that of the Creator, not my actions, that you should seek to emulate. The desires in your heart were placed there by the Creator, and what is in your heart no man can know or judge. Seek to align your will with that of the Creator, and greater works than mine will you accomplish.'

"'I will do my best to correct this error in our thinking,' I promised. 'I will also instruct my people of the coming dangers and the signs we must look for. But I'm not sure you have the right man for this job. I'm not certain I can go through with this.'

"Jesus smiled, reached through the bars, clasped my shoulder and said, 'Right now you must be thinking that I got the easy part in all this,' to which we both laughed. 'Blessed are you when men revile you and persecute you for my sake, Judah. Rejoice and be glad, for great is your reward. Because I gnow the truth of your heart.' Then he leaned in and pulled me closer to the bars, whispering, 'My time draws near... the chief priests and scribes will convene soon and when they do...'"

"This part of the conversation I cannot reveal to you just yet," Teryk apologized. "But soon, very soon, you'll understand just what Judah's part was in all this."

"Are you certain Jesus chastised you for casting out devils and working miracles?" asked Joshua in astonishment.

"Yes, Jesus never wanted his followers to copy his life," explained Teryk. "He wanted us to blossom into the unique aspect of the Creator that we are. I've since learned that Jesus made this quite clear in Matthew 7:21-23, which reads, 'Not everyone that sayeth to me, Lord, Lord, shall enter into the kingdom of Heaven: but he that doth the *will* of my Father who is in Heaven, he shall enter into the kingdom of Heaven. Many will say to me in that day: Lord, Lord, have not we prophesied in thy name, and cast out devils in thy name, and done many miracles in thy name? And then will I profess unto them, *I never knew you*: depart from me, you that work iniquity.'

"I don't know about you," confided Teryk, "but I don't remember reading that verse in Matthew before. I can tell you that when I read the verse anew it scared the hell out of me. I was quite shocked to find that reprimand, in red lettering, coming directly from Jesus himself."

"An irony," observed Raven, "that on the one hand you have those who say miracles do not happen and never did, while on the other hand you have Jesus himself telling his followers not to mimic his works. Yet that's exactly what Church leaders have been instructing Christians to do for centuries. Irenaeus, one of the early Church fathers, wrote, 'those who are truly his [Jesus] disciples actually do drive out dæmons... others heal the sick and lay their hands upon them, and they are completely healthy... even the dead have been raised up, and have remained alive among us for many years.' Irenaeus adds that this power is received in the name of Jesus Christ and that his disciples neither attempt to deceive anyone nor take their money."

"So what is it we're supposed to do?" asked Trisha.

"I believe the answer to that question can be found in the same Gospel. Matthew 25:34-40, to be exact. '...then the 'king' will say, 'Come you blessed of my Father... I was hungry and you fed me, I was naked and you clothed me...' In a nutshell, we are to follow the golden rule," explained Teryk. "'Do unto others, as you would have done unto you.' As you can see, I've been giving this a lot of thought. It is not wrong to heal or drive out dæmons when necessary. What Jesus instructed and demonstrated to his followers was to perform acts of kindness toward one another and to show mercy for the hungry, the sick, the homeless and especially toward those who view us as enemies. In short, we are to love others as we love ourselves. But before you can learn to love others you must acknowledge every aspect of the creation that you are—without judgment. You must accept and love who you are at this moment unconditionally, as the perfect creation you were meant to be. You may not be able to project that perfect aspect of Creator past the fleshy exterior you inhabit but you must acknowledge that it is there. Only then can you learn to love others as you love yourself. Please do not look at me as though I am some sort of saint—I am far from it."

Darkest Before Dawn

"The full Sanhedrin convened in order to form a proper court while it was still very dark," Teryk explained. "There were seventy-one members plus witnesses. The chief priests were determined to find something to accuse Jesus of, and possibly to pull jurisdiction over Pilate. And maybe, just maybe, postpone Jesus' trial. Court was not held in the official building. It was held in the house of Caiaphas. The main gathering room was packed.

"The Great Sanhedrin of seventy-one members contained twenty-four chief priests, each representing one of the twenty-four priestly divisions. The other forty-six members were elders chosen from among the Pharisees, Sadducees and scribes. The high priest, Joseph-bar-Caiaphas, was not only the overseer. He was also a voting member. This ensured a decision by majority vote. Despite the mass corruption, the court still ran pretty much as originally intended, on the principles of impartiality and the proof of evidence by two credible witnesses.

"'In case you haven't figured it out yet, you're one of the witnesses,' snapped Annas.

"According to Jewish law, a witness was required to make the arrest and bring the accused before the Sanhedrin. When the accused was found guilty, the honor of throwing the first stone fell to the witnesses.

"Two other witnesses came forth but their testimonies varied slightly. One maintained that he heard Jesus say, 'I will destroy this temple that is made with hands, and in three days I will build another made without hands.' The second man accused Jesus of saying, 'I am able to destroy the temple of God and build it in three days.' The first offense was cut-and-dry sacrilege, the penalty for which was death by stoning. The second offense bordered on sorcery: The witness only heard him say that he had the power to destroy the Temple—not that he would do it.

"Perhaps I should explain the process of becoming a witness. First, you must be present at the time of the incident. It cannot be hearsay. Second, you must warn the suspect that what he is doing is in contrast to the law, then you must explain the penalty or punishment. After this, if he continued breaking the law, you were considered a witness and were within your rights to arrest this person and bring him before the Sanhedrin. By contrast, if a Roman court lacked witnesses, a person could be convicted by pleading guilty, usually under torture. This was not permitted in Jewish courts. And unlike Roman and modern US courts, the accused was considered innocent until proven guilty. The problem in Jesus' case was that the testimonies of these two men did not match up perfectly. According to Deuteronomy, the judges must make careful inquiry and should the witnesses' testimony be proved false, the court was to do to the witnesses what they wished done to one of their brothers. As it stood, these two were in danger of becoming false witnesses.

"The inconsistency was evidence of how poorly these people had understood Jesus' message. This was getting us nowhere and we had precious little time left. It must be understood that these men were not bearing false testimony against Jesus. Their testimonies were true, but proved false in that they did not agree. By agree I mean they both had to have heard him say the same thing at the same place, and on the same date, even down to the same hour; such was the precision demanded under Jewish law. Under Jewish laws, women, children, slaves and the mentally incompetent were not considered credible witnesses and could not be permitted to testify. As mentioned earlier, they did not permit the testimony of tax collectors either, but this was not due to Jewish law.

"Gamaliel tried to dismiss the whole thing by asking, 'Could he simply have been boasting?' All looked at one another, realizing that the trial might go nowhere. Gamaliel then asked me, 'Judah, you know him best. Could Y'shua simply have been boasting?'

"I turned and looked at Jesus, who was glaring back at me as if to say, 'Don't even think about it.' 'Y'shua hates those who boast and put on charades, almost as much as he hates hypocrites,' I said as I turned back toward the assembled members of the Sanhedrin.

"'Judah was with him for the past several years. Why can he not be called to validate the testimony of one of these witnesses?' asked a scribe.

"'It is well known that an enemy cannot serve as witness but neither can a friend of the accused, and Judah is one of his closest companions,' argued Joseph of Arimathaea.

"'But Judah was commissioned to spy on him before he became his friend,' countered a chief priest.

"'Not exactly,' interjected Gamaliel, 'He was commissioned to join with and spy on Johanan the Baptizer. Yehudah was never commissioned to spy on Y'shua.'

"'But Yeshua was a disciple of this Baptist and so we are well within our jurisdiction,' the chief priest countered with unbridled indignation.

"'Y'shua was merely baptized by Johanan. To our knowledge, he was never one of his cousin's disciples or else he would have been subject to his authority,' explained Gamaliel.

"'Cousins, you're saying these two were kin? They were related?' asked an astonished elder.

"'As are most of his disciples,' I answered, to their dismay.

"'Having wasted almost four years of your life, what can you tell us about him?' asked Annas.

"'I can tell you that the Creator of All is with him and works incredible deeds through him. And I can tell you that he is the long awaited Messiah of Israel, the warrior king and prince of peace,' I answered with all the authority I could muster.

"'Careful, Judah,' cautioned Annas. 'It is not enough for one to say that he is the long-awaited Messiah.'

"'Nor that others say it as well,' I countered. They wanted to dismiss the whole Messiah thing but there were two witnesses whose testimonies now agreed: those of both myself and the young blind man whom Jesus had healed on the Sabbath. I have always been mystified by the audacity of men sitting in council to judge the works of God: works they considered to be hoaxes or dæmonic in origin.

"Eleazar-bar-Ozias was brought forth by the guard and questioned as to the particulars of his healing. 'State your profession,' said one of the scribes, well acquainted with the law.

"'I... I have no profession,' answered the youth.

"'What do you do for a living? What trade did your father teach you, young man?'

"'My father did not teach me a trade. He could not. I was blind and could not perform my father's trade until recently.'

"'A father who does not teach his son a trade teaches him to be a thief!' proclaimed the scribe, waxing vehemently in his self-righteousness.

"*Considering my skills as a treasure hunter, being a thief is a trade in itself,*' I mused.

"'So you're an Ebonite, a misfit subsisting on the good graces of others. This *healing* you speak of, where did it take place? And more importantly, did it occur on the Sabbath day?' demanded the scribe.

"'It was at the pool of Siloam. Miracles sometimes take place there. When I heard a commotion and realized the miracle worker from Galilee was passing by, I called to him. He took pity on me and healed me.'

"'How did he heal you? Did he utter magic words? Did he cast a spell? Come, man, tell us what you know.'

"'I could not see what he did—I was blind.'

"'Again with the blindness! Surely, you must have heard something!'

"'I was told the man made a salve with his spittle and placed the clay over my eyes. He instructed me to bathe my eyes in the waters of the pool. I did as he instructed and began to see. I thanked the man and wanted to run home and tell my parents but I did not know the way. So I had to wait by the pool until they came for me. I then had to wait for them to speak to me in order to know who they were, for I had never seen them before.'

"'I understand your parents are in here with you now?'

"The boy nodded and the scribe looked around as an elderly man stepped forward. 'You sir, what is your name and what is your relation to this young man?'

"'I am Ozias-bar-Symeon. Eleazar is my only son.'

"'Why have you neglected to teach your son a profession, as you are commanded to do? The man is almost of age and does not yet have a wife or the means with which to support a family, all thanks to your negligence.'

"The scribe was speaking of the five duties the Mishnah commands of a father. A father must redeem his son with a sacrifice at the temple. A good Jew is required to circumcise his son on the eighth day. His mother must also be present but, because she is considered unclean for seven days after giving birth, she cannot appear sooner, hence the eighth day. He must instruct his son in the Torah. He must teach him a trade. And he must find him a suitable wife before the age of twenty, or the young man shall be considered accursed of God. The man was clearly troubled and feared being excommunicated: cast out of the synagogue.

"'My son was born blind, sir. Every physician we took him to said it was hopeless. As such, it was not possible to teach him my trade. And what father would give his daughter in marriage to a blind man?'

"'Tell me what you think of this man, this Galilean?' asked the scribe, pointing toward Jesus.

"'Sir, I am not called to give witness, nor did I observe the man commit a crime on the Sabbath day. I beg to be excused if you have no more questions.'

"Not getting the answer he wanted, the scribe dismissed the man with a wave of the hand. Normally witnesses and those called to be questioned were not treated so disrespectfully. The scribe stood before the young man and tried to intimidate him but the young man was enthralled with the splendor of the high priest's palace and all the finely dressed priests around him, some whose robes clearly weighed upwards of fifty pounds.

"'So you were blind but now you see,' surmised the scribe, rolling his eyes in disbelief. 'The day on which you were healed,' he said, forcing the words out, 'was our Holy Sabbath day and any man that performs such works on the Sabbath is not of our Heavenly Creator but is in fact a wicked man.'

"'But only the Heavenly Creator could have healed me. No wicked man could have such power. I do not know if the man who stands accused of a crime is a wicked man or not,' said Eleazar, looking at Jesus. 'You say it is a crime for this man to have healed me on the Sabbath. Yet you approve of the Maccabeans desecrating the Sabbath by shedding blood. Indeed, sir, you celebrate their deeds on the day of Hanukkah. I do not know how our Heavenly Father views these matters, but I do know that I was blind, and now I see. I have prayed since I was a child that I might see; then I resigned myself to a life of blindness. After that I prayed that I might know the Messiah, the promised king of God before I died, and by that I meant that I would know of his arrival. And although there are two in this room who look alike,' he said, not taking his eyes off Jesus, 'I believe I am looking upon the promised Messiah at this moment. And I know that only the power of the Almighty could have made this so. For He does not hear the prayers of a sinner. And although faith may produce miracles, miracles do not necessarily produce faith.'

"'You wretch,' cried one of the chief priests, approaching the young man. 'You were begotten in sin. You were born in sin and have lived with the sin of blindness for your evil acts. And now you presume to stand here and preach the law to us? That man has a devil in him,' he cried, pointing at Jesus, 'and we know who put it there. No man sent of the Almighty would have healed on the Holy Sabbath.'

"The man's foul breath caused Eleazar to take a few steps backwards. Guards laid hands on the youth and forcibly removed him from the room. A scribe next to me sat down and began filling out the necessary documents of excommunication. Without Eleazar's testimony to back up my own, we would be back to one witness. I felt I should bring this blunder to their attention, but thought better of it. With Eleazar gone, I could return the thirty pieces of silver and there would be nothing they could do about it. Deuteronomy was very specific: If only one witness was forthcoming then the suspect could be arrested and held in custody but could not be tried. By the letter of the law, neither of us should have been allowed to stand as witnesses. To be considered a witness, one would have had to first warn Jesus of his criminal act on the Sabbath day and explained the penalty for violating it. Assuming that violating the Sabbath was the crime they were going to slap him with, and neither of us had. As matters stood, Jesus remained unaccused of any crimes and not subject to the authority of the Sanhedrin.

"Other than myself and the young man they had excommunicated, they did not really have any witnesses left. Joseph-bar-Caiaphas looked exasperated as he walked to the center of the tribunal and stood before Jesus. He turned and faced the members of the Sanhedrin. 'You men of Jerusalem, who is the man whom you accuse?'

Incredulous

"They answered in unison, 'In the name of every loyal Jew, we accuse this man from Galilee, Y'shua-bar-Yehosef, who assumes to be a son of the Elohim.'

"Caiaphas called for silence so that the assembled group could hear a scribe read the charges leveled against Jesus. The scribe stood, opened a scroll and declared, 'Most honored men of the Sanhedrin and Jews of Israel, the highest duty a man can render to his nation is to protect it from its enemies. The man named Y'shua-bar-Yehosef blasphemes the Most High, saying he and the Creator are one, that he in fact is the Son of the Elohim, that all men...'

"I could not hear what else the scribe said, as the room became too loud from all the shouting that broke out. To be honest, I think high-school teenagers of my time are far more respectful and well behaved than these men were. Caiaphas again had to call for order and the scribe continued.

"'He claims that all men are the sons of the Elohim. He profanes our Holy Sabbath by all manner of healing and other works. He declares that he will destroy our temple and in three days raise it up again.' Caiaphas motioned for the scribe to continue while he tried to keep order, as we were quickly running out of time. 'He does not stop those who proclaim him to be the successor to our King David. He touches lepers whom the Almighty has made unclean. And he does not wash his hands, exposing us all to contamination. He has declared that he will drive out the inhabitants of Jerusalem as he drove out the merchants, that every Sadducee and Pharisee will be exiled and never again return to the Holy Land.'

'*I stand corrected,*' I thought. '*They are not as dumb as they look—maybe they did understand the parable about the king who made a wedding feast, and just what part they played in it.*'

"After the reading, Caiaphas approached Jesus and demanded, 'I adjure you by the Almighty, by the Gracious and Merciful living Elohim, do you claim to be the long-awaited Messiah, Israel's Anointed King?'

"I objected. Being a scribe also made me a lawyer. Caiaphas had just placed Jesus under our most powerful and fearful oath allowed under the law. 'It is not legal for Caiaphas, the high priest, to cross-examine the accused. It is unheard of under our laws.' I was right and everyone knew it, but they said nothing. Caiaphas knew full well that he was out of line and that it was illegal for the oath to be put to an accused when an answer of 'yes' meant his death. This kangaroo court was now in full session, with the honorable Caiaphas presiding. Their train of thought had jumped the rails of reason. And Jesus was being railroaded.

"Annas turned to me and said, 'Scribe, you missed your calling. You are as wise as a serpent. Perhaps you should have specialized in law.'

"'Perhaps, if you *obeyed the law*, I would have.'

"Jesus knew that to remain silent when the 'Oath of Testimony' was put to you was considered an unforgivable offense and thus he replied, 'If I answer no, I would be no better than the men in this courtroom. If I answer yes, you will not believe me. The time will come when you will see the Son of Man upon the throne of power, coming in the clouds of Heaven…'

"'Just answer the question!' snapped Caiaphas. 'Are you the Messiah, the promised Anointed King?'

"'So you have said.' Jesus was not being evasive. To have answered with a direct yes or no would have been considered extremely uncourteous and rude to the cultured Jewish crowd that stood before him. This is the manner in which one was required to reply to a question of such grave importance. In the proper Hebrew, there were many more powerful ways to proclaim that you were the Messiah than to just come out and say it.

"Annas stepped forward and addressed the Sanhedrin. Holding up a hand for silence, he approached Jesus. Annas played his last wildcard offering to ordain Jesus. If he accepted, he would be elevated to the position of priest. Jesus was already considered to be a prophet. I thought that only Annas would see this as a promotion. In exchange, all Annas required of Jesus was for him to plead not guilty to the charges leveled against him by Rome. Annas would then provide witnesses who would protest his innocence.

"'Many do not feel that you deserve to be ordained,' snorted Annas, 'on the grounds that you violated the Sabbath and keep the company of publicans and harlots, to say nothing of ridiculing our scribes and chief priests. As a newly appointed priest you *will* put a stop to this behavior!'

"*Clever, very clever*, I mused. This proposition was seldom made, and when offered was not to be refused. The title and duties associated with the priesthood were entirely hereditary. Priestly families took great care in maintaining the records that linked them, through intricate patterns of intermarriage. Jesus could never accept the ordination, of course; it would place him in a subordinate position to the chief priests.

"Neither Caiaphas nor Annas had to explain to anyone present what his silence meant. If it was true that the prophesied Messiah had arrived, then an immediate and bloody clash with the Romans would ensue. The Roman garrison under Pilate's command in the city totaled two full legions plus reserves, mostly composed of mercenaries. Pilate, as usual, was well prepared, and if he needed help, I'm sure he could summon Vitellius's legions, which were stationed only two days' march from Antioch. War would spread throughout the land. Even if the rebellion was successful, Rome would undoubtedly retaliate with a punitive expedition, annihilating everything these men had worked so hard to rebuild.

"The disastrous rebellion under Judah of Galilee, just twenty-five years earlier, could not have faded from memory so easily. After the death of Herod the Great, Judah-bar-Hezekiah instigated a revolt by plundering the Herodian palace in Sepphoris. Varus, the Roman governor of Syria, easily suppressed the rebellion with fewer soldiers than were under Pilate's command. In an exhibition demonstrating the power of Rome, Varus burned the city and crucified more than two thousand rebels. The remaining inhabitants of Sepphoris, he sold into slavery. The consequences of Jesus' silence were unimaginable.

"Supposing Jesus was the Messiah and could somehow, through miraculous means, destroy any armies Rome sent against him, the supreme position of the high priest would be eclipsed by this young firebrand. As the nation's deliverer and the representative of God, he would impose policies that were absolute. After all, that was the meaning of the word Messiah: the one God anointed to rule over all!

"'We are undone!' bellowed Caiaphas in an overly theatrical display of emotion, tearing his priestly robe from sheer aggravation. 'You bring destruction upon all Israel!' he shouted, having torn his robe at least a palm's length, the required length to express shock or grief under Jewish custom.

"It is in fact a rule of Jewish law that upon hearing the name of God desecrated, the court and the witnesses must rend their garments. Jesus, however, did not utter the unspeakable name of God. No, Caiaphas tore the holy robes of his office because he understood that Israel was only hours away from engaging the Roman armies in battle. It is an ancient and well-known custom for Jews to rend their clothes upon hearing of great misfortune or the outbreak of war. Caiaphas could not make Jesus see his point of view. In the eyes of the Sanhedrin, Jesus stubbornly pushed toward a disastrous outcome; his recklessness would surely destroy the nation of Israel and the Sanhedrin along with it. Caiaphas had failed in his efforts to make Jesus see reason and accept their guidance. Perhaps this was not the best time to remind him that tearing the high priest's robes was considered sacrilege under the laws of Leviticus.

"'If we hand him over to the Romans for execution, the Zealots will not rest until we are all dead men,' cried one of the chief priests.

"'The Zealots believe he is their Messiah. By now they must know he was arrested and charged with sedition against Rome. There is only one punishment for sedition and the rebels know it well,' said Annas, standing next to me.

"'Still... if there was a way out of this, would you take it?' I asked him in a cold and calculated tone.

"'It is all well for your Messiah to excite the people with his talk of another world while we have to live in this one. We are hemmed in from every side,' exclaimed Annas in exasperation. 'What possible way could we have out of this?'

"There I was again... all eyes were on me. I had to turn away from Jesus. I could not look upon my friend and utter the abomination now forming in my throat. In his cell Jesus had reminded me that long ago shofars were not only blown to signal twilight and dawn: Their reverberating sound had also been a call to war. If I could not do what was asked of me, a bloody battle would soon follow the blast of those silver trumpets. The Zealots would soon raise the battle cry, 'No Ruler but God'. How long I stood there I do not remember. Someone touched me on the shoulder, bringing me back to myself and what I had to do. Betray, or obey… tearing my white linen robe and turning to point an accusing finger at my Lord, I shouted, 'He is a *false prophet!*'

"I stood there, transfixed, as I saw them turn on him. They were like drowning rats in a sinking ship, clutching at any straw of hope, and I had just thrown them the Titanic. Never mind that my accusation was ludicrous. These were desperate men and they would scurry onboard this sinking ship without ever giving it a second thought, in order to save their precious hides, so strong was their sense of self-preservation. Jesus gnew this 'generation of vipers' better than they knew themselves. The efficacy with which he maneuvered them into a position where they would be forced to proceed against him defied understanding. How many times had Jesus taught us not to be so damn predictable? Be unpredictable, he would say, turn the other cheek. Do something your adversary does not expect you to do. And now we had them—right where they wanted us.

"I heard an infernal shriek and likened it to a rooster crowing. An icy chill ran up my spine. I thought of Peter warming his hands in one of the fires outside. My own hands were freezing. I had noticed that it always gets colder just before the dawn, but this chill seemed unnatural, like the diabolical sound of that hellish chicken. It sounded again and my hand began to shake; I wondered if it was from the cold but suspected it wasn't. I turned and stared at one of the fires outside in the courtyard. I recognized Peter, who was standing transfixed, his gaze focused upon Jesus.

"Gamaliel stood before me, his hands firmly on my shoulders, shaking me. 'What have you done, Yehudah?'

"In the distance I heard Peter let out a cry of anguish. I saw that the priests had thrown Jesus' tallit over his head and were assaulting him, asking him to divine who had struck him. I believe they would have killed him then and there, had it not been for fear of what Pilate might do to them. Mordechai and his guard rushed in and attempted to get them off of him. Mordechai drew his blade and slapped a scribe's head with the flat of his sword. His men followed suit as others from the guard dragged Jesus away from the mob.

"I turned to my old teacher and said, 'I have set into motion… events that cannot be stopped.' Looking down, I realized I was clutching my Damascus steel blade and was surprised I had not killed someone with it. I wasn't thinking straight and I wondered if I was in shock.

"Then Caiaphas, who did not appear to have slept at all this night, cried out, with his fist held high over overhead, 'It is far better for this one rabble-rouser to die for the good of all than for the whole nation to perish for his foolishness. The Lord warned his people in the Holy Torah: If there is a prophet among you, or a dreamer of dreams, and he shall speak of other gods, you shall surely put him to death. Do not listen to him for the Elohim are testing you.'

"That wasn't exactly the way it went in Deuteronomy but these men needed an excuse to avoid genocide, and this was as good as any. The entire concept of the Elohim is what kept these men from understanding what Jesus meant by Creator. When Jesus referred to God he meant the true Creator of All; a supernatural omniscient being to whom even the Elohim must answer. Having failed to discredit his works and teachings, they leveled charges against the messenger himself. The Sanhedrin's vote was swift and unanimous. No pretense was given to the custom of younger members voting first, so as not to be influenced by the older priests. Joseph of Arimathaea and Nicodemus, both legislative members of the Sanhedrin, were present and must have voted in favor of execution.

"If the visions of Israel's dreamers had truly ceased long ago, along with the prophets of old, then surely these men offered worship to a God that had long since departed. Jesus had promised them that the sign of Jonah was yet to come. Like Nineveh, the people of Israel had been forced to make a simple decision: Accept God's messenger and what he preached, or reject him and be destroyed in the process—they had chosen the latter..."

"Commander, it is important to consider the fact that under the laws set by Moses a unanimous vote for Jesus' death required the Sanhedrin to wait one additional day, to see if anyone had changed their minds before the sentence of death was carried out," interrupted Kortney, our expert on Judaic Law. "Why would the Sanhedrin bother to uphold all the seemingly trivial laws of the Torah only to blatantly disregard this one important directive?"

"Commander, I could find nothing stating that Judas Iscariot was anywhere near the proceedings," said Noraia apologetically.

"It's in Matthew," said Raven, glancing at her *Bible*. "He states that Judas *saw* that Christ had been condemned, implying he was present at the trial. I know it's slim, but it's all we've got so far."

"According to a long-established Hebrew custom, the only accusers in a Jewish criminal trial were the witnesses," said Phoenix. "Any other form of prosecution would have been illegal. It was the duty of the court under an elaborate judicial code to protect the interest of the accused in every way possible."

"According to Jewish laws, it should have been the witnesses who arrested Jesus and brought him before the Sanhedrin. Upon his being found guilty, the witnesses would be required to throw the first stone," explained Kortney. "This is similar to the case involving the woman who had been caught in the act of adultery."

"I've always been curious about that incident," said Katharine. "What exactly was Jesus writing in the sand regarding the woman taken in adultery, Teryk?"

"When the two witnesses, who claimed to have caught the girl in the act of adultery, dragged her before Jesus, he asked them, 'And, where is her partner?' Jesus was implying the obvious, without actually stating it," said Teryk. "You see the Law of Moses, as it is found in Leviticus, specifically states that both were to be put to death. When challenged again by these men, Jesus did not immediately reply. He stooped down and began to write with his finger in the loose sand. He wrote down the Ten Commandments, as light gusts of wind playfully swept his writing away. In their original form, the writing is quite terse: 'Do not steal', 'Do not murder,' and so on. But not all of the inscriptions were blown away. It was uncanny how some segments remained, despite the efforts of the breeze to erase them. Jesus gazed down in wonder, then looked up at the two witnesses and asked that the man who was without sin cast the first stone. Although there were many in the crowd who had already rushed to find a choice implement with which to bludgeon this poor soul, by law, they were not permitted to cast them. If neither of the arresting witnesses cast the first stone, no one would be permitted to stone her."

"Commander, this story appears only in John 7:53 through 8:12," said Hypnautica, "The wording and style of this text make it apparent that it does not belong there. This story does not appear in the oldest manuscripts attributed to John. The writing style of this passage differs from the rest of John and contains words and phrases not found elsewhere in this Gospel. It appears to have originally existed in the Gospel of Luke, perhaps at the end of chapter 21, but must have been removed…"

"That doesn't surprise me!" said Raven in a sarcastic tone, finishing the sentence for Hypnautica. "You see, Hypnautica, the early Church fathers refused to forgive the sin of adultery. Honestly, what the hell was Jesus thinking?"

Trying to suppress a laugh, Kortney added, "According to the Mishnah, testimony fell into one of three classifications. The least effective was *vain testimony*, which the judges recognized as irrelevant and worthless. Then there was *standing testimony*, evidence which was taken more seriously but could not be accepted until it was confirmed. The accused were literally innocent until proven guilty. And finally you have what is referred to as *adequate testimony*, which occurred when the statements of two witnesses agreed."

"If the two men claiming to be witnesses were deliberately inventing these charges, under Jewish Law they would have been put to death. What's more, they both knew it," said Athena. "To give distorted, fictitious or misleading information during a trial for life was a grave offense."

"Subtleties of Jewish jurisprudence should not be present in a trial whose outcome had been prearranged," admitted Kortney. "It doesn't make any sense. If the Sanhedrin's trial was so illegal, why is there a consistently strong undercurrent of legality to it? The high priests had gone to great lengths in order to obtain Jesus in their custody from the Romans. Having secured witnesses, why overthrow and reject their statements, statements believed to have been fabricated by the Sanhedrin in a deliberate attempt to destroy Jesus? Look at our own corrupt court systems. Nothing could have been easier. Something obviously led them to believe that Jesus would not escape execution."

"The Sanhedrin's accusations, as they are put forth in the Gospels, were lame at best," said Winter. "When the priests came before Pilate, having plotted for weeks to destroy Christ, they could not even tell Pilate what Jesus stood accused of."

"We must remember that it was their Passover. The last thing in the world the priests would have wanted during a Passover feast would have been to go before Pilate and talk him into an early morning execution of a fellow Jew," reasoned Kortney. "Could Teryk be right? Could they have originally sought to protect Jesus by imposing jurisdiction over him?"

The Praetorium

"The Palace Antonia was originally erected to defend the city from the north. The outer walls of the fortress were covered in smooth flagstones, which not only added to its appearance of impregnability, but also made it impossible for anyone to scale the walls. Antonia's pavement, the large outer courtyard called the Hall of Polished Stones, was the official place of judgment for crimes in Jerusalem. It was located north of the temple wall and directly east of the Fortress Antonia: the exact same location where the arresting cohort had assembled on the previous night.

"The pavement was called 'Gabbatha' by the Jews. The stones were ancient and incredibly massive. No one then living knew who had placed them there or why. The blocks were polished like smooth marble. I could actually see my reflection in them. As one stood on the magnificent 'Hall of Judgment' awaiting a verdict, the immense polished stones seemed to evoke a sense of one's own insignificance.

"The impenetrable Herodian palace served as a Roman fortress that permanently quartered a full cohort. During the festivals, Pilate garrisoned an entire legion in the palace with an additional legion plus reserves strategically positioned throughout the city. Pilate's headquarters were in Cæsarea Maritima, but he came to Antonia for most of the important Jewish holidays, bringing with him additional reinforcements to handle the increased number of pilgrims.

"At the Palace Antonia, Mordechai was met by two helmeted legionnaires, one armed with a sword, the other with a shield and spear. The soldier holding the spear and shield removed the shackle from Jesus' right wrist and placed it on his own right wrist. The other soldier, armed with only a sword, took the shackle that was chained to his own left wrist and attached the open end to Jesus' right wrist. Then they escorted him before the praetor or provincial governor, Pilate, who was standing in ceremonial armor at the top of the steps.

"The Gospels refer to this place as the Praetorium. Pilate's actual Praetorium was in Cæsarea Maritima, but Herod's palace served this purpose in Jerusalem. As I understand it, the 'Praetorium' was anywhere the Roman magistrate decided to hold court. I entered with a hand-picked group of unimportant chief priests following close behind.

"Jesus was brought before Pilate, who saw the condition of the prisoner and demanded, 'What is the meaning of this?'

"Caiaphas had refused to enter and was standing at the bottom of the stairs on the stone pavement. From Gabbatha, he proclaimed, 'We have found him guilty!'

"Pilate exclaimed in surprise, 'You have found him guilty? What accusations do 'you' bring against this man?'

"'He stirs up the people against Cæsar,' said a chief priest standing next to me.

"'Your people don't need any help being stirred up against Cæsar!' Pilate retorted, then turned to enter the Praetorium, knowing Caiaphas would not follow.

"Jesus should have been unharmed when he was brought before Pilate, but his face was beginning to bruise. Pilate called for Livius, the tribune who made the arrest. As Livius entered, Pilate held out a hand toward Jesus and asked, 'What is the meaning of this?'

"Livius took one look at Jesus and suspected why he had been summoned. Bowing and placing his right fist to his chest, he said, 'Prefect, Joshua was shackled but unharmed when we handed him to the temple police.' Livius looked into the crowd. Seeing me, he pointed and said, 'This is the witness who identified Joshua for us.'

"Pilate called me forward. 'State your name and relationship to the accused?'

"'I am Judah-bar-Simon. I have been a disciple of Joshua for over three years now. I am the witness who identified the accused.'

"'Was this man unharmed when my tribune handed him into the custody of the Temple Guard?'

"'Joshua was in no way harmed by your Roman soldiers,' I said, feeling the eyes of the priests on the back of my neck.

"Turning to the priests, Pilate asked, 'Is it your custom to beat a man before he has been convicted of a crime?'

"'In the course of the night, our court convened and found him guilty of blasphemy, a crime for which he should be put to death,' said a chief priest I did not recognize. Most of these men held lower positions in the temple, which is why they were in here—they would not be needed to perform the Passover ceremonies later that day. 'He was found guilty of practicing sorcery and inciting Israel to apostasy. The man is a false prophet and under the laws of Moses he is subject to death.'

"After that day, all these men, me included, would be considered unclean because we'd entered a place of idolatrous worship. To the Romans, Cæsar was God and as such, a shrine had been erected to him. Pilate, as governor, also filled in as high priest and was required to perform sacrifices to Augustus Cæsar's graven image. Cæsar's statue was not the only idol in the building. Most Romans kept several idols in their homes, which was why entering their dwellings was forbidden to the Jews.

"Pilate again turned to me for validation. I explained that, 'The Sanhedrin held court during the night. In the process, they lost all self-control and attacked the accused. The priests were beaten off the prisoner by the Temple Guard,' I added, pointing toward Mordechai, 'who removed Joshua from their court and brought him here.' It wasn't exactly what happened, but it sounded good.

"'This man has committed sacrilege and according to our laws he is deserving of death!' said a chief priest who seemed to be in charge. 'If he were not an evil-doer and a sorcerer, we would not now be delivering him up to you for execution.'

"Pilate sat back slightly on his *sella*, a judgment seat traditionally reserved for Rome's highest dignitaries, pondering the situation. 'This may come as a shock to you, priest, but Roman law does not convict a man to death before he is tried. He is first given a chance to defend himself before his accusers.'

"I noticed Pilate's aura, the energy field around his body, light up for an instant. Turning to one of his court advisors, he summoned him, and they spoke in hushed tones. Pilate stood and motioned for his guard to take Jesus outside, which is where he was headed. Two soldiers stationed next to one of the banner holders opened the curtains, referred to as the *velum*, that were normally kept closed during a trial. Pilate had a mischievous look on his face as he waited for Jesus to be brought forth. His advisors stood just inside the Praetorium. I stood with them.

"Pilate's attitude took on a different air. He turned to the crowd that had begun to gather and pointing to Jesus, asked the chief priests, who would not enter the Praetorium, 'What accusations do 'you' bring against this man?'

"Having considered Jesus' arrest and execution a foregone conclusion, most just looked around in astonishment. Then Caiaphas, who was standing in front with his father-in-law, shouted, 'If he were not an evil-doer we would not have delivered him back to you.' He wanted to look good in eyes of the attending Zealots, I suppose. Caiaphas then signaled to a scribe. The man stepped forward and handed Pilate the charges, which the temple scribes had transcribed into the language of the Roman court.

"'He is a prisoner of Rome. It is not lawful for us to put him to death,' declared someone in the mob.

"Pilate glanced over the charges and considered for a moment. 'Being deserving of death!' he read aloud. Then, gesturing toward Jesus in a grandiose manor, he offered, 'Take him, then. Judge him according to your laws. I make a gift of him to you on this your day of celebration,' he said. 'Take him and stone him. That is within your powers. I promise not to interfere in your affairs.'

"Caiaphas's mouth dropped, as did his father-in-law's. Pilate turned to walk away, a smug look of triumph on his face. I could not imagine what sort of jaded game he was up to but he nearly stopped in his tracks at the next utterance from the high priest.

"'He calls himself a king, the Anointed of the Most High,' shouted Annas insolently.

"Pilate continued walking as if unfazed by the outburst. He slowed down when he got near me and one of his advisors turned and fell in step with him.

"Could this be the surviving son of Antipater?" asked the advisor. "His mother's name is Mariamne...'

"*Oh shit!* I had forgotten about this guy. Antipater was the son of Herod the Great by his first wife Doris. Rome did not recognize multiple wives, so if Herod had a successor to his throne, he would have to come from his first wife. Emperor Augustus had decreed that Antipater would be king after Herod, but in a rage Herod had murdered his son. Antipater's wife Mariamne, a Maccabean princess, had disappeared while pregnant with the heir to the Jewish kingdom. She was never seen again. The child, who would then be about Jesus' age, was the only other king whom Rome would recognize. Augustus 'the god' had decreed it and so it could not be revoked. Clearly the man was well versed in our history. I could see why Pilate kept him at court.

"Just then Cornelius, the Roman centurion from Capernaum, approached me and said in butchered Aramaic, 'I came as soon as I heard.' With a heavy heart Cornelius left my side and took the place of the soldier to Jesus' right.

"Cornelius was the centurion who had requested that Jesus heal his servant. He must have been in Jerusalem with his unit. I remembered how upset John the Baptist had been with Jesus when he heard of the incident. I never did understand why John was so offended by it. I knew the Baptist was an Essene. It was an unclean thing for a pious Jew to enter the dwelling of a Gentile. The fanatical Essenes considered physical contact with Gentiles more offensive than the touch of a diseased swine. But Jesus never entered the man's house. In fact, we were miles from the man's villa. John was so angry that he sent two of his disciples to ask Jesus if he was the promised one to come, or should they look for another. I don't know if it went well with John when his disciples returned with Jesus' reply. '...fortunate is the one who is not disturbed upon hearing the things I do.'

"Some of the chief priests walked past me and took their positions in the inner courtroom, where they waited for Pilate to summon Jesus again. Pilate motioned and his guard, fronted by our friend the centurion, started forward. Waiting for them to pass, I noticed how much more Jesus' face had begun to swell where that ox of a temple guard had struck him. To his credit, not one of Mordechai's men had struck Jesus while he was in their custody. I hoped the fool who had struck him would not cross my path anytime soon. Just then I was startled out of my thoughts by a commotion inside the Praetorium. As I prepared to enter with the rest to see what was the matter, I noticed Nicodemus and Joseph of Arimathaea– walking up the steps of the Praetorium.

"Where do I begin? To start with, Pilate was furious that Cornelius had removed his cape and placed it on the steps for Jesus to step on as he entered the inner courtroom, called the secretarium. This was a sign of royalty Pilate did not wish extended to Jesus, but that was not what had caused the disturbance. The priests were accusing the banner holders of lowering the ensigns, which bore Cæsar's image, as Jesus entered. It was this action more than the centurion's which had angered everyone in the room. Two legionnaires were ordered to bring the banner holders before Pilate, who asked them why they had done such a thing. The men replied that they had not. They were Greeks and cared not whether the accused was considered Jewish royalty.

"The priests were beside themselves, so Pilate ordered the guard to take Jesus back out of his courtroom. He then instructed the priests to select a dozen men from among themselves to hold the banners. He would order Jesus to enter again. If the banners did not bend of their own accord as implied, the two Banner Holders would lose their heads.

"At this command the two soldiers holding the banner holders drew their swords. The two men were terrified, but what could they do? The priests placed six of their own men on either side, to hold the poles that bore the banners over the steps by which Jesus was to enter. Pilate read from the scroll again, 'blaspheme… enemy of Rome…forbids payment of tribute to Tiberius…King!' He looked up and motioned for the guard to bring Jesus in. The rest of us waited to see what would happen.

"The centurion moved ahead of Jesus and once again laid his red cape on the stairs, saying, 'Lord, walk upon this and enter, for the governor has called for you.'

"Pilate exhaled in exasperation. When Jesus entered it was evident that the poles, held by a half dozen men on either side, never moved. The images of Tiberius were another matter. Both profiles faced inward toward Jesus, and as he entered they became animated and bowed reverently to the King of Kings, returning to their previous position once he had passed. Pilate had been prepared for anything but this. He was visibly shaken by the experience, as was I. An odd combination of fear and exhilaration coursed through my veins.

"The advisor, whose name I learned was Timonides, leaned over to Pilate and whispered, 'Could this be their Messias, their Christos, the anointed king promised by their God. The one Herod the Great sought to kill shortly after his birth?'

"The governor fought to regain his composure as Jesus approached. When the guard stopped, Jesus did too. Pilate drew near, demanding, 'Are you the Messias, the King of the Jews?'

"This was improper protocol, perhaps. Pilate was still shaken. What he should have said was, 'State your name, for the record.' And what's more, Jesus knew it, so he replied, 'You have said so,' which of course was the formal Jewish method of answering a blatant statement or a question of great importance. Just then, I noticed a man standing in the background who acted a lot like the informant the Romans had used during Jesus' arrest, but my attention was diverted to a chief priest who was rushing toward Jesus demanding that he answer.

"Cornelius turned toward the priest, grabbing the hilt of his sword, and drew it slightly. The chief priest recoiled and turning toward Pilate, warned, 'Did we not tell you he was a sorcerer.' Having regained his nerve, the man turned toward Jesus. Standing just out of the centurion's reach, he demanded, in an insolent tone, 'Do you not claim to be the Anointed of the Lord, the King of all Jews?'

"'Perhaps,' said Timonides, in an eloquent tone, 'a king who must constantly remind others that he is king—is no king at all.'

"'Are you the son of Antipater, heir to the Jewish Kingdom?' asked Pilate. Judging a king was well beyond the governor's power.

"'What? This man is no such thing! He is a Galilean, not an Idumaean,' challenged the chief priest.

"'He's Galilean? If this man is from Galilee then he is a subject of Herod-Antipas and that is who should judge him.' Pilate ordered that Jesus be taken to Herod in chains. He sent along the scroll containing the charges against him and asked that Herod pass judgment on the case."

"Commander, many scholars have speculated that the priests would have been too busy to attend the proceedings," said Kortney. "With the exception of Caiaphas, the high priest, none of the five thousand priests due to attend the temple for Passover would have been missed."

"How long would the necessary purifications take if the priests entered Pilate's court and defiled themselves as the Gospels claim?" asked Cassandra.

"Roughly seven days," proclaimed Kortney. "It is difficult to say for sure based on the information in the Gospels. Their authors do not go into any details as to why the priests would be defiled. It was considered scandalous for a pious Jew to enter a Roman dwelling. You really had to understand the mindset of the Jews in that time."

"The United States is a nation founded by Christians under the principles of Roman government. Has anyone given much thought to why the founding fathers would impose a separation of Church and state?" asked Teryk, seeming to stray from the conversation. "Few of us today can comprehend the concept that a person appointed to rule, such as an emperor, was a divinity. The emperors of Rome were considered divine, and temples of worship had been built in their honor. Pontius Pilate was not only the acting governor, he was also the high priest responsible for enforcing the worship of these divine beings. For this purpose, Pilate had a shrine of worship erected inside the Palace Antonia, where he could make the necessary sacrifices to the divine Augustus every morning while in Jerusalem.

"Separation of Church and state prohibits Congress from establishing a religion and imposing it upon the people. Fearing Congress might pass a law establishing a state religion, President Thomas Jefferson said there should be a 'wall of separation between church and state'. He explains this in a letter addressed to the Danbury Baptist Association, dated 1 January 1802. The DBA was a religious minority who complained that its members' right to worship was being viewed as 'favors granted' under the current administration, not an immutable right under the Constitution of the United States. Separation of Church and state has nothing to do with keeping religion out of government. That letter was taken out of context in the same manner that the Apostle Paul's epistles have been taken out of context. Each of those letters aimed to address a specific situation or concern that was topical at that time." Teryk's voice took on an edge. "Like those who twist scripture, they were not asking what does it really mean but rather what can we make it mean?

"Separation of Church and state has nothing to do with teaching the *Bible* in school or praying at an assembly. Separation of Church and state means that the government cannot declare the president or any other ruler divine and force its citizens to worship him, as in the case of the Roman emperors. Due to the Constitution having been stripped and many laws twisted, should the Illuminati ever succeed in forming their New World Order, there will be little to stop them from declaring their new world leader a deity and imposing mandatory worship on the people of Earth.

"Any priest who entered the Fortress Antonia would have been defiled because he had entered a pagan temple. The priests would have had to purify themselves in a ritual bath for seven days, missing the week long festivities," explained Teryk.

"Exactly!" exclaimed Anakah. "Why would Pilate hold court on a day when the principal witnesses could not attend? Simple logic would dictate that a Roman governor would simply postpone judicial proceedings for such a serious crime and hold prisoner the man accused of sedition against the emperor until after the festivities. Yet all four Gospels make it quite clear that Pilate went ahead with the trial."

"The Gospels also state that the priests were extremely upset when Pilate failed to endorse the verdict they had arrived at earlier that morning in their own court," added Winter.

"Any Jew who displayed such open hostility toward another Jew in favor of the Romans risked death at the hands of the Zealots," cautioned Kortney. "It would have been completely out of character for priests to behave in that manner."

"They had committed themselves," explained Joshua. "The status of their high priestly position would never recover from the blow of Jesus having been set free. It would have devastated their reputations and authority in the eyes of the people. This, more than anything, they could not have allowed."

"Pontius Pilate has been referred to as a procurator in the Gospels, but this title did not appear to be a formal Roman title of that time," said Cassandra. "The title stemmed from the fact that these governors were responsible for 'procuring' tribute to Rome. The earliest reference we could find dates after Emperor Claudius in 41 CE."

"As with all things biblical, historians doubted that a man named Pontius Pilate ever lived, much less governed Judaea. Doubting Jesus had ever existed, why would these intellectuals believe Pontius Pilate could have presided over his trial?" asked Raven. "All that changed in the summer of 1961, when Dr. Antonio Frova, an Italian archaeologist in charge of a dig, discovered a stone that bore the inscription 'CÆSARIENS TIBERIE'VM PONTIVS PILATVS PRAEFECTVS INDAEAE DE'DIT'. It translates into 'Pontius Pilate, prefect of Judea, has presented the Tiberie'um to the Cæsareans'. A Roman prefect—governor—would have had a lot more military responsibility than a procurator. The title of prefect for Roman governors of Judea appears to have shifted to procurator under the rule of Emperor Claudius. The second piece of evidence for the existence of this man comes from the writings of Tacitus. Concerning the great fire that devastated Rome in 64 CE, he mentions Pontius Pilate by name. 'Nero fastened the guilt and inflicted the most exquisite tortures on a class hated for their abominations, called Christians by the populace. Christus, from whom the name had its origin, suffered the extreme penalty during the reign of Tiberius at the hands of one of our procurators, Pontius Pilate.' Those words are from section 15.44 of *Annals* from 115 CE."

"Apparently Pontius Pilate was a member of the Ordo Equester. He served in combat under the famous Roman general Germanicus, in Germany. Germanicus avenged the defeat at Teutoburg Forest and recovered the Legion's eagles lost in that battle. According to my sources," said Athena, "Pilate's status was only that of the Roman equestrian or knight, a middle-class order. The very name Pilatus—Pilate—means 'armed—with-a-javelin'. Pilate was appointed governor of Judea around 26 CE, under Sejanus's recommendation. He accepted the post but requested permission to take his wife. The Lady Claudia was a daughter of Tiberius's third wife, and granddaughter of Augustus Cæsar. His request was granted, a very unusual privilege for a military commander. It seems unusual that Pontius Pilate, not being a nobleman, would have been married to such a prominent member of the royal family.

"We are fairly certain Jesus died during the tenure of Pontius Pilate," continued Athena, "but there is a minor controversy over which years the Roman-installed governor was actually appointed prefect of Judea. Pilate either ruled from the year 26 until the year 36 CE, or from the year 27 to the year 37 CE. This discrepancy will not affect our results. We have used the ancient rabbinical method for setting the start of every year to reproduce the literal dates of every Passover during the reign of Pontius Pilate."

"That was so long ago," declared Adriana. "How can you be certain that any of this information is accurate?"

"The Hebrew calendar, like the early Roman calendars, had short years and long years," explained Clifton. Anakah's friend was somewhat of a recluse, keeping much to himself. Clifton was rather unconventional when it came to troubleshooting problems. He had originally joined Teryk's team of inventors specializing in devices that detected paranormal phenomenon, which was unusual considering Clifton flat out refused to be physically present during supernatural events. He relied instead on video recordings, personal interviews and the readouts of an investigation's electronic equipment. His permanent residence was one of Antares's secret observatories positioned in the mountains of Antarctica. "Confirming the accuracy of the actual date of the Passover would appear to be difficult at first," continued Clifton, "but unlike the Romans, whose calendars were also set by the priests, the Hebrew calendars were set back to the same starting point every nineteen years."

"What starting point? And why weren't the Romans doing the same thing?" asked Jidion.

"If you recall, the Julian Calendar was created by Julius Cæsar," Clifton informed her. "Cæsar decided to standardize the calendar precisely because the priests kept changing the lengths of the years at their whim. At that time, Rome was governed by appointed rulers who served an eight-year term. This was before emperors were established. If the priests did not like the new ruler, his years would be shortened—literally. If they favored the appointed ruler they would add months to his years of service. Cæsar's new calendar had only twelve months and each had either thirty or thirty-one days in it."

"If that's so, how did February end up with twenty-eight days?" inquired Trisha.

"Commander, we're getting off track here," advised Shakira.

"Just answer this last question, Clifton, then we'll move on," advised Teryk.

"Yes, sir. When Julius Cæsar was assassinated, the Romans chose to honor him by naming a month after him. The Romans considered odd numbers to be lucky and the number seven even more so. They renamed the seventh month July, except it only had thirty days, which was considered unlucky. So they took one day from February, leaving it with only twenty-nine. Later, when Emperor Augustus died, they named the eighth month in his honor. Although it was an even month, it was considered lucky because it was the first month after July; except it too had only thirty days, so another day was taken from February, leaving it with twenty-eight days.

"The Julian calendar was much like our modern day Gregorian calendar, in that it was used primarily for commerce," explained Clifton. "It was handy for knowing when the rent was due and when to pay taxes. Like the Mayan Calendar, the purpose of the Hebrew Calendar was the worship of their deity. To this end the priests would add leap months to their calendars in order to have the Passover coincide with the sprouting of new grain and the maturing of young lambs. The priests were aware that they were not keeping the original Exodus Passover. In the Mishnah, they distinguish between 'The Exodus Passover', which Jesus and his disciples kept, and 'The Permanent Passover', which the Jewish community still keeps to this day."

"You have to understand, that back then 'evening' was considered the dawning of a new day to the Pharisees," explained Kortney. "The Sadducees, who counted days from sunrise to sunrise, celebrated the Permanent Passover. By their reckoning, both Passover lambs were eaten on the fourteenth of Nisan. The lamb of the Exodus Passover was sacrificed and cooked on the afternoon of the thirteenth and eaten at twilight, the dawning of the fourteenth. The lamb of the Permanent Passover is killed and prepared on the afternoon of the fourteenth and eaten that same evening. The fourteenth of Nisan, in the Hebrew Calendar, shifts every year to another day of the week because it always falls on a full moon."

"How could the Jews have been so damn accurate back then?" argued Trisha.

"The Hebrews owed their accuracy to the Babylonian Calendar," explained Clifton. "As far back as 700 BCE, the Zoroastrian astronomers of Babylon, in Persia, were cataloging and predicting solar and lunar eclipses more than fifty years in advance with incredible accuracy. The geometrical and mathematical precision behind the measurements was borrowed by their Hebrew captives when they were released. This knowledge later spread to both Greece and Rome."

"As to the hour of the actual trial, that information can be found in the Gospel of Matthew, which states that Jesus was brought before Pilate early in the morning," said Sarina. "The Gospel of John states that Pilate's trial was well underway by about the sixth hour. By Roman calculations, that would have been roughly 6:00 AM."

"If the priests wanted Jesus dead, and it turns out that it was a Roman arrest for a Roman offense against Cæsar, I can begin to see why the priests could not understand Pilate's refusal to follow through," said Shakira. "Teryk, in order to speed up this process I'm going to request that you take us through the trials and up to the point of the execution, unless you have any major objections."

"I can't think of any right now. As always, if someone has a question that cannot wait, please feel free to interrupt." Teryk inhaled deeply and collected his thoughts. He looked about the Round Table and acknowledged the presence of his first officer Monique by nodding to her. Monique had entered earlier and placed an aluminum carrying case on the table before her.

She opened it, revealing a luminous gem suspended within an elongated pyramid of dark glass. For the benefit of those at the Round Table, Teryk summed up the events pertaining to the exorcism in Colombia and how it had led to the discovery of the object now sitting before them. "In addition to your assigned tasks, I am adding one more. It is imperative that we locate and retrieve the second stone and ultimately the Ark of the Covenant itself.

"In regard to Pontius Pilate, I would like to compliment all of you on your excellent detective work. You are correct in your supposition that the chief priests could not understand why the Roman governor, who originated the arrest, was hesitant to execute a rebel like Jesus. In the end, the Jews accused Pilate of being less loyal to the emperor than they were. Pilate responded by washing his hands of the entire debacle."

The Tribunal of Herod-Antipas

"Jesus was taken across the viaduct to the Hasmonean Palace to stand before Herod-Antipas, tetrarch of Galilee. Herod's title, tetrarch, meant that he ruled one quarter of the territory. When Jesus was brought before him, Herod-Antipas exclaimed, 'I am pleased to see you in my court. I have heard much about you and your works. It was very decent of Pilate to have made such a conciliatory gesture.' Then Herod motioned for the scroll containing the charges to be given to him. Cornelius handed the scroll to Herod's guard. Herod's eyes seemed to widen more and more as he read. The tetrarch took his seat and asked, with intolerable arrogance, 'What do you have to say about these charges, King of the Jews?'

"Jesus remained silent. Legally, he did not have to answer. I recalled Isaiah's words, 'As a sheep before her shearers is dumb, so he opened not his mouth.' I then remembered something Jesus said when asked why he wasn't performing as many healings. Jesus explained that as one began to master the powers of the Universe, he would accomplish more and more by doing less and less. One example of this principle was that hundreds were now being healed by the sixty disciples we'd trained and sent out ahead of us. But the healings he himself performed were becoming fewer and fewer. And now, Jesus would accomplish everything—by doing nothing.

"Herod-Antipas taunted and teased, promising to release Jesus if he would just perform a miracle. Exasperated, Herod exclaimed, 'Tongues are wagging all across the land of Galilee that there is a miracle worker running about. It's becoming increasingly embarrassing that the ruler of Galilee has never seen this miracle worker perform a single one.' He then asked Jesus if he was Johanan, the Baptizer come back to life, or perhaps one of the prophets of old, maybe Elias or Elijah. Herod soon lost patience with this insolent Galilean and ordered his Roman guard to beat him until he decided to talk. Cornelius had to unchain

Jesus, after which the guard led him away. While all this was going on I was trying my best not to gawk at the opulence of that place. The fortress Antonia had frescoed ceilings and bronze candelabras but it paled in comparison to this palace.

"Herod soon tired of waiting and ordered Jesus brought back in. When Jesus entered, Cornelius's mouth dropped. Herod's guard had placed Jesus' tallit over his head like an Arab headdress and forced a crown of thorns, a cruel mockery of Cæsar's laurel wreath, over his head to hold the shawl in place. The thorns were long and some of their barbs had pierced the top of his head. From his shoulders hung the cape of a Roman soldier. He had been badly beaten and his beard had been pulled out in places. In his right hand was a rod, presumably the one they had beaten him with. I was not expecting this and struggled to maintain my composure.

"Herod-Antipas thought it was a riot. He called for his servants to fetch a robe: the one given to him by his father-in-law, the King of Arabia: the same king whose daughter Herod had discarded for Herodias, the wife of his brother Philip. The robe was exquisite, scarlet and gold on a dark slate-blue background: a color labeled as 'royal purple' by the nobility. The robe was crowned with rooster feathers around the collar, and covered the entire shoulder area. I later learned that Herod hated the robe for the combination of feathers and scarlet. Antipas would only allow royal purple to grace his personage.

"One of the guards took the rod from Jesus while the soldier's robe was removed. Herod and his entourage laughed hysterically all the while. As two soldiers fitted the king's robe on Jesus' shoulders, the other two men bent one knee and hailed him as king, playing to the crowd. As far as these soldiers were concerned, this was just another religious fanatic with whom they could entertain themselves. The young guard holding the rod stood and slowly raised it high overhead. With a resounding crack, he brought it down on Jesus' head, driving the crown of thorns deep into his scalp. He struck Jesus so swiftly that he had already beaten him four or five times before Herod could put a stop to it. This put an abrupt end to the merriment. Jesus had collapsed to his knees from the onslaught, but he never cried out. The rage in my body was difficult to control. I wanted to draw both my blades and slash at every living soul who had amused himself at my Lord's expense. Cornelius, no doubt would have joined me.

"Herod then called for a scribe and dictated a letter to Pilate which stated that he had examined the charges regarding this seditious rebel and although he considered finding him guilty of the charges, relinquished his authority and yielded to Pilate's superior position as counselor of Rome. He would approve any judgment the prefect would render regarding this insurgent.

"Herod had no love for Pilate. He would be traveling to Rome soon, carrying word of the way in which Pilate handled the situation to his friend the emperor, no doubt. It was Tiberius who had appointed Herod as king over Galilee. If Jesus was truly guilty of sedition against Rome, Herod was not about to let him go that easily. On the other hand, the people hated him for having killed John the Baptist. Herod would not have wanted to add another prophet to his problems.

"Cornelius, the battle hardened centurion, was visibly shaken as he placed the chains back on Jesus in order to return him to Pilate. Cornelius had started out as a mercenary for Rome and had risen through the ranks. The centurion suffered from the misfortune of commanding an army for a nation he did not particularly like, against an enemy he could not bring himself to hate.

"Our small solemn procession wound its way through the wide streets of the Upper City toward the fortress Antonia. In the bright morning sunlight, the beautiful gates and gardens of the Upper City were in sharp contrast to the Lower City's grimy walls, dirt floors, shabby doors and crowded narrow streets," said Teryk, sitting back and sinking into his plush chair. "And I was beginning to develop a splitting headache similar to the one I now feel."

"So they never actually found anything to charge him with?" observed Marileyna.

"The Talmud, an important Jewish work compiled around 200 CE, which incorporated the Mishnah, mentions Jesus, calling him a false messiah, a sorcerer who was justly condemned to death for practicing magic to heal and work miracles," said Phoenix. "It also states that Mary was his mother and that he was a teacher. According to the Talmud, not all the sages of his time agreed that Jesus was a heretic."

"That certainly seems to coincide with Teryk's explanation of things concerning the Sanhedrin. As for the Romans, the official charge against Jesus was 'seditio', meaning sedition," explained Cassandra. "The Gospels maintain that Jesus was guilty of the crime. All I can figure is that Jesus must have done something or said something that the Romans took as an offense against the personage of their emperor Tiberius. I have yet to isolate what that was."

"What evidence is there to support the claim that Jesus was guilty?" asked Marileyna.

Raven stood and addressed the members of the Round Table. "Friends, I am afraid you are at a disadvantage. You see, Teryk confided in me the details of the crime Jesus committed. Teryk has so far given you a lot of hints without disclosing the particulars. I urge you to continue diligently searching for the answer. I assure you, it can be found within the Gospels."

"But all I find is that Jesus was innocent and Pontius Pilate tried at least three times, possibly four, to pardon him," said Joshua. "I realize this is not in line with the character of the historical Pilate. But all the Gospels tell the same story and as you have repeatedly pointed out, that, in itself, is a rarity."

"If I was arrested for a crime and found innocent, would I be pardoned?" Raven stood and asked the assembled group. "Some of you are nodding 'yes'. Most of you in this room originate from the United States. I'm old enough to remember President Richard Nixon crying on national television, telling the nation's citizens how sorry he was, just before the newly appointed President Ford pardoned him. By this same logic, President Nixon certainly must have been *innocent*. Incidentally, Nixon had once been a Broadway actor, one of few actors who could cry tears on demand."

"Perhaps we will never know exactly what 'Tricky-Dick' was guilty of, because he was pardoned before any trial was ever conducted," explained Raven, taking her seat. "The correct answer to my question, however, is *no!* If I was innocent I would have to be acquitted of the charges—not pardoned. The Gospels accurately portray the actions of a Roman Governor repeatedly attempting to pardon Jesus for his actions. I, like most Christians, naïvely assumed Pontius Pilate was proclaiming Jesus' innocence."

The Man Who Would Be King

"Growing up Christian, I accepted Christ's divinity, the Virgin Birth, Judas's Betrayal, and my own sinful origins for which a loving God would cast me into everlasting darkness for all eternity. Marileyna, I look at you and see myself when I was younger. My scruples nearly omitted you from this investigation because you hold these concepts to be truths, as did I a month ago. And I'm not saying you are wrong to cling to those beliefs. I am saying that none of those beliefs were originally part of Jesus' life, his Ministry or sacred scripture.

"I continue my story with great trepidation," said Teryk in a somber tone. "To some of you it may appear that I am taking great liberties in the retelling of these events. I can only say that I take great comfort in the knowledge that Truth is eternal—whereas no Lie can live forever.

"As we entered the Praetorium, it quickly became evident that Pilate had not expected Herod to return Jesus to him," explained Teryk. "Given the enmity between the two, it was obvious Herod was up to something. A servant entered and requested to speak with Pilate. He bore an urgent message from Pilate's wife. Pilate opened the small scroll and read from it. He then rolled the scroll back up and sat there contemplating his next move.

"The governor rose and ordered Timonides, Jesus, the guard, and me to follow him into an adjacent room that had been converted into the Temple of Cæsar Augustus. Upon entering the temple, we found ourselves surrounded by crimson banners embroidered in gold. These decorations hung from the walls, bearing the profiles of Augustus the Divine. This pagan temple, on the Temple Mount, was a constant irritation to the priests because of its proximity to their temple.

"Tapping his open palm with the scroll, Pilate turned to Jesus and said, 'I have the authority to crucify you or release you.'

"Jesus corrected him in an authoritative voice. 'You have no power over me except what has been given to you from above. It is those who have delivered me unto you that bear the greater sin.' Jesus raised an eyebrow toward the chief priests standing at a distance. 'If I called upon my Father, twelve legions of angels would come to my defense at this moment, but then how will scripture be fulfilled?'

"'Then you are a king?' questioned Pilate, amused.

"'I am... for this I was born. And everyone who seeks Truth hears my voice...'

"'Your voice!' interrupted Pilate, 'and not that of the emperor's? By the very act of claiming to be king, you are subverting the authority of Rome,' said Pilate through clenched teeth, trying to keep his voice down so that the chief priests could not overhear. 'At the very least, you must be planning to lead a rebellion in order to establish your kingdom. Either possibility is a political assertion punishable by death!' Pilate calmed himself and in a more civilized tone, added, 'The Kingdom of Israel collapsed long ago and your people were made slaves soon afterwards.'

"'There are few slaves who have not had a king among their ancestors my lord,' Timonides assured Pilate.

"But Jesus made no reply; he stood there crowned with a wreath of thorns, and wearing the beautiful robe Herod had placed upon him.

"Pilate pursed his lips as he considered his next question. 'What then is *Truth* that anyone who hears it should seek it?'

"But the Master remained motionless and would not answer the Governor. 'Perhaps I can answer that question,' I said, looking to Jesus for approval and noticing that the crown of thorns around his beautiful tallit gave him a regal, magisterial appearance when combined with the ornate cape. My headache had worsened. I tried not to think of the incredible pain Jesus must be under. Pinching the bridge of my nose in an effort to quell the throbbing in my head, I continued. 'Some time back we, his disciples, asked that very same question of him. And Joshua answered us by saying, "Truth is Truth even if no one were to believe it. And a lie," I said, looking up while flicking my beard with my index finger, in an effort to minimize an open gesture toward the profiles of the many 'deities' that surrounded us, "is still a lie—even if you were to force the entire world to believe it."'

"'And how do you gnow that that is the *Truth*?' sneered Pilate with undisguised hostility.

"'You don't,' said Timonides, 'unless you do. Truth, like gold, does not tarnish. It may change shape but its essence is eternal.'

"Pilate thrust out his hand toward Timonides and handed him the small scroll. Timonides read it then showed it to me, unsure if I could read Latin.

"The message, from the Lady Claudia Procula, read: 'Have nothing to do with this honorable man: I have suffered many things in a dream this day on his account.'

"'It appears this 'sorcerer' has the ability to influence dreams, the Realm of the Gods,' said Timonides, raising his eyes in the direction of Cæsar's statute.

"Judging by the look on Pilate's face, it was not what he wanted to hear. The Emperor Augustus had believed that dreams were the means by which the gods communicated with us, and no Roman omen of impending doom was complete without a dream to accompany it. Calpurnia, Julius Cæsar's spouse, had been warned in a dream of Cæsar's torn and bloodied toga on the eve of the Ides of March: a warning Cæsar chose not to heed.

"Crazy as it sounds," said Teryk, "Pilate had a custom of releasing a prisoner who would be selected by the people and granted a gubernatorial pardon…"

"The custom, an ancient one, was called *privilegium paschale*," interrupted Jared, "but the earliest account of a privilegium paschale that I could find was around 367 CE. Not all Rome's governors chose to employ it. And men imprisoned for homicides or sacrilege, were not eligible for pardons."

"The incident cannot be discounted that easily," said Raven, "because it appears in all four Gospels. In Acts 3:14, Peter makes a reference to the incident involving the release of a murderer instead of Jesus."

"Adolf Deissmann, in his work *Light from the Ancient East*, speaks of a Florentine papyrus dated to about 85 CE. The document contains a report of judicial proceedings by the governor of Egypt, G. Septimus Vegetus," said Noraia. "Septimus said to Phibion, the accused, 'Thou has been worthy of scourging, but I will give thee to the people.' There are even a few accounts where amnesty was sometimes associated with festivals."

Teryk waited to see if anyone had any further input, then continued. "It quickly became evident to me why this heavy-handed governor would do such a thing. It was for this gubernatorial pardon that such a large gathering, of mostly Zealots, had assembled in front of the palace so early in the morning; and like the dimwits most of them were, they showed up in droves. Pilate was far more clever and subtle than I gave him credit for.

"The insurgent, Joshua-bar-Abbas, was brought out in his blood-stained, faded linen tunic to be substituted for Jesus. I can tell you that my thoughts were not Christian. And I hoped some of the blood was his own. The people had been incited by the priests to call for bar-Abbas. They roared his name in acclaim, as if he were some sort of hero—which to the Zealots he was.

"Pilate raised a hand for silence, and motioned toward Jesus. 'I find no fault in this man and I am of a mind to pardon him of the charges against him. Under your laws this man has been charged with perverting the people. I have examined him and found no fault touching on those things he is accused of. Being a Galilean, I sent him before Herod, who chose not to put him to death.

The Tetrarch of Galilee has approved any judgment I render on this matter. I will therefore order him chastised, and released.'

"While the assembled mass was in an uproar, Pilate addressed the temple's high priest and chief priests who stood with him. In a low voice he said, 'Can you explain to me how it is that the very dæmons this man expels proclaim him your Messias while your holy men want nothing to do with him?' Then, looking directly at Annas, he proclaimed in flawless Aramaic, 'Truly, your wisdom borders on stupidity.' Pilate waxed poetically; in Aramaic the words rhymed beautifully.'

"'Who cares what title you place on a rebel? If you let this man go you are no friend of Cæsar! We have no ruler over us but Cæsar!' shouted Annas. The priests enticed the crowd in the background to take up the call. The excited clamor of the crowd, instigated by Annas and provoked by his minions, shouted, 'You are not Cæsar's friend if you let this man go.'

"'A new fear now overpowered the anxiety that had been gnawing at Pontius Pilate, his mind already bent and twisted from rebelling against what was commanded of him. How does one describe his aura? So undone was the man. He had always been in control, yet was now being swept along by a raging torrent of powers beyond his understanding. His soul had never come in contact with the icy fingers of Fear that now rasped at the tattered edges of his mind. How in the world was Pilate going to explain to Cæsar that he was less loyal to the emperor than an angry mob of Hebrew dogs? True, Sejanus had appointed Pilate, but Tiberius Cæsar was still the emperor and it was he who had issued the orders, and whom Jesus had allegedly offended. No doubt Herod would take great delight in retelling this story.

"Secular historians have argued that Pilate's inflexible and obstinate character was impinged by the execution of Sejanus. The head of Tiberius Cæsar's personal bodyguard was accused of plotting against the emperor two years before the crucifixion in 33 CE. The problem with this assertion is that Sejanus was very much alive at this time. And according to my calculations, he should not have been executed until the Fall Equinox, still another six months away," reasoned Teryk.

"There was another problem that most historians are not aware of: Pilate belonged to a prestigious fraternity called *Amici Cæsaris*, the 'Friends of Cæsar'. On his right hand was a golden membership ring with the image of Tiberius. The only way to leave that influential club was by being exiled after having all your property confiscated. As always, the emperor would allow you to leave your family an inheritance if you performed the required suicide. Cæsar might overlook the outburst of an eccentric holy man but he would not be sympathetic to one who was claiming the throne.

"Pilate stood reflecting darkly on the options available to him. Jesus had been charged with an offense against the dignity of the emperor. If Pilate released

Jesus, he would be liable for high treason under the law *Lex Iulia maiestatis*, sometimes called the *laesa maiestas*. The Law was originally enacted by Julius Cæsar and later re-enacted by Augustus. Laesa maiestas literally meant 'Violated Majesty'. This law was all-embracing and devoid of legal limitations; it did not lend itself to strict definition. Men charged with it could be tortured until they confessed to the crime. In short, the damn thing sounded much like the Bush Administration's P.A.T.R.I.O.T. Act, which I used to think they had come up with all on their own. The law was so wide ranging in its definition that it pretty much covered anything the emperor might consider harmful to the interest of Rome or himself. Its purpose was to secure absolute submission and obedience worthy of the veneration of a god, yet slandering the gods was not considered a punishable offense. If the Illuminati had ever wanted to lay the groundwork for the Antichrist, I'd say they'd succeeded.

"At this point the multitude began to shout, 'His blood be upon us, and upon our children,' as was the custom in Israel at an execution. Not long after this, two servants appeared carrying a large wash basin. They brought it out to Pilate who declared in a loud authoritative voice, 'His blood "be" upon "your heads"' and not mine.' Pilate held his bent arms out before the crowd. He bent over the bowl and lowered both forearms up to his biceps into the bowl. As Pilate raised his arms skyward, he solemnly repeated his words in an effort to placate the Roman gods, or any other gods he may have offended. He put his hands in one more time and said, 'I wash my hands of the innocent blood of this just man. I will not take upon my head the great sin of condemning an innocent man and acquitting a murderer!'

"The priests gazed triumphantly at Jesus the unconquerable Messianic King of Israel: the same man who only days ago had been venerated by some of the very same people now present. Jesus stood before the crowd, condemned to death as a criminal. The chief priests had been right about this heretic all along. How fortunate for the Nation of Israel to have been led by these righteous men of God: men who had not been blinded by the Galilean's sorcery. No Jew would take up arms for a false prophet. No revolt would take place that morning. There would be no Zealot reprisal.

"Historians and scholars have long argued that they find no real motive for the priests wanting Jesus dead. Perhaps it is because their motive was a simple one: self-preservation. What the Sanhedrin lacked was an opportunity to destroy Jesus without the ensuing repercussions. This motive is the fine thread that runs through their trials, their accusations, and their actions. They only sought to save Jesus in order to save their own precious hides. Now that Jesus was no longer a threat to their demise, the means for his destruction lay in the golden opportunity that had presented itself.

"These men could never possibly have understood Jesus, and what men cannot understand they must destroy. I stood transfixed experiencing an epiphany. All at once I understood what their outcry from Deuteronomy meant when it was placed next to a passage from Numbers." Teryk glanced at some notes. "Deuteronomy 19:10 says, '…by failing to prevent the shedding of innocent blood, you take that blood upon yourself,' while Numbers 35:33 says, '…and the land cannot be cleansed of the blood that is shed therein, but by the blood of *him* that shed it.' I realize the scripture was never meant to be read in this manner but I thought it strange that the verses came to me as if they were one."

"Jesus was then taken to be scourged. This was not an additional punishment ordered by Pilate. It was part of the sentence of crucifixion; in fact, it was included in every sentence of death in order to extract the maximum amount of suffering. Unlike Mel Gibson's *The Passion*, Jesus was not tied to a whipping post. He was stripped and suspended by his hands, with his feet just off the ground. This was done so that the skin would be taut, increasing the amount of pain he felt.

"Floggers were strong soldiers, experts in the use of various flogging whips. Two Roman soldiers stood on either side of Jesus. They struck hard and fast, incredibly so. Just as the weights landed on Jesus' body, the soldiers flicked their wrists so that the sharp points would tear off or break small pieces of flesh, leaving bruises and contusions in their wake. The brutal instrument whooshed through the air then made a loud snap as it came into contact with the flesh of Jesus.

"They started at the middle of his back and struck anywhere, both front and back. I was grateful that they stopped at the shoulder area and did not strike his face. If Jesus had been scourged with the instrument used in the movie *The Passion* he probably would not have survived it, with his skin stretched out the way it was. Feeling nauseous, I closed my eyes. I could not watch this— unfortunately, I could hear it; I counted the customary forty lashes, not the thirty-nine most preachers are fond of recounting. If one was fortunate enough to lose consciousness under this type of thrashing, the Romans would revive him with a bucket of cold water. Unlike Cestus and Dysmas, Jesus did not cry out. I had heard that men sometimes bit their tongues in two from the flogging. I could stand no more, and wandered outside Fortress Antonia."

"If Pilate had acted true to form," said Athena, "his overbearing, obstinate, inflexible personality would have taken control of the situation, and he would have done as he pleased regardless of what the Jews wanted. This contradiction has never been explained before. Having instigated the arrest, why would he be averse to accepting responsibility for Christ's execution?"

"Exactly. Pilate even tried to shift the matter to Herod's court," said Trisha. "When that failed he attempted to crucify Barabbas in place of Jesus."

"For the record, Barabbas's full name was Joshua-bar-Abbas," explained Teryk. "Barabbas, as it turns out, is not an actual name. The prefix *bar* means 'son of' as in the example seen in Mark 10:46, Bartimaeus the son of Timaeus."

"I find it strange that the Lady Claudia Procula should have had a dream concerning Jesus on the night of his arrest," said Winter. "Could it have been triggered by the knowledge of her husband's plans to arrest him? The dream mentioned in Matthew 27:19 should not have terrified her if she had no knowledge of what her husband intended with Jesus."

"The only other motive I could come up with for the Jewish Mafia, aka the Sadducees, wanting Jesus dead was material gain," said Kortney. "Normally the Second Messiah, from the line of Aaron, would have presided over the Sanhedrin. But the Baptist had been dead for some time. Annas stood to lose his profitable monopoly if Jesus took over the operations of running the Jewish religion. There is plenty of archaeological evidence to show that these men lived a life of luxury and power."

"Commander, the statement 'it is not lawful for us to put any man to death' is simply untrue," said Raven. "In Acts, Saul of Tarsus, aka the apostle Paul, carries out the orders of the Sanhedrin by stoning Stephen to death. Stephen is not stoned in hiding but at the city gates, without anyone having first obtained permission from the Romans."

"In a reference to Jesus, Flavius Josephus refers to the execution of James, the brother of Yeshua, by the Sadducean high priest Ananias," said Kortney. "The account reads as follows: 'He convened a meeting of the Sanhedrin and brought before them a man named James, the brother of Jesus, *who was called the Christ*, and certain others. He accused them of having transgressed the law and delivered them up to be stoned.' Again, no one seemed concerned about putting a fellow Jew to death without first having officially obtained permission from their overlords the Romans.

"Joseph ben Mattathias, better known as Flavius Josephus," continued Kortney, "was a Pharisee priest, and is considered a Jewish historian. He wrote twenty-eight volumes on his people's history. Born in 37 CE, he wrote most of his work toward the end of the first century. Josephus was the commanding general of the Galilean armies. He surrendered to the Roman general Vespasian during the siege of Jotapata after having drawn lots with his colleagues. By this method, the men would not actually commit suicide but be killed by a fellow soldier. Josephus was the last to win the lot and faithfully killed his fellow soldier, but failed to commit the agreed-upon suicide. When he surrendered to Vespasian, he is said to have convinced the Roman general that he was a soothsayer, predicting that Vespasian would become the next emperor of Rome. Luckily for Josephus, Vespasian did go on to become emperor. And although Josephus is viewed as somewhat of a scoundrel, his accounts of the war have proven to be incredibly accurate.

"The validity of some of Josephus's claims has been questioned by later historians, because at the time they seemed like gross exaggerations. For instance, Josephus claimed that the harbor of Cæsarea Maritima, built by Herod the Great, was as large as the one at Piraeus, a major harbor in Athens. Recent underwater excavations, however, have proved that the harbor of Cæsarea Maritima, located on an inhospitable coast, had in fact been comparable to that of the harbor at Piraeus. The harbor of Cæsarea is now rated as one of the most incredible architectural accomplishments of all time."

To Die Among Friends

> *Those who can make you believe absurdities,*
> *can make you commit atrocities.*
> —Voltaire

"All the laws Jesus lived by, and could so easily quote from, were working against him. The world had gone mad, lies were the truth and the truth was a lie. Everything was happening so fast. Jesus was not supposed to die today. This was Wednesday. The crucifixion was not supposed to happen until Friday. Isn't that why we celebrate Good Friday? Never had it crossed my mind that he might die today, or that my death might follow his. Off in the distance, a camel complained and I realized that I was still dressed in the priest's garb. I headed toward the sound of the camels and entered a marketplace. After purchasing a dark robe with a large hood, I drew the hood over my face and headed toward the place of execution where I waited. Using the shadows cast by the Sun, I judged it to be about an hour before noon. And by noon I do not mean twelve o'clock. Long ago I learned that when shadows show the sun to be directly overhead, the time is roughly 1:30 PM Daylight Savings Time.

"The soldiers on the limestone outcrop were reinforcing the permanent upright beams, or stakes. The beams were square and set into pre-existing holes in the limestone. The soldiers drove wedges in on all sides and aligned the post using a plum-bob.

"Crucifixions were intended to make a public example of the condemned for all passers-by. Although the Persians, Assyrians and Greeks practiced crucifixion, none used it as extensively as the Romans. Rome did not sanction this horrendous form of punishment on just anyone. This exemplary death was reserved for those committing high treason both political and religious, as well as disobedient slaves, pirates, and particularly violent criminals. The location for the spectacle had been carefully selected. Crowds would taunt those condemned to death as they suffered suspended from a cross, hungry, thirsty, tortured by cramps and biting insects they would be helpless to swat away. Many rebels tried to retaliate while dying on the cross. Some tried spitting on their tormentors. Spartacus's rebels were said to have urinated on the faces of the soldiers who crucified them. One could hurl insults, I suppose, but I had heard that the soldiers would simply climb up a ladder and cut out the tongues of those who did.

"The place called Golgotha was not a hill at all, but a limestone outcrop situated within a cemetery. Deuteronomy describes cemeteries as unclean. According to Jewish laws, Jews, especially priests, are defiled if they walk over the dead. For this reason, cemeteries were identified with the sign of a skull. Golgotha, which meant 'the skull' in Aramaic, was located toward the east along the road from the Fortress Antonia. The cemetery was located on the north side of the road, just before the fork that led to Jericho."

"Commander, it is quite possible that Golgotha was a limestone outcrop. Nowhere in the New Testament is it referred to as a hill," said Raven.

"The Dead Sea Scrolls make it quite clear that one would be defiled if they walked over the dead," added Phoenix. "For this reason, graveyards were identified with the sign of a skull, as Teryk just said."

"Matthew, Mark and John refer to the place as Golgotha," said Shakira. "Luke alone refers to the site as Calvary. The Hebrew word *gulgoleth* and the Latin word *calvaria* both mean *skull*."

"As Judah, I had witnessed a few crucifixions while in this altered state, and knew Jesus would be tied to a beam called the *patibulum*. He would be forced to carry the thirty-to-forty-pound oak crossbeam from the Fortress Antonia. It was a Roman custom that a condemned man should walk all the way from his holding cell to the place of execution. The distance wasn't that far, just over a mile, but I could understand why Jesus would have fallen three times.

"From the rocky outcropping, I turned and saw a *quaternion*, a guard of four soldiers, with Jesus being born along. Behind him were Dysmas and Cestus, both of whom were receiving the customary beatings the Romans called *flagellatio*. Just then Jesus fell and did not get up. If one fell with that beam strapped to his arms, there would be no way to protect his face from hitting the ground. I saw a soldier draw his sword and cut Jesus free of the crossbeam as he lay prostrate. They then selected a man from the crowd; according to the Gospels, this would have been Simon of Cyrene..."

"Jesus didn't actually carry his cross then, did he?" questioned Adriana.

"It is a common consensus among scholars that this admonition was put in the mouth of Jesus by later translators," explained Teryk. "What Jesus actually said was, 'We must carry out the mission we ourselves have set before us.' We will want help and think that others should help us, but it would be like helping a young chick out of its eggshell or a butterfly out of its cocoon. There are things each of us must undergo alone in order to become the creation God meant us to be.

"As Simon approached carrying the beam," Teryk continued, "the soldiers waiting at the road's edge took hold of the patibulum and forcibly led Simon to Golgotha. The soldiers then began to strip Simon of his outer garments. Realizing what was happening, Simon screamed for the centurion. It took some time for Cornelius to set the matter straight. Abandoning the patibulum where it laid on the ground, the soldiers walked over toward Cestus. They offered him the customary drink of wine mixed with myrrh, which acted as a narcotic. Myrrh was one of the gifts offered to Jesus by the Magi; it symbolized his mortality.

"Removing the crossbeam, the soldiers stripped Cestus and lay him on the ground over the patibulum. Cestus groaned as they looped the ropes around his wrist and secured them tightly. I guess they figured he would not be requiring the use of his hands anymore. Both Cestus and Dysmas had participated in the ambush of an arsenal that was being transported to Jerusalem. I suspected a trap and told them as much, but Joshua-bar-Abbas and others convinced them otherwise, bragging that 'the Romans could no longer boast that their highways were as safe as the Forum at noon.' To the Zealots, Cestus and Dysmas were not perishing at the hands of the hated Romans. They were sacrificing their lives for the freedom of Israel and joining the ranks of their venerated heroes. Above their heads were the usual placards, each one referred to as a 'titulus' in the Roman tongue. They read *crimen laesae maiestatis*: 'outlaws whose crimes had caused injury to the majesty of the emperor'."

"Commander, I discovered that the two others crucified with Jesus were originally called *lestai* in both Mark and Matthew. The word was wrongly translated in the King James Version as 'thieves'. Its true meaning is actually closer to robbers, bandits or brigands," said Shakira. "They are referred to as *kakourgoi* twice in the Gospels of Luke and Mark. In Greek, the word means criminals or malefactors."

Teryk nodded his thanks to Shakira and continued. "Just then a procession of priests arrived. They waited by the road, and did not enter the cemetery, lest they be defiled by walking over the dead and have to miss the Passover celebrations about to take place. This is why the Romans selected the site: They knew that no Jew would approach. The priests got the attention of a soldier in charge of the execution and handed him a bundle. 'You are not to tie this one,' they said, pointing to Jesus. 'Nail him fast to the cross,' ordered a scraggly bearded chief priest who seemed to be in charge.

"I turned to face those followers of Jesus who were present. John was nowhere to be found, nor could I see Yehosef ha Ramati or Nicodemus. Among the women at the Crucifixion was Miriam, mother of Jesus. Mariamne, called the Magdalene, was also there, accompanied by Jesus' stepsister Salome: mother of the disciples James and John. And Miriam, the wife of Jesus' uncle Cleophas, was also present...."

"You're saying the disciples James and John, the 'Sons of Thunder', were related to Jesus?" asked Marileyna. "That they were his nephews through a stepsister?"

"Yes, and Joseph, the father of Jesus, had only one brother, named Cleophas. His wife Miriam was Jesus' aunt and their only son, was the disciple Symeon the Zealot, Jesus' cousin," explained Teryk. "Joseph, Mary's husband, originally had seven children with his first wife Salome. The oldest was James 'The Just'. He was followed by Salome, who was married to Zebedee. Their sons James and John, the 'Sons of Thunder', were disciples of Jesus.

"Joseph was the third child, followed by his sister Martha. Joseph's name has been translated as Jose, probably to eliminate suspicion that he was Joseph's son. They in turn were followed by Simon, Esther and Judah, who is referred to as Jude by the Church, to distinguish him from Judas Iscariot. Understandably, this information may be difficult to prove, much less believe. All I ask is that you do your best.

"The soldiers were just starting on Dysmas," continued Teryk, "while another group of soldiers was beginning to hoist Cestus into position. The soldier with the bundle of spikes laid it down on the ground just in front of me and opened it, revealing four large rusty iron nails which resembled tapered railroad spikes with exaggerated heads. Two of the spikes were longer, appearing almost seven inches in length. The shorter ones were about four inches in length. There were also two pieces of wood with small holes in their center. These wooden plaques would be used to hold the ankles firmly to either side of the vertical beam.

"Just then, Jesus walked past still wearing the robe. I looked down in despair and noticed that there were now only three nails. I looked about and noticed a small figure making his way through the crowd, moving away from the crosses. Suspecting that he had taken a nail, I hurried after him. When I caught up with the little thief, I grabbed him by the shoulder. As I spun him around, I could feel his bony frame. It was a young boy. He was terrified. Stealing from Roman soldiers was a grievous offense. I knelt down and asked him why he had taken it. But he was too afraid to answer. I assured him I would not hand him over to the authorities.

"He said he had no parents and feared attack at night when he slept. He wanted to fashion a blade from the nail in order to defend himself. Just then the priests noticed that one of the nails was missing. I offered to trade the boy my short sword for the long nail. Concealing the sword underneath my cloak, I

Joseph "Five Eagles"Reyna

handed it to the boy. He exchanged it for the nail. As he turned to leave I offered him a handful of silver coins and asked where he would celebrate the Passover. He informed me that he was not a Jew.

"A hush engulfed us. I turned to see that a Roman herald had motioned for silence. His strong voice rang out as he faithfully read the decree, announcing the offenses of each criminal before the gathering crowd. 'He who hangs naked before you now, Rome and all the gods of Rome condemn him…' First Cestus's account was read, then Dysmas's. They were Jewish malefactors, criminals who had been caught in the act of stealing. The herald did not mention that they had attacked Roman soldiers and stolen swords from an armory. Crucifixion was intended to disgrace and humiliate, such a statement would have declared them patriots.

"I had just placed the nail in my sash when an unbelievable pain shot through my right hand. I then heard the sickening thud of the hammer's first blow. I immediately grabbed for my right hand, fearing that it would not be there! My right arm was paralyzed by a searing pain. As the next hammer blow struck, the pain intensified and I realized they had just driven the nail into Jesus' wrist. I turned to see, fearing I would lose consciousness. I could not make out Jesus from my position. The pain seemed to be coming from the median nerve bundle located deep in my wrist. That's the same nerve bundle that hurts when one is diagnosed with Carpal Tunnel Syndrome.

"Both of my wrists were throbbing. My feet would soon follow suit. Why was I experiencing this pain? Why wasn't anyone noticing me? Then I realized I wasn't screaming. My mouth was open but no sound came forth.

"Hoarse shouts and orders were barked, accompanied by the creaking and straining of ropes as they hoisted Jesus up. I may have lost consciousness for a moment as I felt my arms become dislocated from my shoulders. The pain in my wrist was beyond anything imaginable.

"The pain shot through my feet before I heard the sickening thud of the hammer: a sound not quite loud enough for the metal to have had a direct encounter with the wood. The second blow would have a sharper ring to it. How much more would that hurt? The pain was indescribable. Beyond words, in fact. Knowing there was no word to describe the pain, the Romans had invented one: excruciating, literally meaning *from the cross*."

29

The Crucifixion — Hoax or Historic Fact?

"There are stories and legends, but is there any real evidence that anyone was actually nailed to a cross by the Romans?" asked Adriana.

Kortney shuffled through his notes. "Flavius Josephus wrote that he managed to obtain permission, from General Vespasian, to accompany Roman forces during the siege of Jerusalem. Josephus's accounts of the battle are the most valuable existing volumes dealing with Jewish history from 100 BCE to 100 CE. He documented that hundreds of Jews were nailed to the very walls of the city when the Romans destroyed the temple."

"Two short passages in *The Antiquities* mention Jesus, calling him Yeshua: the name Teryk says he was born with," said Sarina. "Josephus's work survived as a copy made by Christian monks during the Middle Ages. According to the first passage, referred to as the *Testimonium Flavianum Josephus, The Antiquities* 18.63-64:

'About this time lived Yeshua, a wise man, if indeed one should call him a man. For he was a performer of astonishing deeds, a teacher of men who are happy to accept the truth. He won over many Jews, and indeed also many Greeks. He was the Christ. When Pilate, upon hearing him accused by men of the highest standing among us, had condemned him to be crucified, those who had in the first place come to love him did not give up their affection for him. On the third day he appeared to them restored to life, for the prophets of God had prophesied these and countless other marvelous things about him. And the tribe of Christians, so called after him, has still to this day not disappeared.'"

"'He was the Christ... for he appeared alive again on the third day.' This does not sound like a statement a Jew is likely to make about a suspected Messiah figure," argued Kortney. "In 1972, Professor Shlomo Pines of Hebrew University in Jerusalem announced he had discovered a differing, and possibly more original, version of Josephus's writings in an Arabic manuscript dating to the tenth century. This earlier and perhaps unadulterated version of Josephus is believed to be a more accurate statement and more in keeping with what a Jew of that time might have said about a suspected Messiah:

> 'At this time there was a wise man, who was called Jesus, and his conduct was good, and he was known to be virtuous. And many people from among the Jews and the other nations became his disciples. Pilate condemned him to be crucified and to die. And those who had become his disciples did not abandon their loyalty to him. They reported that he had appeared to them three days after his crucifixion, and that he was alive. Accordingly they believed that he was the Messiah, concerning whom the Prophets have recounted wonders.'"

"The word translated as 'cross' in the New Testament has the general meaning of a stake or pole," said Noraia. "In Acts, Peter says Jesus was 'hung on a tree'. And in Galatians, Paul also states that Jesus was 'hung on a tree'."

"Since my ordeal I have done a great deal of research on 'savior gods', of which Dionysus was one," said Teryk. "Like Jesus, he was said to have been 'hung on a tree' yet the image I saw representing Dionysus was that of a crucifix. Instead of a crown of thorns, Dionysus was said to have worn a crown of ivy. Both were draped in purple robes. And both were given something to drink shortly before they died, only to be resurrected days later."

"Teryk, we're trying to prove Jesus was crucified, not disprove it," argued Joshua.

"Agreed. I merely wanted to point out an observation that I had made."

"The cross as a symbol has been used for millennia," said Winter. "To the ancients the four arms of the cross symbolize the four elements—earth, water, air, and fire. The figure on the crucifix represents spirit, the fifth element, bound by nails to the material world."

"Before continuing my story," added Teryk, "I would like to point out that neither of these accounts, attributed to Josephus, mentions a betrayal by a trusted follower. They do, however, mention that Jesus' disciples did not abandon him but remained loyal, believing he was the Messiah.

"Two horsemen, mounted cavalry, rode up. One of the Roman knights dismounted carrying what looked like a flat shield. He gave it to a soldier who climbed a ladder and attached the wide plank to the central vertical post that formed Jesus' cross. The titulus was much larger than I had ever imagined it to be. Upon reading it the priests were beside themselves. The Roman knight did not argue with them. He simply said, 'Pilate has written what he has written, and it shall stand.' I was delirious with pain and wanted to read the inscription on it but realized it would be impossible in my current condition. Whatever it was, it certainly was not 'INRI'.

"At this point the soldiers sat down to watch the men die. Interestingly enough, the soldiers did not remove Jesus' underclothing; by Pilate's orders, I later found out. From the wounds I experienced, there can be no doubt that the nails were definitely in the wrist. And the Romans did not use ropes to help suspend the weight of Jesus' body on the cross. That means the nails exerted nearly three thousand pounds of pressure on the nerve bundles in the wrists. I also observed that his left foot was nailed over his right.

"'Father, forgive them... for they know not what they do.' Jesus had to pause and take in breath in order to complete the entire phrase. I felt parched, as if I was dying of thirst. I cannot imagine what he was feeling.

"This statement had an indescribable impact on the Roman guard. Crucifixion was so painful and unbearable. Those condemned to the cross normally uttered obscenities, not words of forgiveness. The Romans were beginning to see that this was no ordinary man.

"I then saw Joseph of Arimathaea speak with the guard. Nicodemus was with him. The soldier allowed Joseph to move toward Jesus. He was holding up a small wooden cup at Jesus' feet in an effort to collect the blood. It would be needed for the burial ceremony. It did not take Yehosef ha Ramati long to fill the cup...."

"Sorry to interrupt, Commander," Kortney apologized. "According to Hebrew custom, when a Jewish man has been murdered, his blood must be collected and poured over his personal prayer shawl, his tallit. The tallit is considered a sacred thing and must be buried with its owner. The blood is poured upon it so that on the Day of Judgment, the victim can present it as evidence of the crime before the Living God."

Teryk acknowledged Kortney's comments and continued. "The actions of Joseph reminded me of the priest, who only yesterday had collected the blood of the sacrificial lamb in his small golden bowl in order to splash it upon the stone altar as an offering to God. The most important covenants between God and man were always ratified with the shedding of blood.

"'Master... if you truly are the Messiah... save yourself and us as well,' pleaded Cestus, bringing me back to the events unfolding before me. Cestus had always believed Jesus was the Messiah and this was not how the 'Promised One' was supposed to meet his end.

"'You and I are guilty and paying for our crimes. What crime has the Master committed... that he should be condemned... to hang here with us?'

Incredulous

answered Dysmas. Then, addressing Jesus, he requested, 'Remember me Master… when you enter into your kingdom. Remember us… when you come into your glory.'

"Jesus turned toward Dysmas and smiled. Then he turned to Cestus and said, 'I promise you this day… you shall be with me… in the Realm of Souls.'

"He seemed to be saying it to both men. The Realm of Souls in no way resembles Hell. In fact, there is no understanding of what we call Hell to the Jewish mind. If I were trying to describe this place, I would have to say that the Roman Catholic's *Purgatory* is about as close as I could define it; except you do not work off your sins. It is a sort of holding place, sometimes referred to as the '*Bosom of Abraham*'."

"The Realm of Souls? Are you certain, Commander?" asked Trisha. "As I understand it, Jesus was bearing our sins, and should have descended into the pits of Hell for three days."

"Does scripture not say that Jesus had taken upon himself all the sins of the world? Yet you have him promising Dysmas that he will be with him in the Bosom of Abraham. If you'll just bear with me…" Marileyna flipped through her notes. "According to Peter, Jesus was going to Hell. Acts 2:31 says, '…his soul was not left in *Hell*, neither did his flesh see corruption.'"

"That is the standard salvation teaching of the Church," agreed Teryk, "but I would like to ask both of you a very important question. Is it possible for Jesus to tell a lie? Yes or no? Can Jesus promise a dying man that he will soon be with him in Paradise, knowing full well that his own destination is Hell?"

"Jesus is supposed to be the Truth made flesh, so it would be inconceivable that he could knowingly tell a lie, especially one of that magnitude!" reasoned Marileyna.

"The early Church preached against the concept of the Bosom of Abraham and substituted the term 'the spirits in prison' or 'paradise' when referring to the Realm of Souls," explained Phoenix. "Sometimes they even referred to it as Hell. In the King James version of Luke 23:43, Jesus says, 'I promise you this day you shall be with me in paradise.' Much like the New Testament teachings on Hell, the teachings of Paradise are not found in the Old Testament either."

"*The Aquarian Gospel of Jesus the Christ* is the only one I know of where Jesus actually says, '…Behold, for I will meet you in the realm of souls this day,' said Cassandra. "The book was first copyrighted in 1907, by Levi H. Dowling, a chaplain in the US army during the Civil War. Levi explains that he transcribed the book from the Akashic Records. In his work he covers what has come to be called 'The Missing Years of Jesus.' According to Dowling, Jesus was in Persia studying in their monasteries during this time. There is an interesting story I would like to share about this Gospel. I first confronted Teryk about the problem with the promise to meet in Paradise when he arrived at Antares. We were in the archives when I asked him about it. Teryk simply sat there thinking about the question. Then he smiled and said, 'I know the answer to that question, Cassandra, but due to the nature of the investigation I cannot give it to you. As for the evidence you seek, however, I can tell you that it's in one of these books.' He pointed toward the Archive. 'It's in a book I've never seen before.' Teryk got up and wandered around the library shelves, passing his left hand over the books as he walked by. He stopped, pulled a book off the shelf and examining it, remarked, 'The spine has no cracks in it. I doubt this book has ever been opened. The answer you seek is in here.' We opened it and searched for the part about the crucifixion. Not only did we discover that Jesus never said 'paradise' but referred instead to the Realm of Souls. It also mentioned that it was the priests who wanted Jesus nailed to the cross. I must admit I have never witnessed Teryk display his abilities before. To me, his powers seemed almost magical."

"If Teryk is correct, The Aquarian Gospel seems to be the only one that got it right," added Kortney. "It must be understood that the Jews never referred to the Realm of Souls as a sort of paradise. Judaism does not have a concrete concept of an afterlife. To the Jews the holding place they go to in the afterlife is referred to as the Bosom of Abraham, which in no way translates into Hell and suffering for their sins."

"In our modern Gospels Jesus is allegedly quoted as teaching more about Hell than anyone in the entire *Bible*," said Raven, "like the story of the rich man who goes to Hell and the poor man who goes to Heaven. The passage refers to Heaven as the Bosom of Abraham."

"When Jesus was telling that story, we all understood that it was a parable. Because he was referring to young Lazarus and Joshua-bar-Abbas in regards to a question about good and evil," explained Teryk. "Jesus wanted to make the point that money did not change the essence of the immortal soul. To give us a better understanding of the afterlife, he followed this parable with the parables of the lost sheep, the lost coin and the prodigal son..."

"But there is a Hell, Teryk! I've been there. I've seen it!" exclaimed Claudia. "And it is almost exactly as it has been described by others."

"I did not mean to imply there was no such place as Hell, My Lady," Teryk apologized. "No one is more aware of its existence than I. Such an infernal dimension certainly does exist in the lower realms. What I am saying is that Jesus never preached that your eternal soul would be tormented there if you ignored his teachings. The ones who did teach such a heretical doctrine, however, were Paul and every one of the savior gods. When we die, some souls inevitably do go to this inferno. Unable to forgive themselves in this life, I believe many descend into Hell of their own accord.

"Where was I? Oh, about this time, Jesus turned to his mother and proclaimed, 'Woman, behold your son.' Then he looked toward me sitting on the ground behind her and said, 'Son, behold your Mother.' Noticing my condition, Mother Mary turned and hurried to my side. She held me and somehow this act made the pain seem to lessen. How Jesus, in such pain, or perhaps worse, could form comprehensible sentences was beyond my understanding. My hands were covered in blood, as were my feet. Mary Magdalene and Lazarus also came to my side.

"The pain began to lessen slowly and I noticed the soldiers had already divided the men's sandals and anything else that could be resold. They seemed overly excited as they began to cast lots for the fabulous robe Herod had placed upon Jesus. Men convicted and executed under the king or governor had their property confiscated. Luckily Jesus' beautiful tallit, spun of hemp and silk, was on his head under the crown of thorns. It would be needed for his burial...."

"You're saying that Jesus directed the statement; 'Son behold your Mother,' to Judas and not John?" inquired Joshua.

"That is what I observed, Joshua," said Teryk.

"This verse, 'Son, behold your Mother,' is only found in one Gospel: John's," said Raven. "It states, '...Woman, behold thy son! Then saith he to the disciple, Behold thy mother! And from that hour that disciple took her unto his own home. She stays with him for the rest of her life...' This only strengthens my belief that Lazarus was the author of the Fourth Gospel." JOHN

"From what you've said, Teryk, John's mother Salome, Jesus' step-sister, was present at the Crucifixion when Jesus uttered those words," surmised Anakah. "It seems unlikely that Jesus would have placed a responsibility that more fittingly fell to his oldest stepbrother James than upon James's nephew, the disciple John."

"Anakah is correct," explained Kortney. "According to Jewish custom, the responsibility of caring for the mother fell to the oldest surviving son, in this case James the Just: Mary's oldest stepson."

"There is only one other who could claim that right: Jesus' fabled twin brother," proposed Phoenix. "Teryk, did Jesus ever explain why he addressed Judah as the son of Mary?"

"Yes, he did. Shortly after the resurrection Jesus revealed to the disciples that Judas Iscariot was his identical twin brother," said Teryk, to the astonishment of everyone in the room. "On the night of his birth, a second child was born to Mary. A boy: Jesus' twin. This caused concern because the prophecy regarding Y'shua's birth spoke of only one. Mary named her firstborn Y'shua in accordance with Archangel Gabriel's instructions. Since no instructions had been given for the second child, she decided to name him Judah, the boy's great-great-great-great-great-grandfather. Mother Mary also thought it might be best for the second child to be raised by the midwife who assisted at their births.

"Leah-bas-Ezekiel was the wife of Symeon-bar-Boethus, a Pharisee, and high priest of the Sanhedrin at the time. Judah was to be raised a prince of Judaea

Joseph "Five Eagles" Reyna

and educated in the temple. They raised Judah as if he were their own child. Jesus explained to the others that this was why Judas had been among the first disciples chosen and why he had favored him so much and taken him almost everywhere he went. The other brothers and sisters of Jesus mentioned in the Gospels were stepbrothers from Joseph's former marriage to Salome. This is why there are two named Judah in the same family.

"Jesus instructed Judah to journey to the Far East, after the ascension. He was to go to Kashmir: a beautiful land of flowers enclosed by ice-capped mountains. Jesus explained that his mother really loved it there when he was studying in the mountain monasteries. Mother Mary wished very much to live out the remainder of her years in that valley."

"A special bond exists between some identical twins. That might account for why you experienced pain during the Crucifixion," explained Sofia. "If Judah and Jesus were in fact identical twins, that is."

"There is an ancient legend that after the Crucifixion, Mary journeyed with her son on the Silk Road to India from Palestine. She is rumored to have been buried in Kashmir," said Phoenix. "Commander, could you give us more information regarding this journey?"

"I'm sorry to have kept you in the dark regarding that journey. But there was no way I could have added those details earlier," apologized Teryk. "Jesus told me that, when he was twelve years old, he and his mother had traveled to England with Joseph of Arimathaea. When they returned, they traveled by ship down the Red Sea to the Arabian Sea and skirted the southern tip of India. With favorable trade winds, their trip by sea took about two months. Jesus said he studied in many temples throughout the region. He and his mother returned to Palestine via the Silk Road after completing his studies in Kashmir. On his way back, Jesus taught throughout the lands they traveled. He told me the people of those regions referred to him as Saint Issa.

"Judah was to drop this old name and take up Jesus' old title and assume his identity," continued Teryk. "That might account for the legend of Mary journeying with her son on the Silk Road to India after the Crucifixion. As for Mother Mary, she enjoyed the beauty of Kashmir for several years. She used to love to climb a hill that overlooked a valley covered in flowers. From there she could see the snowcapped mountains reflected off a shimmering blue lake. She was loved by all. When she died, a special tomb was constructed for her on top of that hill."

"Jesus did not accompany the two of you into Persia as well?" inquired Jidion.

"I saw him ascend into a bright cloud, My Lady. Except for the incident while fishing in the Sea of Galilee, that was the last any of us saw of him. But we did not travel to Persia alone. I purchased Veronica from the house of Caiaphas without too much difficulty and set her free. We were also accompanied by several of Jesus' entourage, including the disciples Andrew, Thaddaeus and Timothy."

"A Tomb containing Mary's remains would be highly controversial!" exclaimed Joshua. "The Roman Catholic Church teaches that the Virgin Mary ascended into Heaven in what is termed the Assumption, although the New Testament makes no reference to the event."

"This brings up an interesting point," observed Raven. "If the body buried at the tomb of the prophet Yuz Asaf, in Kashmir, is found to have the same mitochondrial DNA as the woman buried in the tomb of Mother Mary, it would raise some serious questions."

"What body? What are you talking about?" asked Trisha.

Raven paused, flashing a sheepish smile, unsure of just how to answer the question. She turned toward Teryk for further instruction.

Looking at his friend and confidante Raven, Teryk rose from his seat and began to pace slowly around the large table. "I suppose this is as good a time as any," he began. "While still aboard the *Defiant*, I ordered Raven to assemble a small but secret group to investigate the possibility that Jesus traveled to Persia during the years he is missing from history. As Judah, I observed that Jesus did indeed spend forty days with the disciples before ascending to the heavens. During that period he made it known to his disciples, and to his own family, where he had been during what the Church calls the missing years. Jesus also explained Judas's part in the arrest, and why he and Judah looked so much alike.

"I hope you can all understand why this information was not divulged earlier. In order to thoroughly investigate these claims, it will be necessary to venture into the Tibetan monasteries in and around Kashmir. A great deal of information has surfaced regarding Jesus having visited that region of the world.

"The tomb spoken of by Raven is in the middle of Srinagar's old town in Anzimar, in the Khanjar quarter of preset-day Kashmir, next to an old Muslim cemetery," continued Teryk. "The building that now surrounds the tomb was a later addition. An inscription explains that Yuz Asaf entered the Valley of Kashmir long ago. His life was dedicated to the search for Truth. Although most Muslims claim that the 'Tomb of the Prophet' is associated with their culture, the structure predates Islam by several centuries.

"Raven's concern is that archaeologists will mistakenly assume that the body of Yuz Asaf is that of Jesus. You see, Mary's tomb, called Mai Mari da Asthan: 'The Final Resting Place of Mother Mari', is also located in Kashmir and was venerated for centuries. I say 'was' because the British desecrated the tomb desiring the location for a military fort. They pushed the blocks of the tomb off the side of the hill. It is not known what became of the body. Should Mary's body ever be found and its mitochondrial DNA match that of Yuz Asaf's body, it would prove that the prophet was her son—which, of course, he was…"

"Many on the Internet have already jumped to the conclusion that the tomb of the prophet Yuz Asaf is in fact that of Jesus," interrupted Raven. "Having already discovered that Jesus spent his missing years in Persia, and believing he survived the Crucifixion, they mistakenly concluded that he travelled to Kashmir and lived the remainder of his life there. Once again we find ourselves with a dilemma. Either Jesus Christ had an identical twin brother or he survived the Crucifixion and his remains are buried in Kashmir!"

"The things you say, Teryk," said Juaquin uncomfortably.

"Search for any information regarding Jesus' travels throughout India, Pakistan or any other part of the Far East," instructed Shakira, whose natural ability to command seemed to have placed her in charge of the entire investigation. "See if anything else in the New Testament could imply that Judas never committed suicide as history maintains."

"As I mentioned earlier," interrupted Cassandra, "*The Aquarian Gospel of Jesus the Christ*, written by Levi H. Dowling, claims Jesus was in Persia studying in their monasteries during the missing years."

"You're right, Cassandra. I'd forgotten you mentioned that," said Shakira. "I would like to stress the importance of finding the evidence in the Gospels themselves."

"The book, *King of Travelers*, by Edward T. Martin was quite informative on the subject," added Raven, "as was his DVD entitled *Jesus in India*."

"It is highly unlikely that a Jewish rabbi would go traveling into India," argued Kortney.

"I think that it has been clearly established that Y'shua-bar-Yehosef was not an ancestor of Aaron or Levi and therefore could not have been a rabbi," Sofia reminded him. "Had Jesus been ordained a rabbi, an extremely rare custom, there would have been some mention of it in the Talmud or other rabbinical literature."

"True enough, My Lady," agreed Kortney, "but I was referring to Judah, who was raised as a scribe and a priest of the Sanhedrin."

"In regards to Judah, I can assure you that he wanted nothing more to do with the Jewish priesthood," confided Teryk. "On a sidenote, I would like to add that many attribute the origins of the 'golden rule' to Jesus. But five hundred years before his birth, Buddha said pretty much the same thing. And Confucius offered similar guidance. Had Jesus been educated in Persia, he would have learned of these two masters. I realize it's a lot to take in. Try to imagine how I felt witnessing it. If that's all for now, I'll get back to describing the details of the crucifixion.

"In Jesus' weakened condition the priests must have reasoned that they could safely despise him without retribution. Feeling emboldened, the priests and scribes moved as close as they dared. With raised fists they shouted, 'He saved others, let Him save Himself. Come down from the Cross now and we will believe in you.'

"It was exactly noon because the Shofars had just sounded, summoning the faithful to worship. As the sound of the Shofars died down, the Earth began to shake violently and the sky began to darken. Everyone looked up and pointed nervously. Within minutes the Sun was blotted out from the heavens. I looked up hoping to see the Sun's corona surrounding the Moon's disk, its flares illuminating the sky, but the darkness was absolute. Over the Sun was an ominous silhouette that seemed far larger than it should have been. As if on cue, the silver trumpets of the temple sounded for the last time. The effect was eerie and no one said a word.

"The earthquake that followed was massive, much more powerful than an eight-pointer I once experienced. The fluid-swaying motion of the Earth lasted for some time. Screams arose from within the city walls as pandemonium erupted. Scribes and priests drew back in terror as the Roman soldiers drew their swords. Lamentations and cries of astonishment broke out all around us."

The Greatest Story Never Told

> *Man will occasionally stumble over the truth,*
> *but most of the time he will pick himself up and*
> *continue on as if nothing had happened.*
> —**Winston Churchill, Commentary on Man**

"There could not have been a daytime eclipse, Commander! Modern-day scholars have come to the conclusion that Luke must have been mistaken," argued Claudia. "With a full moon occurring on the night of the Crucifixion, there is no way that an eclipse could have taken place during the daytime."

"It is true that modern scholars dismiss the eclipse as a dust storm or a very dark rain cloud," agreed Raven, "but the fact still remains that Luke wrote the Greek word 'ekleipo' and no other."

"Commander, the duration of eclipses in general, over a fixed location on Earth, is less than eight minutes. And by duration I mean the total time from when the Moon's disk completely obscures the Sun's light until the Sun's light can be seen again," explained Clifton. "Eclipses take nearly an hour to even begin to blot out the sun. What you are you suggesting..."

"What Teryk is suggesting is *not possible!*" maintained Claudia. "Passovers are held during full moons. Therefore it would be utterly impossible for the Sun to be eclipsed by the Moon on that particular day. An eclipse can only be caused by the interposition of the Moon between the Earth and the Sun."

"The daytime eclipse Teryk described would have been a violation of the very laws of nature," argued Adriana. "Must I remind you that most Christians today believe that the acts of God are in concert with, not in violation of, those laws?"

"That's very interesting, considering that every miracle I have ever witnessed was a direct violation of the known laws of the Universe, a Universe you maintain is only an illusion—my own personal hallucination," chided Teryk. "The best minds of this world seem to have defined our reality as the collective inputs of the five senses we process through our carbon-unit life forms. These five senses are limiting at best and can be easily fooled by those who can manipulate the illusion. Is it any wonder that as I'm trying to explain a larger understanding to you, my own senses are brought into question? What you need to understand is that there is far more to your superficial reality than the perceived physical world. Atoms are mostly empty space. What your mind interprets as reality is made up of less than 5% of what's really out there. You demand physical proof, forgetting that our physical Universe is mostly made up of nothing."

"I see it as a collective consciousness," agreed Anakah, "a holographic matrix-like reality that comprises all life forms in the galaxy."

"I disagree," said Teryk. "I have come to the realization that each of us is simply an interference pattern within the holographic matrix. The Creator, this consciousness, intelligence or life force that comprises our holographic illusion can exist apart from us; whereas we cannot exist apart from it."

"In regards to the Moon, Claudia is correct," agreed Clifton. "What Teryk is talking about could not have been an eclipse as we understand it. Yet I believe that what Teryk has described was caused by our Moon as it maintained a stationary geocentric orbit directly over the city of Jerusalem, two thousand years ago!"

"Think about what you're suggesting, Clifton! The Moon would have had to slow down, reverse direction and move across the heavens in a matter of hours. We are then to believe that the Moon took up a stationary orbit over Jerusalem and tracked Jesus' position for several more hours, after which it would have had to accelerate in order to return to its original position that night," countered Sarina, her forehead supported in her right hand as she contemplated her next words carefully. "Commander, I am seriously considering the possibility that you were delusional, given the circumstances."

"And yet, as a rule, delusional people are not incredibly accurate," observed Sofia. "Teryk's account of what may have transpired has so far stood up to our scrutiny. Up to this point, almost everything Teryk's told us has been verified either by biblical or historical records."

"Ladies, when I'm finished you are going to have far more to debate than a daytime eclipse. That very same night there was a second eclipse: a blood-red lunar eclipse." Teryk raised a hand for all to be silent. "What I witnessed on the day Jesus died were two eclipses that occurred within hours of each other."

"It is going to be impossible to prove such a thing, Commander," stated Sarina. "This event occurred nearly two thousand years ago!"

"Over these past few days, I've listened to the complaints of those who feel that my having assembled the entire research team for this investigation has been a serious misallocation of resources. Well, now you know why I have assembled you all in one location," explained Teryk.

"If I might, Commander," inquired Anakah.

Teryk nodded his consent.

"Occam's Razor, a rule of reason sometimes used in philosophy, might be applicable here," continued Anakah. "It states that if a number of equally valid solutions exist for a given problem, the simplest solution is probably the correct one. If it can be proved that two eclipses did in fact occur on the same day, I am not sure that anyone here would be willing to accept the simplest solution."

"And what would that be?" asked Adriana.

"That our world is orbited by a massive artificial satellite, constructed by beings far more ancient and technologically advanced than we are!" added Clifton, to the astonishment of everyone in the room.

Teryk gazed around at the astonished group and continued. "Upon noticing that no trumpets sounded the Roman legions to battle, Cornelius ordered his legionnaires to sheath their swords. He then ordered his men to fashion crude torches from the tattered remnants of clothing taken from the convicted men. He ordered the two cavalry soldiers to proceed to the Fortress Antonia and procure proper torches in case they should be needed. They were also to find out if Pilate had issued any special orders concerning the darkness.

"As the mounted soldiers rode off, the first of the makeshift torches took to flame. Jesus must have regained his strength, perhaps from the cooling effect of the eclipse. He cried out in Aramaic, 'Eli, Eli, lema sabbachthani!' In the torchlight, I could see that Jesus displayed a sardonic grin of triumph as he uttered those words. The distance to the cross was about ten yards but the expression on his countenance was unmistakable. The words themselves were the beginning of the 22nd Psalm. I thought it interesting that Jesus spoke in Aramaic: the language practiced by all priests of the temple. By this very action, Jesus seemed to be targeting his statement directly at the assembled priests and scribes.

"The 22nd Psalm begins, 'My God, my God, why have you forsaken me?' but Jesus did not utter it in the form of a question, nor did he seem to be directing it at God. It was more of a… triumphal statement with just a hint of cynicism. Priests of the temple memorized a lot of scripture. Holy Scripture is considered to be a living thing and as such, Jews are forbidden to write down verses from it. This particular psalm was one of a few that were required to be memorized by all the young men of Israel, much like the 'Our Father' is memorized in Christian cultures. If I were to cry out, 'Our Father who art in Heaven,' you could automatically recite the remainder of the prayer. In this same manner, all the priests present knew exactly what came after 'Eli, Eli, lema sabbachthani'—and why Jews were required to memorize it.

"The 22nd Psalm written by King David was perhaps his only prophecy concerning the Messiah. David had asked God how the Messiah would die. Think of it as a sort of authentication of the Messiah. After the initial 'My God, my God, why has thou forsaken me?' it goes on to say, '…they shoot out the lip, they shake the head saying, He trusted on the Lord that he would deliver him… the assembly of the wicked have enclosed me… they pierced my hands and feet… they part my garments among them, and cast lots upon my vesture.'

"The look on the faces of the priests, in the torchlight, was priceless— they gnew damn well who he was now. Then one ass shouted, 'He calls for Elijah, let us see if he will come,' and others took up the odious call. Truly these were wicked men, amusing themselves at my Lord's expense. Just then, a massive aftershock threw these men to the ground. An expression of fear covered the faces of many who turned and headed toward Jerusalem with great haste.

"I noticed that the temperature had begun to cool significantly. The pain in my hands and feet had lessened to a dull throb. My eyes adjusted to the darkness and I could clearly make out the stars, their brilliance not dimmed in the slightest. They formed constellations that did not belong in the night sky, at least not at this time of the year.

"I heard Jesus utter the words 'I thirst' in a very raspy tone. At this, a young Roman soldier took a hyssop stalk and dipped it in the posca: a bowl containing the drink of the common military. The young soldier attached it to the end of his javelin. He then held the hyssop to Jesus' lips, allowing him to sip from it—not a single soldier made an attempt to stop him.

"The hyssop acted like a sponge when it was dipped into the bowl. Normally, soldiers did not put the stalk to their lips in order to drink. They raised it over their heads, squeezing its contents into their mouths. Hyssop leaves give off a pungent mint-like aroma. The small bushy plant has blue flowers and is often used as medicine. The mixture of vinegar, water and wine was sour but thirst-quenching. Sailors had originated the habit aboard Roman ships. The soldiers seemed to enjoy the drink, which they found refreshing and a lot safer than the local drinking water.

"There is a theory that Jesus was slipped a narcotic to induce a state that gave the appearance of death. The torches provided sufficient light for me to see that the young guard used the same hyssop the soldiers had been using. To me, it seemed that the soldier responded more out of pity than any spitefulness. I also observed that the other soldiers continued to drink from the substance in the bowl, with no ill effect.

"Then, in a loud voice, Jesus cried, 'Tetelestai.' The word sounded Greek, and I did not know the meaning of it."

"I believe the word means 'the debts are paid for' but it has been mistranslated into 'it is finished'," said Raven.

"Tetelestai is more of a document, really," explained Teryk. "It's a certificate of sorts, prepared by a Roman court when a man is thrown into a debtors' prison and required to work off his debts. Just bear with me, guys, and I'll explain the whole thing."

"Then Jesus cried out in a very loud voice, 'Abba, baddach ephkid rouel...' It is a verse from Psalm 31:5, meaning 'into your hands I commend my spirit'. He did not live long enough to recite the last part of the Psalm: '...It is you who will redeem me, Lord.'

"After Jesus had uttered those words, the light of the Sun slowly returned as the Moon's disk moved away, causing another earthquake, greater than the first. Though seated, I fell over, rolling to one side and protecting my wrists by pulling them in towards my chest. To my surprise, the pain in my hands and feet had subsided.

"I then heard Cornelius utter, 'Surely, this was the Son of God and it is his God that reigns.' I observed that the length of the shadows cast by the upright beams of the crosses seemed slightly longer than the beams themselves. My best guesstimate would put the time at about 5:00 PM.

"In the sunlight I could make out the inscription on the titulus above Jesus' head. It read *I'shua Nazarenus Rex Iudaeorum*—Y'shua the Nazarene, King of the Jews. It was written in Latin, Greek, and Hebrew. I could not help but notice that Jesus' cross created the unmistakable image of the Qabalah's Tree of Life: a cross with an additional but shorter crossbeam above the main crossbeam. Illuminated by blazing torches in the unnatural darkness, the symbolic gesture of Jesus suspended from the 'Tree of Life' between Heaven and Earth would have been unmistakable to any passer-by."

"The Gospel of Mark states that it was about the ninth hour, which should be about 3:00 PM. Why do you think it was nearer 5:00 PM?" asked Joshua.

"Ancient sundials did not keep the same time as our modern timepieces," explained Teryk. "The shadow cast by the sundial's arm varied according to the season. You should check your timepieces against the shadows cast by the Sun at its zenith. The Sun is not directly overhead until about an hour and a half after your watch reads 12:00 PM. To the Romans, however, it would have been the ninth hour, which many *Bible* students take to mean 3:00 PM, our time. It looked closer to 5:00 PM, though, judging by the length of the shadows cast by Sun's position in the sky."

"I looked up to see Jesus' face. The right side was badly bruised, his right eye swollen shut. His nose appeared broken. His knees were bloody, probably from having fallen with the patibulum tied to his arms. I could make out the long sharp barbs in the crown of thorns, emphasized by the brilliant white of his prayer shawl under them.

"Seeing his pierced feet, I remembered the Magdalene's tears washing over them. I also remembered her crying as she anointed his head with spikenard at Bethany. She had snapped the delicate alabaster bottle in two over his thick auburn hair just three days ago. The small alabaster vase, no longer than my index finger, turned out to be a form of blown glass that only resembled alabaster.

"The words of the prophet Isaiah again came unbidden. 'He was oppressed, and he was afflicted... He was taken from prison and from judgment: and who shall declare his posterity...' *Wait a minute*, I thought. *Posterity?* Posterity means his offspring, his children, his successive descendants, the generations not yet born! But Jesus and the Magdalene have no children. Is she pregnant, then? I had lost my train of thought. Where was I? '...and who shall declare his posterity? For he was cut off [killed] out of the land of the living: for the transgression of my people was he stricken. And he made his grave with the wicked and with the rich...'

"Shouting from the priests brought me back to my senses. They were requesting that the *crurifragium* be inflicted, meaning that the legs of the crucified men should be broken in order that they might die and thus be removed from the crosses, in keeping with Jewish laws. Cornelius informed them that when he received orders from Pilate to do so, he would, but not until then.

"With that, a procession of priests, Yehosef ha Ramati among them, proceeded to secure the requested permission from the governor. After what seemed like another hour, Yehosef ha Ramati arrived with an officer from the Place Antonia. He was holding an official consent from Pilate for Jesus' body to be released to him for burial. Cornelius issued an order and a soldier used a large wooden hammer to break the legs of both Cestus and Dysmas just above the ankles. This action by the soldiers was not intended to add torment. Rather, it was an act of mercy, its purpose to end the suffering of crucified men by hastening their death.

"I recalled the prophecy that none of the Messiah's bones would be broken but suspected that it had more to do with the Book of Exodus expressly forbidding the breaking of the Paschal lamb's bones.

"Enough!" shouted an older legionnaire as he approached the soldier who was brandishing the large hammer. The soldier was going to break Jesus' legs in the same manner that he had shattered the legs of Dysmas and Cestus. The older legionnaire drew up his own spear, tipped with a broad leaf-shaped blade, and thrust it into Jesus' left side near the center of his ribcage. The spearhead itself was about a foot long and penetrated deep enough to reach his heart. The soldier then added, 'This man has been dead for some time now and you shall humiliate him no further.' I later learned from Cornelius that this soldier's name was Caius Longinus.

"That Jesus bled blood and water was no miracle. He must have been dead for some time, otherwise I would have probably felt the pain myself. From what I had read on crucifixion, this fluid was most likely extravasated blood that had separated into its constituents: clear plasma and red blood cells. The process is called coagulation and occurs about an hour after death. This fulfilled Zachariah's prophecy, and I wondered if the dull minds of the scribes could recall it: '...they shall look upon 'me' whom they have pierced.' Probably not. A modified crowbar-like device was then used to remove the nail through Jesus' feet and extract the nails from his wrists.

"Cornelius drew his short sword and placed it under the crown of thorns, using the sword as a lever to lift the crown off Jesus' head. This proved difficult even with the assistance of another soldier, because the thorns had been driven deep beneath the skin. I did not think they had penetrated the skull but rather sunk deep between scalp and skull.

"Four soldiers carried the body of Jesus to the nearby road. '*Had Joseph not requested Jesus' body, history would probably never have concerned itself with an empty tomb*,' I thought. The soldiers placed him down on top of a burial cloth that had been folded in two for extra strength. Even folded, the shroud was still longer than Jesus' body. Several of Nicodemus's servants helped to take Jesus' body to a nearby garden tomb that was the property of Yehosef ha Ramati. The body was very pale from loss of blood. His arms were outstretched. Rigor mortis having set in. If the Roman guards suspected for an instant that Jesus could still have been alive, they would never have released his body—because if he was still alive they would soon be put to death.

"Cornelius had the bodies of Dysmas and Cestus removed and placed on a wagon, to be dumped in the Valley of Hinnom. They were not permitted a formal burial. The unauthorized removal of a corpse from a crucifix was a criminal offense. Had it not been for the First Day of Unleavened Bread, called the High Sabbath, all three bodies would have been left to rot on the crosses, as was the Roman custom. Guards would have been posted at Golgotha to prevent family or friends from attempting to remove the corpses in order to bury them."

31

Deathwatch

"The Golal, the stone that covered the entrance to the tomb, was about ten inches thick and stood just over four feet tall. The white paint on its surface had still not dried in the cool evening air. When Jesus had spoken of whitewashed tombs, he had been referring to this white paint, which was intended to warn trespassers that they would be defiled if they entered, because the tomb was occupied.

"The helpers, it seems, did not actually touch the corpse. They had lifted Jesus by holding onto the large linen sheet. They then carried his body the short distance to the tomb. Placing Jesus on the stone slab would have proven more difficult if rigor mortis hadn't already set in. But that posed its own problem because he could not be transported through the small entrance with his arms extended the way they were. Joseph and Nicodemus each grabbed one of his arms and folded it over the body. They then bound the wrists using a piece of Joseph's sash, so that the arms would not extend out again.

"I observed from a distance. Servants had already begun to prepare the thick resin-like substance and were dipping strips of linen into the glutinous amalgamation. They handed the strips to Joseph and Nicodemus who worked as quickly as possible to bind the body of Jesus in the fashion of an Egyptian mummy. They needed both of their hands to wrap Jesus' body in thin one-inch strips, so they could not reach for a lamp when they needed one. Their hands and most of their clothes were covered with the shellac-like myrrh. It reminded me of making piñatas in school, immersing the thin newspaper strips in the mortar-like paste made from flour then wrapping them around a balloon; this process was very similar to that.

"They had both entered the Fortress Antonia earlier and were now touching a corpse. Being priests, this would require them to undergo seven days of purification. As a result, they would miss the Passover week celebrations. In addition to this, Joseph had also walked over a cemetery. I came close and offered to help but, as I was a priest, they did not want me to have to undergo the seven days of solitude they were about to endure for touching Jesus' corpse. I was weak from loss of blood and did not wish to remind them that I was with them in the pagan temple and had walked over a cemetery as well.

"I was startled by someone clutching at my robe. It was Mary Magdalene. She had dropped to the ground beside me. I knelt and held her hand, which was frigid. I removed the heavy cloak I had purchased and draped it over her. She was petite and young. Hollywood always portrays her as a middle-aged woman but I doubt she was even twenty years old. Rising, I said, 'I need to assist the priests because they are running out of time.'

"Mary Magdalene handed me a bundle of flowers she had picked from the garden. They were wrapped in her outer cloak. I carried the flowers to the edge of the tomb and set them down. The two priests were working furiously. There was still much work to do. I picked up the lamp that was set by the mouth of the sepulture. It did not seem to be doing anyone much good there. I entered and held the lamp over the two men. They did not object and I was in a position to observe the procedure. The tomb was almost high enough for me to stand up straight. The old priests were using a rather large amount of myrrh. Fragrances of spice and herbs mixed with that of myrrh, permeating the small space. I noticed that Jesus' body was covered with small purple bruises set in pairs, from the scourging he'd received.

"Wrapping the body mummy-fashion took far more time than I could have imagined, as Jesus was not a small man. Their wrappings came all the way up to Jesus' neck but did not cover his head. There was an additional binding around his jaw in order to keep it shut, making it look like Jesus had a toothache.

"A long shroud, like the one some believe might be the Shroud of Turin, was spread under the body on a shelf hewn from solid rock. This shroud extended from just past Jesus' feet and ran the length of his body. It was bunched up just past his head. When the men were finished, this bunched-up material would be draped over the top of the corpse. Before doing so, they took the flowers Mary Magdalene had picked, from the many varieties that bloomed in the garden at that time of year, and laid them along the edges of the shroud, on both sides of Jesus' body.

"Joseph then reached for Jesus' tallit, which had been folded neatly, but stopped himself upon noticing that his hands where covered in shellac. He asked me to place the tallit over the face of Jesus. I asked why it was not placed under the shroud. Nicodemus informed me that the tallit was considered a holy thing and must be buried with the man to whom it belonged. Being a holy garment, it was not permitted to touch the dead man. For this reason it would lay on top of the shroud over Y'shua's face. The tallit must be what history recalls as the napkin that covered his face. It was not found with the grave clothes, but folded and set aside in a separate place.

"Just then we heard the first blast from the silver trumpets announcing the beginning of the High Sabbath. The first three stars must have become visible. The shofar's broadcast proclaimed a limit on the time that could be spent on Jesus' burial. I stepped out of the tomb and waited for the two priests to exit. Women and helpers hastily prepared to leave in the dimming twilight. A distraught Mary Magdalene, my lamp illuminating her disheveled hair, looked on anxiously from a distance. She was among the last to leave. I watched as she trailed behind the small group heading east over the hill into Bethany, her small frame silhouetted against the tranquil darkness. I turned and saw Joseph pouring a cup of blood over the tallit that was on Jesus' face. He placed the cup in the tomb since it too was covered in blood.

"As they exited the tomb, the two elderly priests hesitated to roll the massive stone over the entrance, explaining that the High Sabbath had begun and no work could be performed. I thought this odd, and asked them if they ever went outside their homes on the Sabbath. They both nodded that they did. 'Do you leave the doors to your home open when you exit?' I asked. Without answering, they assisted me in closing the tomb. Then the two elderly priests retreated in order to find a mikveh for the purpose of purification.

"Normally a 'deathwatch' would commence: the wait to see if a loved one will return to life. But in Jesus' case this seemed unnecessary. Martha and Mary had informed me that they had watched young Lazarus's body until the allotted time of three days had expired. The loss of a brother is a terrible sadness. Somehow the loss of a king seems far greater and more difficult to put into words. I studied my surroundings and began looking for a suitable tree from which to hang myself. Looking up at the full moon, I noticed a gradual copper-reddish color darkening its forward edge. Placing my hands on my hips, I realized that I had not yet returned the thirty pieces of silver. *I certainly can't hang myself before doing that*, I thought.

"Returning to the temple, I saw that the city was in an uproar. Crews were still clearing rubble and carting off the dead or tending to survivors. Everyone was pointing excitedly at the citron-tinted moon that had become more menacing. Wondering what all the fuss was about, I supposed I should be grateful no one was demanding that I stop and help. This was probably due to the blood-stained priest's robes I was wearing. More likely it was due to the fact that this was the Holy High Sabbath. The last thing anyone needed was a scribe pointing out the fact that no one was supposed to be exerting themselves.

"Near the North Gate I entered a mikveh in order to purify myself. Luckily there was a servant present to attend to me. The man provided me with a clean robe to wear. As I washed my feet and entered the first pool, I was amazed at how bright it was in the chamber. It never ceased to amaze me how much light was given off by those small clay lanterns in the niches. I could make out cracks in the walls. They must have been caused by the earthquake, as they had not been there before.

"How long had I remained awake? It had been twenty-four hours since the Last Supper had begun and as usual we had started out early that morning. I was beginning to feel its effect and was grateful for the bath. The mikveh refreshed my spirits and I guesstimated I had been awake for nearly thirty-five hours. How much longer? I laughed thinking I would soon be catching up on sleep—or would I simply wake up exhausted in the deprivation chamber on board *Defiant*? Why hadn't anyone tried to wake me? Maybe I was in a coma. *Well, no point in worrying about that now*, I thought.

"As I neared the temple, I could see in the dimming moonlight that the entire complex had suffered a lot of damage; probably why it had taken them another thirty years to finish construction on this place. I noticed that the doors to the Women's Court were open. As I passed the gold-plated doors decorated with silver-plated palm trees and flowers, I noticed that the Corinthian gate on the east side remained closed. I approached the temple entrance. The two mighty bronze pillars, Jachin and Boaz, stood to the left and right of the gold-plated temple doors. The pillars were incredibly wide and said to be hollow. Two hundred pomegranates hung from chains attached to the top of the pillars.

"These pillars were replicas of the two built by Adam and Seth. As the story goes, Adam was given the wisdom that concerns the heavenly bodies and their order, meaning that by their signs he knew what was to come. Adam predicted that the world would be destroyed by the violence and quantity of water and again by the force of fire. In order that their wisdom might survive each of the catastrophes, Adam and Seth—being the inventors of many things—inscribed their discoveries upon the pillars. One coded alchemical symbol that stood out was a green lion standing on his hind legs, tearing at the Sun with his claws. It symbolized acid cutting through a given material in an effort to extract the desired substance. Adam had constructed one pillar from fired brick and the other from stone.

"Inside the temple its priests were everywhere trying to clean up the mess. It was difficult for them, accustomed as they were to walking on smooth stone floors. The floor was littered with wreckage and these 'tenderfoots' were having one hell of a time clearing out the rubble. The walls and floor of the temple were made of stone, but their surfaces had been covered with Lebanon cedar: a mighty tree that grows in the mountains of Lebanon. The cedar on the floor, ceiling and walls was overlaid in gold, in the same manner that the Ark of the Covenant had been.

"The solid-gold seven-branched menorah, symbolizing the presence of God, was burning. Towards the rear of the structure, the curtain, often called the veil that closed off the Holy of Holies, was now in shambles. If the curtain had been torn in half I could not tell, since the entire thing had collapsed to the ground. The small enclosure resembled a glorified empty tomb more than a sanctuary of God. And although the Ark of the Covenant was no longer present in the Holy of Holies, the high priest was still required to enter the room once a year on Yom Kippur, the Day of Atonement; to atone for his own sins and those of the people.

"I wondered why Jesus hadn't selected Yom Kippur as the day to die on; somehow it seemed more fitting. On Yom Kippur the high priest was required to cast lots in order to choose between two goats to sacrifice. One goat would be offered as a burnt sacrifice, the ashes of which were then placed in a bag and tied with a scarlet ribbon to the horns of the second goat. The high priest would then lay his hands on the goat and make confession for all the sins of the people, in effect transferring the sins of Israel to the scapegoat. At the end of each confession he would speak God's name aloud. It was the only time the name of God was permitted to be spoken aloud.

"I wondered why the priests had not leveled that charge against Jesus. Plenty of witnesses had heard him utter the name of God during his arrest. That offense was punishable by death. At any rate, the high priest would then cut off a piece of the scarlet ribbon. The beast was then goaded out of the city and into the wilderness by priests, as people lined the road, forming a narrow pathway. The goat was taken to a deep ravine about twelve miles away and encouraged to leap off the steep cliff to its death. Flag messengers would signal back to the high priest that the scapegoat was dead and the celebrations would begin after a final ceremony. The piece of scarlet ribbon was placed over the entrance to the tabernacle, where it would magically turn white overnight. Except that from this time forward the scarlet ribbon never turned white again.

"'Judah, I saw you covered in blood. What happened? Were you hurt during the earthquake?' asked Gamaliel, who seemed to be directing the cleanup.

"'Yes, I'm fine, Master. What are these graven images embroidered all over the curtain? And why are the priests working on the Holy High Sabbath?' I inquired.

"'After the earthquake Caiaphas finally declared a state of emergency. We have been cleaning up and carrying out the dead and wounded ever since. As for your other question, the images are not graven images. Embroidered onto the lintel of the Holy of Holies are two standing kherubim (cherubim) facing each other, their arms extended straight out: one set low, the other raised high. Each kherubim has the torso of a woman with eagle wings extending from her arms, while her lower body resembles that of a lion. Two such creatures sit facing each other on the lid of the Ark of the Covenant, wings outstretched.' He held his arms out in a forward motion. 'Since no such creature is to be found, the law pertaining to graven images remains unbroken.' Behind the lintel was a tapestry as thick as a man's wrist. Herod had had it woven in Babylon. The tapestry, a multicolored panorama of the Universe, was visible through the transparent lintel. The curtain and the lintel were brought down during the second earthquake.

"Do you know what happened to the Ark of the Covenant, teacher?' I asked, rubbing my eyes as they had begun to sting from the smoke of the lamps in the temple.

"He looked at me and then around to the other priests but no one seemed to be paying much attention to us. 'The Maccabees record that the prophet Jeremiah, having been warned by God, gave orders that the tabernacle and the Ark of the Covenant be placed in hiding to protect them from an impending attack on the city. Jeremiah hid the Ark and Tabernacle, along with the Altar of Incense and many golden vessels and instruments used in temple ceremonies, in a cave on the Mountain of the Elohim. Jeremiah then concealed the cave's entrance.'

"'Also, a replica of the Ark was taken to Ethiopia by Solomon's firstborn son, Menelik, who had been raised according to our customs. The Queen of the South had requested that priests accompany her on the return to her Kingdom, so that they might instruct her child. The boy's mother sent him here to be recognized by his father the King on his twenty-first birthday. As you can imagine, it did not go over well with the priests. Solomon was informed in no uncertain terms that Menelik could never inherit the throne and must be sent away. Solomon said if his firstborn was to be sent away, then all firstborn of the priests must be sent away as well. So the firstborn of all the Levite priests were sent away. Solomon ordered that replicas be fashioned by his craftsman so that the young priests would have everything they'd need to perform their duties in his son's kingdom. The firstborn are the overseers of the Ark, you see. A special wagon was constructed in order to transport and protect the Ark over such a great distance. The wagon, however, suffered the same fate as David's wagon: It could not support the great weight of the golden mercy seat.'

"'I thought that it had to be carried by a procession of priests? If the Ark was that heavy, how could a handful of priests carry it?'

"'Priests were required to carry it but none of Solomon's craftsmen could duplicate the 'lightning stone': the light-radiating Schamir that King Solomon had fashioned into a ring in order to prevent the priests from using it.'

"'Lightning stone? I didn't know the Ark was supposed to have a lightning stone. What did it do?' I asked.

"'By itself the stone could do nothing, but when combined with the Schethiy , the 'stone of perfection', the 'lightning stone' glowed with a ruby-red radiance and became a weapon of unspeakable power and destruction. It could cut through glass and stone perfectly and silently. That is how Solomon's craftsmen were able to cut the massive blocks of stone without the sound of hammer and chisel,' explained Gamaliel.

Joseph "Five Eagles" Reyna

"'If the temple was to be built without the sound of hammer and chisel, how is it Herod the Great was able to construct it?' I asked.

"'Herod's craftsmen employed a secret compound that when poured into a form took on the dimensions of that form and hardened into stone. It is how they were able to create the massive blocks of stone used to build the surrounding walls of the temple. I understand this method of construction was employed in the building of the great Sea Port of Cæsarea Maritima as well.'

"'Concrete, the massive stones are a form of concrete?' I asked in astonishment, forgetting that the word or concept would be foreign to someone unfamiliar with it.

"'It was a closely held secret passed down from the construction of the pyramids. I do not know its name,' admitted Gamaliel. 'The Schamir and the Schethiy were not only used for construction and destruction. They were also needed for the transportation of the Holy Ark of the Covenant. Its solid gold lid was far too heavy for a handful of priests to carry. When the stones were placed one inside the other and set in their proper resting place upon the Mercy Seat, the Ark would rise off the ground a height of three fingers,' he said, holding up his hand in a modified Boy Scout salute: three fingers extended to give me some idea of how high the Ark levitated.

"'The young priests transported the Ark to Ethiopia. The stones were returned to Solomon. These same stones, referred to as the 'regalia', were inherited by the kings of Solomon's line to the seventh generation. King Joash was the last to possess them. None of the priests now living have any idea where the Ark or the stones are hidden,' he said, his voice trailing off.

"'*The chamber will not remain empty for long,*' I thought as I prepared to hurl the open moneybag over the navy-blue barricade that was once the curtain, and against the back wall of the chamber.

"'What is the meaning of this?' snapped Caiaphas, imposing his self-importance. Surprised at my presence, he added, 'And what are *you* doing here?'

"'Since my services as a witness were not required for the Sanhedrin to pass judgment on Y'shua, I have come to return the thirty pieces of silver I was given, from the temple treasury, for acting as the arresting witness!' I said in a surprisingly belligerent tone. It's amazing how your attitude changes when you know you're about to die.

"'Judah, you gave the testimony that sealed his fate. You are required to keep that money as a token of good faith,' muttered Caiaphas through clenched teeth, barely able to restrain himself.

"'If that testimony sealed his fate, why was there not a second witness to back me up? Two witnesses are required for the court to render a verdict. The testimony I gave your court, for which this payment was rendered, and the only one backed by a second witness, whom you excommunicated, was that 'Y'shua was the Anointed Messiah from the line of David, the Anointed Messiah from the line of Aaron having been John the Baptizer. Since you did not accept my testimony, I cannot in good conscience keep the money.'

"'You claimed he was a false prophet! You said it before everyone. We all heard you,' retorted Caiaphas.

"'That was no testimony—that was an accusation, one your priests have been making for years. And if you believe that was a testimony, I assure you it was false. By the letter of the law you are witness to it, and are required to sentence me to death by stoning.' Returning the pouch to my sash, I stooped down for a good sized chunk of broken masonry that was decorated with a gold-plated lily resembling a fleur de lis. I placed the stone in Caiaphas's hand and held out my arms, palms up. I motioned at the rubble around me, saying, 'By law you are required to cast the first stone. There are plenty of rocks here for everyone. And it certainly won't be the first time the blood of a priest has been shed within this sanctuary.'

"'I suppose we should all just go home and return in three days, after Y'shua has rebuilt the temple?' roared Annas, walking up behind Caiaphas. The remaining priests stopped what they were doing and turned toward the commotion. Shimmering in his gold-and-white robes, he proclaimed, 'You heard it from his own lips…'

"I cut him off. 'It is well understood that no man can bring an accusation against himself under our laws! In fact, the law is quite clear. It expressly forbids subjecting the accused to answer a question that would condemn him to death if he were to answer! And to make matters worse, the holy Mishnah states that a unanimous verdict of 'guilty' in a capitol trial has the effect of being rendered an acquittal. In other words, the entire Sanhedrin, by voting unanimously to put Y'shua to death, inadvertently acquitted him of all charges! And to top it all off, when a sentence of death is rendered, our holy law requires that execution be suspended until the following day, during which period the court must observe an entire day of fasting. After the fast, another vote must be taken to see if everyone is still of the same opinion. This allows for a full review of the evidence. That is why capital crimes are not judged during the feasts. You Sadducees pride yourselves on adhering to the laws of Moses. I cannot even begin to count how many of those sacred laws you've broken during this grave miscarriage of justice!'

"Annas displayed a cold, plastic smile that only the truly insincere possess. His shifty eyes gazed at me through slits of undisguised hostility, but he said nothing. This disturbed me more than usual, but I was just getting started. Pointing at him, I shouted; 'You have slain the promised Messiah! And for that the Almighty shall bring this temple down on your miserable heads. You shall wander the earth without a home until the End of Days.' Then, pointing toward the heavens and raising my voice even louder, I shouted, 'The Blood-Moon is a sign from the heavens that you have shed the innocent blood of his Anointed. This land shall not be cleansed of the blood you have shed, nor shall any sacrifice remove his blood from your hands, until he that shed it returns to take his rightful throne!'

"Removing the moneybag from my sash, I added, 'It is only fitting that the symbol of that which you worship and love above all else should reside in this holy sanctuary. May the Most Holy have mercy on you and your descendants— for no one else shall!' I hurled the open moneybag over their heads and into the Holy of Holies. I heard the coins bounce off the back wall and rattle onto what sounded like a stone floor.

"'I can no longer bring myself to call you hypocrites,' I shouted as they forcibly removed me from the temple. They dragged me outside, where a deafening thunderclap caused all who had assaulted me to run back into the temple for cover. None ventured out. I was infuriated and drew comfort from the fact that within a generation the Sadducees would be hunted down like dogs and wiped off the face of the Earth. Within a generation, Titus, commanding more than half the legions of Rome, would sack this city. According to Josephus, there will not be enough crosses for all the bodies or enough room to place the crosses. Some will be nailed to the very walls. Soldiers will have to twist the bodies into grotesque postures just to be able to find a clear spot on which to crucify them. Generations of Israelites will have to pay for the stupidity of a handful of Jews. They didn't all reject him, of course. A great many who accepted him will take his advice and flee to the mountains when the armies of Rome begin to close in around Jerusalem. Those who delay in escaping the city will be flung over its walls by the Zealots themselves.

"Just then I noticed my old teacher Gamaliel standing at a distance. He approached hesitantly and asked, 'By what power and authority do you do such works?'

"We walked away from the temple doors. Turning to him, I said, 'By a power you neither know nor recognize, old friend, but perhaps one day soon you will. Recalling the reason I had wanted to see him, I said, 'Y'shua was nailed to the cross, but Pilate gave no such order. Do you know which of the priests ordered it?' I was unable to disguise the irritation in my voice.

"Gamaliel stopped and sat down on the steps of the temple. He looked up at me, his face barely illuminated by the darkened moon. 'Yehudah, crucifixion is the most agonizing and humiliating form of death. Did you know that one of my nephews was crucified while you were away?'

"'No, Master, I was not aware of this.'

"'The Romans nailed him to a cross. At first I was outraged. Crucifixion was bad enough but I soon saw it as a blessing in disguise. My nephew died during the night while the rest of those crucified with him continued to endure their torment for days. Wondering if the nails had something to do with it, I speculated that the nails may hasten death by introducing wounds that cause much blood loss. So I ordered one of my servants to drive a nail, a smaller nail of course, through my hand. I know that crucifixion nails go through the wrists but that might have done irreparable damage.'

"I looked at him in astonishment. 'You always were too curious for your own good.'

"'Yes, well I finally convinced my servant to drive a nail through my hand,' he said, as the thumb of his right hand caressed and massaged the center of his left palm. 'Judah, I cannot tell you the extent of the pain I was in. My mouth opened but my servant assured me no screams came forth. I thought I would surely defecate myself. It seemed almost impossible to form and hold a coherent thought in my mind. Before I could endure it much longer, Yossi, my servant, pulled the nail out of my hand.'

"'Y'shua formed complete sentences while on the cross,' I said.

"Turning to look at me while still massaging his left hand, he added, 'So I've been told. Still, he did not suffer long. And I pray God will forgive me for what I've done.'

"Gamaliel stood and walked toward the Court of Women. He beckoned me to follow. The old man stopped on the steps leading to the Court of Priests and gazed at the rusty reddish moon. 'The blood of that innocent man hangs over our heads,' he said, nodding. 'Annas and the others act brave but they are frightened half out of their minds.'

"'Well, they certainly had me fooled.'

"'There is a state of near hysteria among the people, a feverish drive to locate the long-awaited messianic personality. That's why the Baptist caused such a stir... but Herod had him executed. Do you know that I have been waiting for the Messiah all my life? The prophet Daniel said the Messiah would appear sometime during the four hundred and ninety years from the time of reckoning, following the decree to rebuild Jerusalem. The moment for the Anointed to make His appearance has nearly run out, Yehudah.'

"'Johanan made it clear that he was not the expected ruling king and singled out Y'shua as the one we were looking for,' I corrected.

"'I have looked forward to his arrival and dreaded it as well. The period of history when the anticipated prophecies are fulfilled make it quite clear that it will be a time of great tribulation and testing for Israel. That is why I devoted myself to studying the expected signs that would herald this period of time. What you said to the Sadducees just now caused all those old fears of mine to resurface. The Sadducees, Pharisees and Essenes represent a very small part of the population but each was formed as a result of men looking to interpret every event—political, social or economic—as relating to a Sign of the Times. The power struggle has endured for over a hundred years. Had Annas not seized upon imposing heavy tariffs during his term as high priest, the Sadducees would not have gained as much power as they now yield. Having done so, they have become high-handed, loving power, wealth and the position they hold over others.'

"'Yehudah, do you remember the reaction from my students when I got to the part where the Israelites, fresh out of Egypt, cried out against Moses? Everyone in the class swore they would never have acted in that way. I, too, feared the Romans would destroy us if we proclaimed Y'shua-bar-Yehosef the Messiah. He had just been arrested for a capital crime. If we proclaimed him our King, would not the whole of Israel rise up only to be ground into the dust by the iron-clad heel of Rome? Yes, we were afraid, but not as afraid as we are now. Yehudah, do you recall the prophecies of Joel and Amos concerning the Messiah?'

"'No, honestly I cannot recall any of their prophecies that might relate to the Messiah at this moment. One prophecy of Amos that comes to mind may be fitting though.' Gamaliel cocked his head and seemed to wonder what that prophecy might be. 'I will send a famine in the land, not a famine of bread, nor a thirst for water, but of hearing the words of the Lord,' I said. Amazed that I had recalled it in its entirety, I turned to face him. His face appeared ashen in the dim light.

"Looking up at the blood- moon that was almost eclipsed by the Earth's shadow, he quoted from Amos. 'And it shall come to pass in that day, saith the Lord God, that I will cause the Sun to go down at noon, and I will darken the Earth in the clear day. And I will turn your feasts to mourning...' Without turning to look at me, he continued. The prophet Joel said, 'The sun shall be turned into darkness, and the moon into blood...'

"'Don't you see, Yehudah, all of Heaven is proclaiming your Master as the Anointed One. To the Jewish mind, lunar eclipses are regarded as tokens of the Creator's anger. And the most dreaded and worst possible omen is the blood-red moon. A solar eclipse, on the other hand, is regarded as a bad omen for the entire world. But that was no normal eclipse, was it?' Turning toward me, he grabbed both of my arms for emphasis. 'The Moon stood before the Sun... for hours. The Babylonians, who could foretell a solar eclipse years into the future, feared them as a sign from the heavens that a king was about to die. I fear a king has died. And we are responsible for his death. What shall the Elohim do to us this time, I wonder?'

"'Forgive you as always, of course,' I said in a sarcastic tone, because at that moment I could not think of one reason why all those priests should not be put to the sword. 'You, my friend, are forgiven... not expressly, but by reasonable implication.'

"He gave a dry chuckle and released me. 'You always were an optimist, Yehudah. I do not feel the God of our fathers will forgive this offense so easily.

Fiery shields were seen flying over the temple. The priests on duty heard a host of voices shout in unison, as the heavy curtain collapsed during the second earthquake, 'Let us depart from this dwelling.' Annas played it off as just the rumbling of the earthquake, but I am troubled. The priests I speak of are Sadducees. They do not believe in angels or the resurrection. If they were making it up, they would have said they heard one voice, not many voices speaking as one.' His weary voice was becoming melancholic.

"'And still you refuse to believe who he was,' I demanded. 'Many prophets and righteous men have longed to see what you have seen, and have not understood. And to hear the words you refused to listen to. It seems the only reason priests ever went to listen to his words of wisdom was so that they could twist them into lies in order to accuse him of wrongdoing.' Gamaliel had a puzzled look on his face, not sure what to make of me.

"'Father, forgive them for they know not what they do." Did he not forgive you already? I heard him myself as he uttered those words from the cross. You sit here under the blood moon on the day he was put to death. What else must happen before you understand who he was? What else does he have to do to prove to you he was who he claimed to be? You know the pain of being nailed to a board.' I thought, *Unfortunately, so do I.* 'Could you have found it in you to utter such words?'

"'His feats have always bordered on the supernatural, his abilities almost superhuman,' admitted Gamaliel.

"'And still your priests tried to twist his words. The disgrace and humiliation of the cross was not enough punishment for those men's liking. While Y'shua lived, his words were a healing balm for the infirmities of Israel. Just as the lies of the priests are a festering sore that constantly irritates our nation, each morning these appointed 'holy men' pour out their hatred upon Satan, shaking clenched fists toward Heaven and each evening basking in his blessings.'

"Shaking his head slowly, he said, 'We had our chance and now it's gone. Once again we put our demands on God instead of allowing his will to be done. We followed the laws and the scribes when we should have been following our hearts.'

"'Teacher, I know that the Book of Daniel is your favorite. What would you say if I told you that my Master had read to us the message from the Sealed Book of Daniel: an additional sacred book that has been hidden in plain sight? What if I told you that you could read it as well?'

"'How is this possible? What does it say? Does it speak of the Messiah?'

"'The theme of the Messiah is a thread that runs through the entire tapestry of the Sealed Book of Daniel. The Sealed Book is almost twice as long as Daniel's original work. Most of the text is written as if God were speaking directly to us! God speaks of working through His Son among the children of Israel. This 'Son' is given many titles; among them are the Instrument God, the Pure One, and the Anointed. Near the middle of the book, God's Messiah is mentioned by name—and his name is Y'shua!'

"'Y'shua? Will you read it to me, Yehudah? I very much wish to hear what it has to say,' pleaded Gamaliel.

"'You can read the Sealed Book of Daniel for yourself, Master. But first you must promise to me that what I am about to disclose, you will never divulge to another living being, not even on your deathbed. For the End of Days has not yet come upon us and as far as you and I are concerned, the Sealed Book of Daniel must remain sealed—for now.' Gamaliel wasted no time in taking the necessary oath. I reminded him that Y'shua had once said, 'One jot or one tittle shall on no wise pass from the Law, until all be fulfilled.' But more importantly he told us that 'the last shall be first and the first last'. In order to read the Sealed Book of Daniel, you must start at the end and work towards the beginning. Your ability as a scribe will allow you to easily parse the text. The text speaks of our ancient history in order to set the stage of future events. You will find that the text reads perfectly in reverse order!'

"'It would seem that the student has become the Master. I only wish I had not burdened my mind with all the expectations imposed upon me. I wish I'd had the courage to sit at your Master's feet and listen to his wisdom and council as you did. Few Jews had any love for the prophets of old while they were still alive, refusing them even the title that was rightfully theirs. That is why Caiaphas refused to proclaim Yohanan-bar-Zebedee, the Baptizer, a prophet: because it was evident that Yohanan had come in the spirit of Elijah, the prophet of old reborn as prophesied. If Elijah had indeed come, then it should stand to reason that Israel's Anointed King was also here. But a living prophet is always regarded as a troublemaker. Well, Master Yehudah, what would you advise your old teacher to do now?'

"'I cannot speak for myself, but in time some of his followers will cross paths with the Pharisees and scribes. When that day comes, keep in mind that if what these men are doing is of God, you cannot hope to stop it. Should you persist, you will only find yourselves fighting against God. By the same rod you measure these men, God shall measure you. Isaiah said you would not know him when he came. But perhaps all is not lost… there may still be hope for you. You may still get your wish and sit at my Master's feet, listening to him as he dispenses pearls of wisdom. I am not so sure God was leaving you when the veil of the 'Holy of Holies' collapsed today. In fact, I think it is a sign that God has removed the last obstacle separating him from his people.' Gamaliel looked at me, puzzled.

"'The Sanhedrin tried to convict Y'shua of saying that he would destroy the temple and in three days raise it up again. When he said those things he was not speaking of this temple,' I said, holding my arms out and gazing up at the imposing structure behind us. 'He was speaking of this temple,' I explained, placing my hands over my heart, 'in which dwells the Holy Ghost. This, then, was the meaning behind the words, 'Destroy *this temple*,' implying his body, 'and in three days I shall raise it up again.'

"Gamaliel's bushy eyebrows were furled as he tried to comprehend what I was saying.

"'Gamaliel, in three days the man who has fulfilled these prophecies is going to rise from the dead!'

"His eyes flew wide in astonishment. 'His body will not see corruption,' uttered Gamaliel almost to himself. He turned abruptly and climbed the stairs back into the temple, where some of the other priests still lingered, afraid to venture out, while others continued to clean up the mess from the earthquake. Gamaliel then stopped, composed himself and returned to me. 'All may not be lost, indeed. Yehudah, you are aware that the prophecy requires that two anointed Messiahs reign over Israel. Yohanan-bar-Zecharia, the Baptizer, fulfilled the prophecy that Elijah must come first.'

"'Yohanan is dead, Master...'

"'But you, Yehudah, are very much alive. Should your Master return from the Realm of Souls, he would have a Scribe from the priestly line of Aaron, a miracle worker, to preside, at his side, over our nation! The fact that the two of you look so much alike...'

"'You cannot be serious!' I interjected.

"Without answering me he turned and hurried up the stairs again. 'He'll what?' was the only thing I could make out from their dialogue with him. He seemed excited, though they did not seem to share his enthusiasm.

"I thought it best to leave the temple and so headed east toward the garden of Gethsemane, near the Mount of Olives."

"Teryk, you mean to tell me that you were able to break the code and read the Book of Daniel in reverse? Is it anything like the Atbash Cipher found in the Qabalah, or the Dead Sea Scrolls?" asked Kortney.

"Yes, I was able to read it," confirmed Teryk. "I'm not sure I'm qualified to answer your question regarding the Atbash Cipher, though."

"The Atbash Cipher is a Jewish cryptogram," volunteered Trisha. "It is a simple substitution code based on the twenty-two-letter Hebrew alphabet, where the first letter of the alphabet is substituted for the last letter. The second letter is substituted for the next-to-last letter, and so on. The Atbash Cipher dates back to five centuries before the time of Christ and can be found throughout the Old Testament.

"As a scribe Judah had an understanding of the Atbash Cipher, Trisha," explained Teryk. "The Book of Daniel is unlike anything I have ever seen. It reads both forward and backwards!"

"But who in antiquity could possibly write a book that can be read both forwards and backwards?" asked Adriana.

"Who indeed?" agreed Teryk. "Phrases used in the forward version are repeated in the reverse text. The reverse text contains words that are not used anywhere else in Hebrew scripture except the Book of Daniel. Much of the text is part poetry and most of that is discernibly written in Parallelism. One example of Parallelism can be found in Luke 15, where Jesus asks which one of you having a hundred sheep does not leave the ninety-nine in the wilderness to go searching for the one that is lost. This incident is followed by the woman who had ten silver coins and lost one. She lit a candle and swept the house searching until she found the lost coin. Both rejoiced once they found the one that was lost. This sets up the backdrop for the next story, the Prodigal Son and his return to his father.

"Kortney, you are well versed in Hebrew and Aramaic. See if you can disprove what I've just told you." Turning toward the rest of his team, Teryk commanded, "See what can be found on the possibility that someone in our time has already broken the seal on the Book of Daniel. Need I remind anyone that if the seal has indeed been broken, there can be no more doubt that we are in the End of Days?"

"Such a discovery should have made front-page headlines around the world!" exclaimed Kortney.

"As should the discovery of a massive pyramid complex in Bosnia, dating back twelve thousand years," reasoned Teryk. "That discovery was made years ago but our custodians and their media minions have never deemed it worthy of the public's fickle attention."

CHAPTER

32

Dead Man Walking

"Passing through the Court of the Temple and under a structure called the Court of the Israelites, toward the Women's Court, I stopped. Before me lay the Nicanor Gate and guarding it was Ya'akov, the temple guard who had struck Jesus in the face. There were few guards the size of that lumbering ox. I stood there fingering the blade at my side. I paused and closed my eyes in an effort to control the rage I felt for this man. Should I kill him? Why not? What the hell, this was all some sort of wild hallucination anyway. What if it wasn't? For God's sake, I'm Judas; I'm going straight to Hell anyway! What does one more sin matter? I was barefoot and made no sound as I came up behind Ya'akov thrusting my dagger just below his left shoulder blade. Removing it quickly, I moved back into the shadows.

"He was certain someone had bumped into him. He turned but could see no one. Wincing in pain, he brought his left arm down against his side and fell to his knees with a sharp exhalation. Drawing his sword, he squinted into the darkness. 'Who's there?' he challenged through clenched teeth, inhaling sharply as his body fell back against the column. A figure moved toward him from the shadows without a sound. His eyes grew wider.

"'Divine for me—who has killed you, jackoff?' I asked in a cold and steely voice. He tried to call for help but there were few guards on duty that night. I knew I'd pierced his heart. How many men Judah had dispatched in this manner I could not remember and didn't want to. Killing never came easily for me, nor should it have, but this fool had been a dead man ever since he'd dealt that crashing blow to Jesus' face as he stood before the high priest. '*You really should see the look on your face,*' I said, chuckling as he fell backwards, his legs folding under him.

"'What a sweet memory,' I mused, but it was only that: a memory, and one I had created to help me deal with the raging emotions that swirled within my mind. Could I have killed this fool? That goes without saying. Should I have killed him? Now that was another question entirely. Had not Jesus forgiven his offenders from the cross? If so, who was I to judge this man? Making new memories to override bad memories was a technique I wished I had learned when I was much younger. I learned that memories are like recordings; we can record over those that cause us pain. You know that you created the new memory, but your heart does not seem to feel the impact of the original memory once you have recorded a new one over it.

"As I passed the guard, Ya'akov gave a start then regained his composure. 'Sir, the East Gate was closed at sundown and cannot be opened until dawn,' he said to me, noticing I had not turned left or right.

"I raised one hand in acknowledgement but continued in that direction. Maybe a long walk would do me good. As I approached the massive bronze gates, I could feel a presence like that of the Holy Spirit. A tall figure stood before the Corinthian gates. I had not noticed it until it moved. By tall I mean at least thirty feet in height. An angel stood before me and was looking down at me. Maybe I wasn't going to make it to the Mount of Olives before I died. The angel held no sickle in its hand. I couldn't make out its face. The angel—for that's what it had to have been judging by its wings, which just grazed the stone pavement—turned and pushed against the imposing structure that could scarcely have been moved by a dozen men.

"The East Gate was fastened with iron hinges to a gargantuan iron shaft that was said to be sunk to a great depth within the solid block of stone below it. The angel's wings spread as the gate began to groan. I could not tell if the cool gust of wind was from the angel's wings or from the opening that appeared in the dark orange-red moonlight. I envisioned Samson pushing two massive pillars as the dim moonlight shone on the angel's outstretched wings. With a thunderous crash the massive doors struck some sort of stop and the angel motioned for me to pass. I heard a guard yelling in the background but continued toward my rendezvous with fate.

"I left the temple and crossed the Kidron Valley to the uneven ridge that formed the base of the Mount of Olives. I passed Roman guards with torches who stood watch over the many camp cities that covered the area. The Moon was a little brighter now and I turned for one last look at the temple. It gleamed like a beautifully illuminated snow-covered mountain, so white was the stone of its construction. I was transfixed by the eerie glow of glittering gold against a backdrop of bright stars that had claimed the night as the Moon's brilliance faded in the wake of Earth's shadow. A gust of cool wind, perhaps from the angel's wings, reminded me that I was on my way to hang myself.

"The lunar eclipse, now a pale salmon-orange, was the only light in the garden of Gethsemane where Jesus lay buried. I opened what looked like

Joseph "Five Eagles" Reyna

a wrought-iron gate. The metal had been bent and twisted to form flowers and geometric shapes. Gethsemane was a beautiful garden, not a graveyard. The Golal sealing the entrance stood out in contrast to the life surrounding it. There were half a dozen hastily painted white brush strokes splashed across the face of the Golal: the hockey-puck-shaped stone that sealed the tomb. The white paint drove home the fact that Jesus lay inside.

"I turned and studied the terrain. I was almost directly across and just slightly above the level of the entrance to the temple, which was not located directly in the center of the Court of Gentiles where most archaeologists put it. I never saw the temple built with the assistance of the Persian King Cyrus the Great, who had defeated the Babylonians. That temple had stood for nearly five hundred years. Unable to place the new temple in the center of the Court of Gentiles, Herod chose to build it between the existing one and the Palace Antonia. The temple or sanctuary was completed in just under two years, but construction at the temple mount had continued and would for another generation, most likely due to earthquake damage. '*It shouldn't be too difficult for my team of archaeologists to relocate this garden and the actual tomb of Jesus,*' I thought.

"Leaving the garden, I closed the gate. 'Well Judas, looks like you're at the end of your rope,' I said, turning to look for a suitable tree branch from which to hang myself, only to find the angel blocking my path. The angel reached down and lifted me high into the air amid a mighty whoosh. The grandeur of the firmament extended out before me and I was awestruck by the panoramic view of Jerusalem. Mount Scopus was covered with tents, as were all the other hills that surrounded the city of David. It was estimated that nearly three million pilgrims from every corner of the empire had come to celebrate this Passover because of Jesus' popularity.

"I wondered if the angel would drop me. That might explain why Judas was found splattered in the field of *Akeldama*, south of Jerusalem on the other side of the Hinnom Valley: 'the field of blood'—*my blood*, I thought. I could hear the howling of pariah dogs and jackals far below me. Looking down on a silent city, I thought, *You had your chance and you blew it.* Just then the angel held me with one arm and pointed the other toward Bethany, where I saw a strange glow on a hilltop. The greenish-blue light increased in intensity then died down again, much like when a transformer blows. I turned to the angel and pointed toward that distant light. He nodded. *OK... I don't know what's going on but I suppose I can hang myself over there.*

"The angel placed me at the foot of the hill. When I reached the summit I found no tree to hang myself from, nor could I throw myself off a precipice. Launching myself off the top of this hill in any direction would only cause me to roll for a few feet. There was a large stone with what appeared to be a natural indention that formed a seat. I chose to sit on it and await further instructions, or perhaps for the light to reappear. I sat there watching the Moon, which was now a yellowish-orange. A brilliant crescent of whitish-blue had appeared at the base of the Moon. I wondered how the Moon could have moved to the opposite side of the world and hovered in position blocking the Sun for hours.

"Anyone who has looked through a telescope at the Moon quickly finds that they have to keep readjusting the telescope's position because within minutes the Moon moves out of the instrument's visual range," explained Teryk. "This is the reason no eclipse has ever lasted much longer than eight minutes or so. A mystery of mysteries to be sure, but such a monumental and catastrophic event must have been recorded by historians. If it could be proved, perhaps those who doubt might one day come to believe that the Nazarene was who he claimed to be—the long-awaited Anointed Messiah."

"Messiahs? Earthquakes! Angels! Eclipses! It is becoming increasingly difficult to believe you, Teryk," interrupted Jidion. "And if the angel had dropped you, what would you have done?"

"Well, I had considered slitting my throat on the way down, but in all likelihood I'd have probably screamed like a little bitch."

The Dirty Dozen

"The morning passed without incident and I awaited the rising of the Sun. In the custom of the Native American shamans, I stood, removed my sandals, and ran my toes through the sand, reconnecting with the Earth. The sand was cold, for the temperature had dropped a few degrees as it always does just before sunrise. Some high wispy clouds drifted across the sky. It was going to be a beautiful sunrise.

"I do not startle easily but I jumped halfway out of my skin as a hand came to rest on my left shoulder. It was the Magdalene. She seemed surprised to see me.

"'Y'shua?' she asked apprehensively.

"I shook my head and answered, 'No, it is I, Judah.' I was wearing white, the color Jesus often wore. On her face she wore the most lost and hurt expression I had ever seen, and I had seen many. That I looked like the Master could not have been easy for her. Did she hate me? Did she see me as a traitor? Remembering the sunrise, I turned abruptly toward it, more to hide the tears in my eyes than to see the sunrise, which might be my last. A brilliant sliver of magenta pierced horizon. Just then I felt her arms wrap around my torso. Her body trembled softly as she cried while holding me. The shofars sounded in the distance.

"She stopped abruptly, took my right hand and examined it, running her hands over my wrist. Then she examined my left hand. She looked at me in wonder. 'Your hands were pierced. I saw you bleeding and in great pain.'

"'Yes they were and I was, but the scars vanished along with the pain,' I explained.

"She stepped back, a look of dismay on her face. Noticing that I wore the white raiments of a temple priest, she asked, 'Are you one of them, Judah?'

"'I am a Scribe and a Pharisee,' I confirmed.

"'Did he know this about you?'

"'Of course, there is little that he did not know about me,' I replied.

"'The others are at my father's home.' She pointed toward Bethany, wiping her eyes. 'Perhaps you should change out of those clothes. If the others see you they might think the worst. They fear the Romans may come at any moment and arrest them as well, not knowing what Dysmas and Cestus may have said under torture before they were crucified.'

"'At this point they should probably fear the Sanhedrin more than the Romans. As for me, let them think what they will. Y'shua knows the truth.' I looked down from the hill toward her family's estate. Its vast lushness resembled a Napa Valley vineyard rather than a desert from my time.

"'You speak as if he were still alive, as if he will explain it all to them.'

"'Is not our God the God of the living?' I asked.

"She did not answer, but considered my words. Her voice changed to its regular joyful, melodious tone as she exclaimed, 'God has returned our friend to us safe and sound. Come, you can rejoin the others.'

"'Open the door! It is I!' announced Mary Magdalene excitedly.

"The doors to most affluent homes were designed to be opened only from the inside. Entering the room, I looked around at the disciples. Ruling the world was the furthest thing from their minds this morning. Everyone froze in place. Some expressed shock, the blood draining from their faces. Then I realized what was happening. I was wearing white. I never wore white. Jesus wore it because of his Essene background, and I had entered with his companion, the Magdalene. I looked at my hands, hoping the stigmata had not returned—it hadn't.

"'It is Judah called *Thomas: the Twin*,' explained Mary Magdalene.

"Mary, Jesus' mother, rushed forward and embraced us both. This seemed to diffuse the apprehension felt by the disciples. I felt a small body hug me from behind and knew it had to be Lazarus.

"'We feared you had been arrested,' said Levi, clasping my shoulder. 'What took place, Judah, after Y'shua was arrested and led away?' he asked.

"Symeon looked at me askance, then it hit me. How could they possibly know what had happened? I was the only one who remained with him. I looked and saw Cephas sitting by the fire with his tallit over his head. It wasn't until I moved toward him that I realized Lazarus and Mother Mary were examining my wrists, for they had both observed my wounds yesterday. 'I cannot explain what happened, Mother,' I said as I kissed her on the forehead and moved toward Peter. The other disciples looked at me curiously, for they in their Galilean fashion always addressed her as *woman*, a term I found condescending. I placed my hand on Peter's shoulder and tugged at the prayer shawl to remove it from his head, but he pulled it tighter.

"'I became frightened when the girl at the gate questioned me. And when the priests set upon him I feared to remain any longer. As I made to leave some in the crowd accused me of being Galilean and one of his followers. I denied I even knew him,' he said through uncontrollable sobs. 'I am so weak.'

"I shook my head. 'What happened has only made you stronger, Cephas. The girl at the gate, Veronica, knew I was one of Y'shua's disciples. From your Galilean accent, she must have reasoned you were one as well.'

"'I should never have followed.'

"'Well, I could not deny I was one of his disciples. They knew damned well I was.'

"'You were leading that mob… you arrested him,' James exclaimed in an accusing tone.

"'I was acting under orders,' I said, standing to face them.

"'Whose orders, the Sanhedrin's or Rome's?' asked another. I think it was Symeon but his voice sounded the same as his father's.

"'I acted under the orders of our Master, the Messiah of Israel. It's a long story but if Symeon the Zealot does not sheath his sword I will never be able to tell you what I know.'

"'Come let us break fast and we will hear what Judah has to say,' said Salome, assisting her two sons, the hotheads, toward the main dinner table.

"I pulled up a cushion and sat Indian style with my back against the wall as the women served us. I noticed Peter had pulled the tallit off his head and onto his shoulders. I would like to say his gaze upon me was comforting but it was not. Symeon, who had not sheathed his sword, stood over me to my left, the better to swing at me I suppose.

"'I will have your sword first,' demanded Symeon.

"'I am not carrying a sword. In fact, I don't have one anymore. I traded it for this,' I said, removing the long nail from my sash. I laid it on the table to the astonishment of all. Then I removed my dagger and handed it to Symeon.

"'No! A Zealot must never be without his blade,' he said, sitting down where he had stood. 'It's true, then. They did nail him to a cross.' Taking the nail in his hands, Symeon hefted its weight and tested its sharpness with his finger.

"'Was this one of the nails they used to crucify him, Judah?' asked James.

"No it is not, but it would have been. I'm getting ahead of myself. Perhaps I should begin with the arrest.'

"'First I would prefer you to explain how you came by this,' said John, who was holding the nail.

"After explaining how I had acquired the nail from the young boy, I sipped some wine from my cup and returned the nail to my sash. I revealed why it had been necessary for me to make the arrest. I told them how the Sanhedrin had assembled on such short notice but had been unable to find Y'shua guilty of breaking any of their laws. I told that the Sanhedrin had reconvened, a much larger force, and not finding something they could use against Y'shua in order to control him, they had decided that it was best to proclaim him a false prophet and charge him with sorcery. In this way Rome could execute him for sedition without reprisals from the Zealots. Having set themselves upon this course, they were not happy when Pilate attempted to pardon Y'shua and release him.

"'You're saying Pontius Pilate—that arrogant, stubborn, inflexible, overbearing Roman—was going to release Y'shua?' asked an unbelieving Symeon the Zealot.

"'Pilate, that cold-blooded, tactless tyrant tried to release him?' asked Philip, a look of astonishment on his face.

"Pilate's wife Claudia had sent him an urgent message during the trial, advising him to 'have nothing to do with that just man' and adding that she had suffered much in a dream because of him. As you know, Romans tend to take dreams very seriously.

"'Three times Pilate sought to release him,' said Mary Magdalene, and that seemed to settle the matter.

"'Three times a Roman governor tried to save him and three times an Israelite had to deny he even knew him,' said Peter, who had now taken a place at the table. 'If Y'shua was innocent, Thomas, why didn't Pontius Pilate simply release him?'

"'That's just it, Cephas. According to Pilate, Y'shua was not innocent of the charge of sedition against Cæsar. Pilate himself assured me of this in no uncertain terms. Apparently the Sanhedrin learned that Emperor Tiberius Cæsar had sent out a decree ordering all rebels put to death. They used that information and threatened Pilate with the accusation that he was 'no friend of Cæsar' if he pardoned Y'shua and let him go. Fearing both Cæsar and the wrath of the gods, Pilate washed his hands of the whole ordeal and handed Y'shua over to be crucified.'

"'Have we not all seen him vanish? Why did he not do so?' asked John. 'I did not think any harm could ever come to him.'

"'We did not think any harm could come to the Baptist and we all saw what happened to him,' I said, uncertain how to reassure them. 'Y'shua tried to prepare us for this day but we simply didn't grasp the meaning of his words.'

"'After you left the Passover Seder, the Master asked us if we had ever wanted for anything when he sent us out without purse or provisions,' said Symeon. 'We had not. But then he added, "Yet now whoever has a purse let him take it, and whoever has no sword let him sell his cloak and obtain one." I knew you carried a sword and told him I had mine, thinking of the battle cry we would raise with the coming dawn. Then Peter raised a sword and told the others you had made a gift of it to him. I felt certain then that we would be going to war!'

"'Should we go back to Galilee, Judah?' asked Thaddaeus.

Joseph "Five Eagles" Reyna

"'No,' I cautioned, 'Y'shua ordered that you remain here, together at least until the end of the Passover feast.' I thought that should be long enough for them to witness the resurrection which I now felt certain would take place. 'There is something I must attend to that has waited long enough,' I said, rising to leave. I had not told the disciples that I had flung the thirty pieces of silver back at the priests. Returning the money seemed like a good enough excuse for me to be allowed to leave, I thought.

"'You wouldn't be telling us to wait here together so that the Romans can catch the rest of the troublemakers, would you?' asked Symeon the Zealot.

"'You would do well to remember the Master's words, *"I have not lost a single one of those you gave to me,"*' I assured them. 'I must see Caiaphas. I am still in possession of the thirty pieces of silver: the customary payment for an arresting witness. I testified that Y'shua was the long awaited Messiah, but my testimony was not accepted during his trial. Duty requires that I return the meager sum.'

"I said my farewells and asked Mary Magdalene to follow me outside. Removing the nail from my sash, I handed it to her and said, 'I would like you to hold onto this for me.'

"Examining the nail, she asked, 'How can the Romans pride themselves on being civilized, boasting of their just courts?'

"'Civilized for the Roman citizens perhaps but not for the rest of us,' I said turning to leave.

"The Magdalene pulled me around and embraced me once more, her fingers kneading the material of my cloak, which she had returned to me. I held her and there were no tears this time. After what seemed an eternity, I gently placed my hands on her small shoulders and tenderly pushed her back. As I looked into her piercing green eyes, I asked, 'Is there anything you wish me to tell him for you?'

"Her eyes narrowed, as she tried to comprehend my statement, then widened as comprehension set in. She quickly embraced me. Nodding her understanding, she said, 'Tell him I will always love him.'

"From Bethany I cut across the top of the hill, as Jesus had done a few days earlier. I passed the withered fig tree, remembering Jesus' teaching of it and wondering just how many of his messages had been lost throughout time. Upon entering the Garden of Gethsemane, I looked around at the young saplings. These would be large, gnarled olive trees in two thousand years when I return—if I return.

"I knew this was not the location where tradition holds that Judas meets his end, but it was close to where I last embraced my Lord. It was close to his tomb and it was where I would meet my end. Perhaps, if I returned to the *Defiant* and discovered that the history of where Judas met his end had been altered, I would have evidence of my experience, even if I was the only one who understood its implications.

"It was still early morning; I'd always thought Judas hung himself in the middle of the night. I unwound the long sash wrapped around my midsection from the temple uniform. This thing had to be at least twelve feet long. I climbed one of the large old twisted olive trees. The gnarls and knotty exterior created excellent footholds. Before I knew it, I was stretched across a large branch. I secured the sash to the branch and wondered how I could remember abstract concepts effortlessly but could never remember the name of the knot I was tying. It was one of my favorites: simple, easy to untie and would not release; it also would not slip around my neck and choke me, so I had to employ a slipknot for that. Thinking it best to leave the hood over my head as I slipped the loop around my neck, I wondered if I could really do this. As I lowered myself, I remained holding on to two smaller branches that jutted out for some distance. Before me was the temple. I marveled at the brilliance of its shimmering gold against the sapphire blue of the sky. I looked down at the deep green hues of the lush grassy fields, and the many red shades of the sand. I wondered if things were really this beautiful in the past. Because if they were, humanity has screwed up this planet far more than anything previously imagined.

"To the south of the city, I could see wisps of smoke rising from the infamous Valley of Hinnom, although some chose to call the place Gehenna, meaning Hell. Garbage was burned there daily, making the place smell offensive. But that is not where its name was derived from. It was called Gehenna because long ago countless infants were offered to the furnaces of Molech, by their own fathers. I recalled the passage that spoke of this in the book of Jeremiah, and marveled that men could memorize entire books! 'And they built the high places of the Ba'al, which are in the Valley of Hinnom, to cause their sons and their daughters to pass through the fire of Molech... which I did not command. Ben-Hinnom was where legend holds that Judas took his life. I thought it ironic that the sacrificed children had all been firstborn. Because that was where the bodies of Cestus and Dysmas would have been cast, both of whom were firstborn.

"The money belt around my waist was not empty and the additional weight was not helping matters. I thought of letting go, but the idea of a broken neck did not sit well with me. Suffocating to death was going to be bad enough. I grabbed the sash and lowered myself to a point where it began to tighten around my neck. This caused the hood to fall over my face. If I were to let go now, there should be no danger of me reaching the ground before I ran out of rope. The sash continued to tighten around my neck. I could either fight it by trying to hold myself up until my arms burned from the exertion, or I could let go and get it over with.

"I decided to let go. The panic to my system was immediate. The thought of drawing my sicarius and slashing the sash came to mind but that would have been counterproductive. My eyes developed tunnel vision and the world closed in around me. To my surprise, my legs were engaged in a running motion, hoping to escape this madness, I suppose. I closed my eyes and began to feel my consciousness expanding.

"My arms dropped to my side. I felt weightless. I opened my eyes and saw that I was drifting above Judah's body, not sensing any attachment to it. I perceived what appeared to be a silvery cord connecting my awareness to his body in much the same way an astronaut's umbilical cord connects him to his spacecraft. Ecclesiastes 12 cautions against this silver cord being loosed. The next instant, I was sucked through a vortex like a bug sucked up a vacuum hose. I felt no fear, however; only a joyous anticipation. I wondered how many times I had done this before. The walls spiraling around me appeared gelatinous. I reached out and touched them. My transparent luminous fingers skirted the edges. Brilliant crystalline sparks of every imaginable color splashed out and spiraled behind me. I could hear melodious sounds, like wind chimes, when I gazed at the brilliant flashes of light.

"Exiting the tunnel, I found myself in what appeared to be a field of brilliant stars surrounding a golden nebula. Synchronous musical tones resonated as swirling golden light surrounded me. And I wished I had been a musician, so that I might somehow duplicate the melody. It felt wonderful to be there. In fact, I felt guilty that it felt so good.

"The life review that followed was not a pleasant sensation," said Teryk as he looked around the table. "In it, I relived every experience of pain and confusion 'Judas the Sicarii' had inflicted upon others. After this, I was permitted to experience the loss of every life I, as Teryk, your commander, had personally been responsible for ending, as well as all the deaths resulting from orders I had personally issued. I experienced not only their pain and suffering in every way imaginable, but also the grief I inflicted on their loved ones. I also experienced every singular act of kindness. This I found odd. Although I endured every consequence of the orders I'd issued, I also experienced the relief and gratitude of those I'd been responsible for rescuing, as a direct result of the casualties I'd inflicted."

"Damned if you do, damned if you don't," commented Juaquin.

"This entire experience was a form of self-judgment," continued Teryk. "There are few who would judge us as harshly as we judge ourselves. Can you imagine what a man like Hitler must have had to endure during the life review? My self-judgment was experienced from the perspective of others, with no access to my own thoughts or motives. I felt their loss, their anger, their fear, terror and pain just as keenly and clearly as they had felt it before dying. I'd once believed that evil was much like a malignant tumor: a cancer that, if left unchecked, would spread, eventually destroying the host. In an attempt to make sense of what was happening, I visualized myself as a surgeon seeking out and destroying these rogue elements. As with all surgeries, there would be bloodshed accompanied by pain.

But before you rush to judgment, let me assure you that I can clearly see the irony of viewing these individuals as a threat to the whole.

"On a spiritual level, I understand that each of us is indivisible from the whole. Consequently, battling what I perceive to be evil, in this holographic illusion, cannot be the answer. In the end the only *one* I truly hurt—will be myself. In time, I ultimately came to the realization that without the difficult experiences woven into the tapestry of my life, I would never have become the man I am today. The loose strings at the tattered edges of my life still bother me but they no longer entangle my mind. There are those who liken life's journey to a maze, with many dead ends that lead nowhere. I have discovered, on my own journey to enlightenment, that it is more like traversing a labyrinth. And anyone who understands the subtle difference, understands that a labyrinth has only one solution—and it can only be solved by moving forward.

"In this illusion, we all must play a part. Without the Illuminati playing their part, we would not now be playing ours. The more terrified the ruling elite become of losing control, the more they'll seek to remove our remaining liberties. Individuals will begin to see their world slowly closing in around them, as more and more liberties are stripped away. Eventually, the only place left for the masses to turn will be inward. And isn't it there, the last place one would think to look, deep within our own human hearts, that we find our connection to Divine Source? *Cause and effect*: fear is driving the ruling elite to maintain absolute control over the global population. Ultimately, their actions will inadvertently trigger the very last thing they would have ever wanted—a mass awakening of the planet's population. Should that happen, it will quickly become evident that the ruling elite serve no real purpose," said Teryk as he sat down and reclined. "Perhaps this sounds like gibberish. I can only say that the more I come to understand these abstract concepts, the less I am able to put them into words. Perhaps that is why some call it a paradox.

"Where was I? Oh yes, as my mind reeled from the effects of this epiphany, I saw a shining, silvery being standing before me. I have read accounts of such an experience. First-hand sources report that when people gaze upon the face of this beautiful being, what they see is their own likeness reflected back, as if their likeness had somehow been transposed onto the beautiful being of light. Since Jesus and Judah both looked identical, I could not be sure that this was in fact happening.

"Then the face on the being of light changed to this face," said Teryk, an index finger pressing his cheek. "I came to the understanding that I and the brilliant beautiful being of light that stood before me were one and the same. I recognized this *'unique awareness'* as *me*. The *me* God had always intended me to be. Apparently, the original intent of separation from Source had been for each aspect of Creator to awaken and become self-aware; expressing its individual uniqueness—collectively.

"I looked around. Cestus and Dysmas were there too. Jesus appeared and informed me that I was in the Realm of Souls. He and his disciples had been spreading the good news to all those who had lived before. Some had been there since the Great Deluge. He then introduced me to all the patriarchs and prophets of old. Jesus' reddish-brown hair was almost identical in color to King David's. Solomon's hair was darker and had a burnt-copper look to it, like the Magdalene's.

"There were many Masters there and all were celebrating Jesus' triumph. To my surprise, some chose not to listen. Much like their living counterparts, they were not too pleased with his message. Then I remembered and gave him Mary Magdalene's message. Shortly after that Jesus informed me that I had to go back, as it was not my time, and I still had much to do as both Judah and Teryk."

34

A Rude Awakening

"I wasn't ready to go back. I wanted to explore this place. I saw wondrous structures, resembling transparent cathedrals that seemed to glow from within. I wanted to remain longer but I was pulled down and away, much like the pull felt when approaching the ramp of an airplane's cargo drop. Yanked away from Jesus, I felt myself falling, a sensation reinforced when my head bounced off the ground. I felt strong hands at my throat. Then a bolt of energy shot through my body. I took in a deep breath that caused me to start choking and coughing as I rolled on the ground. My entire body was tingling, like when an arm or leg falls asleep. I opened my eyes only to see that I was surrounded by an astonished group of soldiers. Above me hung the severed remnants of the sash I'd used..."

"Commander," interrupted Noraia, "I discovered a passage in 1 Peter which corroborates the absurd statement you just made. '...but though his body died, his spirit lived on, and it was in the spirit that he visited the spirits in prison [the realm of souls], and preached to them—spirits of those who, long before in the days of Noah, had refused to listen to God.' Then 1 Peter reiterates the sentiment. 'That is why the Good News was preached even to those who were long dead—killed by the flood....'"

"That cannot be in the New Testament! I do not recall reading anything like that before," argued Trisha.

"Well then, open your Bibles and prove me wrong. You'll find the verses in 1 Peter 3:18-20 and 4:6," countered Noraia.

Upon finding the verses, Trisha gave a loud exclamation as did others in the room.

"Thank you for that, Noraia. I wasn't sure how we were ever going to validate anything in that part of my story. In fact, I had almost decided to omit the incident entirely," confided Teryk.

"Commander, why wouldn't the 'Enlightened Ones', the *Illuminati*, want a mass awakening of the population to occur?" asked Joshua.

"Joshua, do you consider men like the Buddha, Socrates, Mahatma Gandhi and Christ to have been awakened or enlightened souls?" Without waiting for an answer, Teryk continued. "Awakened souls as a rule do not have a need of priests. Enlightened beings tend to ask embarrassing questions, ones not easily answered by the establishment. The free spirits I mentioned earlier had a track record of opposing tyrannical systems of authority whether they were religious, governmental or military. Do you seriously think the controlling governments of the world would want billions of individuals acting as those men did?" demanded Teryk. "No—I think not!"

"Commander, you mentioned you had almost decided to omit that part of your story," observed Sofia. "Are there things you have chosen to omit?"

"Yes, there are," Teryk admitted. The room went silent. All eyes were on him. "Regarding the transcripts of the incident with Asmodeus, I asked Joshua to fill in the events that transpired shortly before my arrival. Does anyone here recall the archbishop's question to the dæmon concerning Blue Apples? I think the reference to Blue Apples may have something to do with the wand Jesus used in the raising of Lazarus."

"A wand, you mean like a Harry Potter, sorcerer-type of wand?" asked Anakah.

"I omitted the details because it seemed too fantastic," admitted Teryk. "As I understand it, when the Israelites first arrived at the land of Canaan, Moses sent out six pairs of scouts, in teams of two, into the region. When Joshua and Caleb returned, they were said to be carrying, what the *Bible* describes as, a massive cluster of grapes they'd stolen from the Nephilim.

"Blue Apples was a term interchangeable with grapes. What these two had, in fact, taken were a cluster of blue gemstone spheres said to have originated from the galaxy's central Sun—what we today would call the super massive black hole at the galactic center. Three of these blue gemstones ornamented the tip of the wand I spoke of. They were arranged in a close triangular setting resembling the suit of Clubs ( ) in a standard deck of playing cards."

"The only link between blue apples and Rennes-le-Château we could find is a visual phenomenon that occurs every January 17th," said Phoenix. "On that day the sunlight shining through a stained-glass window projects an image of three blue spheres, referred to as a cluster of blue apples, on the opposite wall. I find it disturbing that Jesus's wand was fitted with the same number of Blue Apples. Commander, just how large are these things?"

"The spheres are slightly smaller than a standard billiard ball," said Teryk. "They shine with an inner golden luminescence that resembles ribbons of light reflected off water. Phoenix, what is the image portrayed on that stained-glass window anyway?"

"The image depicts Jesus raising Lazarus," said Cassandra. "As strange as this might seem, Commander, it may surprise you to learn that all pre-sixth-century representations of Jesus raising Lazarus from the grave depicted him holding a wand."

"It makes me wonder if that's not the day Jesus actually raised Lazarus on!" exclaimed Raven. "I take it you're not aware that the manifestation can no longer be observed. It would appear that the good Mayor of Rennes-le-Château has covered up that window in an effort to stem the tide of tourism."

"I fear there is more you are not telling us, Commander," chided Sofia.

"Only a few other things come to mind," admitted Teryk. "First, my description of Herod's Temple is inaccurate or perhaps incomplete."

"In what way, Commander?" asked Kortney, adjusting the controls at his station in order to activate a holographic representation he'd created of the temple, using available information.

"Just behind the two massive bronze pillars near the entrance stood what was referred to as the porch. This enclosure rose quite high into the sky. It housed an immense representation of the 'Fiery Serpent' Moses had constructed in the wilderness.

"Another omission is an object Gamaliel described to me. It rests between the two kherubim that sit upon the Ark of the Covenant," said Teryk. "This structure was sometimes referred to as the Pillar of Ashtoreth, the mother goddess sometimes called Ashura."

"The mother goddess worshipped by King Solomon?" asked Sarina.

Teryk nodded, "It seems that once the male-dominated Levite priesthood came to power they introduced the male-only concept of God by eliminating all references to the Shekinah: the female aspect of Creator," explained Teryk. "The Shekinah was the companion of YHWH. To the pagans she was the equivalent of Ashura, the mother goddess. This pillar, sometimes referred to as the 'Mercy Seat', represented the feminine aspect of the Creator God.

"This may sound strange to some of you but I have always envisioned the Holy Spirit as a feminine energy," confided Teryk. "She is the comforter, the counselor Jesus said he would send to assist and teach us. Jesus often addressed this part of the creator as the Shekinah, the female aspect of Source."

"Commander, the oldest and most ancient representations of God always depict YHWH as a serpent or dragon coiled around the pillar of the Universe, aka the Tree of Life," said Phoenix. "The Cathar depictions of this serpent coiled around a pillar depict it with what, up until now, I had taken to be a sort of forked tongue. The protrusion stemming from the serpent's mouth is tipped with three closely clustered spheres matching the description you just gave of the wand."

Teryk closed his eyes to consider what he had just heard. Lowering his head, he said, "I believe... help thou my unbelief, Lord." Turning toward those around him, he promised to be more forthcoming in the future. "There is just one more thing I would like to add before I continue. Gamaliel told me that when he and Symeon, Judah's father, were young men they participated in an expedition to Mount Choreb, the Mount of the Elohim: what we today call Mount Sinai. Both were firstborn and had been selected as part of a special burial detail to entomb the remains of an exceptionally holy man near the mountain's summit. According to Deuteronomy, the Mountain of the Elohim is an eleven-day journey south from Kadesh Barnea. Gamaliel described the holy mountain as rising thousands of feet above a plateau on the Plain of Paran.

"Gamaliel stressed that they were not supposed to go wandering on the holy mountain. Both men disobeyed, hoping to surprise their fathers by discovering the cave in which Jeremiah had hidden the Ark of the Covenant. Instead they were astonished to discover an ancient temple protruding from a massive man-made cave near the top of the mountain. There was also a large spring gushing fresh water nearby. Gamaliel felt certain it was an Egyptian temple but it appeared to have been abandoned for some time. They discovered altars, obelisks, amulets, vases, bowls and wands but felt too afraid to bring anything back with them. He told me he'd never spoken of it to anyone. I suppose we could have ESPionage look into the matter."

"That description of the mountain doesn't sound like the modern day Sinai. That mountain does not stand by itself. It is part of a mountain range," said Phoenix. "The mountain Gamaliel described fits the biblical description of Mount Sinai more accurately. I would really like to be part of any expedition to Mount Sinai, Commander."

"Duly noted, my Lady," said Teryk. Addressing the rest of the team, he added, "There are a few other things that I cannot disclose at the moment. But I promise that before this investigation is over I will have briefed everyone present and explained why I chose to withhold the information."

"Before you continue, Commander, there is one more thing I'd like to ask," said Raven appearing uncomfortable. "This may sound trivial but does Jesus have a horse? More specifically, is it a rainbow-colored horse?"

"Actually, he does but... it's not really ah... Raven, why do you ask?"

"Well, I read a book called, *Heaven is for Real*, about a little boy, not quite four years old, who came close to death and believes he went to heaven," explained Raven. "His father is a pastor and he noticed the child kept saying things about Jesus that he should not have known. Like, 'Dad did you know Jesus has a cousin who baptized him?' Wondering if his child had in fact gone to heaven, the father started to pry, questioning his son to see what else he might tell him. While playing with his toys the boy commented that Jesus had a rainbow horse. He was excited because he got to pet him."

"I can see why a four year old might identify it as a horse," reasoned Teryk. "The creature is not actually a horse, per se. It's... well, it's a unicorn!" Holding up a hand in an effort to maintain control, Teryk explained, "In the *Ars Theurgia Goetia of Solomon the King*, it speaks of the Tahash. According to this work, the tahash was allowed to run on the Earth so that its skin might be used to line the walls of the Tabernacle. It had a single horn on its forehead and was gaily colored like the turkey-cock. It belonged to the class of clean animals; meaning it chewed the cud and did not have cloven hooves. The unicorn's pelt was a brilliant white that shimmered many dazzling colors. Earlier, I quoted from Psalm 22, the unicorn is mentioned in that psalm. According to legend, the creature vanished from the Earth with the destruction of the Temple of Solomon.

"From the look on your faces, I should have probably dismissed that question," said Teryk. "Trust me, this information will pale in comparison to the information regarding humanities true origins.

"A priest accompanying the small detail of soldiers identified me as Judah, one of Joshua's disciples called the Double," said Teryk, continuing his story. "As a soldier helped me to my feet, the centurion leading the troop ordered me to accompany them to the tomb so that I might help identify the body of Jesus.

"'We thought you were dead,' said the priest, a Levite.

"'I was... I was dead,' I assured him, 'and in the Realm of Souls, but I was ordered to return.' He seemed astonished but asked no more questions, only eyed me suspiciously. I suspected he was a Sadducee who did not believe in such things.

"We were not far from the tomb. The small contingency, made up of both Roman soldiers and temple police, rolled back the golal. I entered with the centurion who identified himself as Lucius. After I identified the body as that of Y'shua-bar-Yehosef from Galilee, they replaced the burial cloth and I laid the tallit over the burial cloth on top of Jesus' head.

"The guard allowed the golal to roll back into its recess, securing the entrance to the tomb. *Now what?* I wondered as my hand came to rest on my dagger. *What the hell?* I thought. Turning toward the centurion Lucius, I identified myself as 'Judas the Scariota', which means 'Judas the dagger-man'; it would be like saying 'Mack the Knife' in our culture.

"The Roman guards around me drew their swords and the Temple Guard, not sure how to react, remained motionless. 'Judas the Scariota' was a name that had existed long before I'd been around. To the Zealots he was a sort of Robin Hood, a hero to the people of Israel. Many leaders of the Zealot movement had taken the name. Aside from having once been a Zealot assassin, my name just happened to be Judah.

I raised my arms slowly, placing them on my head as one of the soldiers searched me and removed my dagger. Lucius examined the blade and found it to be stained with blood from the lamb whose throat I had slashed the previous day, but he did not know that. To the Romans, my dagger was called a sicarius because it resembled a sica; a short curved sword, the preferred weapon of robbers and murderers.

"Lucius appointed one legionnaire in charge of the tomb's detail and returned with me to the Fortress Antonia. We attempted to enter through the fortress's eastern gate, but the imposing Hall of Graven Stones, where Jesus had been tried the previous day, was completely destroyed. The massive blocks were pushed out of the Earth in all directions. Some of the blocks were shattered and others were intact. Laborers toiled to clear the area as we made our way through the mangled monoliths. Since it was the Holy High Sabbath, the laborers were most likely Romans or Greeks.

"The prefect was given a full report but Pilate had difficulty believing that I could be the Zealot assassin who had eluded capture all these years. He must have wondered if perhaps I, too, had a death wish. 'This is an interesting blade, Judah. It matches the description of the one used by the infamous Judas the Scariota,' said Pilate. 'Where did you obtain such a fine blade?' he inquired.

"'It was a gift given to my father by a friend, a merchant who obtained it in Persia. The metal is Damascus steel, known for its resilience and ability to maintain an incredibly sharp blade.'

"'I have heard of this legendary metal. And the blood, to whom does that belong?' Pilate asked, holding the blade up to the light.

"'The blood belonged to several sacrificial lambs I had to slay yesterday at the temple. I would like to add that although I am the Scariota, I have not taken a life for several years now. As for the blade, I make a gift of it to you.'

"'The Scariota, huh? How do I know you're not just trying to commit suicide like your Master?' He pondered the question for a moment then withdrew his ceremonial dagger and pointed toward a knot in a decorative pillar some distance from us.

"Without hesitation, and much more swiftly than Pilate expected, I hurled the dagger into the center of the knot. Luckily for me, the blade was heavy, otherwise it would have simply bounced off the hard wood.

"The nearby Roman guards moved in to seize the insolent Jew, but Pilate stayed them with a wave of his hand. As he walked toward the dagger he explained, 'I have sentenced many men to their deaths, Judah.' Turning toward me, he added, 'Never did I believe any of them to be innocent of their crimes.' Holding his chin in thought, he stared at the dagger, admiring my handiwork. Then, removing the dagger, he turned slowly toward me and asked, 'Tetelestai, is that not what your Master uttered just before he died on the cross?'

Joseph "Five Eagles" Reyna

"'It was, although I'm not entirely curtain of its meaning.'

"'Being a wealthy man from an influential family, you wouldn't be. When a man is convicted in a Roman court a 'certificate of debt' is prepared by a court scribe, who itemizes every crime for which the person was convicted. The prisoner is then indebted to Cæsar and must repay him a prescribed amount for those crimes of which he stands accused. This document travels with the prisoner to whatever prison he is sent to, where it is nailed to the door of his cell. There it remains until the sentence is carried out. Once the debts are paid in full, the certificate is taken down and the words 'paid in full' written across it. The document is then rolled up and given to the prisoner. He can never be imprisoned for those crimes again. The Greek word tetelestai means paid in full.'"

"There is a reference to the certificate of debt in Colossians 2:14," said Raven. "'*Having canceled out the certificate of debt, consisting of decrees against us and which was hostile to us; and He has taken it out of the way, having nailed it to the cross.*'"

"That's what redemption means," added Joshua, "to purchase out of slavery and set free by paying the ransom price."

Teryk nodded and continued, "'You see, when a man is thrown into a debtors' prison,' explained Pilate, 'he is required to work off all his debts. The debtor is not released from captivity until he has paid off all his debts and his 'certificate of debt' is marked 'Tetelestai': *the debts are paid for.*'

"'So they list all the man's debts one after the other. They cross them out as he pays them off?' I surmised.

"'Perhaps I should explain further,' suggested Pilate. 'A scroll is laid out like so.' He extended both arms out over a long table, implying a very long scroll. 'When I say all his debts, I mean *all his debts*. A public decree is sent out and all whom this man owes must be present if they wish to be repaid. The first man who brought forth the charges is actually the last to be repaid, because his name and the amount owed are recorded first. The scroll is then rolled up to that point and sealed with wax, then the next party and so on. The scroll could have a score of wax seals on it depending on the number of men the prisoner is indebted to.'

"'When the man enters prison the first seal is broken and that debt is read aloud. The man then begins to work off that debt. As one debt is paid off an official seal is placed upon the scroll. The creditor, the man to whom the debt is owed, will make his mark and receive his payment. Then the next seal is broken and read aloud and the process starts all over. Upon being released from prison, the debtor is handed the document as proof against anyone accusing him of still being indebted to them. So my question to you is, do you know what Joshua meant by Tetelestai? Because when he uttered that word, the ground began to shake violently and the Sun's light returned.'

Incredulous

"Gazing down at the polished marble floor, I thought of the Book of Seven Seals mentioned in the Apocalypse: the Book of Revelation. Hollywood always represents the book as appearing like a large dictionary or thick *Bible* with seven locks on it, similar to locks one would find on a teenage girl's diary. Could the Book of Seven Seals simply be a scroll similar to the one Pilate just described? I shook my head. *How could I ever explain the Lord's redemption to Pilate?*

"'Long ago a covenant was made between the Elohim and the Hebrews,' I explained. 'Joshua came to end that covenant and begin a new one. He said he would atone for the lost so that they might be redeemed back to the Creator of the Universe, the Source of All. This is something that could not have been understood until this moment. Sadly, I'm not sure we understood half of what he tried to teach us. Up until the very end, Y'shua tried to teach me that 'all men' are the sons of the Creator.'

"'Including the Romans?' Pilate asked, raising a brow.

"'Especially the Romans,' I assured him. 'Yesterday I witnessed our priests, the holy men of our tribes, calling for Y'shua's death.' Turning to Pilate, I added, 'And I witnessed a Roman governor trying to release him for a crime committed against the emperor. I saw pity in the eyes of those I would have called my enemies, and murder in the eyes of my own people. Never did I expect mercy from your legionnaires.' Then, looking down into my empty hands, I explained, 'As his pupil, I am afraid I have failed my Master.'

"Admiring my sicarius and wishing to change the conversation to a lighter topic, Pilate asked, 'You wouldn't by any chance know the secret of the Damascene process for making this type of steel, would you?'

"In fact, I did know. During the monsoon season blacksmiths would use caves cut deep into mountain sides that funneled the typhoon winds into their small kilns in order to superheat the metal. The blade's hardening process was barbaric. It was accomplished by superheating the blade then thrusting it into the body of a muscular slave or criminal, after which the blade was tempered in cold water and reheated. The nitrogen in human flesh produced a chemical reaction that hardened the steel. Damascus steel was characterized by the distinctive patterns of banding and mottling reminiscent of flowing water. This may be an elaborate hallucination but I was not about to risk giving away such a secret to the Roman Empire. Blades made from such metal were worth their weight in gold. Shaking my head, I said, 'I'm afraid you'll simply have to be content with owning one of the legendary blades.'

"'I shall treasure this gift always and display it in a place of honor,' said Pilate, turning to walk out an archway decorated with banners portraying the profile of Tiberius. His guard stood at the ready for his order to arrest one of the most wanted assassins in Judea. Pilate stopped just past the opening, turned to me and said, 'As far as I'm concerned 'The Scariota' is no more.' Pointing with the curved blade in the direction of Golgotha, he stated, 'The man I executed there yesterday, died in his place—'enemy of my enemy' you are free to go.' The guards turned to Pilate in astonishment then quickly regained their military bearing, but a tribune named Caius objected. His friend, a centurion, had been killed by a Scariota.

"'When did he die?' I asked.

"'Not two months ago.'

"'It could not have been by my hand, then,' I explained. 'I've killed no Roman for over three years. And up until this afternoon that blade had remained unbloodied.'

"'This man is an enemy of Rome. He cannot be released so easily, Governor,' said Caius, trying to contain his rage.

"'Well, Judah, it would seem that I have been backed into a corner once again.'

"Turning to Pilate, I suggested, 'Perhaps if you offered the man a chance to kill me?'

"Pilate considered then returned the dagger to me.

"'No!' objected the tribune. 'Prefect, I request duel by sword.'

"'I'm afraid it's not for you to decide. The man who is challenged by right chooses the weapon,' explained Pilate. At this, soldiers on either side of me grabbed torches and motioned for me to follow.

"*I lived through the noose only to be cut to pieces by this vengeful Roman officer. Maybe I should have thrown myself off a cliff*, I mused as we entered a large room. The soldiers holding the torches gathered in an oval and Pilate stepped forward to offer me my dagger. The centurion was fully armored and looked anxious to spill my blood. There was no formality; Pilate simply gestured for me to attack him. I shook my head at Pilate's gesture and proclaimed, 'It shall be swords.'

"Pilate moved toward me and handed me his beautifully engraved and elaborately decorated gladius.

"I whispered, 'I hope I do not embarrass such a fine blade.'

"He smiled, taking my dagger and trying to contain a laugh as he returned to the circle.

"As I turned to study my opponent for a moment, I wondered if this short sword was actually intended for fighting. Caius's helmet was gleaming in the light of the torches and his breast plate appeared impenetrable. His forearms and shins were also protected and his long red cloak almost touched the ground, making him appear like some sort of superhero. 'I am not accustomed to using a weapon such as this,' I admitted waving the weapon wildly. 'Why don't you simply rush in and kill me?' I entreated.

"He wasted no time. I parried and swept his feet out from under him. For an instant the man floated horizontal before me. I raised the sword up and over him, driving it into the center of his breastplate, the force of which drove him down onto the stone pavement. The helmet protected his skull from cracking but I was certain the impact must have stunned him. I dropped my left knee over his sword arm, and pressed the tip of my blade into his throat. There was no fear in his eyes, only surprise and then an understanding that he had blundered right into a trap. 'I am sorry for your loss, Caius. The centurion must have been a good man to have a friend such as you. But I did not kill your comrade, as I am not about to kill you. Before I allow you to stand, however, I must know that this matter between us is at an end.' His pride was bruised but he nodded his consent.

"As I helped him up I added, 'Tribune, you should always keep in mind that youth, strength and agility are no match for patience, prowess and treachery, but, more importantly, you should never, ever act in anger.'

"'Wise words to live by,' agreed Pilate, walking forward to sheathe his sword. 'I trust this matter is settled.' The tribune nodded again. Pilate gestured for me to follow him. Two guards with torches walked with us.

"*Damn, I wish my people were this well trained,* I thought as we walked into what appeared to be some sort of food-storage area. Pilate stopped and picked up a large apple. Holding it up for me to see, he crushed it with his hand. He handed one to me. I tried to crush it with all my might but failed to even break the skin.

"'You are lucky that he did not get his hands on you,' cautioned Pilate.

"Realizing how close I'd come to dying reminded me to inquire about the nature of the crime Jesus had been accused of. 'Joshua's arrest was carried out by a Roman tribune, allegedly for a crime against Cæsar. I wish to know exactly what my Master said or did that got him arrested.'

"'I thought I had made that perfectly clear yesterday,' protested Pilate. 'Joshua was arrested for sedition against the personage of Emperor Tiberius Cæsar,' he explained.

"'Yes, but what exactly did he do? What did he say that could have been taken for sedition against Cæsar?' I asked, trying to clarify the issue.

"Pilate turned and said something I didn't catch to one of the torch bearers. The soldier snapped to attention, nodded and quickly left the room. 'He will return shortly with one of my informants. Perhaps he can explain it to you better than I.'

"The guard returned, escorting a man into the room. He took one look at me and exclaimed, 'The Double! What is he doing here?'

"Pilate held his hand out, silencing the man. Turning toward me, Pilate implied that I should address my questions to his informant.

"Studying his pocked countenance, I could have sworn this was the same man who was keeping to the shadows on the night of the arrest. I composed myself and addressed him. 'I wish to know the exact nature of the charges brought against Y'shua-bar-Yehosef.'

"'Yes, I see,' he nodded, understanding. 'As I recall, you were not present during the incident at the temple. Your Master Joshua was in the Court of Gentiles when he was approached by several priests who inquired of him if it was lawful to pay tribute unto Cæsar. An obvious trap, you see. If he answered yes, the people would despise him. If he answered no, the Romans would arrest him. Your Master chose to respond with a question. He asked for someone in the crowd to show him the tribute of which they spoke. Many in the crowd held up coins. I myself held up a Roman Denarius.'

"'Your Master singled me out of the crowd and asked whose image was upon the coin. He never touched the coin. Having done so would have made him unclean due to the graven image it displayed. I answered simply by saying, "Cæsar's." Turning toward the crowd once more, he said, in a voice loud enough for all to hear, "Then render unto Cæsar the things which are Cæsar's, and unto God that which is God's, and unto me that which is mine." The man just stood there, looking at me, with an expression that seemed to say, '*Is it not obvious to you?*'

"'Judah,' said Pilate, 'what you fail to comprehend is that to the Romans their emperor *is* God. To state otherwise openly is punishable by death. Yesterday, when you were speaking of Truth, did you not also imply something similar?' said Pilate, leaving the question hanging in the air.

"Holding up a Roman denar, Pilate proceeded to read its inscription. '*Tiberius Cæsar, son of the divine Augustus.* Why, carrying a single coin displaying the image of the divine Tiberius into a brothel is punishable by death. The Emperor Tiberius has put men to death for criticizing anything he has ever said or done. Your Master was not the first to die for this offense, nor will he be the last. Yesterday, I sought to pardon your Master…'

"'But to have done so,' I interrupted, 'would have offended the divine Tiberius, and invited total ruin.'

"'All the emperors are worshipped as gods, Judah,' Pilate explained. 'As the acting governor I am not only the prefect but also the presiding high priest of this province. As such, each morning I am required to perform a sacrifice in the temple to the divine Augustus.'

"That statement, that clever contrivance of words had brought about his execution? *I was in shock!* Could the most perplexing enigma concerning Christ's Crucifixion be that simple? In that moment, I came to the realization that Jesus truly was master of the situation, which is why he cautioned us not to be so damn predictable. I was in awe of the man. My Lord… my King… the Unique Son of

God had waited until the last possible moment to set into motion events that could not, would not, be stopped."

Teryk looked around the table. All were silent. "You wanted to know what crime Jesus was arrested for? Well, now you know. Sedition against the emperor was punishable by death. This explains why Jesus' arrest and execution were carried out by Roman soldiers. It also explains why Jesus was not simply stoned to death by the Jewish Sanhedrin and why his disciples were not arrested as well."

"Up to this point, I had believed the entire crucifixion story was a myth concocted centuries later," admitted Adriana. "It would be interesting to learn what your research teams uncover regarding this part of your story."

"I had planned to close today with this part of the story," said Teryk, "but I need to share with you what I learned about the beliefs of the ancient mystery religions, beliefs that should have no place in Church dogma."

"Teryk, I'm sorry but I've always understood that Christ was not actually executed," argued Jidion, "that he somehow survived or was substituted by another who took his place on the cross. Although what you've just told me seems to make more sense, I'm having a lot of trouble believing it. The Universe simply does not work that way. If Jesus was as good a person as you claim, karma would not allow for such horrible treatment. And I cannot bring myself to believe that an all-loving God of kindness and mercy would delight in inflicting so much suffering on one of the greatest Masters who ever lived."

"Agreed!" admitted Teryk. "But the Universe would hold you accountable for violating a man-made law, even if you were not aware of its existence," said Teryk continuing his story. "While still in a state of shock, I felt a gentle hand on my shoulder and turned to see the Lady Claudia Procula. She was demure and incredibly beautiful, with perfectly arched eyebrows and a graceful manner. Wrapped around her beautifully sculptured neck, and suspended by a thin gold chain, hung a familiar gold talisman—a crucifix. A man's image, like that of the Christ, was inscribed into the crucifix. Forgetting myself, I reached for the amulet. Claudia's personal guard clasped my wrist. I apologized for my behavior. Introducing myself, I asked, 'What is the meaning of the talisman you wear, my Lady?'

"'It is Dionysus,' she said, examining my features. 'It is incredible how much you look like him, Judah.'

"'Yes, many have taken to calling me *Thomas* because of it.' She looked puzzled, not grasping the meaning of the Hebrew word. 'The word means 'twin' or 'look-alike',' I explained. Pointing to the talisman, I admitted that I was not familiar with the story of Dionysus. 'Could you please tell me about him?'

"'I know a few things about him but perhaps you should direct your questions to Timonides. He is Greek and well versed on the subject,' she offered.

'From what I know, Dionysus was born of a virgin. He became a traveling teacher and healer, who like your Master performed many miracles. He is best known for changing water to wine at weddings. Dionysus met a tragic end. He was betrayed then crucified, but after three days in a tomb he rose from the dead and ascended into Heaven.'

"I studied the cruciform, which had a crescent moon at the top, facing up like the horns of Taurus. At the bottom of the vertical crossbeam was what looked like an arrowhead or perhaps an anchor, like the ones I've seen with Christ crucified to a ship's anchor. There were Greek letters at the bottom that meant nothing to me, and seven small diamond-shaped squares that formed an arch over the top of the crucifix."

At those words, a holographic image of the talisman appeared in the central chamber and slowly rotated for all to see. "The talisman you see before you was discovered among the World War II contraband stored aboard the Nazi U-Boat," explained Raven.

"'Who was your Master, Judah?' asked Pilate.

"'Was he one of your prophets?' inquired the Lady Procula.

"'I do not think so. No, not exactly. You see, prophets do not normally develop a following or train disciples to do what they were capable of doing themselves. But most importantly, prophets speak for God much as a spokesman would speak on behalf of someone else. A prophet, you see, is a messenger from God. In fact, the Hebrew word prophet actually means 'one who speaks for another'. The prophets introduced a phrase with "*Thus saith the Lord*" and were held accountable for everything they said. If their words prove false they were immediately stoned to death. Prophets would often speak with no regard for their own wellbeing or safety, warning men that only doom awaits those who turn away from the Elohim.' She was not Jewish and did not have a core belief from which to draw upon. *Hell*, I thought, *the Jews are taught these core beliefs from childhood and they have trouble understanding Jesus.*"

"'Y'shua,' she said, pronouncing his name properly, 'did not speak falsely and yet they demanded his death.'

"'Y'shua did not utter "*Thus saith the Lord*" either, my Lady. He spoke with his own authority in the manner of Moses, who drew this authority directly from God. This was something new to the priests of the Sanhedrin, something they could not understand. And it is human nature to fear what one does not understand. In two days, however, everyone will come to understand exactly who he was. Yesterday at about noon you witnessed the moon standing before the sun....'"

"'The Babylonians believe that an eclipse is a bad omen signaling the death of a king,' she interrupted, tilting her head and scrutinizing me, perhaps wondering if I understood the implications of her statement.

"Although I was not aware of this Babylonian belief, Gamaliel had said as much. 'Last night there was a second eclipse,' I continued. 'The Moon turned to blood. The priests understood all too well that it represented the blood of a prophet hanging over the heads of the Jewish people for demanding his death.'"

"'Ever since awakening from my dream yesterday, I have feared that we have somehow incurred the wrath of the gods,' she confided in a trembling voice.

"'I was just about to explain to your husband that I do not believe our God will hold him responsible for Y'shua's death. Y'shua assured us that 'No man would take his life, he would freely give it' as well as telling us he would lay down his own life and three days later take it up again. He declared this to us many times.'

"'What does that mean... exactly?' inquired Pilate, his eyes betraying his cool military bearing. Pilate's astonishment was evident and a look of concern had begun to cloud his facial features.

"'It means that after three days in the tomb, Y'shua will rise from the dead as he predicted, just as your Dionysus is said to have done.' I did not think it was possible for Pilate to turn any paler than he had the previous day, but he did. 'In the morning the chief priests will ask to see you. They will request that a guard be placed at the tomb for three days. They would have met with you today but it is a high Sabbath day. If I were you, I would hand pick a detail to guard the tomb until the time has passed. The guard will have much to answer for if the body is missing on the fourth day,' I added.

"'I do not hold that he could be Dionysus come back to life but, even if he were to rise, he could never get past a Roman guard I just posted outside his tomb,' boasted Pilate. 'High Sabbath or no, your chief priests were here this morning.'

"'Last night Joshua rendered your entire cohort defenseless with the utterance of a few words,' I explained. 'And he did it not once, but twice.'

"Pilate looked to his spy, who confirmed the account with a jittery nod. The spy looked concerned that Pilate was just now receiving this information, especially since he had been one of those who had fallen, and was still wearing the scorched garment to prove it. Pilate, like Herod the Great, employed a security system of spies and informers, which is one of the reasons Jesus spoke in parables.

"Pilate left us and re-entered the Praetorium. He gave orders I could not overhear. His servant left us and returned with an ornately decorated box which Pilate opened, revealing a healthy supply of red wax, a spool of red thread and some sort of large signet. Turning toward the tribune who had arrested Jesus, he ordered, 'Make the tomb as secure as you know how.'

"Livius, the tribune who had conducted Jesus' arrest, appeared apprehensive. 'Prefect, never have I refused to follow your orders but if I could be spared from this detail I would be indebted to you,' he said, right fist closed over his chest, left hand resting on his sword.

Joseph "Five Eagles" Reyna

"A young tribune stepped forward and asked for the honor. Pilate eyed Livius, a man he clearly trusted. The young tribune, Petronius, had come highly recommended from Rome. He had arrived only the previous day. The tribune was a friend of Lucius, the centurion, charged with guarding the tomb. Turning toward Petronius, Pilate ordered him to make the tomb as secure as he knew how. Turning to Tribune Livius, he ordered, 'Make certain there is no other way in or out of that chamber, and assure yourself it contains the body of the same man Judas helped Lucius identify. Should you require Judas to positively identify the body again, take him with you. Assure yourself that Joshua-bar-Josef is in fact dead and account for all entrances to the tomb.'

"'There is only one entrance to the tomb, Prefect. I have made certain of it,' said Lucius.

"Pilate nodded then ordered, 'Inspect it again and do not allow the 'Seal of Tiberius Cæsar' to be set across the tomb's entrance until you are certain of it. Livius, I will require you to personally hand pick Petronius's guard.'

"'How many men will make up the guard, sir?' asked Livius.

"'It will be a full guard: sixteen legionnaires not including Lucius, the centurion overseeing the detail,' said Pilate. 'Petronius, I will expect a full report. Ensure that your men are supplied with enough torches and provisions to remain at the site until the first day of the new week. Although you are a tribune, I am making you personally responsible for the guard. You are not to rotate these men. You will be the only soldier allowed to leave the area and only for the purpose of reporting to me, as you are not far from the fortress. Have a mount prepared for this purpose. I will remain in Fortress Antonia during the entire week of festivities.' Clasping the man's forearm, he added in an ominous tone, 'There are few men I would trust with this task, Tribune. Yesterday you were held up, unable to enter the Port of Cæsarea due to the unnatural darkness. I believe that darkness was somehow directly connected to the death of the man whose tomb I am now entrusting you to guard.'

"The tribune's eyes widened slightly in understanding, then, placing his right fist over his heart, Petronius replied, 'As you command, Prefect,' and was gone to make the necessary arrangements for the guard detail.

"Pilate signaled for the spy and his officers to leave us. When they were gone he said to me, 'Judah you seem to keep implying that I had no part in your Master's death.' He held a hand up for me not to speak and continued. 'The truth is that I am directly responsible for his death. As you have observed, I am no statesman. To make matters worse, I have great contempt for your Jewish laws and have sought for some time now to eradicate your nation from the face of the Earth. Sejanus, who appointed me to this position, informed me that he hates the Jews and ordered me to take steps to exterminate the entire race. Sejanus's parting advice on governing was "The vain voices of the people must not be listened to."

"'When I first arrived here I ordered soldiers of the Twelfth Legion to hang ensigns by night bearing the image of the emperor and other insignias of the legions. They hung them all over the city of Jerusalem. As I anticipated, the population was in an uproar. I was besieged at Cæsarea for six days and nights, after which I surrounded the deputation with an armed force, ready to hack them to pieces if they did not go home. Do you know what these fools did?' he asked, a look of perplexity on his face.

"Grasping at the collar of his armor, he explained, 'They pulled back their garments and stretched out their necks, the better for the legionnaires to lop off their heads. They would rather risk death than have their laws violated. Truly, I had never faced such fanatics as these. All the cities under Roman rule display these ensigns, but not this city. In the end, I capitulated and removed the ensigns. Julius Cæsar owed a debt of gratitude to King Herod for assistance he received during the Egyptian campaign. Tiberius has always been a great follower of Julius Cæsar, and it is for this reason I was forced to withdraw the ensigns.

"'I then took money from the sacrosanct temple treasury, the Corban of the Galileans. The money went to the building of an aqueduct from the pool at Bethlehem, ensuring a safe water supply to my fortress and the city when the pools in the surrounding area run dry. In truth, I was surprised to see how much wealth was in one synagogue's vaults.'

"'Did it have to be the Corban you raided?' I asked. 'Didn't you realize that fund was used exclusively for religious purposes and is considered sacred? That was only half the insult. Solomon's pool is considered sacred to all Jews for its healing waters. And to make matters worse, any Gentile who enters the temple's interior, where the Corban is stored, is supposed to be put to death.'

"He looked at me askance and nodded in agreement. 'If you recall, I was trying to incite a riot? I have never wished to understand your people, Judah. My desire has been to destroy them. I was here, in the Fortress Antonia, when the crowd assembled in the Court of Gentiles to protest my actions.'

"'I remember, you ordered your soldiers to disguise themselves as civilians and mingle amongst the Galileans. They were to club everyone in sight when they received their signal. The Galileans were in their place of worship, unarmed and defenseless.'

"'*Defenseless!* They didn't even try to put up a resistance. I witnessed men throwing themselves in front of their women and children before my soldiers, only to be bludgeoned to death. Once Roman soldiers begin killing, Judah, they become drunk with bloodlust. I can assure you, Tiberius reamed my ass for that one.'

"'So you're saying you ordered the arrested of Y'shua in order to incite a riot in Jerusalem, which is at this moment overcrowded with Jews from all over the world?'

"'My heavy-handedness had placed me under the Emperor's scrutiny, so I knew the next time I tried to incite a riot, I must look blameless. Sejanus is, after all, the co-ruler, not the emperor, of Rome. When your Messiah made that blatant statement of sedition before so many witnesses, and during the Passover Feast, I could not resist. The holiday commemorates Israel's release from bondage and persecution by another nation. The fervor for freedom among your people would be at its highest. If a revolt were to be ignited, then Passover, when hundreds of thousands swell Jerusalem's population, would be the time to set it ablaze.'

"'Putting down a full-scale revolt would have given me the opportunity to show Rome just how valuable I might be elsewhere, perhaps Egypt. You see, Judah, I am not of Roman aristocracy. My ancestry is rooted in the Sannites, a mountain-dwelling warrior nation that held out longest against the Romans. My forefathers were all members of the legendary Legio Linteata: a special corps of golden-armored warriors bound by extreme vows. I distinguished myself in battle on the northern frontiers, fighting Germanic tribes alongside Tiberius. Although great honor and privileges have been bestowed upon me, the title of prefect is a military title not associated with the ruling class. At best, all I could ever hope to be is a low-ranking aristocrat...'

"'Had you succeeded,' I interrupted, 'you'd finally get to rub shoulders with Rome's elite. To say nothing of the percentage of the wealth, seized from the enemies of Rome, the Senate would offer you as a prize for your incredibly swift victory,' I added, admiring the brilliant strategic maneuver. I had not noticed the Lady Claudia leave us but I then saw her walking toward us with a sheet of parchment that bore an imposing imperial Roman seal. She handed it to me at Pilate's request.

"'This came from Rome just days ago,' explained Pontius Pilate.

"It was in Latin. The message basically stated that Tiberius wanted to impose a period of peace that Rome had once enjoyed: the Pax Romana. Any overt act against Roman authority was to be swiftly and severely dealt with. Immediately! All suspected revolutionaries within the Roman provinces were to be crucified by order of the emperor.

"'Were not some of Joshua's own disciples arrested for attacking a transport, carrying swords from the armory at Cæsarea?' demanded Pilate. 'The information we extracted from the captured Zealots indicated they were planning a full-scale revolt at the start of the festivities. So I decided to help things along by ordering the arrest of your Master.'

"'Is that when Joshua-bar-Abbas was taken prisoner, during the attack on the transport?' I asked.

"'He and the other two who were to be crucified with bar-Abbas yesterday. The rest are still being...' Pilate searched for the right words, '...encouraged to cooperate,' he added, in reference to their torture. 'I suspected that murderous scum of being a spy for the Sanhedrin as well. So I offered bar-Abbas's release to see how the priests would react, and to identify the Zealots in the crowd. Perhaps I should have offered another in his place.'

"'I myself selected bar-Abbas as one of five disciples to personally train,' I added. 'Perhaps it would have been better if you had killed him.'

"Pilate offered me the dagger. 'He lives still. Are you sure you do not want to hang onto this, a little longer?'

"'Do not tempt me!' I pleaded. Still trying to suppress a chuckle, I asked Pilate to clarify something that had been troubling me. 'Prefect, why did you deem it necessary to dispatch an entire cohort to conduct Jesus' arrest? Was that another attempt to start a riot, and if so, how were you going to explain that to Rome?'

"'Rank has its privileges, Judah. Was Joshua not proclaimed your Messiah, your King?' asked Pilate. 'Such an exalted position called for nothing less than a full army to perform the task!'

"'The title '*Joshua Nazorean Rex Judæorum*', what made you place that over his head?'

"Slowly shaking his head, Pilate proclaimed, 'Rome does not consider this province important enough to appoint a quaestor to judge criminal cases and so that responsibility falls to me. I placed that title over his head because I did not wish to offend the gods any further. I have told you this because I want you to understand that I am not entirely innocent of this man's death. I had hoped for a riot.' Turning away, he added, 'I now fear I have offended the gods and know not what they will do to me, to my family, or to Rome.'

"What a tangled web of intrigue, strategy, conspiracies, plots and counterplots—'*You can't write stuff like this!*' I thought, finally beginning to understand. Bowing to the Lady Procula, I said, 'I must go, My Lady.' Turning toward Pilate, I cautioned, 'I leave you with this question, Prefect. If the man you say you are responsible for executing is witnessed—by many who knew him—walking, talking and eating with them throughout Judaea, can you be held legally accountable for his death?'

"He looked at me, pondering such an unusual possibility. 'If the man was seen alive by credible witnesses, under Roman Law one would have to be acquitted of the charges,' he explained.

"I nodded in agreement and added, 'Likewise should your soldiers return with the news that the tomb has been found empty! Consider this burden lifted off your shoulders. I believe Roman soldiers accused of being asleep on post are crucified, are they not?' I inquired.

"'Only those who are not Roman citizens. The others are flogged to death.'

"'Yes, of course... much more civilized,' I quipped as I walked toward two Roman soldiers standing guard at a nearby entrance. I stood before them at a distance of about four paces. Raising my right hand, I moved it in a sweeping gesture. The legionnaires collapsed unceremoniously onto the polished stone floor. I turned to see Pilate walking up behind me, a look of astonishment on his face.

"'Are they dead?' he asked.

"'No more than the soldiers who arrested Joshua,' I assured him.

"'I am no stranger to death, Judah. I have seen my share of horror during my command under Tiberius, fighting the Germanic tribes. But I had not known fear until yesterday,' he confided in me. 'And even now I am not sure I completely understand what is going on.'

"'I will leave you with these words of wisdom, Governor. If you truly fear the anger and wrath of our God, I suggest that you not persecute the followers of the Galilean. I assure you, if Y'shua's tomb is found opened and the corpse missing, it will not be by the work of human hands. If the God of the Jews could summon such massive earthquakes and position the Moon to block out the rays of Rome's invincible Sun-god, his messengers could easily break the seal of Tiberius Cæsar. You might want to take that into consideration when his followers proclaim, to any who will listen, that the tomb could not hold the one whom God had promised to send.' Motioning to the two soldiers who were just picking themselves up off the floor, I added, 'And I would advise that you *not* punish the men ordered to stand guard at the tomb. Governor, you have my assurance as a Zealot commander, there will be no full-scale uprising.'

"'You *really* do want me to crucify you, don't you?' he blurted. We both laughed. 'You are asking an awful lot of me, Judah. In the past Rome has hunted down the followers of any troublemakers, nailing their leaders to crosses and enslaving the greater part as an example to others. If your Master is whom you claim him to be, I will do my best to ensure that his followers remain unharmed.'

"'I have one last request, sir. Might it be possible for you to send your advisor with the detail inspecting the tomb? I desire to speak with him concerning matters pertaining to the mystery religions.'

"He nodded his understanding and authorized me to accompany his officers to the tomb for the purposes of re-identifying the body before the seal of Tiberius was set upon the entrance. After that I was free to go.

"'Timonides,' ordered Pilate, 'I am charging you with the sealing of the tomb. Ensure that the seal of Tiberius Cæsar is placed in such a way that it will be broken should the stone be moved. Upon your return to the fortress, send out heralds announcing the placement of the seal upon the tomb, and the penalty of death by crucifixion for anyone foolish enough to break it.'

"'As you command, my Lord,' said Timonides, bowing low.

"Pilate ordered another servant to carry the necessary supplies for the seal, and we headed toward the tomb. As we walked to Gethsemane, accompanied by a small guard, Timonides remarked that he thought Jesus' definition of Truth was a flawless interpretation for such an abstract concept. On the one hand, it seemed to give no answer, yet it could answer every question he had ever asked concerning Truth.

"I liked Timonides, who considered himself a student of logic and reason.

"'I understand your Master healed many in Judaea,' said Timonides. 'Did he really do this free of charge?'

"'He never charged,' I assured him. 'Freely we had received and freely we were to give.'

"'Remarkable,' exclaimed Timonides. 'The sick who frequent the temples of Asclepius, the Greek god of healing, are expected to pay when they consult the priests for a remedy.'

"'What sort of remedies?' I asked.

"'Mostly herbs or a ritual bath. Sometimes the priests even prescribe exercise to the afflicted.'

"I had many questions for the governor's advisor, a slave whom Pilate had renamed, but they all revolved around one central concept: *the Christ*. What did Christ mean to the Greeks? Was it simply the translation of the word *anointed* or did it imply more? I also needed to glean what I could regarding the savior-god Dionysus.

"'Dionysus was semi-divine,' explained Timonides, 'a deity half-man, half-god. Stories of gods bearing children are common in Greek culture. Dionysus' mortal mother was the beautiful princess Semele, a virgin. She was impregnated by Zeus. Dionysus was born during the Winter Solstice, in the presence of three shepherds and a future disciple bearing a cross with a crucified figure upon it. The crucifix was an omen of what awaited the child. His followers, 'the ones who gnow', believed themselves born again through baptismal rites. Dionysus was somewhat of a traveling teacher who performed many wondrous works, like turning water into wine at marriage ceremonies. In fact, he performed this feat so often that he is remembered by the Greeks as the 'god of wine'. He was called 'The Beginning and the End', 'The Alpha & Omega', and 'God's only begotten Son'. Like your Joshua, Dionysus entered triumphantly into the city of Athens, riding upon an ass as people waved branches and spread their cloaks before him.'

"'To many of the Greeks, the teachings of Dionysus were considered heretical because, like the other savior-gods before him, he taught that those who refused his teachings would perish in Hades. Unspeakable terrors in the deepest bowels of the Earth awaited those who declined to accept his beliefs,' continued Timonides. 'Those who received his teachings would be rewarded with everlasting life in a celestial paradise of which there were seven levels, that is to say seven Heavens. Like your Master, Dionysus was crucified during the Spring Equinox. After his betrayal and crucifixion, his followers claimed that Dionysus had descended into the Underworld. They claimed that his death was a sacrifice for the sins of the world. After three days, Dionysus resurrected from the dead. He brought Semele, his mother, up from the Underworld and renamed her Thyone. Dionysus ascended with his mother to Mount Olympus. It is said he will return at the 'End of Days' during a great apocalypse to judge the quick and the dead.'"

"I had difficulty believing what I had just heard—for it smacked of Church dogma," admitted Teryk. "In scanning the memories of Judah, I found nothing to support the concept of a fiery Hell."

"Hell is a pagan concept better understood by the Greeks," interrupted Phoenix. "Salvation and damnation were concepts preached by Paul and his disciples. The Christian concepts of Heaven and Hell, as they are taught by the Church, have no place in the Old Testament. The savior-god religions, however, preached that those who rejected their teachings would be cast into a place of everlasting torment during the afterlife. Such a belief would have been foreign to the minds of Jews during Jesus' time. Part of this Gnostic doctrine was the belief that there were actually *seven levels* of Heaven. In 2 Corinthians 12, Paul describes how he was '...caught up as far as the 'third' Heaven.'"

"I think we should seriously investigate the possibility that the Apostle Paul was himself one of these *Gnostics*," suggested Noraia, finding the word distasteful.

"Where was I?" Teryk said, half to himself. "At this point I asked Timonides, 'How long have people believed these teachings?'"

"'As far back as anyone can remember,' responded Timonides, holding his chin. 'You see, Dionysus was not the only one to bring this message to the world. The first one to resurrect from the dead, I believe, was Horus, who was Egyptian. Later it is said that Tammuz, a Babylonian, also rose from the dead. History is filled with their legends. Attys, the Hittite, Adonis the Syriac, Dionysus, who was Minoan, and Mithra, a Persian, all rose from the dead. Every one of these saviors was born of a virgin and all were born during the Winter Solstice. They were baptized, traveled with a band of disciples teaching, and performing miraculous works. All were betrayed and crucified during the Spring Equinox. After two or three days of entombment, they resurrected and ascended into the heavens. And it is said that they will return to judge the living and the dead during the Last Days.

"'Mithra's followers differ slightly from the others,' Timonides added. 'They practice a blood sacrifice called the Taurobolium, or bull sacrifice. This involves slaughtering a bull on a perforated platform while the initiate, standing beneath, is bathed in the bull's blood, or 'born again', as they refer to it. For the poor, who cannot afford to sacrifice a bull, a lamb is substituted. This sacrifice is called the Criobolium and they refer to themselves as those 'who are washed in the *Blood of the Lamb.*'

"'Washed in the Blood of the Lamb!' I blurted.

"But that is not why they are considered strange. To join the ranks of their celibate priesthood requires voluntary self-castration!' To a man, the Zoroastrian priests are *eunuchs, for the kingdom of Heaven.*

"We arrived at the tomb and I hesitated to enter, whispering, 'It feels strange to me... that he is dead.'

"'In the presence of Death, there are no strangers,' said Timonides, placing a reassuring hand on my shoulder and motioning for me to enter.

"Upon entering I noticed that the soldiers had already pulled back the burial cloth. The shellac, coating made of mummy-like strips, had begun to harden into a fiberglass-like finish. For the most part the coating was still very sticky and its fragrance filled the small chamber. In some places it had hardened and was smooth to the touch. The wild flowers Mary Magdalene had picked were strewn on the burial shroud along both sides of Jesus' body.

"I caressed his bruised cheek, which felt cold to the touch, and proclaimed him to be my Master, Y'shua-bar-Yehosef. I pointed out to the tribune the blood-soaked strips of linen under the semitransparent veneer. Petronius questioned the blood marks in the center of Jesus' feet. It was not normal for a crucified man to exhibit this type of wound. Longinus, who had pierced Jesus' side, explained the discrepancy, which strengthened our testimony that this was the body of the man they were to guard.

"Having touched him, I was reminded of my position as a scribe. I would have to undergo a seven-day cleansing ritual for having touched a dead body. *If I lived that long.* Then again, if I was Thomas, Judas could not have killed himself! Could he?

"Caius Longinus then pointed out the massive bloodstain on the left side, where he had thrust his spear into Jesus' heart to verify that he was already dead. This had prevented the breaking of his bones. Caius then reached into the moneybag that hung at his side, and produced two coins. These he placed over Jesus' eyes.

"Turning to me, he explained, 'It is for the ferryman, Charon, to carry his soul across the River Styx to the land of the dead. If your master does not have payment for his fare, his soul must wander forever.'

"I nodded my consent. This tradition was not among our customs but I did not have the heart to remove the coins. Pulling the burial cloth over the length of Jesus' body, Petronius called for a length of rope but none could be found. He then removed his dagger and cut a strip from the edge of the shroud. It was about the width of a human palm and extended the length of the shroud. The soldiers used this long strip to wrap the burial cloth securely around the body. They tied one end around the feet then looped it around the knee area. About half way up they looped it again, just over his hands, then continued towards the head. When they had finished I returned the bloodstained tallit, woven of silk and hemp, to its original position: folded upon the face of Jesus. By then the body resembled that of a sailor's about to be buried at sea, wrapped as it was.

"Petronius carefully examined the stone walls once more, prying at the corners with his dagger. Assured there was no other entrance into the tomb, he ordered the guard to roll the massive golal back into its depression. Timonides and the servant who assisted him placed the seal on the tomb. At this point Petronius approached me and questioned the darkness of the Crucifixion. He wondered what I might know about it. I related Joel's prophecy about the Sun growing dark at noon and the Moon turning to blood, and what I thought it meant.

"Overhearing our conversation, Timonides added, 'You don't really think he is one of the savior-gods, do you? I mean, even if he did resurrect from the dead, this seal cannot be broken.'

"'If the God of the Jews truly darkened the skies on the celebration day of Sol Invictus, our Sun God, raising his servant from the dead should present less of a problem,' remarked Petronius. 'If such a God chose to break the seal of Tiberius, what power do you suppose Rome could muster against Him?'

"At this, I noticed that the seal consisted of a string held in place by two blobs of red wax imprinted with the image of Tiberius Cæsar. 'You keep saying the seal cannot be broken, but it seems rather flimsy to me,' I remarked.

"'The seal itself is fragile, but if someone were to break the seal of Tiberius Cæsar, all the powers of Rome would not rest until the perpetrators were hunted down and crucified,' Petronius assured me.

"Finally understanding what they meant, I thanked Timonides for sharing what he knew of the savior-gods. Petronius, having no further need of us, told me I was free to go. Still alive and not sure what to do, I traveled past Bethany toward Jericho, to the old mikveh of the Baptist for my required seven days of purification. There I found Yehosef and Nicodemus, who had already been there one day and still had six to go.

"Now you know the crime for which Christ was arrested and executed," said Teryk addressing those seated at the Round Table. "The task set before you now is to either validate my version of events with credible historical data or to discredit it. When this investigation began, I had no idea it was going to become this involved. Some of you were upset when you first learned that I was questioning the story surrounding the Crucifixion and subsequent resurrection. If I have offended anyone, I assure you that it was never my intention to do so. That said, I would like to ask all those who see no point in continuing this investigation to please exit the room. Where this investigation is headed… is not for the faint of heart. If you found fault with me questioning the credentials of the 'Only Son of God', you're sure as hell going to be upset when I question the very existence of a jealous, vengeful and vindictive God. The story Jesus told concerning the Exodus, during the Last Supper, had nothing to do with Moses freeing the Israelites from bondage in Egypt. The Israelites had been in positions of power ever since Joseph had been appointed second in command by pharaoh. These Shepherd Kings, called the Hyksos, were not released from bondage by Ramses. It was the brother of Moses, Pharaoh Ahmose, that exiled the Hyksos, hence the title of the book: Exodus!"

"Moses was the son of an Egyptian pharaoh," added Jared. "The priesthood established by Moses later fabricated a believable story and set it centuries after the actual events had transpired. They did not do this to hide the fact that the corrupt activities, of the Hyksos, had been milking both Egypt and Babylon dry for centuries. The priests were trying to hide the fact that their greatest prophet, Moses, had been born half Egyptian. The catastrophes that plagued Egypt, during the Exodus, did in fact happen. They were recorded by many civilizations all over the planet four centuries before the alleged Jewish Exodus."

"I am not about to tackle that can of worms just yet," said Teryk. "Let's keep that one on the back burner for now and concentrate on the conundrum at hand. Having accessed the memory of a first-century scribe, it may surprise you to learn that when Hebrew scripture addressed God it was almost always in a plural form, rarely in the singular. The term used to identify God in the Old Testament is the *Elohim*; a descriptive term meaning 'those who came from the sky'. In fact, the term Elohim is used to identify God over three thousand times in the Old Testament."

"Where the scripture read 'the Elohim', the gods, the translators of the King James' version rendered it as God, singular. Where scripture read 'the Lord of the Elohim', they translated it as the Lord God. The Torah, the original source of this information, clearly states that the planet was already here when the Elohim arrived! And that man was already in existence when the Elohim chose to place their image upon him in order to make him, in their likeness! " Teryk gazed around the table slowly. "I'm not sure where that investigation will lead. To be honest, I'm not sure I want to know. For the moment, however, we are still investigating events that transpired two thousand years ago.

"I did not see anyone run out of the room! I'll take that to mean that everyone present wishes to continue with this investigation," said Teryk as he pulled up a calendar on his iPad. "We are nearing the end of the year. No sense in dragging this investigation through Christmas and New Year. Perhaps it would be best if we break early for the holidays and reconvene toward the end of January. I need some time to recharge. My mind feels a bit scattered. Today's session really took its toll on me."

"On a sidenote, this year's treasure-recovery operations have been especially profitable thanks in part to a newly implemented metallurgic technology," announced Teryk. "As a result, I am allocating $293,081 bonus for each citizen of Antares, in addition to all other bonuses. Joshua, I would like you to try and re-establish a link with Artimus and update him on the situation here. Check with Jared for the necessary passports and security measures. I hope you understood that the bonus extends to our newest arrivals as well."

"That should more than cover all my travel expenses."

"I will cover all travel expenses," explained Teryk. "The bonus is for you to spend on things you want. While you're in Europe, might I suggest you look into flying off the Swiss Alps in a wingsuit? They're a lot of fun."

"Thank you, Commander. That's very generous of you," said Shakira. "I still haven't spent last year's bonus." Addressing those gathered at the Round Table, she added, "Well guys, we have our work cut out for us. We've found a couple of references to a daytime eclipse but I would like us to try and locate more. Two eclipses on the same day, accompanied by massive earthquakes, would have been a monumental event. As always, the crucial documentation of Judah's presence at the trials seems to elude us. And now we have an additional task: locating historical references to his having been Jesus' identical twin brother, as well as the one called Thomas.

"Jesus' resurrection will be scrutinized from every angle," she continued. "The Shroud of Turin appears to be the smoking gun. Jared, please set the shroud as your forensic team's highest priority. Perhaps the clues at Rennes-le-Château in France can shed some light on the matter. The Gnostic influence on Christianity is evident, but we need to know just how deeply they infiltrated the emerging church. If there's nothing more to add, you are dismissed until the end of January."

"Commander, isn't that bonus a bit excessive?" asked Trisha. "How can you afford to do that?"

"This year Antares's submersible treasure fleet recovered nearly two trillion in gems and precious metals alone," replied Teryk. "Do you recall the recent bank bailouts and the trillions spent trying to jumpstart the US economy? If your government had spread the wealth among the citizens, who would have used the money to pay off bills, created new businesses and splurged the remainder back into the economy; each US citizen would have received a check for roughly $145,000. So no, I don't think it's excessive. Unlike the United States, Antares is not operated as a non-profit organization."

Later that evening, Teryk had decided to brush up on his urban tactical assault skills in one of Antares's terrestrial chambers. The chambers could simulate any environment from blizzard to monsoon conditions. Upon exiting his captain's quarters, he was confronted by three members of his research team.

Raven handed Teryk a clearance authorization for Katharine. She explained, "A conference of solar physicists and geophysicists will be gathering in

Rio de Janeiro, Brazil, to discuss the emerging problems with Earth's protective magnetic fields. Aristides has been studying this problem for some time. Mikhail is attending because fellow Russian astrophysicists will be lecturing on an interstellar energy cloud that the solar system is entering. Mikhail is convinced that this energy cloud is affecting the Sun and every planet in the solar system. He informed me that the Max Planck Institute, Germany's equivalent of MIT, has conducted a number of studies confirming that the Sun has not been this turbulent in at least the last eleven thousand years. Katharine will require a false passport if she is to attend along with the team of scientists we are sending."

"When is this conference in Brazil scheduled for?"

"The conference is in January, Commander. Katharine just found out about it. I realize that she hasn't been with us long but I..."

"Understood, Raven. Get started on the authorization," said Teryk as he signed the necessary documents.

Raven held up a jewel case containing a gold talisman of Dionysus, similar to the one Teryk had described. "Two of these were found aboard the U-Boat. Does this look anything like the talisman the Lady Claudia Procula was wearing?"

"That's it exactly," Teryk assured her, taking the talisman from her and examining it. "I did not get to inspect the original closely, but this looks very similar to what I remember in both size and design."

"Commandant," said Monique, handing Teryk a file stamped with seven seals, "enclosed is a full report on the Nazi submarine U-3047, which was not brought to Antares's docks as you requested. We originally thought the submarine safe. According to the captain's log, all torpedoes had been jettisoned. But during the removal of artifacts some were found to be booby-trapped. Technicians discovered that the sub's ballast tanks contained natural gas and were rigged to explode."

"I ordered the warship taken aboard the mobile docking station, Voyager, positioned east of the Lesser Antilles," continued Monique. "Due to the amount of corrosive damage sustained by the German U-boat's outer hull, the explosives demolition team has advised us not to bring it aboard Voyager just yet. They will be employing 'avatar droids' in an attempt to flood the sub's ballast tanks, displacing the explosive gas and neutralizing the threat. The explosive devices will be disarmed afterwards. Buoyancy compensators will prevent the U-boat from sinking during the procedure. Enclosed you'll find a list of what has been removed from the sub so far. A full manifest will be drafted once everything is off the U-boat."

Examining a photo of some strange-looking instrumentation, Teryk asked, "Has Devereaux been informed of this?" He showed the photo to Jared.

"Oui, monsieur. It was Devereaux who identified the instruments as belonging to a secret UFO-type craft he believes the Nazis were working on," answered Monique.

"Note that the instrument markings are divided into thirty-degree segments, Commander," added Jared. "We know of no German aircraft outfitted with this type of equipment during World War II. Devereaux informed me that only top-secret Nazi flying-saucer experiments utilized such instrumentation. At the moment we are not sure where to house what appears to be UFO wreckage recovered by the Germans. For now, Devereaux, Mikhail and Aristides are analyzing the metal's composition in their labs."

"Most of the metals are a form of aluminum with high concentrations of pure iron," Jared informed him. "In some specimens they have identified as many as seven different metals. What is unusual about their composition is that the individual metals retain their unique qualities. When observed through a powerful microscope, the material resembles particle board or granite. Each of the individual metals is bonded to those around it while retaining its unique properties. We've uncovered maps and encoded records containing the locations of other Nazi submarines. Most appear to have been hidden in Antarctica. Devereaux thinks this was done to better preserve the bodies of downed alien pilots he believes are aboard those U-boats."

"You said the documents were encoded. How did you manage to break the code so quickly?" asked Teryk.

"We found an Enigma encoding device aboard the sub. Trisha, a big fan of Alan Turing, has been a big help in operating the contraption," Jared explained. "Turing was the MI6 mathematician, cryptanalyst who is credited with cracking the Nazi's unbreakable enigma code by developing the first computer-like 'thinking machine'."

Teryk pulled out a photo from the file and exclaimed, "Wow, is this supposed to be a painting of Leonardo's Mona Lisa?"

"The painting is still being analyzed," Raven assured him. "We lack the proper experts to complete a thorough investigation of the artwork. According to Hypnautica, the renaissance painter Raphael recorded having seen this painting while visiting Leonardo da Vinci just before he died. According to Raphael, next to Leonardo's deathbed was a painting of the Mona Lisa. Raphael noted that the woman in the painting was strikingly beautiful in comparison to the known Mona Lisa, currently at the Louvre in France. The only difference Raphael could detect in the painting was that the Mona Lisa in Leonardo's possession had eyebrows."

"You mean the Mona Lisa at the Louvre doesn't have any eyebrows? No wonder she looks so weird," exclaimed Teryk, looking more closely at the photo then at the next one, which showed a golden Nazi swastika surrounded by a diamond-covered wreath. "What's the story behind this bejeweled Nazi paraphernalia?" he asked.

"History records that a much larger solid-gold swastika wreathed with diamonds was presented to Adolf Hitler by Heinrich Himmler, head of the Gestapo," said Monique.

"The golden swastika, commissioned by Himmler, a former chicken farmer, was made from the gold fillings of Polish Jews. If Heinrich Himmler commissioned this swastika as well, it could be what's giving off so much negative energy aboard the submarine," deduced Raven. "Commander, am I to understand that it was the dæmon Asmodeus that led you to this site? Because some of the information I've uncovered on the dæmon leads me to believe that it was once one of the Nephilim, but no one is entirely certain just what that arcane word means."

"Why do you suppose the Church is after the Ark of the Covenant, Commander?" asked Jared.

"I couldn't say, but I can assure you they have no intention of informing the Jews or returning the Ark to them, should they find it," said Teryk. "They were obviously after Asmodeus because the dæmon presides over the realm of Secrets and Buried Treasure. There's also the possibility that the dæmon assisted Solomon in the building of the First Temple. At any rate, the dæmon agreed to give me information that would lead us to the Ark of the Covenant, in exchange for its eventual release."

"In addition, Asmodeus warned me of the dangers associated with my having consumed the manna. Apparently manna affects the soul, so it would not have mattered what body I was in when I consumed it. Raven, see what the researchers can find out about those claims. I will question Asmodeus further when I get a chance."

"Yes sir, but regarding the Ark, I've heard that all archaeological finds of a religious nature are considered property of Israel and by law must be handed over to the Israeli authorities," said Raven.

"That law only applies to archaeological artifacts the Israeli authorities are aware of," explained Teryk. "Apparently, the Knights Templar were successful in locating the Ark about a thousand years ago. Contrary to popular belief, it would appear that the Templars got wind of their betrayal and arranged for the removal of the Templar treasure from Europe. Their entire fleet, which comprised eighteen galleys, sailed out of La Rochelle on the night before the event. Asmodeus assured me that the Ark of the Covenant was among the cargo of treasure along with the golden ritual objects of Solomon's Temple." In an effort to lighten the mood, he added, "There will be a full moon tonight. Raven, please inform our new guest of this evening's festivities."

Joshua stood near an observation port. Outside, dolphins displayed incredible agility as they toyed with mackerels. "Well, I think I'll take this time to brush up on the history of the savior-gods you guys keep referring to," he said to Raven upon seeing her approach. "I had no idea that there were so many, and all born on December 25th of virgin mothers, just like Jesus. That they all supposedly resurrected after having been crucified is a little unnerving. I find the similarities between this Dionysus character and Jesus quite fascinating, though."

"While you're at it, you might want to team up with Cassandra. The Gnostics and ancient cultures seem to be her specialty," suggested Raven. "Might I recommend that you focus your studies on one savior-god in particular: Mithra, a Persian who preceded Jesus by about four centuries. As far as I know, Mithra was the last of the savior-gods. Like Christ, he, too, was born of a virgin in a sacred birth-cave during the winter solstice. Mithra is credited with raising the dead, and healing the sick and the lame. He restored sight to the blind and exorcised dæmons. Strangest of all, he celebrated an almost identical Last Supper with his twelve disciples shortly before being betrayed and crucified; or hung on a tree. He was entombed in a rock and a few days later resurrected from the dead. Although it is well documented, few people realize that Mithra was revered and worshipped by the Romans. Mithra's ascension was celebrated during the spring equinox now known as Easter."

"That all sounds very interesting," admitted Trisha joining the two. "But I feel the need to reacquaint myself with all four Gospels. It's been a while since I've read them."

"Trisha, you've been inquiring about our intelligence-gathering programs, so Teryk has made arrangements for you to explore our ESPionage facility. He would like you there by 1800 hours this evening," Raven informed her. "Will that be a problem?"

"Not at all. I've wanted to see the place ever since I got here."

"Tonight will be the first time you guys experience Antares during a full moon," said Raven. "The city will surface, sea conditions permitting. There will be all sorts of great activities for you to participate in. There's volleyball, wind-surfing, tow-boarding and jet-skiing. It's a lot of fun. If we were on an actual beach I would invite you to go surfing by moonlight with us. You have not surfed until you've done it on a hydrofoil board."

"Sounds like fun," admitted Joshua, "but I'm a country boy. I've never surfed in my life."

"Not a problem," Raven assured him. "We have several training tanks onboard and most are used for surf training, both recreational and beach assault. But I think the best way to learn to surf is by being towed behind a jet-ski."

Joshua had been jet-skiing when he noticed Trisha standing on the dock. "These jet-ski helmets are outfitted with night vision, Trisha! It's awesome. You've got to try it," advised Joshua as he maneuvered his jet ski closer to one of Antares's surface docks. "Hey, by the way, how did things go at ESPionage?"

Trisha shook her head slowly, saying, "These guys really are a threat to national security! As a demonstration of their abilities, they described my workplace to its smallest detail. They described the colored lines in the hallways for repair and service people to follow. When servicemen enter our facility they are transported inside of windowless vehicles. When they arrive they are not permitted to look up. They must look down and stare at the colored line that applies to them: green, yellow, red, and blue. These lines direct them to their assigned work areas. The remote viewers perfectly described the raised floor. They identified the Sun Microsystems computer bank consoles by name and described them as being dark gray with bright blue and green LEDs. They identified and described the Liebert Precision Power consoles as being beige with gray name plates. I was most impressed with how accurately they identified all the buildings and each of their functions at the SCIF."

"What's a SCIF? And why do repair men have to look down at the colored lines?" asked Joshua.

"Repair men have to look down because if they look up and see our maps or instrumentation panels, they could be forced to recall the information if they are captured and hypnotized. SCIF stands for Secret Compartmented Information Facility. It's basically a small city contained within a large building disguised to look like a warehouse," explained Trisha. "ESPionage even pinpointed the building's location through something called dowsing. Teryk said that dowsing has been around for hundreds, perhaps even thousands, of years, like that's supposed to validate it or something."

"Just because you don't understand how something works, Trisha, doesn't mean you can't learn to use it effectively," argued Joshua. "Electromagnetism is a phenomenon that has never been fully understood, yet we use it every day. Incidentally, the marines used L-shaped dowsing wires during Vietnam to locate land mines and tunnels."

"That's stupid. Why not simply use a metal detector?" asked Trisha.

"You're assuming every platoon had one of those things. Besides, the more advanced land mines are made out of plastic so that metal detectors can't locate them. Dowsing is the only way to find those things. I myself have dowsed for land mines, underground water pipes and power lines."

"Has anyone ever blown themselves up using those things?" she asked in disbelief.

Joseph "Five Eagles" Reyna

"To date, I haven't heard of any marines or combat soldiers who have. I sure hope that guy with the TV show called Jackass never attempts it. He might be the first."

"I wonder if his ratings wouldn't go up?" asked Teryk, joining the conversation.

"Commander, we did not notice you there," apologized Trisha.

"Sorry to interrupt the festivities," said Teryk. "Katharine has been chosen to accompany members of my research team to a conference in Brazil. We have reason to believe Earth's population could be in great danger. Based on the information we have, we can expect to start seeing massive Earth changes taking place within the next decade or so. And Katharine believes that you could be of some assistance in the matter, Trisha."

"Changes like what?" asked Trisha intrigued.

"A few years back, the National Aeronautics and Space Administration— NASA—announced that the United States would suffer trillions in damage if it were suddenly struck by a high-intensity solar radiation storm," explained Teryk. "The damages would most likely result from the upcoming Solar Max; when the Sun's magnetic poles are due to flip again. It could take the United States as much as a decade to recover from such an impact, due to its aging electrical infrastructure. I think you and I both know that without proper authorization, NASA would never have gone public with that information. My teams need to know what, if anything, is being done by your government to address these issues."

Upon entering Teryk's accommodations, Trisha gave a long slow whistle, "Wow! It's good to be the king," she said, looking around at Teryk's spacious living quarters. The thick acrylic outer walls provided a breathtaking view of the ocean. Soft blue lights illuminated fluorescent fish as they swam by. One bulkhead displayed what looked like a miniature cliff dwelling. In the cliff's recesses were tiny fires that cast an eerie glow. Upon closer inspection, the delicate flames turned out to be puffs of cotton illuminated by hidden LEDs. A miniature waterfall cascaded into a pool surrounded by a miniature forest of bonsai trees. She touched the trees, not believing they could be real. Some jutted out from the cliffside, their roots anchored into the rock face. Above her, thousands of tiny stars flickered within a whirling galaxy.

"The stars are really cool, aren't they?" commented Raven. "Each is composed from a fiber-optic strand," she explained.

"Artists are a commodity we have in abundance at Antares," added Monique.

"It's beautiful," exclaimed Trisha.

"Hypnautica, before we begin I need you to record and categorize the following. Use the monitoring systems in my quarters to make an accurate record of this information for others to study," instructed Teryk. "In other words, do exactly what you've been doing for the Round Tables.

"Trish and Joshua, I don't believe you've met Devereaux, he's one of our best special projects scientists and a member of Jared's ESPionage team," said Teryk. "Although Anakah and Athena are Mothers of Lemuria they are also members of ESPionage. Our specialists on languages and ancient cultures Sarina, Cassandra, Marileyna and Kortney you already know."

"What you might not know is that they've become quite concerned about an ancient cosmic interloper that appears to be reentering our solar system," announce Shakira who had requested this impromptu gathering in Teryk's quarters. "The recent actions of the world super-powers disturb me. The urgency with which they seek to complete monumental projects at remote inhospitable locations, like the Svalbard Global Seed Vault, troubles me greatly. Russia is at this moment completing work on five thousand *additional* underground bunkers. China has squirreled away an entire naval fleet, dry-docked within enormous tunnels, deep inside their mountains. And the US is rumored to have over a thousand Deep Military Underground Bunkers spread across the globe. Trisha, without compromising your oaths of secrecy, what can you tell us concerning any massive Earth changes that US naval intelligence may have been aware of?"

"Have you ever heard of something called the Schumann Cavity Resonance?" asked Trisha.

"Schumann's Resonance is an electromagnetic pulse sometimes referred to as the heartbeat of the Earth: 7.8Hz—a frequency close to that of human brainwaves. When we sleep our brains link to these pulses through entrainment," replied Sofia; another of the Lemurian Mothers who was regularly consulted in order to find a more peaceful solution to a problem.

"That's correct. The Schumann Cavity Resonance is a wave, a negatively charged pulse emitted from Earth's surface. It rises as high as 30,000 feet into the ionosphere," explained Trisha. "It normally fluctuates between 7 and 8.5 Hz. The frequency averages around 7.83 Hz. It is believed this frequency has remained stable for hundreds, possibly even thousands, of years. But ever since the 1980s it has been increasing steadily. This has become a problem because many of the navy's top-secret submarine communication systems are based on this frequency. The system used to operate flawlessly. Top-secret messages could easily be superimposed upon the Schumann Cavity Resonance, which acted like a carrier wave. All a submarine had to do was drag a long wire through the water, and this simple antenna could easily receive and transmit messages from anywhere on the planet. Last I heard, the pulse was over 13Hz; meaning that the length of the wave has shortened. This presents a problem because the navy's massive antenna arrays are drilled into solid bedrock and go for miles, making any sort of alterations, in order to adjust to the changing frequency, nearly impossible."

"Wow, I'm impressed. I had no idea you understood radio transmissions and wave propagation that well," said an astonished Joshua. "The carrier wave was Marconi's contribution to radio when he infringed on Nikola Tesla's patents. But if the wave was 7.83Hz and it's changed that much, how can a human retune to the changing frequency? It would be like your favorite radio station changing its broadcasting frequency from 103.5MHz to 165.5MHz. Standard radios are just not configured to tune into that high a frequency."

"Well, stress certainly doesn't help," said Anakah. "You should certainly learn to meditate and watch what you're consuming. Insomnia has already become a serious problem for many women. Normally human brainwaves link to these pulses through entrainment in the same way that a baby links to the heartbeat of its mother. Liquid crystals within the human body detect these waves and..."

"Liquid crystals!" exclaimed Katharine. "What sort of liquid crystals?" she asked, intrigued at the possibility.

"It is believed that the human heart is a seven-layer liquid crystal oscillator," explained Anakah. "Humans have a natural physical rapport with Earth's low frequency isoelectric field. This is why so many women today are having trouble getting a decent night's sleep. If the frequency of the Earth increases that much and our body's frequency remains the same, we feel anxious."

"Strong electromagnetic fluctuations have been linked to increases in Extra Sensory Perception and bursts of human creativity due to possible influences upon the pineal gland," explained Athena, "but most humans are resisting the change to this outside influence. There is some speculation that the human collective consciousness is somehow affecting the Schumann Resonance. But that would be like the tail wagging the dog— we should think outside the box by looking for a very powerful external electrogravitic influence."

"Mikhail might be able to shed some light on the subject," said Jared. "He has been compiling data on something he calls the Photon Field: a massive, dense, highly electrified interstellar energy cloud first detected by the Russians in the early '60s. Mikhail claims that it is affecting every planet in our solar system. And if it's powerful enough to perturb every planet in the system, it could be what's affecting the Schumann Cavity Resonance, which in turn could be affecting the collective consciousness.

"Gregg Braden, a bestselling author whose pioneering breakthroughs have helped bridge the gap between the hard evidence science demands and the mysterious nature of spirituality, also believes Earth's frequency is being affected by the Photon Field," continued Jared. "For years, the Russians have been measuring increasingly high amounts of plasma and photon activity which they believe are having a profound effect on our Sun. NASA scientists did not confirm the existence of this energy field until July 14, 2010. Since then, both NASA and the European Space Agency have warned that mega flares resulting from the cycle 24 Solar Max could knock out the Northern Hemisphere's technological infrastructure, setting us back at least two centuries. Considering the economic troubles plaguing the past decades, I find it inconceivable that space agencies, from around the world, had the financial resources to launch a virtual flotilla of solar satellites.

"It would appear that the rising frequency is adversely affecting the planet's rotation. It's slowing down! Aristides believes that as the Schumann Resonance increases, Earth's electromagnetic field decreases, effectively leaving the planet without protective shields," warned Jared. "It's entirely possible that the Earth's rotation could stop if the Schumann Resonance gets strong enough. After a few days, it is believed that the Earth will begin rotating again, but this time in the opposite direction. It's likely this has occurred in the not-too-distant past. Accounts in the records of ancient civilizations state that the Sun used to rise in the west. I once heard someone say that a prophecy pertaining to the Second Coming of Christ spoke of the Sun rising in the west. The Hopi have a similar prophecy and warn that when we see the Sun rise in the west we should prepare for a great shaking of the Earth. I looked for the prophecy in the Book of Revelation, but could find no reference to it..."

"Well, I suppose that it's my turn to add my two cents," interrupted Athena. "I doubt any of you have ever heard of a man named Ned Dougherty. He wrote a book after his 'life-altering' near death experience, or NDE. As some of you already know, I, too, had one of those experiences and my life hasn't been the same since. Like me, Ned was shown visions of possible futures. He witnessed the Sun expanding and appearing very large in the sky. Shortly after this, solar flares began bombarding the Earth," Athena paused for emphasis. "After that it gets bad; the earth's rotation begins to slow and all its volcanoes erupt, filling the atmosphere with thick clouds of smoke and ash. He saw the earth tilting off its axis, causing mega-earthquakes that change the shape of entire continents. Then a gigantic tidal wave struck the eastern coast of the United States and new land masses rose out of the oceans. Shortly after this, the Earth's rotation stopped completely for a few days. When it did begin spinning again, its rotation was in the opposite direction."

"There is just such a prophecy in the Qur'an," announced Shakira; who specialized in ancient cultures and was of Arabic descent. "'*The Hour [of judgment] will not come until the sun rises from the west, and when it rises from the west and when the people see it, they will believe...'* Quran 6:158. Other signs include a sky filled with smoke and a phenomenon referred to as The Three Eclipses. The passage reads, 'A night will come on the people that shall be prolonged for three nights...' If the world were to stop rotating for the duration you speak of, then one night would not see sunrise for about three days. How scholars interpreted that passage as pertaining to three eclipses, I'll never know. When the Sun does finally rise it will do so from the west. According to the prophecy, this will herald the return of the Christ, who will unite the Muslims and Christians under one banner. This prophecy also speaks of al-Masih ad-Dajjal, or Messiah-Liar. He is the expected Antichrist, the Deceitful Messiah who will make his appearance to the Jews in their part of the world.

"Egyptian records give two accounts of a reversal in the earth's rotation," affirmed Shakira. "We find only one account of such a reversal in records of South American civilizations. Both state that the Earth stops rotating for about three days before the Sun is seen rising in the horizon it normally sets in."

"I was not aware that the Qur'an contained anything like that, Shakira. Thank you for that information," exclaimed Jared. Addressing the group he continued, "As a result of these Earth changes, the human body is becoming more sensitive. This phenomenon has already improved the efficiency of our ESPionage teams."

"I wonder if this photon field isn't somehow affecting the underground cauldron at Yellowstone," speculated Monique.

"Yellowstone National Park?" asked Trisha, glancing toward Katharine. "Why? What is your interest in the Yellowstone caldera?"

"Teryk's old mentor warned us of a danger that lurks beneath it: a danger of apocalyptic proportions," exclaimed Monique.

"When I first entered the priesthood I researched and looked for the prophecies that related to the Second Coming of Christ and the Apocalypse," Teryk explained. "There were many events of interest but most fizzled out. For a time I even wondered, as others did, if the meltdown of the Chernobyl facility near Kiev, in April of '86, was not the long awaited sign called 'Wormwood', a catastrophe mentioned in the 'Trumpet Judgments' from the Book of Revelation."

"What does this *Wormwood* have to do with Yellowstone?" asked Katharine.

"By an incredible coincidence, the word Chernobyl, in the Ukraine, means Wormwood," explained Teryk. "When it melted down, many considered the possibility that it might be a sign of the End of Days. To me, Chernobyl was one of those events that fizzled out because the biblical Wormwood will affect one third of the planet. Yellowstone's detonation would certainly accomplish that. By comparison, Chernobyl's meltdown was insignificant."

"As I recall, the Russians seeded the clouds in order to stop the radioactivity from reaching Moscow; poisoning thousands in the process," announced Trisha.

Katharine stared at her friend in disbelief.

"Oh don't worry, that information is not classified," added Trisha. Then, turning toward the others seated around her, she disclosed that she had been a US Naval Intelligence Officer.

Katharine confided in those around her that, "Yellowstone had been a major contributing factor in the decision to end our lives. My life was shitty enough already. I mean, who wants to wait around for that to happen?"

"Cat seemed so convinced of her finding," added Trisha, "that I began to question the people I thought should have the answers. I learned that our government was aware of the danger associated with Yellowstone's caldera but had made no specific emergency or recovery plans to deal with it. FEMA is primarily prepared for run-of-the-mill natural disasters. And we've all seen how inept those preparations were."

"Are they just playing it off then?" asked Jared.

"Not exactly," admitted Trisha. "I learned that the US government intends to preserve its armies. Why do you think they have been creating wars on the other side of the world? They needed an excuse to mobilize the major portion of their armies out of harm's way. In the event that an eruption demolishes half the nation, the United States has every intention of remaining a superpower by preserving its fighting force. While at the Pentagon, I entered a briefing room with a peculiar map that caught my attention. It was a map of the United States that displayed new coastlines and an inland sea stretching from the Mississippi to the Great Lakes. I was swiftly escorted out of the room upon inquiring why Wisconsin, most of the East Coast and Florida where gone."

"Do you think you could recreate the map?" inquired Jared.

"I've done some research of my own into that subject, and you will find a fairly accurate reconstruction of the Navy map by Googling; John Moore, navy flood map," replied Trisha. "The web site, www.thelibertyman.com, belongs to John Moore, an ex-Navy Seal turned homicide investigator. Because of his background, some time back, Moore was tasked by a friend to look into the possibility of something called Planet X and its effects on our planet. At the time, John states that he thought his friend needed a tinfoil hat. That is until Moore was informed that everything his friend had suspected was true and that the US government has known about this threat and has been preparing for it since about 1979. As evidence of this, Moore, a self-styled whistleblower, draws attention to the Pentagon's February 2010, Quadrennial Defense Review Report. Based on the findings of the US Global Change Research Program the Quad Report emphasizes pre-emptive measures in anticipation of an upcoming global crisis. The Report stresses that the Department of Defense should take precautionary measures in order to deal with the potential threat of mass migrations of civilians displaced in part by the rising ocean levels, multiple or simultaneous natural disasters, the spread of disease and the scarcity of drinking water."

"This would help explain why US cities are equipping their police force with military grade weapons," surmised Jared. "In the event of mass riots, a militarized police force will no doubt employ them in an effort to control the population."

"John Moore believes that the current administration is pushing the manmade Global Warming agenda in an effort to keep the public from realizing why our weather has become so chaotic," explained Trisha. "For instance, the media has been unusually silent on reporting the fact that the North Atlantic Thermohaline Conveyer, the Gulf Stream, is dead in some places and dying in others. This happened in the summer of 2010 when the media's attention was focused on the British Petroleum oil spill. Moore points out that in university level physics experiments were a colored stream of warm sea water is introduced into a long tub of cool sea water the thermal boundary is clearly visible. The conveyor is driven by salinity. Two things are known to disturb this balance in the thermal boundary, desalinating the water solution or introducing oil to the mix. It is believed, that the Gulf Stream is what regulates the Jet Stream. With the Gulf Stream effectively gone, we can expect to see a shift in the Jet Stream accompanied by erratic weather patterns and sustained areas of drought."

"Katharine, concerning Yellowstone, do you have any idea what kind of devastation we can expect to see should it erupt?" asked Athena.

"Basically, the worst parts of the *Bible*" explained Katharine. "The movie *2012* did a pretty good job of simulating the Yellowstone eruption up until the last scene. Once the volcanic dust envelopes the Earth, it will begin to settle. If you breathe in the volcanic dust, your lungs will become filled with a suffocating, pasty acidic cement, to say nothing of inhaling tiny shards of volcanic glass. The accumulating cement slurry is believed to cause a slow, painful and agonizing death. Should Yellowstone erupt, the explosion will most likely be heard on the other side of the planet. The last scene in the movie *2012* is a view of three massive ships sailing under sunny skies. If that thing goes off, the Earth's atmosphere will be blanketed, effectively plunging the world into darkness. The resulting nuclear winter could last decades."

"As it stands now, what is the likelihood that the Yellowstone caldera will actually erupt?" asked Anakah.

"Based on all the data accumulated so far, it could erupt at any moment," explained Katharine. "Yellowstone's caldera is already classified as being in the 'Red Zone'. The last eruption is believed to have ejected at least two hundred and fifty cubic miles of magma into the atmosphere, roughly a thousand times more than the Mount Saint Helens eruption in 1980. No one knows exactly what to look for, but generally the signs of an impending eruption are an increase in earthquake activity. Also you should look for unusual animal behavior and a sudden drying up of water wells and natural springs in the area.

"There are several thousand volcanoes on the planet. The majority of them are located along the Ring of Fire surrounding the Pacific Ocean. Yellowstone National Park, however, is located in Wyoming, Montana and Idaho. It's in the center of a large tectonic plate, nowhere near the Ring of Fire. This had led some to speculate that the massive magma reservoir under Yellowstone was being heated in part by radioactive material—which is where your Wormwood would come in," explained Katharine. "A recently discovered Mantle Plume, which extends down into the crust at least four hundred and fifty miles, appears to be what's causing the hotspot. This enormous chasm is acting like a chimney stack, venting heat from the planet's interior and heating up the cauldron. Geologists have located almost twenty of these hotspots worldwide. Yellowstone's caldera is roughly the size of Mount Everest and sits just five miles below the surface. I would like to add that I, too, believe something external is affecting the planet. Since recorded history there were never more than a half a dozen volcanoes erupting on the planet at any one time. Now, there are over forty active volcanoes. And the temperature of the planet's core is a thousand degrees hotter than it has ever been measured before."

"Yellowstone is the least of our worries," added Trisha. "The navy has discovered two larger active cauldrons, one in the Pacific and the other in the Indian Ocean. There is some speculation that the approach of Planet X could trigger them off."

"I also think there is an outside influence affecting the planets," confided Sarina, a specialist on ancient cultures. "But my research has led me to believe that it is not being caused by a planet but rather an approaching smoldering, brown dwarf star that frequents our inner solar system. In 1976, Zecharia Sitchin was one of the first to bring attention to what he calls Nibiru (nigh-beer-rooh) with his book *The Twelfth Planet*. The information came from King Ashurbanipal's Library in Nineveh, which had originally contained scrolls as well, but they were lost when the city was sacked and the library burned. While translating the clay tablets, Sitchin discovered Sumerian references to an additional planet. The word planet originally meant 'wanderer' and was used to describe any celestial body that moved through the heavens. Like the Maya, the Sumerians identified Earth as the seventh planet because they were counting from the outer solar system toward the Sun. And like the Mayans, the Sumerians should not have known how many outer planets our solar system contained, much less what they looked like."

"It is possible that Planet X and Nibiru could be one-and-the-same," added Kortney. "In his documentary *Are We Alone?*, Zecharia Sitchin interviewed Dr. Robert S. Harrington, chief astronomer at the US Naval Observatory. At the time, Harrington had been searching for Planet X for over a decade and believed he had found it. Like so many other astronomers, He died shortly after publishing, *The Location of Planet X*, in The Astrophysical Journal, July 1988. Not being associated with NASA, I guess he never got the memo."

"At first, I thought it was just an interesting legend," explained Marileyna. "I began assisting Sarina, Cassandra and Kortney with their investigation because they believed the object's last passing coincided with the Exodus. We've made this investigation a sort of hobby, and have been sharing information for about a year now. This object's gravitational interference is well known but it's only half the problem."

"The Sumerians maintained that this wanderer was captured by the gravitational influence of the larger outer planets, wrenching Uranus off its axis and dislodging Pluto, Neptune's largest moon," added Cassandra. "As a result, it has an extremely large elliptical orbit that brings it through our solar system approximately once every 3,657 years; much like a comet. This time period was referred to as a SAR (Shar) by the Sumerians. Our best guesstimate puts its last fly-by at about the time of the Exodus. Effects similar to the ten plagues that devastated Egypt were recorded by the ancient Native American civilizations and the Chinese as well...."

"Based on our latest findings, however," interrupted Sarina, "we now have reason to believe that the SAR's time period was drastically altered due to a collision with a Saturn-sized world that once existed between Mars and Jupiter. The larger asteroids, in this region of space, all spin on the same axis and they orbit the sun at about the same speed. We believe this smoldering interloper is dragging the remnants of the destroyed planet in its gravity well. Its collision with the massive, celestial body appears to have affected the orbit of Mars as well."

"Rahab is the Bible's name for this missing world," added Marileyna. "The Sumerians identify the destroyed world as Tiâmat. What we found fascinating are the correlations between this object's arrival and Earth upheavals dating all the way back to the flood of Noah. Since about that time, all ancient cultures watched the skies for the return of the dreaded red dragon, a fiery-comet that periodically attacked Earth and its inhabitants. The Maya were among the last to track it."

"My best guesstimate for the Exodus puts it sometime around 1500 BCE. That is nowhere near when the Jews claim it occurred. What reason would the scribes have had to alter the timeframe of such a pivotal point in Jewish history?" asked Kortney. "Like the destruction of Troy, the destruction of Jericho had been considered a legend until archaeologists discovered the ancient

Canaanite city. According to archaeologists, Jericho was destroyed exactly as the Israelites claimed. The grain, weapons and clay idols of Jericho's inhabitants were all found buried with them in the rubble. There's just one problem, carbon dating places Jericho's destruction between 1616 and 1530 BCE: centuries before the Exodus.

"The proposed date of the Exodus's commencement has ranged from 1313 to 1145 BCE," continued Kortney. "Conventional scholarly thinking places the Exodus sometime around1250 BCE. In 1 Kings 6:1 it is stated that the Exodus occurred four hundred and eighty years before the construction of Solomon's Temple. This would place the Exodus somewhere around 1450 BCE, during the reign of Pharaoh Ahmose, 1500 to 1400 BCE. In *The Exodus Decoded*, directed by James Cameron, Simcha Jacobovici, *The Naked Archaeologist*, arrives at a similar conclusion. He places the Exodus date at around 1500 BCE, except that he attributes the Egyptian plagues to the eruption of the Santorini caldera. Neither Cameron nor Jacobovici seem to be aware that manifestations similar to the Egyptian plagues were recorded by many civilizations all over the world."

"Subtracting one additional Shar from the Exodus, we arrive at about the beginning of the last Mayan B'ak'tun," explained Marileyna. "Incidentally, the Mayans recorded that a major planetary upheaval occurred at that time. I believe that fly-by roughly coincides with the time of Noah. This time period is more than double the timeframe accepted by conventional biblical scholars. Up until the time of Noah, the red comet had passed through the heavens without incident. Hence, Jesus' ominous warning '...*it shall be as in the days of Noah.*'"

"If a failed star last passed through our inner solar system during the time of the Exodus," hypothesized Katharine, "it seems possible that its gravitational influence could have triggered the explosion of the Santorini caldera which lies under the circular Santorini island group in the Aegean Sea, Greece. If that's the case, I don't see why its next fly-by would not trigger the Yellowstone volcanic cauldron, since it is already in the Red Zone."

Joshua laughed nervously as he shifted in his chair. "You know, when Nostradamus was speaking of fish boiling in lakes and fire in the sky in his quatrains, I didn't really think he meant *fire in the sky*! Come to think of it, the Apocalypse also speaks of the Sun scorching one third of Earth's inhabitants. Athena, what is the name of Ned Dougherty's book? I don't believe I've ever heard of it."

"His book is called *Fast Lane to Heaven*," replied Athena, "I find it disturbing that his book clearly depicted the destruction of the Twin Towers more than half a year before the 9/11 incident." Biting her lower lip, she then asked Teryk, "Do you honestly believe that such a cacophony of catastrophes could befall us? I mean, is the Universe really that chaotic?"

"I think it is," answered Katharine, "in terms of cyclical catastrophic events, anyway. Mount Tambora, on the Indonesian island of Sumbawa, erupted in 1815 and is the greatest single volcanic event in recorded history. Its explosion threw so much material into the atmosphere that it spread around the world, changing the climate of the entire planet so much that 1816 became known as 'the year without a summer'. It snowed that year in June, not only in Europe but in the United States as well. What is not commonly known is that hundreds of thousands starved around the world as a result.

"Has anyone ever pondered how the Dark Ages came about?" Katharine asked those assembled in the captain's quarters. "History doesn't really explain it. The Dark Ages began one century after the fall of the Roman Empire, and lasted for nearly a thousand years. The burning of the great libraries, like that of Alexandria, didn't help matters. Although the Roman Catholic Church had placed a stranglehold on the scientific community of Europe, most Arab nations were flourishing at the time. Nothing in the history books explains why the entire world's population regressed so drastically. Had humanity's progress not been thwarted, it is conceivable that Columbus could have been the first man to walk on the Moon. Can you imagine the world we would be living in today?

"In my own personal research, I concluded that our regression was most likely due to an eruption of Krakatoa. We know a lot about the 1883 eruption that killed over thirty-six thousand people. That explosion is believed to be the largest in recorded human history. Reports of the explosion were recorded nearly three thousand miles away. After the 1883 eruption, the skies of the world were said to appear red and yellow, while the Moon looked pale green and intense 'Sun glows' at dusk lit the sky red for hours after sunset," said Katharine. "But we know almost nothing about a far more destructive, deep underground, cauldron-type explosion that occurred around the year 535 CE. Before that time, the islands of Sumatra and Java were joined as one. The massive eruption created the Sunda Strait of Indonesia.

"The majority of the research work on this event was done by a science writer turned historian named David Keys," explained Katharine. "He estimates the volcanic explosion equal to two billion Hiroshima-size bombs! According to his findings, diseased populations of wild rodents had always existed in East Africa. Massive shipments of grains during this catastrophic time period, coupled with migrating barbaric hordes, enabled the diseased rodents to spread beyond their normal territorial boundaries. John of Ephesus, a Syrian bishop, documented an event that occurred within the 535-536 timeframe. He says that there was a sign from the Sun, which only showed for about four hours each day. Many feared that its light would never return. According to the bishop, this unnatural darkness lasted for a period of eighteen months."

"It's no wonder they called it the Dark Ages," added Shakira. "One and a half years of darkness would have decimated the world's population and would have crippled any flourishing civilizations. The Justinian plague occurred about this time, along with massive crop failures."

"According to David Keys's findings," said Katharine, "tree rings from this time period are almost non-existent and don't show normal growth for about fifteen years afterwards. Droughts destroyed some lands, floods destroyed others. Crops failed for seven years and the majority of available drinking water became polluted, causing drastic declines in Earth's population."

"When we reconvene at our next gathering, I would like to make the Round Table aware of these findings. You guys have given me a lot to think about," admitted Teryk. Turning toward Athena, he added, "To answer your question, My Lady; I suspected something, but secretly hoped the research teams would come up empty handed. I certainly had no idea it would have the potential to be so disastrous. I've been doing some research of my own. And the archaeological evidence that our world has been subjected to cyclical cataclysmic events, followed by the periodic rebuilding of our world, since the beginning of recorded history, is overwhelming."

"In *Fingerprints of the Gods*, Graham Hancock argues convincingly that every great civilization that preceded us has in some way attempted to warn future generations of these, intense but short-lived, recurring cataclysms," announced Cassandra, who specialized in ancient world cultures. "It would seem that everyone has a small piece of the puzzle but never stopped to consider that these pieces could go to a much, much larger picture. Personally, I'd thought these oddities were an interesting curiosity, until now."

"It has become apparent to me that the ancients built massive stone monuments in the hopes of warning future generations so that they might be better prepared for the devastation this time around, but the knowledge they left behind has been deliberately repressed," added Teryk. "If catastrophes of that magnitude once again strike our world, humanity will be caught off guard."

"Academia insists civilization as we know it began with the Egyptians five thousand years ago," agreed Cassandra. "Archaeologists have repeatedly ignored, concealed and even destroyed evidence that proved otherwise. I don't remember ever being taught in school that Sumeria was just as advanced as the Egyptians and predated them by thousands of years. Incidentally, Sumerian writings mention the Great Pyramid of Giza a thousand years before Khufu allegedly built it. When you recalled us, Teryk, I was investigating a pyramid complex in Bosnia that predates the Egyptian pyramids by seven thousand years. That's twice as far back as our recorded history goes!

"When I left the site, *National Geographic* was in the process of documenting the discovery. Commander, the Pyramid of the Sun near Mexico

City is some two hundred and twenty feet high. The pyramid in Giza is around four hundred and forty feet tall: twice the height of the one in Mexico. The main Bosnian pyramid is taller than both of these combined—it is the largest and most ancient pyramid on the planet!" said Cassandra excitedly. "I personally met with Dr. Semir Osmanagich, PhD. 'Dr. Sam' was the first to discover the pyramid complex in the spring of 2005. His discovery should have been heralded as the find of the century! You will not believe the opposition this man has had to deal with. Soviet scientists, on the other hand, were so impressed with the work of Dr. Osmanagich, that they made him the youngest member of the Soviet Academy of Sciences.

"Thanks to the assistance of a materials scientist named Dr. Joseph Davidovits, Sam discovered that these pyramids, as well as the ones in Mexico and Egypt, were constructed using some form of ancient concrete-like mix," continued Cassandra. "Such an innovation would have saved thousands of man-hours. If the Egyptians cast those massive two-and-a-half-ton blocks, it would explain why they are so smooth and perfect. Dr. Semir Osmanagich also discovered an elaborate tunnel system that links all the pyramids in the complex. Surprisingly, these tunnels were deliberately filled in and sealed many thousands of years ago."

"These findings, of pre-historic concrete, were verified by the Institute of materials from the University in Zenica, Bosnia-Herzegovina," explained Devereaux. "The concrete blocks were cast from a crushed limestone sludge fortified with dollops of kaolinite clay, silica and natural desert salts. Lime hydrate was used to bind the grains of gravel. This ancient artificial stone-like ceramic has almost zero porosity and surpasses the hardness of any modern industrial concrete available today. The ceramic blocks used in the construction of these pyramids are stronger than the naturally quarried stone they resemble. Mikhail and I were successful in recreating the process outlined by Dr. Davidovits. The amalgamation, referred to as a geopolymer, gives off a pungent odor and has a jellylike feel to it. We discovered that the nearly perfect stone spheres found around the world are also made of this artificial ceramic material. We suspect that the processes was utilized, along with a form of injection molding, to create the enormous ancient Inca stonework structures found throughout Peru. The only structure that does not appear to incorporate this technique is one of the submerged pyramids you located in the Bermuda Triangle: It's translucent, larger than the Giza pyramids, and appears to be made entirely out of massive quartz crystal blocks."

"According to the history books, humans were chucking spears and rocks at each other twelve thousand years ago, not building pyramids of this magnitude. This new evidence drastically alters not only the history of engineering—but that of humanity itself!" declared Cassandra. "Incidentally, that pyramid complex

Aurora discovered, just south of the straight between the Cuban Peninsula and the Yucatan, was filmed by National Geographic in 2003. As far back as July 2001, a Russian scientist named Paulina Zelitsky filmed the submerged ruins. She recorded roads, buildings and pyramid structures of granite in circular and perpendicular formations at a depth of 2,200 feet. The layout is similar to that of Teotihuacan near Mexico City. National Geographic purchased the copyrights to film the pyramid complex. Unfortunately, that documentary has never seen the light of day. I believe the documentary being filmed when I left the Bosnian Pyramid Complex will be doomed to the same dusty subterranean archives as its predecessor."

"Based on my findings and those of my team, it would appear that one of the main objectives of all secret societies has been to keep information concerning mankind's true history from ever reaching the rest of humanity," declared Jared.

"Well, it appears that we have our work cut out for us," said Teryk, drumming his fingers and considering his next words carefully. "When we conclude the current investigation I would like to devote all available resources to investigating the possibility that a brown dwarf star is inbound. We will need to bring the remaining members of the Round Table up to date on the subjects we have just discussed. Jared, please see to it that everyone in my captain's quarters has the necessary security clearances to continue with this investigation."

"Commander, if I may, the reason I'm here is to show you what we've just uncovered regarding documents found aboard the Nazi U-boat," announced Devereaux as he approached Teryk holding a document emblazoned with a Nazi letterhead. "The rest of you might want to remain as well," he advised. Removing the letter from a protective folder, he placed it on a flat surface. Devereaux adjusted a small jeweler's viewing lens to a section of the document. Stepping back, he motioned to Teryk. "Please take a look, sir."

Teryk peered into the small device for a moment then straightened abruptly. "What does this document pertain to?" he asked, stepping aside and motioning for Jared and Raven to inspect the page. Noticing Devereaux's hesitation, Teryk reminded Devereaux that everyone in the room was scheduled to be assigned a level-seven security clearance.

"The encoded document pertains to the locations of additional German submarines hidden throughout South American and Antarctica," explained Devereaux.

After Raven had examined the document, she suggested, "Trisha, I think you should be next."

Trisha gazed into the lens and focused the device.

Observing Trisha's aura flashing red, Teryk exclaimed, "I take it you recognize that symbol! You should. It's on the back of every US one-dollar bill."

Trisha stood, saying nothing. She removed the magnifying device and stared at the period that ended the last sentence on the page. It looked like a normal dot to the unaided eye. Handing the magnifier to Joshua, she exclaimed, "It's the 'All-Seeing Eye' atop the unfinished pyramid: the symbol of the Illuminati!"

Joseph *"Five Eagles"* Reyna

Author's Note

I sincerely want to thank you for your interest in my work. Had I known what I was getting myself into, I would probably never have attempted it. I fully stand behind the well-researched and meticulously documented evidence presented. I am in no way attempting to merge the brilliance of the great men referenced throughout my work with my own discoveries or beliefs. I am simply offering the reader additional academic, scientific and archaeological avenues to pursue and I wish to raise awareness of their incredible contributions.

In 1980, I discovered that our moon was an artificial satellite. That it was linked to the Resurrection of Christ came as somewhat of a surprise. Preserved within the oldest known manuscripts of the Gospels is a version of events that has survived to the present day. Ancient historians, throughout the Middle East, recorded that during the spring equinox of 31 AD, a solar eclipse occurred within hours of a blood-red lunar eclipse. They noted that the solar eclipse was totally unexpected and was accompanied by massive earthquakes.

It is my hope that the astonishing explanations provided may someday help resolve many of the puzzling inconsistencies associated with Christ's betrayal, arrests, trials and crucifixion. The evidence that Jesus was guilty of sedition against the Roman emperor and not innocent, as we have been led to believe, is disturbing. If the possibility that Mary Magdalene may have been Jesus' wife could be considered blasphemy, then the irrefutable evidence that Jesus Christ had an identical twin brother would certainly be considered sacrilege.

Among the best and brightest researchers of our time there is little doubt that great civilizations, predating recorded history, built massive stone monuments in an effort to warn future generations that our world is subject to catastrophic cosmic cycles of destruction that brought their advanced civilizations to an abrupt end. Agents of the Illuminati's shadow government have managed to suppress these discoveries by destroying the evidence and dismissing these ancient accounts of unimaginable devastation as mere legends or myths. However, recent discoveries and advancements in the fields of geology, astrophysics, archaeology, and genetics seem to suggest otherwise.

The Mayan Calendar was not tracking the eclipsing of the galactic center by our Sun. Instead what the ancients were tracking was the point at which our world would collide with an enormous interstellar gravitational energy-field emanating from the super-massive Sayfert energy-source located at the center of the Milky Way galaxy; a galaxy 10,000 times larger than our own.

Two thousand years ago, The Resurrection of the Nazarene successfully demonstrated that a physical human form could metamorphose into an eternal lightbody. Within this highly energized region of space, that is exactly what human DNA is designed to do. The theological implications of these new findings extend beyond anything your carefully molded mind is capable of conceiving. You can refuse to believe the startling revelation of humankind's true origins and our ultimate destiny, but due to the overwhelming amount of evidence, you can no longer afford to ignore it.

If you feel particularly strong about the contributions this book may have made to your own life, please share and discuss the evidence presented with friends and fellow seekers. I kindly ask that you not reveal too much information and spoil it for them. When you turn the page, Kindle will give you the opportunity to rate this book and share your thoughts through an automatic feed to your Facebook and Twitter accounts.

Thank you for reading
—Joseph "Five Eagles" Reyna

The author resides in Texas and continues his extensive research into the origins of our creation and the manipulation of Human DNA.

This story concludes with the second book,

DRAGON SLAYER

CPSIA information can be obtained
at www.ICGtesting.com
Printed in the USA
FFOW02n1310120718
47408705-50593FF